T0247778

Praise for

WATERGATE'S UNEXPECTED HERO

"In 1974, ninety million Americans watched an unlikely group of big-city liberals, southern Democrats, and independent Republicans join together to hold Richard Nixon responsible for the Watergate cover-up. They were introduced to a new American hero—the committee's chairman, Peter Rodino, who was catapulted to national fame and lauded for his calm leadership and bipartisanship during a time of crisis. *Watergate's Unexpected Hero: The Life of Peter W. Rodino Jr.* tells this dramatic story along with the rest of the chapters in this great man's life. Thanks to Dr. Spinelli's painstaking and amazing effort, a new generation will be introduced to Peter Rodino and also be reminded of what can be achieved when our political leaders work together."

CHRIS MATTHEWS, host of MSNBC's *Hardball* for two decades, author of *Bobby Kennedy: A Raging Spirit*

"This valuable book shows that heroes are neither born nor made but emerge from a steady combination of character and circumstance. Peter Rodino's honorable life—and brave conduct when courage counted most—is a reminder that quiet decency is an essential quality in American politics, and one that we need now more than ever."

TODD S. PURDUM, author of *An Idea Whose Time Has Come: Two Presidents, Two Parties, and the Battle for the Civil Rights Act of 1964*

"Peter Rodino finally has a biography worthy of his exemplary career. *Watergate's Unexpected Hero* highlights Rodino's leadership and courage during the crisis spawned by the Nixon presidency but also grounds Rodino's New Jersey experiences, both political and personal, as the key to his character and his success. A must-read for anyone who seeks new insight into the Watergate crisis."

LONNIE G. BUNCH III, founding director, National Museum of African American History and Culture

"Larry Spinelli does a masterful job of capturing the life and service of Peter Rodino, one of the most impressive and impactful leaders of the modern age. The Nixon impeachment inquiry that transfixed the nation was Peter Rodino's finest hour but, as Dr. Spinelli's book shows, his lasting legacy for good was much larger. The son of Italian immigrants, Peter Rodino enlisted in the Army at age thirty-two and fought in North Africa and Italy in World War II. He worked menial jobs for ten years to put himself through law school and embodied the American story. Readers of this book will learn the depth of his contributions to our country, in civil rights, consumer protection, antitrust regulations, fair housing, and many other areas before his crowning chapter of protecting our Constitution during Watergate. He was a champion for the underdog and spoke for those who did not have a voice—a humble man who never sought the spotlight but who was tough as nails when he needed to be. The life and service of Peter Rodino should be a model for future generations that people know about, and Dr. Spinelli's book captures his remarkable journey extremely well."

WILLIAM S. COHEN, former Secretary of Defense, U.S. Senator, and member of the Nixon impeachment committee

"A true American hero."

ROBERT PINSKY, three-time U.S. Poet Laureate, author of *Jersey Breaks: Becoming an American Poet*

WATERGATE'S UNEXPECTED HERO

THE LIFE OF PETER W. RODINO JR.

LAWRENCE SPINELLI

amplify
an imprint of Amplify Publishing Group

www.amplifypublishing.com

Watergate's Unexpected Hero: The Life of Peter W. Rodino Jr.

For more information, please contact:
Amplify Publishing, an imprint of Amplify Publishing Group
620 Herndon Parkway, Suite 220
Herndon, VA 20170
info@amplifypublishing.com

Library of Congress Control Number: 2024905870

CPSIA Code: PRV0424A

ISBN-13: 979-8-89138-081-3

Printed in the United States

FOR CARL PRINCE—

RESPECTED SCHOLAR, DEDICATED TEACHER, AND CHERISHED FRIEND

CONTENTS

INTRODUCTION

DURING THE HISTORIC SUMMER OF 1974, I was working in the town of Secaucus as a New Jersey Department of Community Affairs intern. A reporter for the *Jersey Journal* newspaper learned that I once held a similar position in the Washington office of Congressman Peter W. Rodino Jr., and she wanted to interview me. At the time, Rodino was chairing the Nixon impeachment inquiry, and the televised hearings made him one of the most recognizable public figures in the country. This national prominence sparked considerable press interest in the relatively unknown representative at the center of these momentous proceedings, and even the personal insights of a former intern were now considered newsworthy.

I was happy to bask for a brief moment in the glow of the congressman's newfound fame. I recounted the story of our first meeting six years earlier when he visited Belleville High School, where I was the president of the school's political club. I explained how this singular encounter and my enthusiastic interest in politics led to an invitation for me to coordinate Rodino's young campaign volunteers and to spend two magical summers on Capitol Hill. According to the reporter, this relatively modest connection had transformed me into "a sort of minor celebrity."[1]

I never imagined then that this was just the opening chapter of a long and fruitful relationship that would fundamentally influence my future. In the decades following the publication of that article, I moved to Washington and, after becoming a college professor, spent my free time between semesters working for Rodino on a variety of legislative issues. Consequently, when he needed a new press secretary, he offered me the position, opting for familiarity over experience, personally conducting my on-the-job training. As a former historian, I was an attentive audience for his countless stories about the past, and he frequently sought me out to share a particular memory. I cherished these opportunities and regret that it was not possible to record or transcribe what were usually spontaneous moments of recollection. Thanks to his willingness to take a chance on an eager novice, I was a witness to the events that marked the final years of his stellar congressional career, and it was my somber task to shut out the lights and close his office door for the last time. Happily, our personal relationship continued after that occasion through phone calls and visits. I was among the hundreds of mourners bidding him farewell in 2005, and I was honored to serve as a reader at his funeral mass.

Reflecting on Peter Rodino's acclaimed leadership of the Nixon impeachment inquiry, former Speaker of the House of Representatives Tip O'Neill wrote in his memoirs that "when the rest of us are all forgotten, he's the one who will be in the history books."[2] O'Neill's prediction of his friend's ultimate legacy was partially correct; the bipartisan and deliberative process Rodino pursued established an enduring template regarded by those involved in subsequent presidential impeachments as the "gold standard."

Yet the full scope of Rodino's life, beyond this professional high point, remains largely unknown. Unlike others involved in the Watergate affair, Rodino was unwilling to profit from his experience and declined lucrative offers to write an autobiography in the immediate aftermath of the Nixon impeachment. He conducted his formative work on immigration and civil rights policy in the shadow of a committee chairman who rarely shared the credit, and, as a result, he went largely unrecognized. Many of his later successful efforts in Congress involved blocking action, rather than passing legislation, and these important efforts were not always accorded the same attention.

My goal in writing this book is to redress this scholarly imbalance and present the rest of his story. The son of an Italian immigrant, Rodino succeeded in escaping the constraints of poverty and prejudice, and he was determined to help others do the same. Surrounded by lawlessness in his ethnic neighborhood, he chose a different path and became a fierce defender of the rule of law. I hope that in revealing the forgotten or overlooked details of Rodino's rich narrative, the breadth of his contributions as a legislator will be more fully appreciated and his ability to help steer the country through a national crisis better understood. If Peter Rodino was an *unexpected* hero in 1974, the pages that follow will demonstrate that he was not an *unprepared* one; he brought a wealth of experience to the formidable task he faced.

While personally knowing a subject or witnessing aspects of their life is a benefit for a biographer, it is a knowledge that must be measured against the rigorous standards of objective historical scholarship. I began my research at the Seton Hall University School of Law's Peter W. Rodino Jr. Law Library Center for Information and Technology, where Rodino's papers are located. The collection includes all of the available material from his personal and public life, including audio recordings, scrapbooks, and photographs. The congressional material is heavily weighted toward the final two decades of his time on Capitol Hill after he moved his office to the new Rayburn House Office Building and encompasses both his personal office and House Judiciary Committee files.

Particularly valuable are the oral histories Rodino recorded for Columbia and Yale universities, as well as an extensive series of interviews conducted in the late 1990s by Dr. Bill Berlin for a Rodino autobiography that was never completed. Although the quality of the latter recordings is not optimal, and they require considerable verification, Dr. Berlin managed to capture Rodino's unique perspective, creating a valuable historical resource in the process.

My initial visit to the archives was facilitated by Congressman Rodino's widow, Joy, who was an early supporter of this project. She introduced me to special collections librarian, Dianne Oster. Dianne was extraordinarily generous with her time and knowledge of the material on many subsequent occasions. Following her retirement, both Deborah Schander and Christy Smith were equally helpful in accommodating my requests for extended library visits.

My inaugural research foray beyond the Rodino archives was to the Lyndon Baines Johnson Presidential Library and Museum in Austin. Allen Fisher provided the introductory orientation to the complex world of presidential papers, and I could not have asked for a better guide. His enthusiasm for what was the first request by a researcher to view the Rodino folders was infectious, and his detailed explanation of the organizing structure at the Johnson White House benefited me enormously in identifying other potentially relevant documents. His National Archives colleagues at the Kennedy, Nixon, Ford, Carter, and Reagan presidential libraries were always quick to respond to requests in person or virtually, and they patiently answered repeated follow-up questions. Adam Berenbak at the Center for Legislative Archives in Washington offered invaluable insights into the voluminous records of the House Judiciary Committee and saved me considerable time by helping to identify the most important files.

Manuscript collections were an important component in evaluating all the aspects of Rodino's congressional career, and the staff members at Boston College's John J. Burns Library, which houses Tip O'Neill's papers, and the Howard Gotlieb Archival Research Center at Boston University, where the John McCormack papers are located, were both very helpful in facilitating my visits. I was a frequent occupant of a seat in both the Manuscript Division and the Newspaper and Current Periodical Reading Room at the Library of Congress, where my endless queries were patiently and politely filled.

I wrote the latter half of this book during the pandemic, and I could not have completed it to my satisfaction without the generous assistance of several archivists at institutions that were closed to visitors. Jennifer Mitchell at the Washington and Lee University School of Law helped me to access the M. Caldwell Butler papers, which contain invaluable insights into Rodino's handling of the Nixon impeachment inquiry, including the transcripts of a "fragile coalition" gathering held a year later. Rachel Henson at the Carl

Albert Congressional Research and Studies Center provided the same support and supplied a long list of important documents detailing the Rodino-Albert relationship. I am especially grateful to Michael Lorenzen and William (Bill) Cook of the University Archives and Special Collections staff at Western Illinois University, where Thomas F. Railsback's papers are deposited. Bill Cook copied and sent me six large envelopes of material, including the congressman's recently opened personal notes. All of these individuals went well beyond their job descriptions to help someone they never met at a very challenging time. They have my deepest appreciation.

I want to thank James Blanchard, Skip Endres, Ronna Freiberg, Frank Godlewski, Ted Kaufman, Joy Rodino, John Russonello, Sandy Sincavitz, and Charles Stanziale for sharing their memories and unique insights about specific aspects of Peter Rodino's life and career. I am indebted to Skip Endres for his "master classes" on the development and enactment of immigration legislation during his long tenure at the House Judiciary Committee. Joan DelFattore was also a helpful tutor, educating me on the transformation in publishing since the release of my last book more than three decades ago and providing valuable advice when I most needed it. Howard Rosenthal was a steadfast friend and a wise counselor throughout this entire process.

Working with the impressive team of professionals at Amplify Publishing Group was a pleasure; they ensured that transforming my manuscript into a book was both a stress-free and rewarding experience. Editorial director Will Wolfslau set the tone for this relationship when he responded to my proposal with enthusiasm and encouragement. Merlina McGovern's talents as a copyeditor far exceeded my expectations and her meticulousness never ceased to amaze me. I am truly grateful for her contributions to the text that follows. Finally, I want to thank senior production editor Myles Schrag for his critical role in overseeing all the aspects of this project, including editorial, design, and publication. He did an outstanding job keeping all these various elements moving forward and on the rigorous schedule he established. His quick response to any question and unflagging patience regardless of the topic were much appreciated.

Writing a book is a relatively solitary undertaking, and I am grateful for the interest and support of family, friends, and former colleagues throughout this long process. It is only fitting that I dedicate this book to my NYU mentor and fellow New Jerseyan, Carl Prince, who reacted with unbridled enthusiasm when I first told him about this project. Carl hired me in 1976 to work at the William Livingston papers historical editing project primarily because he was impressed that I had served as Peter Rodino's intern. He has been my friend and wise counselor ever since.

I want to honor the memory of my parents, Frank and Sigrid Spinelli, who supported all my youthful political activities, including two summers on Capitol Hill, that required a financial subsidy. They finally met Peter Rodino on what was his last day as a voting member of Congress.

Finally, I must thank my wife, Arlene, for her constant encouragement, patience, and understanding. She convinced me that it was my destiny to write the first Rodino biography, willingly deferred many retirement activities, and demonstrated an unlimited capacity to listen to stories about Peter Rodino during nightly walks with our beloved dog, Gracie Allen. Without Arlene's love and friendship, none of this would have been possible.

CHAPTER ONE

A MAN ABOUT TO MAKE HISTORY

Peter Rodino was not in Washington, DC, when he first heard the news that would fundamentally change his political life. Since becoming a Democratic member of the House of Representatives, he had religiously left the city following the final vote of the week, returning to Newark, New Jersey, to undertake a full schedule of activities in his congressional district. Rodino had worked hard for more than two and a half decades to forge a reputation for outstanding constituent services. Even his ascension to the chairmanship of the powerful House Judiciary Committee at the beginning of 1973 had not altered this sacrosanct routine. Completing a busy program of local events on a Saturday that was unusually balmy for late October, Rodino had just returned home when a special news bulletin interrupted the television program he was watching and ended his restful evening. In a stunning development that the press dubbed the "Saturday Night Massacre," both the attorney general of the United States and his deputy resigned, refusing to comply with President Richard Nixon's order to fire the special prosecutor investigating the ongoing Watergate scandal.

Coming in the wake of shocking revelations of wrongdoing by Nixon administration officials, the announcement dramatically heightened the already palpable sense of crisis that was gripping the nation's capital. It provoked an immediate outpouring of calls for Congress to begin impeachment proceedings against the president, a constitutional process that was likely to involve Rodino's committee. The rookie chairman decided to do something he had never done before: cancel all his remaining district appointments and return to Capitol Hill before the weekend was over. With this simple action, Rodino was taking the first step across a sharp line of demarcation, and there was no turning back—whatever the outcome. He was now, as the *Miami Herald* would observe, "a man about to make history."[1]

The actual catalyst for Rodino's abrupt departure was an event that took place on another Saturday sixteen months earlier. In the predawn hours of June 22, 1972, five men were arrested for breaking into the Democratic National Committee's headquarters on the sixth floor of the Watergate office complex located on Virginia Avenue in the District of Columbia. Because the men were carrying a full complement of electronic equipment used for bugging telephones, which was a federal crime, the local police turned the case over to the Federal Bureau of Investigation and the Department of Justice. One of the burglars was James W. McCord Jr., coordinator of security for the Committee to Reelect the President (CREEP), the Nixon campaign organization. Largely thanks to the dogged efforts of *Washington Post* reporters Bob Woodward and Carl Bernstein, evidence emerged in the days following the break-in that established a clear link between the burglars and CREEP. By the end of the month, the press was referring to the incident as the "Watergate caper," and Judge John Sirica was selected to preside over a grand jury empaneled to consider the matter.[2]

The initial reaction from the White House was to dismiss Watergate as a "third rate burglary attempt" and hope the issue would fade away before the November election.[3] But with a constant flow of new disclosures and demands for the appointment of a special prosecutor to supervise the case, the president was forced to respond. Speaking at a press conference at the end of August, Nixon assured the public that no one currently working on his campaign or in the administration was involved in this incident. He had instructed all employees, he told reporters, to cooperate with the ongoing Department of Justice investigation because "what really hurts is when you cover it up."[4] Two weeks later, the grand jury indicted the five burglars as well as their immediate supervisors, E. Howard Hunt and G. Gordon Liddy (both former employees at CREEP and the White House), on charges of conspiracy to steal documents and eavesdrop.[5]

Congressman Wright Patman was not finding much evidence of this promised spirit of cooperation as he began the first congressional inquiry into Watergate. Concerned over reports of fundraising abuses and the possible violation of banking laws, the Texas Democrat and longtime chairman of the House Banking Committee instructed his staff to examine CREEP's financial operations. The preliminary findings he presented in September revealed that more than $100,000 in campaign contributions had been laundered through a Mexican bank and that they could trace a portion of these funds to the account of at least one of the Watergate burglars.[6]

The Nixon reelection campaign offered little assistance in unraveling the complicated web of its financial transactions, and officials refused the committee's requests for records of expenditures and lists of donors. When Patman announced plans to continue the investigation, the White House quietly lobbied Republicans and southern Democrats, who comprised a majority of the banking panel, to block the effort. Without their support, Patman was unable to subpoena reluctant witnesses and could not secure a quorum to hold a hearing. A week after the staff released its final report, which charged CREEP with extensive violations of campaign finance rules, President Nixon defeated George McGovern in the presidential election and was reelected with more than 60 percent of the vote, carrying every state except Massachusetts.[7]

But the president's impressive electoral mandate was not enough to shield him from the accumulating political fallout of a dizzying blizzard of Watergate-related bad news. Before a jury found the burglars guilty in March 1973, the *Washington Post* had uncovered evidence that the break-in was part of a political sabotage campaign against Democrats on behalf of President Nixon's reelection and that officials at CREEP and in the White House directed this clandestine operation through a secret slush fund. James McCord, appearing at the preliminary sentencing hearing for the burglars, dropped another bombshell when he informed Judge Sirica that the group was pressured to plead guilty and remain silent. Charging that perjury had been committed at the trial, McCord offered to provide evidence of a wider conspiracy and cover-up, which prompted the grand jury to reopen its probe.[8] If McCord was the first domino to fall, the rest followed in quick succession as the acting FBI director revealed that presidential counsel John Dean, in charge of the White House's own Watergate investigation, had destroyed evidence and lied under oath. Dean in turn met with the grand jury prosecutors to negotiate immunity for his secret testimony against senior presidential aides Harry Robins (H.R.) Haldeman and John Ehrlichman.

With the Watergate scandal now directly linked to the inner circle at the White House and seriously undermining the president's own credibility, Nixon decided to take drastic action. On April 30, he fired John Dean and accepted the resignation of Haldeman, Ehrlichman, and Attorney General Richard Kleindienst. In a televised address that evening, the president declared that there can be "no whitewash at the White House." He assured the public that his nominee to replace Kleindienst as attorney general, Elliot Richardson, would have absolute authority to direct the Watergate investigation, including the power to appoint a special prosecutor if necessary. It was a promise he would come to regret.[9]

At the start of the Ninety-Third Congress in January 1973, Chairman Patman's unfinished examination of CREEP's questionable financial activities was resurrected when the Senate launched a much broader inquiry into Watergate. Sam Ervin, the folksy senior senator from North Carolina and chairman of both the Committee on Government Operations and the Subcommittee on Constitutional Rights was selected by Majority Leader Mike Mansfield to lead a special panel created to conduct the investigation. The Select Committee on Presidential Campaign Activities, which quickly became commonly known as the "Watergate committee," included four Democrats and three Republicans, including Vice Chairman Howard Baker from Tennessee. In a bipartisan vote, the Senate appropriated $500,000 for the panel to hire staff and complete its work within a year.[10] Almost immediately, members began meeting behind closed doors to hear testimony from a litany of former White House and CREEP officials. The committee also initiated what would prove to be a bitter and protracted battle with President Nixon over his broad claim of executive privilege to deny the committee critical documents and information.

On May 17, Chairman Ervin rapped his gavel before an array of microphones and television cameras in the historic Senate Caucus Room and called the Watergate committee's first public hearing to order. The following day, Attorney General Richardson appointed Harvard University law professor Archibald Cox Jr. as the Watergate special prosecutor responsible for all aspects of the Justice Department's investigation.[11]

Except for irate soap opera fans mad about the preemption of their favorite serial, the nationally televised Watergate hearings were widely praised and quickly attracted a substantial audience. Viewership soared with the decision of the fledgling Public Broadcasting Service (PBS) to re-air the hearings at night, making the proceedings readily available to those unable to watch the daytime live broadcasts. For the next three months, more than twenty witnesses provided the committee and the public with a detailed narrative of the illegal campaign activities that culminated in the break-in at the Democratic headquarters and the subsequent intensive efforts to hide these actions. All the major participants in this covert plan appeared before the panel and several, including John Dean, who offered five days of riveting testimony, maintained that President Nixon actively participated in the cover-up.[12]

The most startling revelation from the hearings came from someone not directly involved in the scandal: former presidential aide Alexander Butterfield. On July 16, he told the committee that there was a secret tape recording system in the White House. According to Butterfield, the electronic equipment installed in 1970 routinely recorded every presidential telephone call and all conversations in the Oval Office, the Cabinet Room, and the president's hideaway office in the adjacent Old Executive Office Building. This stunning disclosure transformed the hearings, raising the possibility for the first time that tangible evidence existed to either confirm John Dean's story or exonerate the president.[13] Chairman Ervin immediately requested that the president provide the panel with recordings of conversations from key dates in the chronology of the alleged cover-up. When Nixon again invoked executive privilege and refused, the committee issued a subpoena for several critical tapes. Special Prosecutor Cox quickly followed with his own subpoena, sending the dispute to the courts and opening a new chapter in the Watergate saga.[14]

On the other side of the Capitol, Peter Rodino was initially skeptical about the impact of events unfolding in the Senate. Recently elevated to the chairmanship of the House Judiciary Committee, Rodino was still finding his footing when the Watergate committee began its investigation. He primarily focused his attention on reorganizing his own panel. Although members of Congress were increasingly besieged with letters and petitions calling for President Nixon's removal from office, Rodino rebuffed all attempts to even discuss the future possibility of impeachment, an innate caution shared by the Democratic leaders in the House of Representatives.[15] After the shake-up at the White House and President Nixon's television address on April 30, California Representative John E. Moss announced his intention to introduce a resolution to establish a special committee to prepare for impeachment. Most of his colleagues dismissed the effort as premature. Speaker Carl Albert, who had supported the Patman inquiry and endorsed further investigation, publicly voiced his opposition to what he considered an overreaction. "I know of no evidence direct or hearsay that the President approved the flagrant abuse of power and the abrogation of the law by the people on his staff," he wrote to one of his constituents in Oklahoma.[16] Rodino, declining to comment on the Moss resolution, chose to respond to Nixon's speech by introducing legislation to create a special Watergate prosecutor that was independent of the Justice Department.[17]

As the Senate hearings continued through the summer, eliciting new revelations about the Watergate cover-up, Rodino recognized that he could no longer ignore the issue of impeachment. “I began to see the nucleus of something that was bigger than what they were focusing on,” he later noted, “the question of the president’s involvement and how far that involvement went.”[18] Rodino decided he needed to expand his limited knowledge of the subject and asked his staff to prepare a bibliography of relevant scholarship. The United States Constitution mentions impeachment only four times, and the framers provided few details to guide the process. Under the article establishing the legislative branch, the power to impeach or level accusations of wrongdoing against federal government officials, including the president, was vested in the House of Representatives. Impeachable charges were defined as bribery, treason, or other high crimes and misdemeanors. Responsibility for conducting the trial was given to the Senate, and a person found guilty by at least two-thirds of the senators would be removed from office. Congress had invoked this provision just twelve times prior to 1973, and it had primarily used it against federal judges. The sole presidential impeachment of Andrew Johnson in 1868 was a highly partisan proceeding, and historians largely dismissed it as an unworthy precedent.[19] Rodino began what he regarded as purely an academic inquiry and deliberately kept his research activities confidential. When a seatmate on a shuttle flight to New Jersey commented on the fact that Rodino was intently reading a book about the Johnson impeachment, the chairman began wrapping his reading material in plain brown congressional envelopes.[20]

Rodino did take a few small tangible steps to prepare for an event he still believed was highly unlikely to occur. In early July, he instructed the Judiciary Committee staff to contact the Senate Watergate committee and discreetly raise the possibility of future information sharing between the two panels.[21] He also sent the staff to meet privately with Archibald Cox. Entering through the guarded door, they were quietly ushered into Cox’s office for an on-the-record discussion of Rodino’s legislation to strengthen the independence of the special prosecutor and an unofficial briefing on the status of the Watergate investigation. Cox told them that he was focusing his efforts on the pending criminal cases and not currently investigating Nixon’s personal involvement in

Watergate. He offered to notify the committee if he did uncover any evidence of presidential misconduct.

News of the gathering leaked to the press, sparking rumors that the purpose of the visit was to consult on impeachment. Anxious to dampen this speculation, Rodino downplayed the importance of the meeting and claimed it was merely a part of ongoing departmental oversight. It was the latest indication of the revived public interest in this once arcane topic.[22]

A few weeks later, Rodino was finally compelled to break his silence on impeachment. Father Robert Drinan, a liberal Democratic congressman from Massachusetts, introduced the first House impeachment resolution on July 31, following revelations that President Nixon had ordered the secret bombing of Cambodia as part of the Vietnam war effort. Unlike the earlier Moss proposal that addressed the *possibility* of congressional action, Drinan's brief resolution was an immediate call for "impeaching Richard M. Nixon, President of the United States, of high crimes and misdemeanors," and it was referred to the House Judiciary Committee. Although Drinan was a member of the panel, he received little support from his fellow Democrats, and both Speaker Albert and Majority Leader Thomas P. "Tip" O'Neill considered his action ill-timed.[23]

Receiving no advance warning of the introduction of the resolution, Rodino viewed it as part of Drinan's ongoing anti-war activism, and his initial reaction was to ignore it. But strong interest from the press made this impossible, and Rodino issued a public statement the following day. In announcing that the committee would take no formal action on the Drinan proposal "at this time," Rodino stressed that "only the most careful, the most sensitive, and the most thoughtful deliberation will precede any action taken by the Committee on the Judiciary."[24] He repeated this view a month later when he appeared as the guest on the CBS news program *Face the Nation*. Responding to a question from one of the journalists on the show, Rodino noted that the Ervin committee had not completed its investigation or issued its report and that "the House must of necessity just wait."[25] He prudently decided to accelerate the pace of his impeachment research while he waited for a day he hoped would never arrive.

The unexpected intrusion of another constitutional provision, one he helped to enact, interrupted Rodino's studies. On August 7, the *Wall Street Journal* reported that Vice President Spiro T. Agnew was one of the targets of a Baltimore grand jury's investigation of political corruption in Maryland. Agnew was serving as the state's governor when, in a surprise move, Richard Nixon picked him to be his running mate in 1968. Largely unknown at the time, he soon shed his obscurity and gained notoriety after delivering a series of bombastic and controversial speeches. Attacking anti-war protesters, liberals, and the press, Agnew became the Nixon administration's verbal battering ram and earned the deep enmity of his Democratic opponents. The probe, launched months earlier, had uncovered evidence of Agnew's involvement as both Baltimore County executive and governor in an elaborate kickback scheme to demand payments from businesses seeking government contracts. The potential charges facing the vice president, if the Justice Department decided to move forward to seek an indictment, included bribery, extortion, and tax fraud.[26]

Agnew launched an aggressive counterattack, proclaiming his innocence, denouncing leaks to the press, and vowing to remain in office. If his troubles appeared to offer the White House a respite from the constant drumbeat of the Watergate probe, it proved to be a transitory distraction. Senior aides concluded that the scandal swirling around the vice president was becoming an unwelcomed additional complication for an administration already under siege. With Nixon's tacit approval, they privately urged Agnew to consider resigning, a suggestion he immediately rejected.[27] While Justice Department officials raised the possibility of a plea bargain, Agnew and his lawyers decided to press forward with a legal defense aimed at short-circuiting the judicial process. Raising an unsettled constitutional question, Agnew maintained that a sitting vice president was not subject to criminal proceedings unless Congress first impeached and removed him from office. At the vice president's request, Speaker Albert agreed to discuss the issue and asked senior leaders from both sides of the aisle, including Peter Rodino, to participate in the meeting. Agnew presented a letter outlining his appeal for a congressional inquiry into the charges leveled against him. He compared his situation with that of his predecessor John C. Calhoun, whose request in 1826 that Congress investigate claims he was a war profiteer led to the creation of a special committee and his official exoneration. Concluding his presentation, Agnew informed the participants that he would send all of the original documents in his pending case to the clerk of the House. Albert agreed to "study the matter and get back to him."[28]

Following the meeting, the Democrats in attendance remained in the speaker's office to discuss their strategy. Rodino argued that, if there was an inquiry, his panel—where every member was an attorney—should be responsible, not a special select committee. However, believing the House should do nothing to "impede the orderly administration of justice in the courts," he joined with Majority Leader O'Neill in opposing Agnew's proposal for a congressional inquiry.[29] Beyond the legal arguments, many members of the group expressed strong reservations based on the suspicion that Agnew was cynically hoping to exploit a protracted House investigation to derail, not just defer, the criminal prosecution against him. This potential scenario gained some credibility when Attorney General Richardson called Speaker Albert later that day to inform him that an Agnew indictment was imminent, hinting that the timing of the vice president's visit to Capitol Hill was not an accident.[30]

Rodino returned to his office and, assisted by the Judiciary Committee staff, began a long evening of research into the question. The next morning, he advised Albert that the precedent was irrelevant since Calhoun was not involved in any pending legal action, and he recommended that the speaker refuse Agnew's request. He also warned him that the House should not take possession of any documents to avoid getting entangled in the case. Albert issued a brief statement announcing that with the matters outlined in Agnew's letter before the courts, he was not prepared to take any action at this time. Rodino told the *New York Times* that, in his opinion, the vice president's assertion of immunity from prosecution "appeared to be almost without foundation."[31]

Agnew continued to press his claim of immunity. A few days later, his attorneys asked a federal court to stop presentations to the grand jury in Baltimore of evidence or witnesses that might lead to an indictment. The Department of Justice, previously ambivalent on this constitutional question, responded with an explicit declaration that a sitting vice president, unlike the president of the United States, *is* subject to criminal prosecution. A hearing was scheduled for October 12, and the judge ruled that the grand jury could continue to accept testimony until there was a ruling. Faced with certain indictment and a mountain of overwhelming evidence, Agnew finally bowed to the inevitable and accepted a plea bargain two days before the start of the hearing. The once defiant vice president pleaded "no contest" to the charge of income tax evasion, receiving a $10,000 fine and three years of probation. He then submitted his resignation.[32]

The immediate impact of Agnew's forced departure from Washington was that it triggered the first implementation of the Twenty-Fifth Amendment. Prior to its adoption in 1967, there was no constitutional provision for filling a vacancy in the vice presidency, even though the individual holding this position was responsible for replacing a president who died, resigned, or was removed from office. The Constitution left the post empty and empowered Congress to determine a subsequent line of successors, which it had done on three prior occasions, most recently up until that point in 1947, when it designated the Speaker of the House, followed by the president pro tempore of the Senate. On eighteen occasions, for a combined total of 38 years, the United States was without a vice president. The expanding size of the federal government and development of nuclear weapons in the postwar period, however, soon made this an unacceptable risk to national security. As Peter Rodino observed in advocating for what he considered an overdue change, "we have relied too long on luck and wishful hopes."[33]

The momentum for correcting this defect accelerated following the assassination of President John F. Kennedy in November 1963. When Vice President Lyndon B. Johnson assumed the presidency, the next officials in the line of succession were seventy-two-year-old Speaker John W. McCormack and Senator Carl Hayden, who was eighty-seven. Political pundits questioned if the two elderly leaders were capable of handling the burdens of the modern presidency, and these doubts prompted a broader reappraisal of the entire succession process.[34]

At the same time, Congress had wrestled for a decade with the thorny question of who was in charge of the country when a sitting president was temporarily incapacitated, a possibility that the Constitution also did not address. After President Dwight D. Eisenhower suffered a massive heart attack in 1955, which forced him to spend weeks in recovery, the House Judiciary Committee began a series of hearings on the issue and later considered a variety of legislative solutions to address the problem.[35] By early 1965, all of these concerns were merged together in a single proposal for a constitutional amendment that outlined both a procedure for replacing a vice president and an arrangement for the temporary transfer of presidential powers in case of a presidential disability. Reflecting bipartisan unity and a sense of urgency, the amendment was overwhelmingly approved by Congress in June and sent to the states for ratification. Twenty months later, the Twenty-Fifth Amendment was officially proclaimed part of the Constitution.[36]

Despite the preparatory hearings and extensive debate, several important questions about how to fill a vice presidential vacancy still remained unanswered when Spiro Agnew resigned his office in October 1973. The amendment clearly authorized the president to make his vice presidential replacement selection, and confirmation of the nominee required the approval of a majority in both the House and the Senate. Yet the actual mechanics of the process were not delineated, and they remained subject to interpretation, an undertaking complicated by the current atmosphere of mistrust between the executive and legislative branches of government. "As one who had been a cosponsor of that Twenty-Fifth Amendment," Rodino recollected, "we thought we had eliminated all the bugs, all the pitfalls, but we found out there were lots of bugs, lots of pitfalls."[37]

The first unsettled issue was whether or not Congress should hold joint confirmation hearings. Considering the historic rivalry between the two chambers, it was not surprising that congressional leaders quickly decided to follow separate paths. In the House of Representatives, which had no previous experience in confirming *any* nominees, the speaker needed to assign the task of conducting the hearings and managing the floor debate prior to a vote. Rodino, particularly after helping Albert respond to the Agnew request, expected to get the job. But several committee chairmen were lobbying for the prominent appointment, and other members, anxious to be part of a high-profile event, pushed for the creation of a special panel. As the next person in the presidential succession line, Speaker Albert was particularly sensitive to any appearance of partisanship, and he wanted the House's confirmation process to be fair, deliberative, and above reproach. He rejected the idea of an unwieldy and unpredictable select committee, concluding that the calm and prudent Rodino and his panel of lawyers were the best choice to manage a potentially volatile process. Meeting with reporters after the announcement of his appointment, Rodino promised a thorough investigation and diligent inquiry that might take several weeks.[38]

The next day, President Nixon announced his selection for vice president. Politically weakened by Watergate, he was unable to muster enough support for his first choice, former Texas governor John Connally, and was compelled to select Gerald Ford, the House Minority Leader and a Republican representative from Michigan. Ford's long tenure and popularity on Capitol Hill made him a safer choice to win majority approval, and many Republicans anticipated a relatively quick confirmation. Rodino had come to Congress with Ford in 1948 and considered his classmate a friend; he dashed their hopes when he declared that Ford's status as a member of Congress "will give him no advantages in the confirmation process."[39]

Preparatory work for the Ford nomination hearings was just beginning when the Saturday Night Massacre occurred and forced Rodino's abrupt return to Washington. While the Agnew affair had competed for attention, Watergate had never disappeared from the headlines throughout the summer and fall, as the Watergate committee heard from the last major witness and aired its final live broadcast. President Nixon responded to the end of the hearings with another nationally televised address to declare his innocence and attempt to persuade the country "to get on with the urgent business of our nation."[40] But it was difficult to change the subject when the president was personally engaged in an ongoing and heated battle to keep the White House tapes from Chairman Ervin and Special Prosecutor Cox. On October 12, the US Court of Appeals for the District of Columbia rejected Nixon's claim of unlimited executive privilege and required him to surrender the requested tapes to Judge Sirica for possible presentation to the grand jury.

Unwilling to either comply or appeal the case to the US Supreme Court, Nixon instead countered with an offer to prepare an edited summary of the relevant conversations. He then instructed the special prosecutor to stop all further legal action to secure the tapes and any additional Watergate material. At a midday press conference on Saturday, October 20, Cox declared his objection to the president's order and his intention to continue the fight for the release of the tapes.[41] This provided Nixon with an excuse to abolish the office of the special prosecutor, an action he had contemplated for months. Executing his directive proved more difficult; Attorney General Richardson and his deputy, William Ruckelshaus, were unwilling to renege on their promise to Congress to protect the independence of the investigation. They both resigned rather than fire Cox. That evening, Nixon appointed Solicitor General Robert Bork to serve in their stead as the acting attorney general, and Bork carried out the president's instructions. Following direct orders from the White House, FBI agents entered and seized the offices of the special prosecutor and impounded all the files. The shell-shocked staff, prevented from removing even personal items from their desks, gathered in the law library with reporters to hear a press officer read the final and brief public statement from the Watergate prosecutor. "Whether we shall continue to be a Government of laws and not of men," Archibald Cox warned, "is now for Congress and ultimately the American people to decide."[42]

If Nixon thought that firing the special prosecutor on a Saturday night in the middle of a three-day weekend would minimize the fallout, he was seriously mistaken. "For the first time tonight," the *New York Times* reported, "members of the House of Representatives began talking publicly and seriously about impeaching President Nixon."[43] On Monday, most members of Congress were at home celebrating the relatively new Veterans Day holiday and were unavailable for immediate comment. But, like a slow political tsunami, the harsh negative response to Nixon's action began to overtake the capital as the weekend progressed. Several representatives announced their intention to introduce impeachment resolutions, and both Democrats and Republicans predicted a flood of activity when the House reconvened at noon on Tuesday. Equally troubling was speculation that this hostile firestorm might spill over and seriously delay Gerald Ford's confirmation.[44]

Watching the dramatic images of the FBI raiding the office of the special prosecutor, Peter Rodino's immediate and practical concern was for the protection of the voluminous files amassed during months of investigation, material that was a potentially vital and irreplaceable resource for any future inquiry. After contacting Archibald Cox, Rodino called Robert Bork at the Justice Department and cautioned him to preserve the documents, an admonition he repeated in a follow-up letter. Returning to his small apartment near Capitol Hill twenty-four hours later, Rodino prepared for what would be the most consequential meeting of his public career.[45]

Early Monday, Rodino entered the largely deserted Capitol building to attend a meeting with the speaker, the House parliamentarian, and the few other senior Democrats in Washington. The previously reluctant Albert had come to believe that impeachment was the only option, and he wanted to ensure that the House conducted a serious inquiry before taking any action. Once again, the speaker was under enormous pressure to establish a special panel similar to the Watergate committee to handle the impeachment. Members, hoping to lead or serve on the panel, were already lobbying Albert, suggesting that Rodino was not aggressive enough to challenge Nixon or maintaining that the Judiciary Committee was distracted by the Ford nomination. Rodino presented his case at the three-hour meeting, assuring Albert that his committee was capable of handling these responsibilities and promising to fulfill the speaker's request to complete the Ford confirmation before turning to impeachment. The Judiciary Committee had jurisdiction over constitutional issues, Rodino argued, and this was likely to be an important component of the inquiry and subsequent debate. With the stakes even higher than before, Albert astutely recognized the political dangers of creating a new panel filled with partisans on both sides, and he remained confident in Rodino's ability to manage two important tasks at the same time. Rodino remembered that Albert simply told him, "Pete, I think that you're responsible, you're fair and I think that's where it ought to be, and I'm not going to be pressured."[46] Rodino spent the afternoon drafting a statement and preparing for his new assignment.

The growing tide of anti-Nixon sentiment finally hit Capitol Hill with full force. Congressional offices, reopening after the holiday, were flooded with telegrams and phone calls from irate constituents demanding action on impeachment. At a morning meeting, the returning members of the House Democratic Steering and Policy Committee endorsed the selection of Rodino to conduct the inquiry, clearing the way for the speaker to make a public statement at his regularly scheduled daily press briefing. At eleven forty-five in the morning, Albert, accompanied by Rodino, entered the Speaker's ceremonial room, crowded with reporters. Albert read a statement deploring the president's actions on Saturday and expressing the hope that this would not impede consideration of Gerald Ford's nomination. Signaling the change in his position on impeachment, Albert announced that all resolutions on the subject "will be referred to the Committee on the Judiciary, where I am confident, consideration will begin without delay." Rodino followed with his brief remarks, acknowledging that the "events of the past few days leave us little choice at this time but to move forward with preparation for impeachment proceedings."[47]

When Albert gaveled the crowded House chamber to order at noon, a long line of members rose to condemn the president's decision to fire the special prosecutor and to declare their support for an impeachment inquiry that was no longer considered "premature." Before the end of the legislative day, more than two dozen impeachment resolutions were introduced and sent to the Judiciary Committee.[48]

Peter Rodino was now at the center of two momentous undertakings:

impeaching a sitting president and selecting his potential replacement. "Upon no other member of Congress—even the redoubtable Sam Ervin—has fallen the weight of responsibility now carried by Representative Peter W. Rodino," a *Washington Star* editorial observed.[49] Yet, for the past twenty-five years, he had carried out his public duties and recorded his significant legislative achievements largely outside of the national spotlight. As a result, he was an unknown figure to most Americans, and many wondered if this obscure politician from New Jersey was up to the task. Did he have the skills and character needed to steer the country through a challenging moment in history? Was he prepared for this time and this purpose?

CHAPTER TWO

NEWARK

ONE FACTOR ABOVE ALL OTHERS shaped the destiny of the place where Peter Rodino was born and spent most of his life: location. From its very beginning as a Lenni Lenape settlement and a new promised land founded by Puritan dissidents, Newark's physical site played the most critical role in its development. The thirty families that left the colony of Connecticut under the leadership of Robert Treat in 1666 hoped to find a safe sanctuary for their strict religious practices and a new home where they could prosper. After considering several possible alternatives along the eastern part of the Jersey coast, they finally purchased land from the local native peoples on the western bank of the great River Pesayak that was the most geographically advantageous. The river, which the Puritan settlers later anglicized to Passaic, gently flowed into a large bay before reaching the Atlantic Ocean. Its navigability offered easy portage and a pathway to abundant fishing. The extensive marshy meadowlands surrounding the area provided an additional source of food, with a network of small creeks and brooks bisecting the land and supplying multiple sources of fresh water. The original Newark settlement, named in honor of England's Newark-on-Trent, comprised sixty-two square miles beginning at the river and extending to the foothills of the Watchung Mountains.[1]

Although Newark was founded as a religious haven, its location fostered the settlement's development as an important transportation crossroad, and commerce soon overshadowed theology.[2]As a transportation hub with easy access to New York City and other markets, Newark became a desirable place to do business. The original settlers were primarily devoted to farming. But even in its formative decades, Newark attracted artisans, and the earliest industry to develop was the tanning of hides from livestock and the crafting of quality leather goods like shoes and harnesses. By 1860, Newark was considered one of the leading centers for innovation and manufacturing in the United States.[3]

After the American Civil War, a new wave of industrialization dramatically accelerated the growth and diversity of the businesses in the city. Larger facilities replaced modest workshops and factory smokestacks now competed with church steeples for prominence along the city's skyline. Marveling at this industrial might, the *New York Times* informed its readers that "the trunk you travel with is nine cases out of ten of Newark manufacture, the hat you wear was made there, the buttons on your coat, the shirt on your back, your brush, the tin ware you use in your kitchen, the oil cloth you walk on, the harness and bit you drive with, all owe to Newark their origins." [4]

Maintaining this position of dominance required a steady supply of workers to keep factories operating at full capacity, and Newark increasingly looked overseas for a solution to this problem. The first group of immigrants to come to the city in any significant number were the Irish who arrived in the 1830s. Attracted by opportunities in the leather industry and construction, they initially settled "down neck," an inhospitable area along the bend of the lower Passaic River, abutting the marshy meadowlands with its mosquitos and smells. The Germans followed, finding work in the jewelry industry and the growing number of breweries and saloons, further establishing the "Neck" as the unofficial inaugural home for newly arrived immigrants. Within a few decades, these groups had succeeded in moving up the socioeconomic ladder to become foremen or supervisors and relocated to better neighborhoods. Many were no longer willing to do menial jobs paving streets or hauling goods because they "found something better to do."[5]

Fortunately for the city, the insatiable demand for industrial workers coincided with significant changes in eastern and southern Europe that precipitated a tidal wave of new immigrants to the United States. The unification of Italy in the 1860s ended decades of war and almost a thousand years of foreign domination of its territory. With such a difficult and fractured history, there was no unifying "Italian" identity that could instantly engender a new loyalty and commitment to the unified nation as had occurred in neighboring countries. Province and village remained the most important political entity in an individual's life and the focus of their allegiance and identification.[6]

This was particularly true in the southern regions of Italy, where the authorities in Rome were regarded with suspicion. The national government was dominated by the wealthier northern provinces, and its initial actions only deepened existing regional tensions. The ending of internal customs barriers between regions hurt the small industrial base in the south, which could not compete in an unregulated market against larger, established businesses in the north. At the same time, the government imposed external tariffs to protect these northern industries from foreign competition, which inflated the cost of goods throughout the entire country. The final blow was the enactment of additional taxes that placed a disproportionate burden on the already-struggling poor and further tightened the economic squeeze.[7]

The negative impact of Italian unification on the largely agrarian south was exacerbated by a series of natural disasters that had plagued the region in the preceding years. Most villagers were agricultural workers who lived off the land and worked for local or absentee landlords as tenants, sharecroppers, or farm hands. A sustained drought had diminished arable land and seriously reduced seasonal yields. Regardless of the weather, the workers had to pay landlords their share of any harvest, dipping into their own food supplies to make up for any shortfalls. The region also suffered from the devastation caused by periodic earthquakes, which left many villages either destroyed or in a serious state of disrepair.[8]

Facing this chronic adversity, families struggled to eke out a meager subsistence. Everyone was forced to work from sunrise to sunset on the small plot of land they rented on the outskirts of the village. School was a luxury few could afford, and an estimated 70 percent of the population in southern Italy older than five was illiterate.[9] Many lived in substandard housing under unsanitary conditions, and the scarcity of clean drinking water contributed to significant increases in diseases like cholera and malaria. The optimistic promises of Italian unification were hard to reconcile with the harsh realities of hunger and hopelessness that the Italian people faced every day.[10]

The solution for many Italians was to seek a better life in the United States. What started as a trickle in the 1870s became a great Italian exodus before the end of the century. Stories of unlimited opportunities from the first wave of departees encouraged others to follow, with many of these emigrants sending money home to assist with the journey. Several American companies, desperate to find workers, dispatched representatives to travel throughout the Italian countryside to recruit future employees with promises of a guaranteed job and a cash incentive. Agents from the steamship companies were not far behind, eager to sign up new transatlantic passengers. A network of "padrones" with backing from interests in the United States operated in direct violation of the American ban on contract labor, exploiting potential immigrants by offering to pay their passage in exchange for absolute control over where they would work and live. The Italian government, anxious to ease the strains of southern poverty, largely encouraged these departures, and more than four million Italians left their homeland, making them the largest ethnic group migrating to the United States from the 1890s until the passage of immigration restrictions in 1924.[11]

Despite the severe deprivations at home, it was not easy for someone living in southern Italy to leave. The initial barrier was paying for a ticket that cost more than most peasants earned in a year. Once funding was secured, the hopeful immigrant needed to travel to the port city of Naples, which boasted a dozen shipping lines and was the major point of embarkation for southern Italians.

Because most of the villages in the region were located far from any railroad, a horse-drawn cart was most often the fastest available transport. But many could not even afford such an option and were forced to walk the fifty miles to Naples carrying what few possessions they had with them. Each shipping line operated on a different sailing schedule, and completion of the overland section of the journey required careful planning. A delayed arrival would leave too little time to complete the requisite paperwork; too early of an appearance would result in having to spend limited funds on lodgings or sleeping in the street. For a traveler who had never ventured beyond village boundaries, Naples was an overwhelming and dangerous place that was rife with pickpockets and con artists.[12]

On the day of departure, every passenger was screened and their name entered into the ship's manifest. After 1891, shipping companies at the port of exit were responsible for examining, vaccinating, and disinfecting all passengers before a sailing. Unlike the perfunctory screenings of shipping companies from other countries, the Italian lines carefully assessed the health and physical condition of each individual to ensure that they would not be sent back for failing the medical examination in the United States. They required all passengers to provide certain background information, including the amount of money they possessed and the details of any criminal record. Officials would then ask these same questions of the passengers upon arrival to check for any inconsistencies.[13]

While ships offered first- and second-class cabins, most immigrants traveled in third class or steerage. The third-class fare from Naples to New York, with one or two intermediate stops, ranged from $15 to $28. Third class was located below deck with no ventilation, low ceilings, and little light. It was divided into three compartments: single men, single women, and families. Passengers slept on thin mattresses in double or triple bunks. They received two meals a day. With seasickness rampant, sanitary conditions quickly deteriorated. Many passengers preferred to spend the day up on deck in the small area designated for the third class to avoid the smelly, crowded, and noisy conditions below. They were forced to endure this discomfort for the next two or three weeks as their overcrowded ship crossed the Atlantic Ocean.[14]

The ordeal of the steerage passengers did not end with their arrival in New York. Immigration and customs officials on board the ship processed the first- and second-class passengers. All third-class passengers, prior to 1892, were examined at the considerably less hospitable Castle Garden immigration station, located at the southern tip of Manhattan and under the jurisdiction of New York State. As the flow of immigrants dramatically increased, and immigrant composition began to include more individuals from southern and eastern Europe, there was a growing demand for stricter screening and tougher enforcement of immigration laws. Coupled with this heightened apprehension about the demographics of the new arrivals, a myriad of public scandals involving corruption and mismanagement at Castle Garden underscored the shortcomings of the entire operation. As a result of these concerns, the federal government assumed responsibility for the management of the immigration service and agreed to build a screening center that was isolated from the pernicious influences of the city and better suited to sifting out the undesirables.[15]

For the immigrants arriving as third-class passengers after January 1892, the opening of this new immigration processing facility on Ellis Island in New York Harbor brought greater scrutiny and delay in stepping onto American soil. While first- and second-class passengers leisurely disembarked at the ship's berth on the Hudson River waterfront, steerage passengers were sent to a waiting area on the pier, where they were given an identification tag with their ship manifest number and then herded onto barges for transport to the island. Once they entered Ellis Island's main building, passengers were met by stern uniformed officers and then forced to temporarily surrender all their worldly possessions. They then climbed a long staircase as doctors carefully watched from the landing for any sign of physical impairment. During the next five hours, they underwent a series of medical and mental examinations. Inspectors, assisted by translators, rechecked the accuracy of the information provided on the ship's manifest. The unlucky were detained for further evaluation, and some were sent home; the others returned to Manhattan to either meet waiting relatives or find their way in this new country alone.[16]

Immigrants arriving from Italy faced an additional burden. Unlike earlier arrivals from northern Europe, Italian immigrants were regarded as "undesirable citizens from the land of the vendetta, the mafia, and the bandit."[17] This prejudice was rife among Ellis Island inspectors; they disproportionately detained Italians for extended periods and used minor infractions committed years earlier to justify deportation. More than eight hundred Italian passengers from the Anchor Line's *Bolivia* were detained on Ellis Island in April 1896, causing severe overcrowding, and more than 250 were eventually sent back home. When questioned about the situation, federal Superintendent of Immigration Herman Stump defended this harsh treatment and argued that "this undesirable class has to be examined more carefully than others…with the exception of the Italians, the immigration now coming here seems to be a superior class."[18] Clearly, being Italian was not something that was going to increase the prospects for a smooth entry into the United States.

These obstacles were not enough to keep Pellegrino Rodia from joining the great migration from Italy. Rodia, whose surname would go through several iterations in the US before finally becoming Rodino, fit the profile of the average Italian immigrant: young, male, single, and from the south.[19] He was born on May 30, 1883, in the village of Atripalda, a part of the Avellino province in the landlocked Campania region about fifty miles from Naples. Located in the valley of the Sabato river, which ran through the town, Atripalda was a farming village dotted with small tenant holdings and noted for its hazelnut trees. Like much of Avellino, Atripalda suffered from the hardships brought on by Italian unification and natural disasters.[20]

Pellegrino, which means pilgrim, was the son of Pellegrino Rodia and his wife, Antoinette Rosano. His large family of seven brothers and one sister struggled to survive as peasant farmers, and, by the time he reached his late teens, both his father and several of his brothers had died. Although able to read and write, it is unlikely that Rodia had any formal schooling. But from an early age he did show skill in working with his hands, which led him to learn the basics of the carpentry trade. It may have been this talent that singled him out as the one chosen to make the journey to America.[21]

In March 1900, Rodia said goodbye to his family and left the village of

Atripalda for the first and last time. His sixty-five-year-old relative, Vincenzo Melillo, had made the crossing three years earlier, sailing on the *Patria* from Naples to New York before settling in Newark, New Jersey. No doubt Melillo wrote home about the job opportunities in America and encouraged Pellegrino to follow him. Considering the Rodia family's financial situation, he probably sent a prepaid ticket or contributed a portion of the money needed to pay the fare. His ticket was for the Italian liner *Manilla,* which was one of the workhorses of the steerage trade.. The well-worn ship carried 1,310 passengers with sixty in first-class cabins and the remaining 1,250 in third class. With ten dollars in his pocket and wearing an identification tag around his neck, Rodia set sail for his new life.[22]

The arrival of the *Manilla* in New York on April 6 was ill-timed. A few years earlier there had been a devastating fire on Ellis Island that had destroyed several wooden structures, including the main processing center. During the rebuild, immigration inspections were relocated to the old Barge Office in New York City, which was used for customs inspections before the opening of Ellis Island. It was inadequate for the number of immigrants being processed and was soon overcrowded, making a disorienting entry experience even worse.[23] The same five-hour disembarkation process was carried out here as it was on Ellis Island, except now inspection lines, medical examinations, baggage handling, railroad ticket agents, and money changing desks all competed for the same small space. "From the time a foreigner leaves his native land to seek a new home in the United States until he runs the gauntlet of the blue coated guardians of the New York Barge Office's front door," the *New York Times* reported, "his lot is anything but a pleasant one."[24]

As a steerage passenger, Rodia was transferred on a small boat from the *Manilla*'s arrival pier to the Barge Office in lower Manhattan. Because the building was so small, passengers were forced to wait on the boats regardless of the weather until there was space to enter the station and begin the long inspection process. According to the ship's manifest and his affirmation at the Barge Office with the aid of a translator, Rodia was in good health, had never committed a crime, and his passage had not been paid for by an agent. He listed his occupation as "laborer," Newark was his final destination, and his sole contact in the United States was his "uncle" Vincenzo Melillo. He passed all the various checkpoints without any complications and walked out the front door of the Barge Office into the chaos outside.

Rodia began the last leg of his trip at the nearby landing for the trans-Hudson ferry that conveyed passengers to the three railroad terminals located in New Jersey. The train ride transported him across the meadowlands—thirty minutes later he had arrived in downtown Newark. Like earlier immigrants to the city, he headed to the Italian neighborhood around Mulberry Street and the extended "down neck" area, where "uncle" Vincenzo and other relatives lived in close proximity to the riverside factories and rail yards. In the short walk from the train station, Rodia was introduced to the overwhelming sights, sounds, and opportunities of his new home.[25]

When Pellegrino Rodia stepped off the train, there were almost 250,000 people living in Newark. The city was booming and boasted 225 miles of improved streets, seventy miles of electric streetcar service, and six railroads—all offering employment for unskilled laborers. More than 3,300 manufacturing plants within the municipal boundaries employed an estimated 50,000 workers and hired more every week. Among the major construction projects underway were a new city hall, the building of a monumental French gothic cathedral, and the transformation of an old stone quarry into a public park.[26] But alongside these economic achievements, there was a parallel story of malnutrition, chronic illness, and premature death. The situation had only deteriorated in the decade since the last census labeled Newark the "unhealthiest city" in the United States, with the most cases of tuberculosis and typhoid and the highest rate of infant mortality. The enormous influx of immigrants created serious overcrowding and squalor; buildings designed for sixteen families instead housed sixty or seventy, with five families crushed into a single apartment. The New Jersey Board of Tenement House Supervision found "foul malodorous privy vaults, filled to the yard level…sleeping rooms so dark that even in broad daylight objects at a distance of only a few feet were indiscernible."[27]

If Rodia's transition to this new reality of startling contrasts was difficult, at least he was not alone. There was already a sizable Italian community in the city and their number would exceed 20,000 by the end of the decade.[28] Most Italian residents were non-English-speaking unskilled laborers from southern Italy willing to work in the difficult and dangerous jobs no one else wanted, ten hours a day, six days a week. The railroads, transit companies, and municipal engineering departments were the first to hire large numbers of Italians. They frequently used the services of an agent who recruited work crews in the neighborhood, charging the laborer a monthly fee and a percentage of future wages. Others were hired directly by factories, where they started at the bottom doing menial, unpleasant, and underpaid jobs. Considering his skill working with his hands, Rodia was able to move up quickly from laborer to factory worker and cabinetmaker before securing a position as a machinist.[29]

Beyond employment, the Italian community in Newark provided Rodia with an American version of the community he left behind. The emergence of "Little Italy" neighborhoods helped to ease the transition for newly arrived immigrants by encouraging the maintenance of Italian cultural traditions. These new world villages were firmly anchored by a local Catholic church and dominated by residents from a particular area or province in Italy, which encouraged neighbors and relatives to follow. Inside the colony, language barriers evaporated, and the neighborhood became a source for money, housing referrals, and a social network that sparked friendships and romantic relationships. Equally important, these neighborhoods offered a sense of security in a country that was less than welcoming to Italians.[30]

Newark was one of a handful of cities in the United States that had a significant enough concentration of Italians to support several thriving Italian neighborhoods. Of the four Italian enclaves in the city, the First Ward located west and north of downtown was the largest. The first Italian to settle in this formerly Irish neighborhood was Angelo Mattia from Avellino. After opening a boarding house in 1873, he encouraged other immigrants to join him. As the neighborhood grew and Italians prospered, they were able to purchase land and replace old clapboard houses with tenement housing for the expanding population. A group of Italians purchased the adjoining grounds of the former New Jersey Soldier's Home and subdivided the site to create an expanded street grid. At the center of neighborhood life was St. Lucy's Church, a Roman Catholic church established in 1891. The church was the site of elaborate feast day celebrations honoring the various patron saints of the Italian villages represented by its parishioners, most notably Avellino's Saint Gerard Majella.[31]

By the time Pellegrino Rodia arrived in Newark, the First Ward was a vibrant and bustling place. Eighth Avenue, its main thoroughfare, was lined with bakeries and butchers, cafes and saloons, barbershops, and music stores. The next street over was barely passable because of the pushcarts and street vendors competing for customers. Social clubs and mutual aid societies occupied prominent storefronts, and a streetcar line connected the area with the rest of the city. If no longer a village, the First Ward was still a refuge for Italians that offered the comfort of social intimacy and some distance from the potential perils of the outside world.[32]

This next, and ultimately final, stop in Pellegrino Rodia's long journey is where he met his future wife. Giuseppina Gerardo had lived most of her life in the First Ward. The Gerardo family originally hailed from San Fele in the Potenza province in southern Italy, which was located about sixty miles to the east of Atripalda. When the great 1870s migration began, immigrants from San Fele either went to Buffalo or Newark. Consequently, members of the Gerardo family were among the first wave of Italian immigrants to arrive in the city, establishing a position in the early fabric of the burgeoning Italian community.[33]

Unlike most residents of the First Ward, Giuseppina was born in Newark. Her parents were Rosa Papa and Pasquale Gerardo, who had come to Newark from Brooklyn to pursue job opportunities and stayed to raise a growing family, which included Giuseppina by 1884. Eventually, the Gerardos entered real estate development, constructing and managing tenement buildings along Seventh Avenue. Pasquale was a prominent figure in the community, serving as the first Italian interpreter for the Newark court system, where he helped many newly arrived immigrants navigate the complexities of government. Considering the close-knit social fabric of the neighborhood, it was inevitable that Rodia would come in contact with the Gerardo family either as a tenant, employee, or acquaintance after he moved to the area. His apartment was just around the corner from Giuseppina's home, and the two began a short courtship after being introduced. On May 11, 1905, Pellegrino Rodini, formerly Rodia, and Giuseppina Gerardo were married at Newark's city hall. Justice of the Peace Harry J. Hunter conducted the brief civil ceremony.[34]

The newlyweds rented a small apartment in a First Ward tenement building on Factory Street, where they coped with the daily hardships of no central heating, no electricity, and an outdoor communal toilet.[35] Their first child, a daughter named Ann, was born two years later. The future Peter Rodino, who they named Pellegrino after his father and grandfather, followed on June 7, 1909. The growing family needed more space, and later that year they moved to a larger apartment in a building located on Seventh Avenue in the commercial district. The relocation marked the final transformation of the Rodia name; the *Newark City Directory* published at the end of the year listed the new residents as "Rodino."[36]

Their third child, a son named Patrick, became the first family member born with this new surname. Not long after his birth, the family was confronted with a devastating and unexpected change in their already difficult circumstances. Guiseppina, whose frail health was aggravated by the living conditions in their tenement, finally lost her long battle with tuberculosis in the summer of 1913. Her death at twenty-eight was a cataclysmic event for the family, both emotionally and financially. The senior Pellegrino spent all his time either working or looking for his next job, which left him unable to take care of his three small children during the day. The close-knit social structure of the First Ward helped him through the immediate crisis, and Giuseppina's sister, Mamie, and her husband, Dan, provided a longer-term solution when they agreed to take care of their niece and nephews until the family situation improved. Within a year, the children returned home when their father married Antoinette "Gemma" Paladino, a First Ward widow born in Italy. If practicalities influenced both of their decisions to remarry, it appeared to be a good match, and the couple remained together until Gemma's death thirty years later.[37]

Gemma brought several important changes to the Rodino household. A talented seamstress and embroiderer, she used her skill to sew clothes for her stepchildren and earned extra income by doing outside tailoring, improving their precarious financial condition. She was socially active in the neighborhood and was the secretary for one of the mutual aid societies that were an important part of the safety net for Italian Americans at a time when there was little government support. These local organizations, mirroring village life and regional identification, provided dues-paying members with advice, financial support during an illness, and help with funeral expenses. Hundreds of these societies were established throughout the United States. In Newark, storefronts on Seventh and Eighth avenues served as headquarters for the larger organizations.[38] Gemma's employer was a smaller aid society and every week the members visited the previously quiet Rodino apartment to record their dues in the society ledger. While Ann found it difficult to accept a replacement for her mother, brother Pellegrino welcomed Gemma's arrival enthusiastically. From the beginning, he considered her his "mother, never his step mother." In return, she doted on him and encouraged his innate curiosity.[39]

With Gemma's nurturing influence, the younger Pellegrino thrived within the five square blocks of his gritty urban habitat. His apartment, at the corner of Seventh and Clifton, was across the street from Branch Brook Park, the city's largest outdoor space, which provided easy access to a variety of recreational activities. He was surrounded by a large, boisterous extended family in his tenement building, all of whom were ready to offer help or a meal. Baptized at St. Lucy's a month before his mother had died, Pellegrino and his family made the short walk together every Sunday to attend mass and on feast days to enjoy the special band concerts.[40]

At the center of this compact world was the recently opened McKinley Grammar School on Eighth Avenue, built to meet the needs of the neighborhood's growing population. Here, the primarily Italian American student body initially confronted the often sharp contrast between the immigrant culture they experienced at home and the expected norms of their parents' adopted country. This new reality became apparent on the first day of school when all Italian forenames were automatically Americanized and affixed to official school documents, giving these appellations an appearance of permanency that was rarely challenged. Pellegrino welcomed his new designation as "Peter" and continued the assimilation process a few years later when he inexplicably added the non-Italian middle name "Wallace." Beyond changing names, McKinley encouraged assimilation through music, weekly flag drills, special celebrations of American historical events, and English language classes for parents in the evening. The school's quarterly publication, *The Tattler*, regularly printed patriotic essays and poems written by the students and used this platform to encourage conformity with the Newark Board of Education's version of a national ideal.[41]

Despite these efforts to prepare students for life beyond their own ethnic enclave, McKinley graduates faced considerable obstacles and limited choices as the children of immigrants living in the First Ward. Under New Jersey law, a student was permitted to leave school for regular legal employment when they turned fourteen.[42] The belief that hard work, not education, was the quickest way to achieve economic security was still strong in these families, a sentiment that enticed some students to head to the nearest factory or join a construction crew. Many families desperately needed an additional breadwinner to pay the bills; leaving school was simply a matter of survival. A potential option for those completing their education at McKinley was to attend one of Newark's commercial and manual training high schools. These trade schools prepared students with the skills they would need for a variety of nonprofessional jobs, such as mechanic, secretary, or carpenter. For a select few, the city's prestigious Barringer High School offered an academic program of study, which had rigorous requirements that included mandatory Latin, foreign language training, and a heavy emphasis on the liberal arts. It was a gateway for public school students in Newark who wanted to attend college and have a professional career.[43]

Enjoying school and hoping to continue his education, Rodino decided he wanted to attend Barringer and later recalled his determination to be part of this "beloved academic breeding ground of scholars, doctors, star athletes and many other distinguished alumni."[44] Fortunately, the family's economic status had continued to improve, and financial constraints did not prevent him from pursuing this goal. His father was now regularly employed as a machinist at the Hyatt Roller Bearing factory across the Passaic River in Harrison, where he would work until retirement. He also maintained a part-time carpentry business in the courtyard of their apartment. Father and son always enjoyed a close, comfortable relationship, and the senior Rodino fully supported his son's aspirations and encouraged his ambition.[45] Although Barringer High School was within walking distance of Rodino's Seventh Avenue apartment, it provided a dramatically different environment where, for the first time, Rodino could have regular contact with non-Italians, meet people who lived in neighborhoods he had never visited, and spend time with a group of peers equally focused on achieving upward mobility. After a less-than-stellar beginning, he became a serious student and excelled in all his courses, particularly Latin and French. After school, he participated in several extracurricular activities, including the cheering squad.[46]

Attending Barringer gave Rodino both the confidence and the opportunity to venture outside the boundaries of the First Ward. Thanks to his cousin, he was hired to work part-time in the art department of Hahne & Company, the upscale department store located downtown. He began visiting the nearby nationally acclaimed Newark Public Library and its enormous trove of publicly accessible resources. "My God, all these books here," Rodino recalled of his inaugural foray into the majestic four-story building, "how I wanted to grasp them all, read them all and know what's in all of them."[47] Yet leaving the safety of the neighborhood was not without risk; ethnic stereotyping and overt hostility were potent forces in a city that had experienced a large influx of Italian immigrants. There were few Italians in positions of authority in Newark's municipal government and only a handful on the police force, placing Italian Americans at an immediate disadvantage in protesting discrimination or harassment. Peter Rodino personally confronted this harsh reality during his senior year of high school when he was walking home at night from a holiday party. Two police officers he met on the street accused him of cursing in Italian solely on the basis of his ethnic features and savagely beat him with a nightstick. Rodino lost his two front teeth in the attack and was left bleeding on the ground. Remarkably, he still had the wherewithal to remember the assaulting officer's badge number. In his bloodied condition, he went to the nearest police station, where his complaint was immediately rebuffed.[48]

Unlike many immigrants who were afraid or ill-prepared to challenge authority, neither Pellegrino nor his son were willing to forget the incident and simply accept this injustice. They enlisted the assistance of the Italian Catholic Union, which was an informal liaison between the First Ward and the city government, and received an appointment with Police Commissioner William Brennan. As the father of a recent Barringer graduate, who would later become a Supreme Court justice, Brennan was sympathetic to the plight of the young student in his office and promised a thorough investigation. He honored his commitment, and the final settlement negotiated in the following weeks required the offending officer to apologize and pay Rodino's dental bill, providing a rare victory for Newark's Italian Americans.[49]

With this painful matter resolved and graduation approaching, Rodino began to focus on his future plans and a desire to serve others. He quickly abandoned his initial thoughts of becoming a doctor because of the costs of a medical education. His passion was writing, particularly poetry, and he always carried a notebook to jot down random thoughts or unfamiliar words he could later look up in a dictionary. But he recognized that there were no immediate opportunities to earn a living as a writer and this would most likely have to remain an avocation. Instead, he decided that the most practical and attainable path for him was to pursue a career in the law, a profession that was accorded a degree of social status and provided ample opportunities to help the community. He announced this decision to his family, and the January 1927 Barringer High School yearbook listed Syracuse University as his college destination. In fact, he never applied to Syracuse or any other four-year college. Until he earned the money to fund his higher education, his only destination after graduation was the nearest workplace.[50]

The easiest and quickest way to make money in the First Ward was to get involved in the two leading illegal activities: bootlegging and gambling. These were the latest in a long line of notorious enterprises in the community that cast a shadow over all its citizens and contributed to the narrative linking Italians with violence and crime. One of the first examples of this was the "Black Hand," which operated in Newark in the early 1900s. Taking the name from its warning mark, this loosely affiliated group of criminals had come from New York City to terrorize the Italian immigrants in the First Ward. Using the threat of violence and kidnapping, members demanded protection money from shopkeepers and other honest, hardworking citizens. The press sensationalized the Black Hand's activities, and some observers warned of its connection with the infamous Mafia in Italy. The social isolation of the neighborhood and its residents' innate distrust of the police and the government made the First Ward an easier place to conduct criminal activities. Even as the Black Hand's influence waned, the seeds had already been planted for the neighborhood to be the focal point of regular gang activity and witness to the eventual rise of organized crime.[51]

The enactment of national Prohibition in 1920 accelerated all of this activity. Prohibition outlawed the manufacture, sale, and distribution of distilled spirits in the United States. With its long Atlantic coastline, New Jersey was the center of "rum row" smuggling, and Newark became a key distribution and production center. One of the first Newark locals to see the enormous potential of Prohibition was Abner "Longy" Zwillman, a small-time criminal operating out of the predominantly Jewish Third Ward. Initially providing only transportation and protection for bootleggers, he soon joined their ranks and fought to dominate Newark's liquor trade.[52]

Zwillman found his way into the First Ward through saloonkeeper Joe Reinfeld. Jewish and Italian racketeers mingled with local politicians at his establishment on Eighth Avenue, and Reinfeld directed an extensive liquor-smuggling syndicate. His closest rivals were the Mazzocchi brothers, headquartered at the American Victory Café, a billiard hall and speakeasy one avenue over. Assisted by lieutenant Ruggiero Boiardo, later known as "Richie the Boot," the Mazzocchis operated several large production stills in

Newark, including a facility hidden behind a tenement building in the heart of the First Ward. The decade-long fight for dominance between gangs and ultimately within each gang, led to the ascendancy of Zwillman and Boiardo as the undisputed crime bosses of Newark. It also brought a new level of public violence to the First Ward and contributed to its growing reputation for lawlessness.[53]

Growing up in this neighborhood, Peter Rodino witnessed this firsthand and remembered it as a pretty rough place. Walking to McKinley, he regularly passed the two most notorious streets in the area: Aqueduct Alley and Drift Street. Aqueduct Alley hosted daily dice games guarded by gang members who stood on the corner watching for the police. Drift Street housed a dingy pool hall, constant gambling, and street fights. The saloon on the ground floor of his apartment building attracted a raucous clientele throughout the day and was the site of periodic gunfights. Rodino was only ten when he witnessed his first shooting as he walked to school, and he recalled a later incident *inside* his apartment building when someone rushed past him on the stairway and began shooting on the floor above. He knew at an early age that there were those in his neighborhood "who had taken up what they considered to be an easy life, but it led to a life of crime."[54] Rodino was confronted with this same choice when local thugs offered him a considerable sum of money to unlock the courtyard gate so they could steal the bootleg liquor stored in the basement of the tenement saloon. He refused the offer and, risking retribution, warned the owner. Forced to choose, he had followed his own moral compass.[55]

Unwilling to take the easy path, Rodino found a job as a clerk at the Public Service Corporation's downtown headquarters. The company was one of Newark's largest, with extensive utility and transit operations. While the work was far from challenging, Rodino appreciated the competitive salary and free lunch.[56] Hoping to save enough money to begin evening law classes in the fall of 1928, his plans were derailed by the New Jersey State Board of Education. At the beginning of the year, the board had adopted a higher threshold for admission to law school, replacing the previous minimum requirement of a high school diploma with a new prerequisite of two years of undergraduate education. This was unwelcomed news for both Rodino and the academic institution where he planned to study law. The New Jersey Law School, located near the Public Service building, had been established two decades earlier to provide a convenient and affordable alternative to law schools in New York. From the beginning, recruitment targeted working class men and women, particularly the first-generation children of the state's immigrant population. All classes were held in either the late afternoon or evening to allow students to work full time. In response to the state's imposition of higher application standards, the law school decided to create its own undergraduate college, Dana College. A special two-year prelaw program offered traditional liberal arts courses, and, upon completion, students received a certificate and guaranteed admission to the law school.[57]

Rodino was among those in the college's inaugural class, and, owing to the generosity of his father, he was able to use all his earnings for tuition and books. He continued to work during the day at Public Service and was eventually promoted to assistant foreman in the transit division. He received his certificate from Dana College in June 1930.[58] Once again, his timing was unfortunate; the stock market crash eight months earlier had sparked an economic freefall, triggering the start of the Great Depression. The impact on Newark was swift. Within a year, employment in the city fell by 25 percent.[59] The only government assistance available was a small program operated by Newark's Overseer of the Poor. Established decades earlier to address the temporary needs of indigent families, it was ill-equipped to address a long-term emergency. Consequently, beggars and soup kitchens became regular features of downtown Newark.[60]

The Rodino family was not immune from the harsh economic impact of the Depression. The first blow came when Pellegrino, or Peter senior as he now identified himself, lost his job at the ball bearing factory. Considering the sharp decline in manufacturing, he had little expectation of an early return. Shortly after his father's setback, Rodino lost his job at Public Service. As the family struggled under these challenging circumstances, law school seemed an unaffordable luxury. It was a discouraging realization for someone who had patiently worked on his preparatory studies and watched many of his affluent Barringer friends finish college and begin their postgraduate education. Now he wondered if he would ever achieve his goal and questioned the wisdom of going forward. "I had to decide," he remembered, "whether I would quit completely, or whether I would at least leave school for the time being and then work a bit more, acquire some money, in order to be able to go back to school."[61]

Pushing aside his doubts and propelled by an inner fortitude, Rodino moved ahead and, for the next several years, worked toward his dream of becoming a lawyer while helping to keep the family solvent. Without any particular qualifications or skill, it was not easy to find a job—for every opening, there were hundreds of applicants. Job security had evaporated as businesses hired and fired depending on demand, and most of the positions he secured did not last. Rodino attempted to sell insurance door-to-door, but few could afford the premiums. He worked in several factory sweatshops as a manual laborer and occasionally found a place on construction and street paving crews. Of the many jobs he held, his favorite was working as a ticket agent for the Pennsylvania Railroad. He was the sole operator at the Harrison station during the graveyard shift, and the paucity of customers allowed him to spend much of that time reading books. After his long walk home in the morning and a few hours of sleep, he was ready to accept any available daytime jobs.[62]

Throughout this difficult period, Rodino was sustained by the two great loves of his life: writing and his future wife, Ann. At just seventeen, he had first noticed Marianna "Ann" Stango on the steps of St. Lucy's following eleven o'clock mass. A year behind him at Barringer High School, she was the daughter of a tailor from southern Italy and his Newark-born wife. Along with her four younger brothers, the family lived on the north side of the First Ward. The family, considerably more affluent than the Rodinos, co-owned their large, elegantly furnished two-family house. Rodino was determined to meet Ann and, after several intentionally planned casual encounters, gained an introduction and exchanged a few words. "I knew then that this was the girl that I was going to marry," he recalled. "I was captivated."[63]

Recognizing that they were too young to date, the couple began a secret courtship and pretended to be friendly classmates in public. Following graduation, Ann accepted a job at the Prudential Insurance Company, which was located near the Public Service building, and the two met every day for lunch and walked home together. Their ruse ended when they were spotted by Ann's brother, who assumed her well-dressed escort was an "Americano," a bombshell discovery, considering most of the residents of the First Ward divided the population between Italians and non-Italians. Finally meeting Rodino and learning of his background, the relieved family welcomed him into their home and gave their approval to the match.[64] Everyone understood that the timing of the couple's future plans was dependent on the completion of Rodino's legal education.

With few job opportunities, Rodino revisited the idea of writing as a possible source of income. When his family moved to a new apartment on the corner of Drift Street, he began writing a novel about this notorious place. He could not find anyone interested in publishing the completed work he simply titled *Drift Street*, and he decided to switch to playwriting. Attempting to copy the realistic style of his favorite playwright, Eugene O'Neill, he penned *Black Sheep, Black Sheep*, a dark drama about the complications of an interracial romance. To his great disappointment, neither the play nor any of his other literary works were ever published.[65]

A potentially more lucrative outlet for his creativity was an invitation to use his poetry skills to write popular song lyrics for the music of his friend Anthony Petrolino. They began regularly visiting New York's Tin Pan Alley to pitch their songs to music publishers. Their lucky break came when they were invited to meet with agent Con Conrad and his client Ross Columbo. At the time, Columbo was one of the best-known singers in the country, with a long list of hit records and radio appearances. In a scene straight out of a movie musical, Rodino and Petrolino performed their songs "Girl of the Golden West" and "Never Too Late" for Columbo, who listened politely and suggested the boys might consider moving to Hollywood. No concrete offers followed, and Columbo's death shortly after the meeting closed that door.[66]

This setback did not discourage the novice songwriting team. When superstar crooner Rudy Vallée performed in Newark, they sent him a copy of one of their songs in a big box in a fruitless attempt to attract his attention. The duo's closest encounter with fame came when noted bandleader Paul Tremaine and his orchestra played "Girl of the Golden West" in a radio broadcast segment that spotlighted new talent and featured the unpublished hits of the week. The exposure did not result in any offers from music publishers or performers, and their song catalog never earned any royalties.[67]

While Rodino's writing produced no remuneration, at least his financial situation was beginning to improve after three tough years. His father was called back to the factory, and Rodino finally found a secure job that allowed him to return to school. At the suggestion of a friend, he applied for a position at the Art Metal Works factory, which was located in a seven-story brick building near the Passaic River. A manufacturer of finished metal products, the company was best known for its Ronson "windproof" cigarette lighter—the Depression had had little impact on smoking or the factory's productivity. Beginning on the assembly line, Rodino was quickly promoted to inspector at a higher salary, accelerating his plans to complete his education. He requested to work a modified and earlier shift so he could attend late afternoon classes. The day permission was granted, he registered at the New Jersey Law School.[68]

His new routine as a full-time worker and law student was not easy. Rising before dawn he left home for the factory and began his day prior to the start of the regular shift. At four in the afternoon, he walked ten minutes to school, where, most days, he had both a late afternoon and an evening class. Required courses for first-year students included torts, contracts, criminal law, pleadings, and domestic relations. Once classes ended, Rodino returned to the Drift Street apartment, where he spent several hours studying and grabbed a brief catnap before repeating this routine all over again the next day. He recalled that during this difficult regimen his one constant companion was a much-hated alarm clock.[69] Determined to make the most of his long-delayed law school experience, he still found the time to join the student council and law society, as well as play intramural basketball. His poems appeared regularly in the *Legacy*, the school's yearbook, and he was a writer for the school newspaper. The scope of his volunteerism was recognized when he was elected to the honorary extracurricular club, Seals and Scrolls, where he helped write and perform in the annual gridiron dinner lampooning the faculty.[70]

In addition to these activities, Rodino worked on honing the oratorical skills that were becoming an important part of his identity. At the Art Metal Works factory, he was considered the best debater and was frequently selected to give the remarks when a visiting celebrity was presented with a special Ronson lighter. To strengthen his raspy voice, probably the result of childhood diphtheria, he spent lunch hours in a nearby park reading his and other authors' poetry aloud. He recounted efforts to replicate Demosthenes' practice of placing pebbles in his mouth to improve diction, no doubt a puzzling sight for any passersby. He regularly demonstrated his speaking talents at the law school, serving as a member of the moot court and leading the debate team to a triumphant victory over the University of Pennsylvania.[71]

One of the requirements for admission to the New Jersey Bar was to serve in a clerkship for a total of twelve months, and the school encouraged students to start accruing the requisite hours as soon as possible. The first of Rodino's clerkships was with a real estate lawyer, where he spent most of his time polishing the chandeliers and crystal in the elegant downtown office. He was luckier at his next rotation, when he served as a clerk for municipal Judge Nicholas Albano, who personified the growing political influence of Italian Americans in Newark. The judge, a prominent Republican, was a member of all the major civic organizations and an unsuccessful candidate for commissioner in the last election. Alongside his judicial responsibilities, Albano was the publisher of *The Jersey Review,* a weekly newspaper featuring a mixture of news summaries, business reports, and local events. Impressed with Rodino's writing skills, he assigned him to editing the paper and writing a weekly column, extra duties his new clerk accepted with relish.[72]

The political activism of Judge Albano and his fellow Italian Americans was a relatively recent phenomenon in the city. Many of the early immigrants had eschewed politics either because they intended to eventually return to

Italy or from a general aversion to interacting with the government. The first successful attempt to exercise some political muscle occurred in the First Ward, where the concentration of voters made it possible to elect an Italian American to the city council. This representation at city hall was short-lived; when Newark adopted a commission form of government in 1918, single-member districts were eliminated, and candidates were required to run citywide. As the American-born children of immigrants reached voting age, they sparked an uptick in political participation, and social clubs were transformed into partisan organizations. With the Irish dominating Newark's Democratic machine, many of these new Italian voters registered as Republicans. But an Italian surname on the ballot trumped partisan affiliation, and both parties began offering an ethnically balanced slate that included a proportionate number of Italian Americans.[73]

Despite ongoing efforts from Judge Albano and others to increase political participation, Italian Americans were significantly underrepresented among Newark's registered voters in comparison to their overall population, and they lagged other ethnic groups in applying for citizenship.[74] Rodino, recognizing an opportunity to serve his own community, began visiting social clubs in the First Ward to give lectures on the important benefits of citizenship. Utilizing his fluency in Italian and polished speaking skills, he offered bilingual presentations that were well attended. At the same time, he started teaching English language classes at several sites in the neighborhood and at the downtown YMCA. His growing reputation as a grassroots activist and seasoned orator attracted the attention of the party leaders at the First Ward Democratic Club, and they asked him to join. Rodino had cast his first vote in 1932 for Franklin D. Roosevelt, and he gladly accepted their invitation. Continuing his advocacy for citizenship, he began speaking out on behalf of the New Deal to help solidify support among the Italian Americans in the neighborhood who had deserted the Republican party to vote for Roosevelt. Because of these efforts and his political connections, he was hired as a researcher in the Newark office of the National Youth Administration, created to provide work and education for young men and women, a plum job that allowed him to leave the factory.[75]

Rodino was now directly connected to Newark's Democratic party organization. When he graduated from law school in June 1937, the yearbook described him as an "actor, promotor, and politician," the first time his name and future vocation were linked together in print. His immediate priority was to fulfill his remaining clerkship obligations and pass the bar exam. Successfully completing both requirements the following year, he traveled to the state capitol building in Trenton for the ceremony marking his formal admission to the New Jersey Bar.[76] Perhaps the best example of Rodino's new political stature was the celebration organized to mark this special occasion. Instead of a modest family gathering at the small Drift Street apartment, a testimonial dinner was held in his honor at Vittorio Castle, the most elegant banquet hall in the First Ward. Many prominent Italian Americans attended, and former city commissioner A.P. Minisi served as master of ceremonies. Several local newspapers covered the event and presented flattering accounts of Rodino's determination to become a lawyer.[77]

With a degree from a non-Ivy League law school and an Italian surname, it was unlikely that Rodino was high on the recruitment list for the established White Anglo-Saxon Protestant (WASP)-dominated law firms in Newark. But he had already decided early in his legal education to become a general practitioner, believing this was the best way to serve the most people. He hoped that his reputation and the relationships he developed in the First Ward and among the Italian Americans living in other parts of the city would generate enough clients for him to earn a living as an attorney, not the most solid foundation for building a business. Once again, he refused to take the easy path; from the outset, he was prepared to refuse potentially lucrative legal work "to avoid any clients that might have been in any way tainted, or that might have had a kind of background that was questionable."[78] Confident in his ability to handle a broad variety of cases and different types of law, he opened his law firm in a small downtown office.

Not long after starting his solo practice, Rodino was asked to be one of the Democratic nominees in the 1940 election for the New Jersey General

Assembly. Members of the bicameral legislature's lower chamber were elected in countywide contests, and party leaders wanted a slate that was ethnically and geographically balanced. While the odds of winning in Republican-dominated Essex County were slim, it was an opportunity for Rodino to raise his public profile—he accepted the offer. The *Italian Tribune* newspaper, an early and steadfast Rodino booster, rhapsodized that his candidacy was the "fulfillment of the expressed desire of young Italian Americans everywhere to support one of their own for an elective office."[79] Rodino's name was hard to locate at the bottom of a crowded Democratic ticket led by President Roosevelt, who was seeking an unprecedented third term, and gubernatorial nominee Charles Edison, who was a former navy secretary and son of the state's world-famous inventor. Overshadowed by these more important contests, the assembly race was largely ignored and comparatively uneventful. When not trading barbs with his Republican opponents, Rodino helped new citizens register to vote, spoke at neighborhood political clubs, and appeared at the large "Roosevelt Night" rally that spotlighted all of the candidates.[80]

One issue that did inject some unexpected disquiet into the campaign was President Roosevelt's public criticism of Italian leader Benito Mussolini. Mussolini's rise to power in the 1920s and Italy's embrace of fascism were both regarded approvingly in the First Ward among those who admired his modernization program and restoration of the country's role as a world power. When Mussolini followed his ally Adolf Hitler and declared war on France and Great Britain in June 1940, an outraged President Roosevelt strongly condemned the action. Many Italian Americans were upset by the president's criticism and withdrew their support in the months before the election, further complicating the already uphill battle of the Democrats running countywide.[81] The *Italian Tribune* sidestepped the controversy by simply urging its readers to vote "Italian" and endorsed Rodino and the three other Italian American assembly candidates from both parties. Although Edison was elected governor and Roosevelt won the state, the president did not carry the First Ward as he had four years earlier. As expected, the Republican legislative candidates swept to victory with a 40,000-vote plurality. Rodino finished fifth among the twelve

Democratic nominees; it was a respectable showing for a political novice.[82]

Notwithstanding his election-day loss, Rodino was now part of Newark's political establishment. It was an impressive achievement considering that Pellegrino Rodia had arrived only four decades earlier as an impoverished immigrant. Taking advantage of the opportunities the expanding city presented, the family had overcome considerable obstacles to thrive and ultimately succeed in a tough urban environment. These were the experiences that framed Peter Rodino's world view, and the imprint of Newark on his character was indelible and irreversible. Forced to postpone his education plans and facing bleak job prospects, he learned that patience and determination were the essential tools required to reach a seemingly unattainable goal. Rodino's journey in his early life had allowed him to travel far without ever leaving the boundaries of his neighborhood. Writing in the law school's yearbook a few weeks before graduation, he acknowledge that regardless of these difficulties it was important to keep looking for the next challenge:

> Doth it not seem there's something that we lose
> When that we set ourselves upon we gain?
> The quickening pulse that eagerness endues,
> And expectation's joy and mingled pain.
> Be not content—oh rather let us choose
> Some further shore to seek to find again.[83]

He would not wait long to find his own "further shore," one that was far beyond the city limits of Newark, New Jersey.

CHAPTER THREE

EXPANDING HORIZONS

It was the first time the new Departmental Auditorium in Washington, DC, was serving as a venue for an event of national importance. Built as part of the Federal Triangle project, the ornate structure, with a sixty-foot-high ceiling and gilded carvings, was the only meeting space large enough to accommodate the anticipated capacity crowd of government officials, military officers, and journalists. On the stage, police officers guarded three priceless relics: a strip of yellowed linen cut from the covering of a chair used at the signing of the Declaration of Independence, a long wooden ladle made from a rafter in Philadelphia's Independence Hall, and a ten-gallon glass bowl from a similar event held two decades earlier. Shortly after twelve noon, President Franklin Roosevelt formally opened what he reminded the audience was "a most solemn ceremony." As the wooden ladle was used to stir the almost 9,000 blue capsules in the glass bowl, Lt. Col. (retired) Charles B. Morris stepped forward to place the historic yellow cloth over the eyes of Secretary of War Henry L. Stimson, repeating a task he first performed in 1917. The blindfolded Stimson then selected a capsule and handed it to the president; he declared that the piece of paper inside contained the number "158." With this simple pronouncement on October 29, 1940, the United States began a compulsory peacetime military draft that would impact the lives of more than sixteen million Americans, including Peter Rodino.[1]

Implementing the draft lottery that day was the climax of a turbulent year that had transformed American public opinion on the issue of defense preparedness. As the possibility of war began to cast a shadow over Europe in the mid-1930s, strong isolationist sentiment, well represented in Congress, had both fostered a sense of detachment and proscribed American neutrality through legislation. But Germany's invasion of Poland in the summer of 1939 and the subsequent declaration of war by Great Britain and France made it increasingly difficult to either ignore these events or dismiss their potential future consequences for the United States. The quick and sweeping German defeat of the European democracies during the spring of 1940, climaxing with the fall of France, encouraged a growing feeling of vulnerability. In Asia, Japan flexed its military muscle, waging war in China and forging an alliance with Germany and Italy. A majority of Americans now believed that their country would eventually be drawn into war. President Roosevelt, addressing a joint session of Congress in May, requested more than a billion dollars in new defense spending.[2]

Roosevelt's call for increased spending for the military was long overdue. Starved for resources during the past two decades, the army was using outdated equipment, including rifles, helmets, and tanks left over from the First World War. Equally alarming, the armed forces were woefully undermanned. The US Army ranked a dismal eighteenth in strength worldwide, lagging smaller countries like Switzerland. In fact, it rated even lower than Belgium and Holland, which Germany had easily defeated. This glaring gap prompted the first calls for a peacetime draft, and legislation was introduced in Congress. Although there was strong public support for compulsory military service, a coalition of isolationists, pacifists, and other opponents provided a formidable challenge to passage. In August, President Roosevelt finally overcame his election year caution and endorsed the proposal. When his Republican opponent Wendell Willkie also announced his support, the logjam broke, and the legislation became law on September 30, 1940.[3]

The Selective Training and Service Act of 1940 required all males between the ages of 21 and 36 to register for military service. Because this was a peacetime draft, recruits would only serve for one year, and almost all draftees would be allocated to the army. The system established by the new law was based on the American experience in 1917, when the United States declared war on Germany. The fundamental guiding principles were civilian control and decentralization, with local communities empowered to implement the draft. Each state was required to establish local draft boards, one per 30,000 residents, responsible for registering, classifying eligibility, and selecting draftees based on a national target. The law also created local appeal boards to mediate any disputes. The president appointed all of these voluntary positions, and governors were encouraged to recommend nominees.[4]

Two weeks later, Rodino joined more than 60,000 fellow Newark residents and registered for the draft. A statewide school holiday was declared on October 16 to allow school buildings to be used for the draft, and volunteers from the city's election board and public school teachers staffed the registration tables from seven in the morning until closing at nine at night. Rodino's designated registration site was his former grammar school, where he was asked to provide his age, marital status, number of dependents, and place of employment. The next step in the registration procedure was a notation of race and cursory assessment of his physical characteristics before he finally received a draft card that he was required to carry at all times. The turnout throughout the city exceeded the expectation of draft board officials, and the egalitarian nature of the process unexpectedly brought together a diverse cross section of the community. "Factory hands in overalls rubbed shoulders with white collar workers who drove up in expensive cars and bootblacks waited with the banker," the *Newark Evening News* reported. Even candidates for the New Jersey General Assembly, like Rodino, were forced to suspend campaigning for the day and get in line.[5]

Upon completion of the initial registration, local draft boards assumed authority for the conscription process. Of the twenty-two boards in Newark, the three-member Board 20 had jurisdiction in the First Ward. Assisted by a paid clerk and housed in a neighborhood school, the board's immediate task was to shuffle the registration cards and provide each individual with a randomly selected number for the national lottery to determine the order of the draft call. Following the October 29 lottery drawing in Washington, which had continued until the bowl was empty, Board 20 focused on the challenge of evaluating its first group of potential draftees needed to help fulfill New Jersey's quota. Draft boards had considerable latitude in determining eligibility, which created a variety of standards within the city of Newark, ranging from lenient to strict. All selected draftees were required to fill out and return a detailed questionnaire within five days and submit to a physical examination when called.[6]

Under the selective service act, local advisory boards helped registrants complete these questionnaires, which served as the primary mechanism for making a deferment claim. The day after his electoral defeat, Rodino was appointed to serve on the Newark Advisory Board for Registrants and help provide ongoing advice and counsel to claimants throughout the process. Since the conscription law required both citizens and noncitizens to register, Rodino's language skills coupled with his legal training made him a valuable member of the panel. The two most common deferment claims presented to the draft board were based on either dependents or employment. The employment claim asserted that the registrant was exempt because he held a job that performed essential services; the dependent claim rested on the draftee's financial support of a spouse, child, or other relative. Both were subject to broad interpretation during peacetime and the knowledge that married men were likely to receive a deferment prompted a sharp uptick in weddings. While Rodino's lottery number of 146 was not in the first group of draftees, he was still entitled to claim a deferment based on his "essential service" as a member of the advisory board. Alternatively, he could finally marry the ever-patient Ann and request a dependent deferment. Either choice would help his fledgling law practice, which might not have survived a year-long absence for military service.[7]

Instead, Rodino decided to enlist. Considering how many draftees were eagerly seeking deferments, his colleagues at the draft board were "taken aback" when he informed them of his decision.[8] Early on March 10, 1941, Rodino and seventeen other inductees from the First Ward reported for duty. Rodino was designated as the leader of the group and entrusted with all the trolley tokens for the trip to the induction center at the Newark armory and the train tickets to the Fort Dix training facility. Family and friends from the neighborhood greeted them at Penn Station and presented Rodino with a portable radio as a farewell gift. Reflecting his growing public profile, both daily newspapers reported on his departure. The *Newark Star-Ledger* published an article and sizable photograph of Rodino waving goodbye from the train window; the *Newark Evening News* proclaimed in a pithy headline "Drafter Drafted."[9] No one in attendance could have imagined that more than five years would pass before the "drafter" would return home.

As the United States prepared for its first peacetime draft, one of the biggest challenges was ensuring adequate facilities for a growing army. Under the conscription law, draft quota levels were directly tied to the army's ability to house these inductees. The Roosevelt administration responded to this need by announcing a plan to utilize the Works Progress Administration (WPA) to create new training camps and expand existing military facilities throughout the United States. Fort Dix in rural south central New Jersey, designated as the induction center for New York, New Jersey, and Delaware, received funding to embark on a frenetic expansion program to construct an airfield, a hospital, and hundreds of new buildings to house a projected 40,000 men. "Like a little Western village that suddenly discovers oil gushers under its farms," the *New York Times* reported, "this post rapidly is spreading and building itself up under the impetus of the emergency defense program."[10]

Arriving on a bitterly cold March day, Rodino and the selectees from Newark were escorted to the new Induction Center. Constructed by the WPA in just eight weeks, it was the first prototype in the country specifically designed for the induction process. The building was a maze of rooms and corridors. Rodino's initial stop was a room containing long rows of interview stalls, where an intake clerk asked a series of informational and biographical questions to determine military assignments. Next came visits to the fingerprinting room, locker room, and shower room in preparation for a physical examination. This exam was more detailed than the draft board's perfunctory one, and failure for any reason meant an immediate return to civilian life. Rodino passed the physical without issue and continued to the quartermaster's room to receive his army clothes. Owing to the continued shortage of uniforms, most inductees were given either pants that were too long, an outdated high-collar shirt, or a mismatched hat. However poorly attired, he reported to the barracks to await his assignment to a training unit.[11]

For the next several months, Private Rodino endured the challenges of basic training. The alarm clock he hated during his law school studies was replaced by an equally despised bugler blowing reveille at a quarter to six in the morning. After breakfast, he reported to the field with either his rifle or more likely a broomstick substitute because the actual weapons were still in short supply. Except for a lunch break, the remainder of his day included close-order drilling, physical conditioning, and lectures and demonstrations on a variety of topics ranging from weapons maintenance to military protocol. He returned to the barracks around four thirty in the afternoon to change into his good uniform for retreat and evening mess. Unless on duty, he was free until lights out at eleven at night to listen to his portable radio, write letters, or read.[12]

Special activities or exercises occasionally interrupted the daily routine of basic training. A few weeks after arriving, Rodino participated in the first formal parade of trainees at Fort Dix, marching before an audience of officers, journalists, and invited guests. One reporter in attendance was struck by the diversity of *both* the soldier's uniforms and their ethnic backgrounds.

When Rodino completed basic training, he was assigned to the intelligence unit of the Second Army Corps, formed in 1940 and known as "II Corps," which was headquartered at Fort DuPont near Wilmington, Delaware. Not particularly happy there, living in poor conditions at the fort and mistreated by a hostile sergeant, he impatiently waited for the end of his twelve-month stint. Rodino was not alone in feeling discouraged; the continued lack of proper equipment and absence of a clear purpose for the rigorous training had contributed to the pervasive low morale among his fellow inductees. The letters OHIO, an acronym for "Over the hill in October," began to appear on the walls of army latrines and barracks throughout the country, providing an early warning that there would be widespread departures on the first anniversary of the draft.[13]

This was a potentially lethal blow to defense preparedness just as war clouds seemed to be drifting closer to the United States. In the months following the draft lottery, fear that Germany was preparing to invade Great Britain prompted President Roosevelt to accelerate his efforts to bend the limitations of congressionally mandated neutrality and aid the British by swapping destroyers for bases. In May, the president issued a proclamation declaring an unlimited national emergency requiring that the "military, naval, air and civil defenses be put on the basis of readiness."[14] Two months later Japanese troops invaded French Indochina. In response, the United States imposed an embargo on fuel and barred Japanese ships from using the Panama Canal. Against this foreboding backdrop, Congress narrowly approved legislation to lengthen the tenure of current enlistees for an additional eighteen months.[15]

These events did not alter Rodino's plans to return to civilian life. The draft extension legislation allowed the Secretary of War to defer this additional service time for any enlistee older than twenty-eight. At thirty-two, Rodino was already considerably older than the average inductee, and he hoped his status as a volunteer would further improve his chances of an early release. Expecting to return to Newark when his one year stint was up in a few months, Rodino raised the possibility of marriage during one of Ann's periodic day trips to Wilmington. Years earlier, he had told her he wanted to save at least $25,000 before marrying, a high bar to set and one he was not close to reaching. But he was feeling more confident about the future of his law practice, and the Democratic leaders in the First Ward promised to promote his candidacy to be Newark's boxing commissioner after he left the military. Informed by the company commander that his release from military service was approved, Rodino invited

Ann to come for another visit so they could begin their wedding planning.[16]

Rodino met Ann at the Wilmington train station on a blustery day in early December. They usually ate in the dining room of the Hotel Du Pont, which offered an affordable afternoon dinner on Sundays. After their food arrived, Rodino began the conversation they had both waited years to have. Before he could finish, the background music playing on the hotel's radio was interrupted by an announcement: *the Japanese had bombed Pearl Harbor*. It was around two thirty in the afternoon, and, when the shock and disbelief faded, downtown Wilmington, crowded with servicemen, became a cacophony of horns, sirens, and bullhorn announcements. All leave was immediately canceled, and personnel were ordered back to their barracks. Rodino tried to ease Ann's fears as he walked her back to the train station, but he remembered it as "the saddest departure, a saddest farewell."[17] Later that day, he learned that his discharge orders were rescinded. The United States had declared war on Japan, Germany, and Italy before the week ended.

As part of the II Corps' intelligence unit working with maps, Rodino expected to be sent overseas. Uncertain of the timing, he suggested to Ann that they get married as soon as he could get permission to leave the base. She returned to Wilmington two weeks later on a train delayed by a snowstorm, and they hurried to the city clerk's office for a marriage license only to find it closed. Anxious and determined, they agreed to try again the next week. This time they decided not to leave anything to chance, and Ann's brother and sister-in-law drove them to Maryland, where there was no waiting period and a church ceremony fulfilled the requirements for a marriage license. Fifteen years after meeting on the steps of St. Lucy's Church, Marianna Stango and Peter Wallace Rodino exchanged wedding vows at Baltimore's Basilica of the Assumption cathedral on December 27, 1941. They spent their brief honeymoon at the Hotel Baltimore before Private Rodino reported back to Fort DuPont, and Ann returned to her parents' house in Newark.[18]

Except for their marriage, few things remained constant for the newlyweds during their first months as husband and wife. In February, II Corps was relocated to Jacksonville, Florida, for maneuvers and preparation for overseas deployment. The best thing about the Florida assignment was that recently promoted Corporal Rodino was able to secure married quarters off the base. He asked Ann to join him as soon as possible. This was not a simple request: he was asking Ann to give up her job and family to travel a thousand miles to an unknown place for an uncertain period of time. Wanting to be with her husband no matter the cost, Ann readily agreed and quit her job at Prudential Insurance before boarding a train for Florida. Not long after arriving, Ann learned that she was pregnant and that their first child was due in October. The exact location of II Corps and the father-to-be when the baby was born was far less certain. "Maybe, Australia. Maybe, Libya. Maybe, Dakar. Maybe, Madagascar," a frustrated Rodino wrote to his friend Vince Biunno. "So many maybes to reckon with that methinks I'll eschew them all and drink."[19]

Compared with the rigors of basic training and the spartan facilities of the two forts where he previously resided, life in Florida was a big improvement. Rodino was no longer sleeping on an uncomfortable cot in the barracks, and he could now leave the base at the end of the workday to spend the evenings with Ann in a nicely furnished apartment. There were more social activities for married couples, and the two frequently dined out with new friends. But Rodino still found the work of cataloging and organizing maps tedious, and he applied for a position as an investigator in the office of the US Army provost marshal general. Following Pearl Harbor, all Japanese, German, and Italian noncitizens were required to register as "enemy aliens" and subjected to restrictions that were enforced by the provost marshal's office.[20] Stressing his fluency in Italian and legal education, Rodino submitted an application and attached a letter of recommendation from New Jersey Senator William H. Smathers that his Democratic friends back home helped him obtain. Not initially hired and placed on a waiting list, his prospects for any future openings dimmed when the Roosevelt administration bowed to political pressure and removed Italians from this targeted group.[21]

With no immediate prospects of a more interesting job, Rodino found relief from his daily boredom in writing. This remained his favorite refuge, and he never stopped looking for opportunities to write. When his unit participated in battle maneuvers in rural North Carolina, he brought along a notebook to record his thoughts and composed several poems about the surrounding nature. He appropriated an unclaimed typewriter on the base, and, while he complained in letters that he had little free time, he managed to write several works of fiction that he hoped to publish. His short story entitled "So, You'll Wait For Tomorrow" was the barely disguised autobiographical tale of an aspiring writer, working in a factory and attending law school at night, who witnesses a murder. In the essay, "An Expectant Father in the Army," he directly appropriated his own recent experience and personal anxieties to craft a narrative of a soldier learning that he is going to be a father as he is leaving for an overseas posting. Secretly hoping for a boy, the protagonist acknowledges the possibility that he will never see his child. "When he comes into this life I hope to be able to see him," Rodino poignantly wrote, "but if I never do, and if I never get to hear the great music of the word 'Father,' I believe I shall have done my share for him."[22]

Fiction became reality in June, when II Corps received orders to prepare for an overseas deployment, initially to Great Britain. Rodino helped Ann pack up the apartment and drove her to the train station for the trip to Newark and the return to her parents' house, where she would stay until he returned. Given the uncertainty of the corpsmen's final destination, everyone was inoculated against smallpox, typhoid, tetanus, and yellow fever before traveling to Indiantown Gap Military Reservation in rural Pennsylvania, the staging area for all Port of New York embarkations. The subsequent rail journey across New Jersey to the Hudson River pier was a somber one for Rodino. As the train passed through Newark's Penn Station, he could see the towers of Sacred Heart Cathedral in the First Ward looming on the horizon—a sad reminder that he had expected to be back home by now. It was particularly painful knowing that Ann was only a few minutes away; when he contemplated the next leg of the trip, his melancholy deepened.[23]

Rodino and the II Corps were part of an unprecedented overseas deployment of troops that would send 1.5 million Americans either to or through

Great Britain over the next three years. Even before the United States entered the war, American military strategists had concluded that defeating Nazi Germany was the key to vanquishing *all* the Axis powers. President Roosevelt and British Prime Minister Winston Churchill, meeting off the coast of Newfoundland in the summer of 1941, had agreed that any future Allied action should focus first on Germany. Following Pearl Harbor, an anxious Churchill hurried to Washington seeking reassurance that Japan's attack had not altered the "Germany First" goal. While the American public regarded the Japanese as the greater threat, Roosevelt and American military leaders remained committed to the plan to defeat the Nazis.[24]

A fundamental element of this predetermined strategy was to launch a land attack against Germany as soon as practicable, which required a cross-channel invasion of mainland Europe. Great Britain would serve as the designated staging area for required American troops and equipment before deployment to the Continent. To prepare for this massive influx, a dedicated port was under construction in Northern Ireland, and existing harbors in Scotland and England were modified to accommodate bigger vessels. Largely untested, American troops needed extensive training before they could be considered prepared for their mission. The British converted existing buildings into training centers, erected barracks, and asked their civilians to share accommodations with the country's new allies. A month after Churchill's visit to Washington, the first American troopship carrying almost 4,000 soldiers docked in Northern Ireland, where the country welcomed it as "an impressive vanguard of American military might."[25]

Crossing the North Atlantic was a perilous trip under the best of circumstances. Since the first American convoys had sailed out of New York Harbor, an extensive network of German submarines had gathered in packs off the Atlantic seaboard waiting to attack. Consequently, the arriving soldiers, dressed in their khakis with backpacks and helmets, were required to spend their first hours on board learning the safety rules of the ship. Once in open waters, they would travel in darkness, unable to even use flashlights. The large contingent of troops, closely crowded together on deck, practiced launching and boarding lifeboats and other critical procedures in case the siren sounded to abandon ship. They repeated these drills daily during the crossing in all weather conditions until they could execute them from memory. For Peter Rodino and many of his fellow passengers, it was a particularly numbing experience because it was their maiden voyage on the open seas and the first time they were traveling on a ship larger than the Staten Island Ferry. Rodino vividly remembered his shock at learning that sleeping quarters were in the lower decks of the ship and wondering "if anything ever strikes us what is going to happen?"[26] The transatlantic voyage, he recalled, seemed like the longest ten days of his life.

When Rodino arrived at the Scottish port of Greenock, he learned of his promotion to sergeant and was instructed to report to London for his final orders. He joined his fellow corpsmen walking to the nearby train station, and they traveled together on the seven-hour journey to London. By the summer of 1942, the darkest days of the Blitz were over as the Royal Air Force and antiaircraft defenses challenged German Luftwaffe bombers with increasing success. However, the cityscape still bore the scars of the extensive damage of almost two years of bombing. During his brief time in the capital, Rodino encountered the sobering evidence of wartime destruction and hardship. His next stop was the relatively untouched and tranquil English countryside, where II Corps and its commander General Mark W. Clark were headquartered at Longford Castle. Built in 1588 and the ancestral home of the Earl of Radnor, the castle was located three miles southeast of Salisbury and offered a large area for training troops and easy access to the coast. Rodino was assigned a room in the servants' quarters, allowing him to joke in later years that he had once lived in a castle.[27]

One of the most vexing issues confronting the US Army at this time was the shortage of officers. The peacetime draft had overwhelmed the existing military operation with new recruits, and the wartime draft only exacerbated the problem. More soldiers meant that additional leaders were needed to train them and provide direction on the battlefield. Recognizing that the traditional sources for supplying new officers were inadequate to close this gap, the War

Department approved the expansion of Officer Candidate Schools in the United States and the creation of a parallel program overseas. To encourage participation, admission requirements were revised to make any enlisted man with at least three months army service, a high score on the general classification test, and demonstrated leadership abilities eligible for the program. Those accepted were required to undergo several months of intensive training, and upon graduation they were promoted to the rank of second lieutenant. Although previously uninterested in becoming an officer, Rodino decided to apply, and, in an army where half the inductees did not graduate from high school, his law degree and high test scores made him an attractive candidate; he was selected. Along with his friend Max Zera and thirty-eight soldiers from other units, he was part of one of the earliest officer training classes organized in Britain.[28]

From August 1942 until early December, Rodino resided in the picturesque village of Shrivenham at the American School Center, recently established to serve as a central hub for training activities. He spent most days inside Beckett Hall, a rebuilt manor house and former private girls' school, taking a variety of classes and learning how to be a junior officer. Instructors provided regular evaluations to students on their progress, and judged Rodino's skills as best suited for a noncombat position in the general areas of administration, logistics, or transportation. When not in class, he was engaged in daily and overnight maneuvers in the surrounding countryside that tested physical strength and stamina. It was a rigorous program, and more than a third of the original class were asked to leave before graduation. Rodino, older than most of his classmates, was determined to complete the course; on December 9, he received his diploma and promotion.[29] With training completed, *Lieutenant* Rodino expected a quick return to his intelligence unit at II Corps. Instead, he and Zera were sent to London for a possible reassignment and instructed to wait there for the arrival of new orders. They enjoyed the sights of the wartime city between regular visits to the duty officer for updates. They used this idle time to collaborate on a song they called "When the Yanks Go Rolling Along," with Rodino providing the lyrics including these comical stanzas:

We'll take the hit out of Hitler,
The muscle out of Lini
Every heart will sing a happy song.
We will make no concession
To villains of aggression
As the Yanks go rolling along!

We'll take the hero from Hito
And bury the old meanie
All the weak will be so very strong
There will be jubilation
In every conquered nation
As the Yanks go rolling along![30]

For the moment, however, these two Yanks were not going anywhere.

Unknown to Rodino at the time, his fate was directly linked to a major shift in American military strategy. The realization that the US needed more time to prepare for a European landing had forced Churchill and Roosevelt to reassess their plans. The president remained committed to the Germany First policy, and new ally Soviet leader Joseph Stalin was pushing for the early opening of a second front against the Nazis to relieve pressure on his troops in the east. In the spring of 1942, Prime Minister Churchill proposed that the Allies postpone the channel crossing for a year and instead focus on North Africa, where British forces had been fighting the German and Italian armies for two years. Roosevelt agreed, and in November "Operation Torch" brought the first wave of American troops and equipment to Algeria and Morocco. The following month, Rodino was reassigned as a headquarters staff officer with the First Armored Division, which had already sent half of its troops, tanks, and artillery to North Africa. He would be part of the final contingent leaving in February.[31]

Rodino's arrival in Algeria coincided with a particularly low point for the

American forces. The earlier landings along the Mediterranean coast were plagued by miscalculations and missteps, resulting in significant losses for several divisions including the First Armored. Inexperienced leadership and infighting hindered the offensive against the Axis forces in Tunisia that followed, resulting in a series of setbacks. A major push at Kasserine Pass a few weeks after Rodino took up residence was a debacle ending in a major defeat for the Americans; it confirmed the wisdom of postponing the cross-channel crossing.[32]

Training in the safety of the British countryside had not prepared Rodino and his fellow soldiers for the harsh realities of warfare, and they were stunned by the extensive casualty reports and graphic condition of the returning wounded. Writing in the aftermath of the Kasserine defeat, he observed that "though my officer buddies try to pretend indifference by busying themselves with card games and the like I know their hearts are heavy." He was particularly anxious about the company of enlisted men he had personally trained and escorted to North Africa who were slated to leave for the front line. He listed each individual's name and expressed his deep admiration for these untested soldiers anxious to fulfill their mission and return home. "I suppose my heart can never be wholly in this war," he wrote, "I am too deeply aware of the pain and suffering it has brought thus far. And, I am vividly aware of the yet more brutal consequences to come."[33]

Fortunately for Rodino, he initially spent the bulk of his time away from the fighting at either Allied headquarters in Algiers or the port city of Oran, where overflow military units were housed. Thanks to his French classes and membership in the French club at Barringer High School, he possessed a skill in great demand in a French colony, and he was frequently called to translate documents or to accompany senior officers to meetings and social events as an interpreter. He was also tasked with serving as the First Armored Division's liaison to external organizations like the American Red Cross, and he often conducted outreach to local community leaders, activities similar to those he enjoyed in civilian life. This routine changed in the spring when the Allies began a counteroffensive against enemy armies in western Tunisia. Rodino went to the First Armored Division's forward headquarters a few miles behind the front line. A series of successful attacks pushed the Axis forces toward the capital city of Tunis, where they were trapped and forced to surrender after a five-day siege, effectively ending the conflict in North Africa. Rodino witnessed the endless lines of Italian and German prisoners in nearby Cape Bon, where they were transited to internment camps in Algeria or Morocco. He joined in the Allied victory celebrations on May 20, which culminated in a grand military parade along the main boulevard of Tunis.[34]

The North Africa campaign was the first significant American victory of the war and offered a much needed dose of good news back home. It provided invaluable experience for future operations and resulted in both officers and their troops becoming battle-tested. After the launch of Operation Torch, the Allies agreed that most of the Allied troops would return to Britain for the delayed cross-channel offensive at the end of the North Africa conflict. However, Prime Minister Churchill once again maintained that more time was needed for preparations, and he pushed for another postponement. At a meeting in Casablanca in January 1943, he secured President Roosevelt's agreement to send the North African forces the short distance across the Mediterranean to seize Sicily, arguing that this would lead to the collapse of Mussolini's regime in Italy.[35] Seven months later, the Allies landed. Over the next few weeks, they met little resistance as they easily captured the island.

On July 25, Italy's monarch Victor Emmanuel III, who had supported Mussolini and the fascists for two decades, led a bloodless coup that forced the Italian dictator out of power. This provided the opportunity Churchill needed to press for his real objective: a full-scale assault on the Italian mainland. The possibility of an imminent Italian capitulation, the euphoria over the success of the Sicily campaign, and the lure of finally fighting on the European mainland convinced the Americans to endorse the plan.[36]

In theory, the Allied strategy for the invasion of Italy was relatively straightforward. American and British forces already in Sicily, along with selected units left behind in North Africa, would land in the vicinity of the Gulf of Salerno in southern Italy. Joining together, they would then spend the next several weeks seizing Naples and its important port and then moving up the Italian mainland until they reached Rome. Doubtful that the Germans forces in the country would fight, the Allies assumed they would simply push any remaining Germans northward in their wake. Yet, from the very beginning, nothing about the Italian campaign was simple or easy. The forces landing at Salerno were met by a swift German counterattack, which provided tangible evidence that the Germans were not retreating from Italy anytime soon. This onslaught kept the Allied forces boxed in at their beachhead for more than two weeks until they could finally break free. The British and Americans found their movement north complicated by difficult terrain and inclement weather. Fierce German resistance along defensive lines stretching across the width of Italy, known as the Winter Line, brought Allied movement to a virtual standstill. To crack this impasse, the Allies decided to circumvent the Germans with an amphibious landing of troops at Anzio, north of the battle line and just a few hours from Rome. The landing itself was a success; Allied delays in moving inland allowed the Germans time to counterattack and stop any advance forward. The offensive to end a stalemate resulted in another stalemate that would last for four months.[37]

Because its tanks and artillery were not required for the invasion of Sicily, the First Armored Division remained in North Africa. Rodino, awarded the Bronze Star for the recent Tunisia campaign, was busy exercising his other language skill as a translator to interrogate Italian prisoners of war and using his legal training to serve as a judge advocate.[38] In October, the division received orders to participate in the Italian campaign and sailed from Oran to join the Allied forces at the Winter Line. Rodino and his fellow soldiers spent the next two months entrenched behind this static demarcation, where they endured unusually cold and rainy weather that triggered flooding and created a miserable landscape of mud.

At the beginning of 1944, the First Armored shifted west to assist in defending the landing forces bogged down at Anzio; it played a key role in the successful breakout offensive before moving toward Rome to seize the bridges over the Tiber River. The Allies received a rapturous welcome when they liberated the city on June 5, the day before the twice-delayed channel crossing was finally launched and eleven months after the first soldiers had set foot on Italian soil. For his participation in this unexpectedly difficult achievement, Rodino received his second Bronze Star.[39]

The Rome that the Allies now occupied had endured considerable political upheaval and hardship since the start of the Italian campaign. Following the arrest of Mussolini, the Italian king had agreed to the Allies' demand for unconditional surrender, and subsequently Italy formally declared war on Germany. The German army quickly recaptured the city, forcing the reconstituted government to flee south, and the Nazis unleashed a reign of terror against the populace and partisan street fighters before leaving just as the American troops arrived. While the First Armored Division was ordered to pursue the Germans fleeing to the north, Rodino hoped to leverage his Italian language skills to return to the relative comfort and safety of Rome, which was serving as the operational headquarters for the Allied command. At the end of the summer, his request for a reassignment was approved, and he left the First Armored Division.[40]

Rodino's next and final posting of the war was with a newly created and pioneering military unit: the Military Mission Italian Army (MMIA). It was organized under the umbrella of the Allied Control Commission for Italy, which was responsible for governing and guiding the transition to civilian rule in the country. The MMIA's unique task was to facilitate the entry of the Italians into the war as cobelligerents by helping the Italian army reorganize, providing regular soldiers and partisan fighters with training and new equipment. Housed at the Allied Commission's headquarters in the center of Rome, the MMIA was a relatively lean organization with only twenty-five officers and seventy-three enlisted men to support a far-flung mission that included three field substations on the mainland and one each in Sicily and Sardinia. "Never before in the history of the United States Army has a group of Americans been called upon to fulfill such a peculiar assignment," commanding officer Colonel Clayton P. Kerr acknowledged.[41]

Rodino's assignment was to serve as headquarters commandant, a position that was responsible for all aspects of the unit's administrative functions.

Because the MMIA operated as a separate company, Rodino's duties encompassed those usually performed at a larger battalion or regimental headquarters and included serving as the company's adjutant, personnel officer, supply officer, transportation officer, and chief translator. Aided by two enlisted men, Rodino spent an average day disbursing the company's payroll, organizing transport for the officers, processing the paperwork for personnel actions, ensuring that the substations received their supplies, and regularly interacting with his British and Italian counterparts.[42]

One of the benefits of his position was that it presented opportunities to interact with the Italian royal family, a heady experience for the son of a peasant from Atripalda. As the company's translator, he often accompanied Colonel Kerr to social events, where he met many members of the court. With his language skills and shared heritage, he became an informal liaison to these aristocratic households, helping to arrange meetings and introductions for military personnel and encouraging support for their various charitable activities in a city still plagued by food shortages and overcrowded orphanages. These efforts and his advocacy for American involvement in the rebuilding of Italy brought expressions of appreciation and several honors from the monarchy, most notably the Italian War Merit Cross and Order of the Crown of Italy, which the US Army allowed him to accept.[43]

The MMIA's activities began winding down in the spring of 1945 after Germany surrendered, and the war in Europe ended. In a positive coda to Rodino's military career, he was promoted to the rank of captain after agreeing to serve in the reserves following his discharge, and he was awarded another Bronze Star for "building up a solid, substantial and fully integrated, coordinated and spirited unit."[44] Although qualified to be among the first group returning to the United States based on his length of service and time in combat, the military deemed his work as vital and required him to stay longer. But he didn't need to wait for very much longer. The defeat of Japan and conclusion of all hostilities in September accelerated the schedule for demobilizing American forces, and three months later Rodino received permission to leave Italy. His last two assignments in the military were to return all the equipment he used throughout the war and to serve as group commander for a contingent of soldiers joining him on the voyage back home.[45]

Five years after President Roosevelt read aloud the first draft lottery number, Peter Rodino boarded a ship bound for the United States. He had traveled down a long and at times harrowing road since the day he waved goodbye at Penn Station and had attained a number of significant milestones along the way. Leaving home, getting married, crossing the Atlantic, living in a foreign country, and befriending royalty were just a few of the life-changing events he experienced. He entered the army at the lowest rank and was departing as a highly decorated officer, having developed and honed valuable leadership skills in the process. On a deeper level, he witnessed and was personally touched by the death, destruction, and brutality of war. He was returning a different person, altered in ways that even he could not perceive by the circumstances and the harsh realities he endured.

But if Rodino's was a life changed, it was also a life interrupted. Like his fellow soldiers, he was forced to stop and serve his country just at the moment he was getting started. After all his years of struggle to become a lawyer, he had to abandon his law practice. Finally marrying Ann, he was forced to say goodbye just as they were about to become parents. Climbing up the first rung of the political ladder, military service had required him to step aside. As his ship left the dock in Naples, the cost of this sacrifice and its impact on his future were still to be determined. The final tally would depend upon the answer to one question: what was next?

CHAPTER FOUR

ENTERING THE ARENA

The first peacetime Christmas in five years was approaching, and there was a palpable sense of excitement. Despite the frigid weather and snow blanketing much of the country, travelers mobbed train stations and jammed roads as a record number of them journeyed home for this particularly special holiday. With the end of wartime blackouts, Christmas lights were once again illuminating city squares. Preparations were underway in Washington for the first lighting of the national Christmas tree since Pearl Harbor.

The clearest evidence that the war was over was the presence of so many returning troops who were given priority seating on overcrowded buses and trains. The army promised to make every effort to ensure that these service men and women arrived home in time for Christmas. To achieve this goal, the army accelerated the demobilization process and began operating separation centers responsible for returning soldiers to civilian life around the clock. The best Christmas present, a journalist observed, "was being received by thousands of veterans leaving the service for good."[1]

Unfortunately, Captain Peter Rodino was not among this lucky group. He had sailed from Naples on December 15 along with six thousand other soldiers aboard the carrier USS *Randolph* and was originally scheduled to arrive in New York Harbor a week later. Not long after entering the open seas, the ship encountered gale-force winds and eighty-foot waves from a ferocious winter storm, which forced the vessel to operate at a much slower speed. The battered and damaged *Randolph* belatedly arrived on Christmas morning and docked at an available pier on the Staten Island waterfront. The relieved captain told waiting reporters that it was one of the roughest crossings of his long career and praised the good humor of the troops during the difficult journey. "We kept our promise to get them home—at least to the United States—by Christmas," he quipped.[2]

The welcomed return of millions of American troops after four anxious years had presented the War Department with a major challenge. The end of the conflicts in Europe and the Pacific had come in unexpectedly quick succession and upended plans for the gradual demobilization of American forces. Under intense pressure from Congress and the public, military officials were forced to bring all the troops home as soon as possible. The government hastily erected temporary facilities to process this sudden influx at existing military bases. Fort Monmouth, located in central New Jersey, was the designated site for the state's returning troops. This is where Rodino arrived in an army motorcade when he disembarked from the *Randolph* on Christmas Day. Because the length of his stay was not certain, he was allowed to receive visitors; a few days later, he reunited with Ann for a few hours and finally met his three-year-old daughter, Peggy, who had been born when he was in England.[3]

With the preholiday rush over, the army had resumed its normal schedule of staggered discharge dates to ease the backlog. Rodino's agreement to continue as a reservist made him a lower priority for release, and his final discharge date was delayed until April. Neither a full-time soldier nor a bona fide civilian, he left Fort Monmouth in early January 1946 and hurried home still in uniform to the small apartment in the First Ward that Ann had rented in anticipation of his return.[4]

The major benefit of remaining on the army payroll for the next few months was that it allowed Rodino the opportunity to spend some time thinking about his future. Beyond reactivating his law practice, he was interested in returning to the political arena given an appropriate opportunity. He had already experienced the challenges of seeking office as a Democrat in Essex County, given the unlikelihood of getting elected to the county board of freeholders or the state legislature there, where Republican voters were in the majority. The next municipal election was not until 1949, and he would need to expand his base of support to win citywide in a crowded field likely to be dominated by the current commissioners. While weighing these limited options, Democratic leaders in the First Ward approached him about running as the party's candidate in the Tenth Congressional District. The bulk of this district was in Essex County, and it included a large concentration of voters from seven wards of Newark and the nearby suburban towns of Belleville, Bloomfield, Nutley, and Glen Ridge. Crossing the Passaic River into Hudson County, the remaining area comprised the heavily industrialized municipalities of Harrison, Kearny, and East Newark. With more than three hundred thousand constituents, the largely working class district contained an ethnic mix of Italians, Irish, and Poles.[5]

Representing the Tenth District in Congress was conservative Republican Fred C. Hartley Jr., who was staunchly pro-business and a devout isolationist. He had begun his political career as a local commissioner in the town of Kearny before running for Congress in 1928 against the Democratic incumbent Paul J. Moore. Moore had won the election initially until a recount reversed the results and provided Hartley with a razor-thin margin of nine votes. To help Hartley win reelection, the Republicans in the New Jersey legislature removed Democratic Bayonne from the Tenth District when they redrew the congressional map after the 1930 census. This adjustment, along with a reputation for outstanding constituent services, helped Hartley withstand the political tidal wave of the New Deal to retain a seat in a district that was increasingly regarded as safely Republican.[6]

Recognizing that the odds were against him, Rodino believed that he had a compelling story to tell and a responsibility to fight for his fellow veterans who were confronting a litany of challenges as they transitioned back to civilian life. The first step in making his decision official was to secure the endorsement of the longtime chairman of the Essex County Democratic Committee, William H. Kelly. Kelly was anxious to find a way to mobilize new voters for the Democrats, like the returning soldiers, and he was impressed when Rodino arrived at his office in uniform. Since there were no other serious contenders for what was considered a fruitless undertaking, he immediately gave his blessing, and Rodino filed the required paperwork to be on the June primary ballot.[7] His next stop was to visit his old friends at the *Italian Tribune* newspaper to announce his candidacy for Congress. The result of the visit was a front page article headlined "Peter Rodino Returns Honored and Decorated," which recounted in great detail his wartime exploits, friendship with Italian nobility, and awards from the government.[8] The following week, the *Newark Star-Ledger*, the city's Democratic-leaning morning newspaper, published a follow-up story announcing Rodino's plans to challenge Hartley. Accompanying the article was a current photograph of Rodino in full uniform alongside the newspaper's 1941 photo of his departure for Fort Dix with the caption "Bemedaled Return."[9]

Rodino's return to politics was an impressive debut for a challenger taking on an entrenched incumbent and demonstrated an instinct for self-promotion. It also provided a preview of the narrative he would articulate throughout the campaign directly linking his candidacy with his recent military service. This was not unusual in 1946; it was the year of the veteran in American politics, and many ex-serviceman entered the public arena, including former navy officers, John F. Kennedy and Richard Nixon. Rodino's campaign was largely framed by his identification as a veteran, decorated captain, and war hero. Most of the campaign material he distributed featured photographs of him in uniform. His rapid rise from private to captain in just a few years seemed to especially captivate the press and the public—he was always introduced as "captain" at public events and usually accorded the same title in print. This gave Rodino an immediate gravitas as a candidate that he might not have otherwise had, an unexpected dividend from the time he spent at Officer Candidate School. He was less willing to accept the moniker of "war hero," feeling that he didn't deserve it. He was always forthright about correcting anyone introducing him with these heroic embellishments, reminding the audience that he had not served in direct combat nor performed an act worthy of the honor. With his formal discharge on April 7, he was free to focus his full attention on politics and his legal practice.[10]

Congressional campaigns in New Jersey in 1946 were comparatively inexpensive and uncomplicated undertakings. There were no regular polling, media buys, or high-powered campaign consultants. There were few, if any, organized debates between opponents. Instead, candidates focused most of their attention on supporters, relied on the party machinery to mobilize these voters, and counted on a free press to communicate their message. For a Democratic candidate, the life blood of any campaign was the support of organized labor, which was a potent political force in the state. Setting the pace was the political action committee (PAC) of the Congress of Industrial Organizations (CIO), often a guiding barometer for other labor groups. After the June primary, the CIO-PAC endorsed Rodino and promised financial support. Naively, Rodino believed the endorsements from the CIO and the other labor groups that followed would solve all his problems. "I thought they would just fund me and I would be able to run a campaign," he recalled.[11] But, with Hartley considered unbeatable, labor groups did not earmark any significant resources for the contest, and Rodino was forced to cobble together a makeshift campaign operation on a small budget. He personally assumed the duties of scheduler and press secretary, substituting speeches and releases for the fictional prose of his past writing endeavors. Initially unable to afford his own campaign headquarters, he set up operations at the Park Athletic Club in the First Ward until he was able to rent a nearby storefront.[12]

Rodino's one stroke of good fortune in the early days of his campaign was reconnecting with neighborhood acquaintance Joseph "Joe" Benucci. A fellow alumnus of Barringer High School, Benucci had served in the military intelligence service during the war and joined the Newark police force as a detective following his discharge. Benucci spent his free time volunteering at the First Ward Democratic club. After one weekly meeting, Rodino told him of his plans to challenge Hartley and asked for his help. Benucci introduced Rodino to his network of contacts throughout the city and mined these relationships to solicit invitations for appearances before neighborhood groups and civic associations. Most nights and weekends, the two were together at local meetings or events where Rodino usually delivered brief remarks, and Benucci recruited campaign volunteers from the audience. It was the beginning of a valuable political partnership that would continue for the next two decades.[13]

Rodino did receive some nonfinancial support from the Democratic National Committee (DNC). The publicity director contacted him after the primary requesting background information so they could promote his candidacy, and they sent him a candidate's handbook outlining the party's platform. In September, the DNC invited Rodino to come to Washington for a day-long training session for candidates running against Republican incumbents. He was one of forty challengers from five key states participating in the program. These challengers met with cabinet members and other senior officials from the Truman administration for in-depth briefings on policy issues. Party chairman and Postmaster General Robert E. Hannegan invited them to his plush office for lunch, followed by sessions on campaign tactics and detailed reports about their opponents' voting record in Congress.[14]

The advertised highlight of the day was a meeting with the president, though this was a mixed blessing for many of the candidates. Relatively unknown at the time, Vice President Harry S. Truman had succeeded to the presidency following the death of Franklin Roosevelt the previous spring. The difficult transition to peacetime had unleashed labor unrest, inflation, and a myriad of protracted shortages in the face of pent-up demand. Much of the blame fell generally on the Democrats and specifically on the untested leadership of Truman. As the president's popularity plunged, and the midterm elections neared, Chairman Hannegan had asked Truman not to make any campaign appearances. The request was probably unnecessary; few candidates invited him or even mentioned his name. Not concerned about being linked to Truman, the awestruck Rodino gladly spoke to reporters after meeting the president and posed for pictures outside the White House. It was Rodino's public debut in the nation's capital.[15]

If President Truman was persona non grata on the campaign trail, the name that continued to energize Democrats was Franklin Delano Roosevelt. With the nation still adjusting to his absence after such a long tenure, candidates still invoked FDR and called for the completion of the "Roosevelt program." Many campaigns used his image in their brochures, and some even played recordings of his speeches as if the deceased Roosevelt were still present. No one worked harder to keep his legacy alive than his wife Eleanor. The former First Lady, now a delegate to the United Nations, was a forceful advocate for liberal causes. Unlike Truman, she was much in demand as a campaigner, and her endorsement was coveted by progressive Democrats. On September 11, Mrs. Roosevelt came to downtown Newark to address an overflow crowd at the Office of Dependency Benefits. As she hurried to her next appointment, Mrs. Roosevelt encountered Rodino waiting outside the building. She stopped for a photo with the candidate and told the trailing reporters that "she hoped for a victory by Rodino." It was unlikely that this was a chance meeting; the DNC or state party officials had most likely arranged the photo op in advance with Mrs. Roosevelt or her staff. Whatever the impetus for this brief joint appearance, it provided a big boost to Rodino's fledgling campaign, and the *Newark Star-Ledger* ran the photograph above the fold on the front page with the caption "Nod for Vet."[16]

Following the Roosevelt endorsement, Rodino embarked on a whirlwind schedule of travel throughout the district that left little time for his law practice. He promoted his candidacy in the morning and lunchtime at factory gates before spending the evenings at social clubs, taverns, or house parties hosted by supporters where he might only find a few potential voters in attendance.[17] Regardless of the size of the gathering, his message was usually a blend of his positive progressive agenda and negative attacks on his opponent, a balance he adjusted depending on the makeup of the audience. Speaking to a gathering in Belleville that included independent voters, he emphasized the need to continue the programs of the New Deal and called for the enactment of federal health insurance and an expansion of housing for veterans. At Democratic events, he fired up the partisan crowd with his sharp condemnations of Hartley as a "tool of big business" and the "spearhead of a reactionary clique in Congress."[18] His campaign reflected this dual approach in the advertisements it placed in local newspapers. One featured the candidate in uniform under the positive banner, "Elect Rodino to Defend U.S. Prosperity, Security" and listed the issues he supported; the other warned that "Rodino Will Serve You—Not Hidden Interests" and compared the 1941 date Rodino voluntarily enlisted in the military with the timing of "isolationist" Hartley's vote against the draft.[19]

Hartley never responded to any of these attacks, and, relying on the advantages of incumbency, he did little campaigning except for occasional appearances with other Republicans at large party rallies. The sole encounter between the two opponents occurred at a League of Women Voters forum where Rodino recalled Hartley refusing to debate or discuss any of the issues. Consequently, Rodino dominated the press coverage of the campaign, and the *Newark Star-Ledger* regularly highlighted his activities and speeches. Even the Republican leaning *Newark Evening News* rarely mentioned Hartley or included his comments in relevant news stories.[20] Hartley did receive some unwanted press attention a few weeks before the election when one of Newark's leading Italian American Republicans endorsed Rodino. The surprise announcement from the Eighth Ward's Dr. Virginius Mattia was prominently reported on in both daily newspapers and offered the first indication that Hartley's once solid support within the Italian American community was starting to crack. After praising Rodino for his war service and commitment to helping veterans, Mattia criticized Hartley for failing to speak out against Mississippi Democratic Senator Theodore G. Bilbo's widely condemned comments referring to Italians as "dagos." Bilbo, a leading segregationist and immigration opponent, was a longtime Hartley ally in the conservative coalition opposing the policies of the Roosevelt and Truman administrations. Mattia chastised the Tenth District's representative for abandoning "those among his constituents who for many years have been his most faithful supporters."[21]

From the beginning of the campaign, Rodino's energetic efforts had challenged expectations about the outcome, and the contest began to attract attention from outside the district. The nonpartisan *Congressional Quarterly* included the race on its watchlist, and the *Newark Star-Ledger* reported that "experts are buzzing about the Rodino-Hartley struggle both here and in Washington."[22] The DNC added to this speculation when it claimed that it had a copy of an internal report prepared by Republican officials that prominently featured Hartley's name on a list of congressional incumbents in trouble. Not surprisingly, the Republican National Committee immediately denounced the document as fake and decried the underhanded tactics of the Democrats. Although both Newark newspapers offered competing assessments of the race, without reliable polling in the district, it was impossible to separate wishful thinking from political analysis. But there was general agreement on three salient points: Hartley was facing the most formidable Democratic challenge of his career, he was losing support within the Italian American community, and Peter Rodino was proving to be an attractive and effective candidate.[23]

The perception that the race was tightening added to the usual tension between campaigns, and, when Hartley was booed at a rally in suburban Nutley, he claimed they were Rodino supporters bused in from Newark. A few days before the election, he sent a telegram to Newark's public safety director requesting police protection at polling sites in the predominantly Italian American First and Eighth wards to prevent voter intimidation by his opponent's supporters and provided copies to the local FBI office and the press. Rodino condemned Hartley for besmirching the character of those living in these "notorious" neighborhoods—there were no reported incidents on election day.[24]

The first returns after the polls closed on November 5 were primarily from Newark and suggested a close contest, raising hopes among the family and friends gathered at Rodino's campaign headquarters. But when the suburban vote was counted, Hartley took the lead and was declared the winner. His victory was part of a Republican sweep that elected the party's nominee as governor of New Jersey and gave the GOP control of both houses of Congress for the first time in fifteen years.[25]

If it was a disappointing night for Rodino, he had no reason to regret his decision to challenge Hartley. The final results were considered "Hartley's Hardest Win" by the press, and the congressman's six thousand vote plurality was a disappointing tally in the midst of a Republican tidal wave. Rodino seriously eroded his opponent's formerly strong base of support in Newark's Italian American communities, carrying the First Ward by a four-to-one margin and running even in the heavily Republican Eighth. He improved on the performance of past challengers in the surrounding suburbs, and, across the river in Hudson County, he came within a thousand votes of beating Hartley in his own hometown.[26] Rodino's willingness to take on this stalwart conservative reviled by progressives and organized labor earned him considerable goodwill and raised his public profile beyond the boundaries of the First Ward. Most significantly, he gained the practical know-how of conducting a campaign and ended up doing better than anyone predicted. With Democratic leaders doubting he could win, Rodino was relatively free to operate outside the internal machinations of the party machine, which provided him with a degree of political independence going forward. Once again, he exceeded expectations, overcame considerable obstacles, and profited from the experience.

Rodino's most pressing need after the election was to earn a living to support his family. He finally acknowledged the financial limitations of a solo practice and entered into a partnership with attorney Frank Metro. But he was not planning to fade into the background, assuring his supporters on the night of his defeat that "this was just the battle and that we hadn't lost the war." His non-income-generating public activities remained his top priority.[27] He rarely refused a request to speak at a civic or political event regardless of the occasion or the size of the crowd and returned to the campaign trail the following year on behalf of Democrats running for the state legislature. Hoping to continue his advocacy on behalf of veterans, he accepted an appointment from the American Veterans Committee to serve as chairman of their regional housing committee.[28]

A major focus for Rodino during this period was an issue that was both politically and personally important to him: helping Italy. While he was still stationed in Rome, he had initiated a letter-writing campaign urging Italian Americans back home to send money to those local charities attempting to address the widespread food shortages in the country. He also asked his friends in Newark to organize a "package brigade" to provide supplies to overcrowded orphanages that he had personally visited in the capital city. Returning to the United States, Rodino expanded these efforts and traveled to Chicago to address the Italian Welfare Council, where he presented his eyewitness account of the hardships that Italians faced. "The facts you submitted and the vivid stories you related moved all of us deeply," Joseph R. Salerno, council president, wrote in a thank-you letter.[29] Rodino was always willing to share his personal observations whenever requested and worked with the national American Relief for Italy organization and the Italian embassy in Washington to coordinate this outreach.

The ongoing ability to generate American support for Italy largely depended on the outcome of the fight over the country's unsettled political future. Italian voters had decided in a postwar referendum to replace the monarchy with a republic. The first parliamentary elections were scheduled to be held in the spring of 1948. Italy had the largest communist party in western Europe, and there was a growing fear that they might win the election. Considering the deepening cold war between the United States and the Soviet Union, the Truman administration was actively campaigning to prevent this outcome and threatened to end American aid if the communists came to power.[30] Rodino organized an effort in New Jersey to mobilize Italian Americans to contact relatives in Italy and urge them to vote for the anti-communist political parties. He opened a storefront support center in the First Ward to help translate letters into Italian and personally staffed a similar clinic near his downtown law office. In March, Rodino sent a telegram to Secretary of State George C. Marshall offering to lead a "goodwill brigade" of former veterans to Italy "to sell Democracy."[31] Several dozen volunteers signed up for the nationally publicized trip before the State Department officially rejected the idea because of its diplomatic complications. A few weeks later, the Christian Democrats won an outright majority in the Italian parliament, and the immediate political crisis in the country ended.[32]

All of these public and civic endeavors helped to fortify Rodino's plans to run for Congress in 1948. Encouraged by his strong showing the first time, he was already working behind the scenes with Joe Benucci on a revised campaign strategy based on the previous election results. They focused on the precincts Rodino lost and recruited volunteers to serve as district captains in these areas to create an expanded grassroots network throughout the Tenth District that was independent of the existing party organization. Neither Rodino nor Benucci ever really stopped campaigning and maintained a busy schedule attending social events and regularly meeting with local political clubs and veterans' organizations.[33]

Rodino's electoral prospects were boosted when Fred Hartley confirmed his plans to retire at the end of the current Congress, a possibility he had hinted at during the previous campaign. Following his reelection, Hartley had become the chairman of the House Committee on Education and Labor and coauthored the controversial Taft-Hartley Act, which limited the power of unions and was passed over President Truman's veto. This brought him national attention, as well as the enmity of organized labor, and created post-retirement opportunities on the lecture circuit and in the business community. He was not willing to exchange a lucrative second career for the prospects of a tough rematch with his former adversary, and he refused repeated entreaties to change his mind. Learning from Rodino's example, Republican leaders decided to endorse an Italian American from Newark, and Anthony Giuliano, a former state assemblyman, easily defeated two primary challengers to win the party's nomination.[34]

Hartley's decision not to run again did little to alter the conventional wisdom that the Tenth District was a safe Republican seat. Democratic chairman Kelly told Rodino he was happy to endorse him again in the upcoming April primary, but the party was not prepared to devote any significant resources to what he considered a lost cause. This belief that Rodino could not win was widespread and fueled speculation that he was only entering the congressional race to build support for a planned run in the next municipal elections. The rumors prompted Ralph A. Villani, a Republican member of Newark's Board of Commissioners, to invite Rodino to a meeting in his city hall office. First elected in 1941, Villani was one of the city's most prominent Italian Americans and responsible for overseeing the parks and public property department, where he controlled significant patronage. He was hoping to leverage this power to become the city's next mayor, a position customarily awarded to the commissioner receiving the most votes, and he feared a Rodino candidacy was likely to draw Italian American votes and diminish his chances of securing the top spot. In an effort to forestall this possibility, Villani offered Rodino a job as his confidential secretary at an annual salary of $5,000 and a guaranteed pension. During their two-hour session, Villani assured Rodino he could maintain his law practice and promised to give him a raise after he became the mayor. He stressed the benefits of job security over an uncertain political future and encouraged him not to make a decision until he discussed the matter with his wife. With no hesitation and Ann's backing, Rodino declined the offer.[35]

News of this private meeting was quickly leaked, and Rodino recalled that when he visited Democratic headquarters the following day, chairman Kelly already knew about it and advised him to take the job. Later that week, a detailed account appeared in the "Essex Scrapbook," an anonymously written weekly political column in the *Newark Evening News*. Under the headline "Villani Worked Hard to Sell Rodino Bill of Goods," the skeptical columnist recounted Rodino's public statements that he was running for Congress and noted that "municipal politicos, however, have long claimed that Pete plans to use strength built up in the national election to bolster his bid for the local post."[36] Rodino was upset that his intentions were questioned and sent a follow-up letter to the editor of the newspaper maintaining that any delay in formally launching his bid for Congress was solely the result of his urgent work promoting democracy in Italy. Recounting these efforts and his other experience overseas, he reaffirmed his "sincere interest in national affairs" and argued that he had the "type of experience needed in Washington."[37]

As Rodino began to focus his full attention on the campaign, the broader outlook for Democrats was not encouraging. President Truman, burdened with an unprecedented litany of domestic and foreign policy crises, remained unpopular. His decision to run for election in 1948 after completing FDR's term was not universally welcomed by Democrats. Convinced that Truman was unelectable, a group of party leaders, including Hudson County boss Frank Hague, attempted to recruit wartime hero Dwight D. Eisenhower for the nomination. When he rejected the idea, Truman was selected at the chaotic Democratic convention in Philadelphia, where divisions over civil rights erupted into open warfare. The decision of southern Dixiecrats to leave the convention and select their own candidate further handicapped Truman's uphill battle against his Republican opponent, New York's Governor Thomas E. Dewey. Many pundits were already writing Truman's political obituary and predicting a big Republican win in November.[38]

The 1948 campaign in the Tenth District was largely a carbon copy of the race two years earlier. Although Fred Hartley's name was not on the ballot, he continued to cast a long shadow over the contest. Revenge for the hated Taft-Hartley Act was the national rallying cry for organized labor and fueled their determination to restore Democratic control on Capitol Hill. Rodino benefited from this zeal and the enormous symbolic value placed on capturing Fred Hartley's congressional seat. The CIO-PAC provided him with a considerably larger financial contribution this time and the additional resource of a part-time writer; this proved to be a mixed blessing since Rodino had to rewrite most of the press statements to tone down the socialist rhetoric. The campaign was still on a tight budget, headquartered in a slightly larger First Ward storefront and managing without the usual political accoutrements like campaign buttons. At least Rodino and Benucci could afford to expand outreach efforts and organize more campaign events as well as grassroots canvassing throughout the district. With less press coverage of individual congressional campaigns because of the presidential contest, Rodino had to work harder to get his message directly to the voters, and the additional resources from labor groups funded these activities.[39]

The issues debated on the campaign trail were largely unchanged from the last race, and Rodino continued to push for a full agenda of progressive programs, including federally subsidized housing assistance and expanded benefits for veterans. He was unwilling to soften his New Deal message regardless of the audience. When he appeared before the conservative Battalion Forum in the wealthy enclave of Glen Ridge, he did not hesitate to condemn the Republican Congress for its "errors of omission and commission."[40] He criticized his opponent for opposing government regulation of big business and repeatedly called for the immediate repeal of Taft-Hartley. Giuliano generally focused his attacks on the Truman administration rather than Rodino and promised to carry on Hartley's legacy, which Rodino pointed out to the press included the worst attendance record in the House. Unlike other Democratic candidates, Rodino never shied away from defending the president and his policies. When Truman visited Newark in October as part of his cross-country whistle stop tour, Rodino was one of the speakers at a large rally held in the Mosque Theater and gladly accepted Truman's endorsement. The political fate of the two now seemed inextricably linked, and the *New York Times* noted that though "Mr. Rodino is conceded to be a strong candidate, a genuine cause of concern to the Republicans anxious to hold the seat," his strength in the Tenth District race would be offset by the "trend to Dewey," and it projected a Republican sweep.[41]

Not long after the polls closed on November 3, there were indications that this prediction might be wrong. Governor Dewey was not racking up the projected wide margins in key New Jersey counties, and President Truman and the other Democratic candidates on the ballot were doing better than expected. Spurred by the hotly contested presidential race, heavy statewide turnout far exceeded that of 1946—in the Tenth District, twenty thousand additional voters went to the polls. At Rodino headquarters, tensions mounted as the first returns from Newark were reported. The news was encouraging, with Rodino winning every ward of the city, including Giuliano's home base in the Eighth. Remembering the disappointment of the last campaign, everyone waited anxiously for the results from the Republican stronghold in the suburbs, which had provided Hartley with his margin of victory. Although Rodino did not win these municipalities, he managed to narrow the gap and improve his margins in every town, which enabled him to hold Giuliano to a thousand-vote lead in Essex County. In the Hudson County portion of the district, Rodino carried Hartley's hometown this time and significantly improved his overall vote total. With a final tally of 58,634 votes to Giuliano's 53,052, Rodino was declared the winner.[42]

The realization that Rodino had won the election sparked pandemonium at the crowded headquarters. The excitement soon spilled out into the surrounding streets, where jubilant residents celebrated the success of a "local" and basked in their collective personal pride as Italian Americans. Fireworks, torchlight parades, and impromptu street parties erupted at the win and continued until morning. All the skeptics and naysayers rushed to the headquarters when they heard the news, and Rodino recalled that "I had more supporters, more voters than I'd got votes" on that memorable night.[43] At the same time, Rodino was defying the odds in the Tenth District, President Truman was demonstrating surprising electoral strength nationally to win in a stunning upset over Thomas Dewey that helped the Democrats regain their majorities in both chambers of Congress. In New Jersey, Hugh J. Addonizio competing in the neighboring Eleventh District and Charles R. Howell in the Fourth both defeated Republicans to join Rodino as members of the state's rebalanced congressional delegation. With the Democrats in charge of the executive and legislative branches, Rodino was optimistic about the prospects for adopting the progressive agenda he championed in the campaign. Addressing his supporters on election night, he told the crowd he looked forward to ending "the utter neglect which the GOP-dominated Congress displayed toward such burning issues in domestic politics as housing, inflation, social security and civil rights."[44]

The political irony of a liberal Democrat capturing Fred Hartley's congressional seat heightened press interest in Rodino's unexpected victory. The *Newark Star-Ledger* singled out the Tenth District race as "the most startling upset of the day" in an election filled with surprises, a sentiment echoed in other newspapers.[45] Featuring a photograph of Ann giving the congressman-elect a congratulatory kiss, the *Newark Evening News* interviewed Rodino, who promised not to become "a professional politician" and declared that repealing the Taft-Hartley law was his first priority.[46] Although both newspapers attributed Rodino's election to his plurality in Hudson County, this postelection analysis undervalued the impact of Rodino's activities following his defeat in 1946 that helped to raise his public profile. His outreach efforts to support Italy, frequent speaking engagements, and heightened name recognition clearly made a difference in the Republican-leaning suburbs where his performance improved. A stronger-than-expected showing in Newark against another Italian American local meant that Rodino was only slightly behind Giuliano before the Hudson votes provided the decisive margin. Without Rodino's improved numbers *throughout* the district, the final tally might have resulted in a much closer election or even tilted in favor of his opponent. If Rodino's margin of victory was not overwhelming, the results offered a solid foundation for his new congressional career.

The morning after the election, a weary Rodino met in his apartment with a reporter from the *Newark Star-Ledger* for a follow-up interview. Asked to assess the reasons for his electoral win, Rodino generously credited others, including Joe Benucci, his loyal cadre of volunteers, and the coalition of veterans and labor groups that united behind his candidacy. While these were clearly important contributing factors, the campaign's most important asset and the primary reason for the unexpected outcome was the candidate himself. He had entered the public arena to make a difference and never faltered in his determination to achieve this goal. When no one believed a serious challenge to an entrenched incumbent was possible, he had the self-confidence to undertake the effort. Falling short, he was not discouraged and instead simply redoubled his efforts. Thanks to his own persistence, the questions Rodino pondered about his uncertain future when he boarded that returning troopship in Italy were finally answered.

CHAPTER FIVE

MR. RODINO GOES TO WASHINGTON

IN THE SUMMER OF 1949, political scientist James MacGregor Burns published his first book. Provocatively titled *Congress on Trial*, this inaugural work from a future Pulitzer Prize winner offered a sobering and highly critical assessment of the legislative branch. Burns wrote of a place paralyzed by infighting and obstructionism, a place where members obsessed with reelection were reluctant to address pressing national issues. Feeding this inertia was the outsized influence of lobby groups that made reaching a consensus extremely difficult and a rare occurrence. Burns' pessimistic conclusion was that Congress was ill-equipped to meet the challenges of any crisis that might arise and institutionally incapable of reforming itself. This was the world that Peter Rodino was about to enter.[1]

Burns' harsh critique was particularly stinging because it was written only a few years after the enactment of legislation to modernize the structure and the process on Capitol Hill. Under the new law, most special and select committees in the House of Representatives were either eliminated or absorbed into other panels to avoid duplication, decreasing the total number by more than half and reducing individual assignments from three to one.

All committees were now required to follow standard procedures, including holding regular meetings and issuing reports on final legislative action.[2] Yet these highly touted bipartisan reforms had failed to address the institution's fundamental flaw: the entrenched and anachronistic seniority system. For decades, longevity was used to determine committee assignments, chairmanships, recognition on the floor, office space, and even social standing.[3] Consequently, members who were regularly reelected dominated their respective chambers, and southern Democrats were at the top of this list. Of the nineteen standing House committees remaining after the consolidation, fourteen of the chairmen were from southern and border states, and they controlled most of the major panels. These politically conservative congressional czars were openly hostile to President Truman's progressive agenda and the interests of organized labor. For a liberal freshman from New Jersey elected with the strong backing of the CIO, the path ahead was not going to be an easy one.[4]

At noon on January 3, 1949, the Eighty-First Congress convened, and the brief interlude of Republican rule formally ended as Democrats reclaimed control. Following an encouraging prayer from the chaplain, the first order of business in the House of Representatives was to determine if a quorum was present, and, a majority of the members responding in the affirmative, the chamber proceeded to select its leaders. The genial yet tough Texan Sam Rayburn was elected Speaker, a position he had previously occupied, and John McCormack of Massachusetts was returned to the post of Majority Leader. Asking the members to rise, the new Speaker administered the oath of office to all the representatives in attendance and then formally called the House of Representatives into session.[5] Watching the proceedings in the public gallery were several of Rodino's coworkers from the Art Metal Works factory, along with a large group of family and friends from the Tenth District. After the swearing-in ceremony, the New Jersey contingent joined other well-wishers at an open house in Rodino's congressional office across the street before they all attended an evening reception held in his honor at the nearby Hotel Congressional.[6]

Rodino arrived in Washington with an advantage that helped him to stand out from the other members of the freshman class. As the liberal Democrat who captured the conservative Fred Hartley's congressional seat, he was a political novelty in the capital and attracted more attention from the national press than the average backbencher. Both of the city's daily newspapers singled Rodino out for special profiles, and he was embraced by influential political columnist Drew Pearson. Through his syndicated column, the "Washington Merry-Go-Round," and his weekly radio show, Pearson presented a combination of news, gossip, and investigative reports to a nationwide audience. The liberal Pearson was Fred Hartley's fiercest critic and celebrated his successor in a column published two weeks after the start of the congressional session. Providing a detailed recounting of Rodino's upbringing in a rough neighborhood and struggle to become a lawyer, he lauded the new congressman for remaining true to his humble origins. Peter Rodino, Pearson informed his readers, was "the man a great many people will be watching."[7]

While there were benefits to being identified as Hartley's replacement, it was also a potential burden. A critical step for new members of the House of Representatives was securing a committee assignment, a decision that could determine the future trajectory of a congressional career. For Democrats, the primary responsibility for this selection resided with a panel comprised of the party's Committee on Ways and Means members. Rodino had already decided that, based on his interest in world affairs and connection to Italy, he wanted to serve on the foreign affairs panel with the judiciary committee as his second choice. But the leaders of organized labor had other plans for him and wanted the symbolism of Rodino leading the effort to repeal Taft-Hartley. When he arrived in Washington, he discovered to his dismay that the CIO, without his knowledge, had secured his appointment to the House Education and Labor Committee. Rodino had hoped to pursue a wide range of progressive policies rather than championing a single, all-consuming issue for which he lacked a deep knowledge. But refusing to help his major political backers achieve a goal he campaigned for was not an easy choice.[8]

Rodino decided to turn to Majority Leader John McCormack for advice. The two had established an immediate bond through their mutual involvement in the Knights of Malta, a Catholic service organization. Explaining that the Education and Labor Committee was not his choice, he requested a reassignment to his first or second preference. A sympathetic McCormack was unable to make this change unless another member was prepared to swap and not surprisingly, no one on either panel was willing to exchange seats. At McCormack's suggestion, he next approached Charles Howell, a fellow freshman from New Jersey, who was slated to serve on the House Committee on Veterans' Affairs. Howell was worried about the political pressures he might face on the committee as a nonveteran, and he gratefully accepted when Rodino proposed a trade.[9]

Rodino must have had some inkling that his new assignment was not without its own challenges. The chairman of the House Committee on Veterans' Affairs was the ill-tempered John Rankin from Mississippi. He was notorious for his unapologetic racism and frequent anti-Semitic remarks. Among a stable of autocratic chairmen in the House, he was considered one of the most tyrannical; he refused to establish subcommittees and rarely held hearings.[10] Although as a junior member Rodino was expected to keep quiet and defer to the chairman, he violated both of these precepts during his first month in office when he was embroiled in a public fight with the chairman that threatened his fledgling career. The dispute began over Rankin's legislation to provide a monthly pension to every veteran at the age of sixty-five. Rodino joined the Truman administration and a few courageous veterans' groups in opposing the measure because of its astronomical price tag that would drain resources from other needed programs. On February 15, the chairman convened a markup session to approve the bill without proper notice or the prior distribution of the legislation. Repeated attempts by Rodino and others to offer amendments were either ruled out of order or simply rejected without a vote, triggering a heated debate inside the closed-door meeting. As tensions mounted, seven Democrats, including Rodino, walked out in an unprecedented protest.[11]

The drama quickly shifted to the House floor, where the protesters went to lodge a complaint with Speaker Rayburn. A furious Rankin followed them and, storming down the aisle, requested permission to speak. Taking aim at the rebels, he accused them of running out on veterans and dismissed them as "uninformed." An angry and stunned Rodino sat listening and wondering how to react. With quaking knees and a quavering voice, he rose and asked for unanimous consent to address the House. Drawing upon his oratorical skills, he began speaking without notes, reminding his colleagues of his status as a new member of Congress and an honorably discharged veteran before responding directly to Rankin: "The veterans fought to preserve our democratic way and as a member of Congress it is my solemn duty to continue to fight to preserve that way…This opportunity I do not believe was afforded to us because of the objectionable way in which the chairman of the House Veterans' Affairs (VA) Committee conducted today's meeting."[12]

When Rodino sat down, the chamber erupted with applause. Fittingly, it was his maiden speech in the House of Representatives.[13]

Rodino's courage in confronting the formidable Rankin was widely praised by the press and provided a second round of national coverage in less than a month. Both the *New York Times* and the *Washington Post* singled out Rodino and the three other freshmen rebels for initiating a long-overdue challenge to Rankin's abuse of power. The *Washington Times Herald* hailed "the popular youngster who beat Fred Hartley" and quoted extensively from Rodino's floor speech, noting that "for once John Rankin had no answer."[14] But Rankin was already planning his next move, and a few weeks later he used parliamentary maneuvers to force a vote in the House over the objections of the Democratic leadership. With the backing of Speaker Rayburn and President Truman, the opponents managed to defeat the popular bill by a single vote. A furious Rankin announced in a pique that the committee would not consider any pension legislation during the current session, which prompted some criticism of Rodino from disappointed veterans. Although the public fight further damaged Rodino's already strained relationship with his chairman, it earned him the gratitude of the large contingent of Rankin critics in the House of Representatives, including Majority Leader McCormack and House Judiciary Committee chairman Emanuel Celler.[15]

During his first weeks in office, Rodino settled into a routine that he would continue to follow with little deviation for the rest of his time in Congress. Thanks to the G.I. Bill, he had recently purchased his first home at 205 Grafton Avenue in a residential area of the First Ward, which made relocating the family to Washington financially difficult. He and Ann decided that the most practical option was for him to commute every week, and he accepted an offer to share an apartment with his colleague Hugh Addonizio, whose neighboring district contained Newark's central wards. The two had developed an instant friendship on the campaign trail, and the press quickly dubbed the roommates and frequent traveling companions "the twins."[16] Rodino's work week usually began in the dark early hours of Monday morning, when he left his house to board the train at Newark's Penn Station. Arriving in Washington by eight in the morning, he hurried to his office where he read the mail piled on his desk and dictated responses. The remainder of his morning was taken up by committee business, and he set aside his afternoons for meetings with visiting delegations and constituents. Since House proceedings were not broadcast, Rodino and his colleagues spent a considerable amount of time on the floor monitoring the debate or in the adjacent cloakroom where members could socialize, make telephone calls, and have a snack. He spent most nights working in the office unless he was invited to a social event, not a frequent occurrence in his early years. After the final vote on Friday, he boarded the train for the return trip back to Newark.[17]

Unlike other people, Rodino did not enjoy the luxury of relaxing on the weekend. Instead, he started a hectic two-day marathon aimed at building and maintaining the relationships that were critical to his political survival. Every Saturday, he held visiting hours in his downtown office, and the waiting room was regularly crowded with constituents needing some form of assistance. Rodino personally met with everyone, conversing in Italian when necessary, and did not leave until he had resolved all requests or processed them for additional action. In the evening, he attended weddings, anniversary parties, and a whirlwind of other social events, often accompanied by his wife. Most Sundays he visited churches and traveled throughout the district to speak before civic or veterans' organizations until late in the evening.[18] The one thing he did not do was spend much time at his Grafton Avenue house.

Rodino was not without help in managing his congressional operations; every member received an annual staff allowance and could hire up to seven employees. He had asked Joe Benucci to serve as district director and enlisted his sister-in-law, Marge, to be his personal secretary, the same position she held at his law firm. Accepting the recommendation of the CIO, he hired Selig "Jack" Bendit who had worked on Capitol Hill for fifteen years, to run the Washington office.[19]

However, delegating did not come naturally to the self-reliant Rodino, and he provided detailed instructions to Benucci on how he wanted the office to operate:

"Remember, Joe, that I must adhere to certain policies, and there may be times when a conflict may arise, which I must resolve myself and which I cannot permit others to resolve for me! More than that since the responsibility will be mine alone for whatever is done, I am assuming full responsibility of affixing my signature. Whether here or in Newark, no one will sign my name for me at any time!"[20]

Rodino served as his own press secretary, working hard to maintain good coverage in Newark's two daily newspapers and writing most of his floor statements and speeches. Because long distance telephone calls were expensive in 1949, letter writing was the primary method of constituent communications. Rodino's higher public profile generated a significant amount of mail either seeking help or opining on a current issue. He drafted many of the responses and personally contacted the relevant federal agency or Truman administration official if required to resolve a problem. This demanding pace soon took its toll, and in late February his doctor ordered several days of bed rest after he arrived home groggy and feverish. Admitting to reporters that he was still dictating letters and greeting a steady flow of visitors from his sickbed, Rodino confessed that his workload was so great that "if I didn't tackle some of the stuff, by the time I got back on my feet I'd be so far behind I'd never catch up."[21]

Rodino's initial legislative roster was an eclectic mix of issues that were important to the district, elements of the Truman administration's agenda, and subjects of personal interest. The first bill he introduced was a measure to modify the immigration rules to make it easier for fiancés of resident aliens to enter the United States, addressing a problem voiced by his Italian American constituents.[22] None of his proposals were considered in the House and garnered little notice outside the Tenth District.[23] The one exception was the repeal of the Taft-Hartley Act, which continued to push Rodino into the spotlight. He agreed to a request from his labor allies to be the lead witness at the first congressional hearing on repeal, symbolism not lost on the press. Rodino used his testimony to outline a long list of the law's shortcomings and warned that, left unchecked, it would destroy the labor movement. Rodino then suggested that Fred Hartley refused to seek reelection because he knew he would be defeated by the broad opposition to the law he authored, a claim that was not supported by the facts. This set off a bitter partisan debate between subcommittee members over Hartley's current role as a business lobbyist. The contentious hearing received extensive press coverage. While an outraged Hartley condemned Rodino, a grateful CIO expressed its appreciation.[24]

Frozen out of any meaningful role in his own committee, Rodino continued to look for other opportunities. In December, there was an opening on the House Judiciary Committee when one of its members unexpectedly died. Although the usual practice was to select a replacement from the same state, Rodino expressed his interest in the vacancy. His opposition to Rankin provided a reservoir of goodwill from some members, and his friend, Louisiana Representative Thomas Hale Boggs, was on the selection committee and vigorously promoted Rodino's candidacy.

But the most important advocate for Rodino's judiciary membership was the panel's chairman, Emanuel Celler. Celler had hoped to recruit Rodino after the 1948 election, writing to New Jersey Congresswoman Mary Norton that "I note that Peter W. Rodino, Jr., a lawyer, will be part of the New Jersey delegation. I wonder if you could interest him in applying for membership in the Judiciary Committee."[25] The CIO's intervention in the selection process had derailed this possibility. Now Rodino's impeccable progressive credentials and challenge to Celler's archenemy inspired the chairman to try again, and he worked to ensure Rodino's nomination, which the House unanimously approved on January 26, 1950.[26]

Although the House first established a panel to oversee issues related to the judiciary in 1813, the modern committee Rodino joined was a byproduct of the recent congressional reorganization, which had significantly enlarged its jurisdiction by adding the previously independent panels on patents, immigration, claims, and law revision. This had transformed the House Judiciary Committee into one of the chamber's major committees, with legislative responsibility over a broad range of national issues and oversight authority for a large portion of the federal bureaucracy.[27]

Leading the twenty-seven members who were all attorneys was Brooklyn Democrat Emanuel "Manny" Celler. First elected to Congress in 1922, the sixty-two-year-old grandson of German Jewish immigrants was known for his sense of humor and formidable debating skills, which he never hesitated to use against his conservative opponents on the House floor. If not an absolute authoritarian in the Rankin mold, he did not hesitate to exercise the considerable power at his disposal under the seniority system. Celler was responsible for hiring and firing the committee's professional staff—a move that ensured that their primary duty was to serve him, not the other members. He controlled the referral of legislation sent to the committee, and this provided important leverage in determining the fate of a proposal or rewarding a loyal ally. There were four numbered subcommittees loosely organized around the inherited jurisdictions, and Celler could either send a bill to one of these panels, create a special subcommittee to handle a particular issue, or simply retain jurisdiction at the full committee. Choosing either of these last two options allowed the chairman to remain personally involved in the process and influence the final outcome.[28]

Despite these levers of power, managing a large group that was rife with conflicting views and healthy egos was not an easy task. Celler was an unabashed liberal, and not all of his Democratic colleagues on the committee shared his commitment to the Truman administration's agenda, making votes on key legislative issues difficult to predict. Other members who previously occupied senior positions in the abolished committees resented the loss of influence and openly clashed with Celler, who had only ascended to the chairmanship in 1949. Consequently, his first committee vacancy presented an opportunity for Celler to strengthen his control; adding the equally liberal Rodino guaranteed another reliable vote and a natural ally. Beyond their ideological compatibility, the two quickly developed a warm, personal relationship fostered by an appreciation of their shared immigrant heritage and mutual love of Italian opera. Rodino became Celler's loyal protégé. From his humble berth as the junior member of Subcommittee 2, responsible for the unglamorous subject of claims, he was ready to serve a chairman he respected.[29]

Joining the House Judiciary Committee was the capstone of an extraordinary freshman year for Rodino. Back home, the *Belleville Times* was already declaring that "there are many in these five suburban towns who consider Rodino an excellent Congressman."[30] Looking ahead to the November election, he appeared to be in a strong position with a well-oiled constituent service operation in place and an army of volunteers like the Rodino Ladies Auxiliary eager to start campaigning. But Rodino understood that an incumbent was most vulnerable facing reelection for the first time, particularly in a non-presidential, low voter turnout year, and he began preparing for a tough fight. New Jersey Republicans signaled they were doing the same and announced that recapturing the three congressional seats they lost in the past election was the party's top priority.[31]

No longer the challenger, Rodino could now claim tangible achievements when he launched his reelection campaign under the banner of "Service Not Self." In advertisements and stump speeches, he extolled his liberal voting record and near perfect attendance. He highlighted his influence in Washington by featuring laudatory quotes from Drew Pearson and Majority Leader McCormack. His opponent, Essex County Freeholder William H. Rawson, was a lackluster candidate and could not compete with Rodino's level of activity on the campaign trail. Once again, the press predicted a close race, underestimating Rodino's political skills and the ability of his labor allies to get out the vote. On election day, Rodino won with a 20,000-vote plurality, a threefold increase from 1948, and this time he captured most of the suburban towns in the district. Considering that the Democrats suffered losses on both sides of Capitol Hill, it was an impressive victory and one that prompted the *Newark Evening News* to conclude that Rodino "showed solid entrenchment in the 10th."[32]

When the new Congress convened in January, Rodino ascended a few steps up the House Judiciary Committee's seniority ladder and received an additional assignment from the chairman. Celler was a longtime foe of big business, and he had created a special subcommittee to investigate the economic impact of monopolies and anticompetitive practices. Holding a series of high-profile hearings on specific industries, the panel published its findings in several highly critical reports and proposed changes to close loopholes in the existing antitrust laws. Celler had already announced an ambitious series of hearings in the upcoming session of Congress that were a blend of highly technical issues, like interlocking directorates, and more broadly appealing topics, including baseball's antitrust exemption. Rodino readily accepted Celler's invitation to fill a vacancy on this high-profile panel.[33]

Sitting through hundreds of hours of hearings over the next ten months, Rodino participated in a congressional version of a master class on a subject he knew little about before he joined the subcommittee. His access to voluminous background information and regular briefings from committee staff provided a privileged weekly supply of educational materials on the social consequences of economic concentration. With the exception of a few days in October when his son Peter was born, he rarely missed a public or executive session. At these sessions, he was exposed to a wide variety of economists, business leaders, and senior government officials. Although initially low-key, he gained confidence as the hearings progressed and grew noticeably more comfortable expressing his criticism of the business community and their monopolistic practices. Celler often called on him to chair the hearings in his absence; he would become passionate about the issue by the time he left the subcommittee at the end of the year. When Celler created a permanent antitrust subcommittee a few years later, Rodino was one of the original appointees.[34]

Rodino's departure from a subcommittee he enjoyed was the result of his selection to serve on another special congressional panel created to investigate a scandal involving bribery and corruption by political appointees in the Truman administration. At the time, federal tax collectors were located in major cities throughout the United States, and these positions were among the most sought-after patronage jobs. When several collectors were charged with accepting kickbacks to reduce tax liabilities, the trail of allegations led back to Washington, where the failure of the Department of Justice to prosecute these cases or investigate misconduct sparked charges of a cover-up. A besieged President Truman was forced to fire the head of the tax enforcement division, and he ordered Attorney General J. Howard McGrath to initiate an internal review of the department's conduct. The Republicans in Congress were outraged, arguing that McGrath, a former Democratic National Committee chairman, was incapable of overseeing a fair and independent inquiry. Securing bipartisan support in the House, they passed a resolution requiring the House Judiciary Committee to create a special seven-member subcommittee to investigate the Department of Justice.[35]

Without the advantage of foresight, it seemed unlikely in 1952 that Peter Rodino would benefit from serving on a panel conducting a nonpartisan investigation into the misconduct of executive branch officials. The formation of the subcommittee was announced in February, and straddling the line between witch-hunt and whitewash was expected to be a daunting task in an election year. Rodino's appointment was regarded back home as a mixed blessing at best. The *Newark Evening News* sympathetically noted that he was given a difficult job that might continue into campaign season. While recognizing the challenges, Rodino told reporters, "I shall do as my judgment directs for a thorough, fair, nonpartisan job based on the facts as presented."[36]

The responsibility for leading this politically sensitive undertaking was given to Kentucky Democrat Frank Chelf, who ranked sixth in seniority on the full committee and was a former prosecutor. Chelf assured the members of the panel, including New York Republican Kenneth Keating, who authored the resolution triggering the probe, that he was determined to operate on a strictly nonpartisan basis. Rodino supported Chelf's decision to conduct the hearings in public sessions and urged him to select "a good, reliable, thorough counsel and smart investigators."[37] The problems confronting the congressional investigation were apparent even before the hearings began as the subcommittee grew frustrated over the attorney general's lack of cooperation. McGrath refused to provide any requested documents until his internal review was completed, and Chelf was reluctant to proceed without them. When Rodino joined with the Republicans to pressure the chairman to move forward, he finally agreed to schedule a starting date.[38]

On March 26, the Special Subcommittee to Investigate the Department of Justice held its first public hearing. Setting the tone for the group's year-long undertaking, Chairman Chelf declared that "our investigation will be searching and painstaking lacking the carnival ballyhoo which many would like."[39] The sole witness was Attorney General McGrath. McGrath faced tough questioning from the Republicans and attempted to defend his leadership in several hours of testimony, which he completed the following week just before he was fired by President Truman. Rodino was highly critical of McGrath and welcomed his departure. But he was equally concerned that the investigation remain focused. In executive sessions, he frequently opposed Republican efforts to either broaden the probe or weaken the rules of evidence.

The details of these closed door meetings were leaked to Drew Pearson, a frequent critic of the scandal-ridden Justice Department. In a May 25 column, he condemned Rodino for opposing a thorough investigation of corruption. "Congressman Rodino has had a good record on most things," Pearson wrote, "he should not blemish it by serving as a cat's paw for the whitewashers." The column included a photo of Rodino with the caption "favors whitewash."[40] Because there were no transcripts of the closed meetings, and the public hearings were not yet printed, Rodino was at a disadvantage in defending himself and demonstrating his tough questioning of witnesses. This was Rodino's first encounter with Pearson's sharp sting, and he was worried about the political fallout in an election year. He immediately called Pearson to refute the charge and urged him to print a retraction. The columnist agreed to investigate, and the following week he offered an indirect retraction when he included a quote in his column from Chairman Chelf vouching for Rodino's commitment to a thorough investigation. Upset about the leak from the subcommittee, Chelf spoke to the *Newark Star-Ledger* to confirm that the Tenth District's representative voted on every occasion "for a full, free investigation," and Republican subcommittee member Patrick J. Hillings offered his own letter of support.[41]

The early adjournment of Congress in July for the upcoming campaign did not end the subcommittee's work. The delayed release of documents from the Truman administration required the subcommittee to double the size of its small staff and led to a broadening of the investigation beyond the original tax fraud cases. The discovery of unethical conduct and illegal activity by a wider range of government officials forced the panel to meet throughout the summer to interrogate a long list of new witnesses. In September, the panel issued the first of several reports in which members unanimously condemned the absence of ethical standards at the Justice Department, most notably the ability of government lawyers to engage in outside legal work, which created numerous conflicts of interest. The members' harshest criticism was reserved for former Attorney General McGrath, who they accused of incompetence and gross mismanagement. The panel continued to follow the unraveling trail of misconduct for the remainder of the year and held its final hearing in late December, just days before its mandate ended.[42]

Fortunately for Rodino, the time-consuming work of the special subcommittee was largely regarded in the Tenth District as a positive reflection of his growing stature in Washington. When he launched his reelection campaign in July, the press noted he was on a rare break from the investigation and was expecting frequent "call backs" during the campaign. When he needed to return to Washington a few weeks later, the *Nutley Sun* praised his sacrifice and "devotion to duty." Rodino certainly encouraged this narrative, providing regular updates on his subcommittee activities, and he released a telegram from Chairman Chelf applauding his willingness to work on the investigation even "at risk to his political career."[43]

This was not a view shared by Rodino's opponent, Newark Housing

Commissioner Alexander J. Matturri. Four days before the election, the Republican challenger sent out a political attack ad focused on the investigation. Reproducing the initial Drew Pearson column criticizing Rodino, the Matturri broadside included the tagline, "Lets [sic] wipe out White Washing and Crime, Corruption, Confusion, Communism."[44] A panicked Rodino called Pearson for help, and the columnist immediately sent a telegram incorporating a strong statement of support: "As I wrote subsequently I later became convinced that you were doing a bang up job on the Chelf Committee...I regret therefore that anything I wrote several months ago may injure a man whom I regard as an able, conscientious and valuable public servant."[45]

That night, Pearson included a story about Rodino and the campaign attack in his Saturday broadcast. While it was unlikely that the charges would gain traction, Rodino was not taking any chances in an electoral climate that did not favor the Democrats. His campaign quickly launched a counterattack with their own flyer condemning Matturri and his "Big Lie." Rodino proactively called reporters and traveled nonstop throughout the district in the final days of the campaign, condemning his opponent's "gutter tactics."[46] The Republicans did achieve an impressive victory on election day, with presidential nominee Dwight Eisenhower crushing his opponent, Illinois Governor Adlai Stevenson, and the party regaining control of both chambers of Congress. In New Jersey, Eisenhower had received the largest plurality for a Republican since Calvin Coolidge and easily carried Essex County. Despite this Republican tidal wave and Matturri's last-minute attack, Rodino equaled his previous electoral margin to win handily and again demonstrated his personal popularity in the Tenth District.[47]

Rodino encountered a decidedly different Capitol Hill when he returned for the start of the new Congress in January 1953. For the first time, he was a member of a political party that did not control either the legislative or executive branches, and he faced all the limitations of being in the minority. His mentor Emanuel Celler and friend John McCormick were sidelined and no longer able to provide help. The Eisenhower administration controlled the federal agencies that were critical to maintaining good constituent services.

The outcome of the election reversed the partisan balance on the Judiciary Committee, and as a result Rodino lost his spot on the claims subcommittee. The new conservative chairman, Chauncey W. Reed of Illinois, had no intention of continuing his predecessor's progressive policy agenda and abolished the special monopolies panel before burying the antitrust issue in the subcommittee on patents.[48]

With a smaller legislative portfolio, Rodino focused his full attention on a cause he had been pursuing for the past several years. John Hvasta was a Czechoslovakia-born naturalized citizen. He lived with his parents in Hillside, a town five miles from Newark within New Jersey's Sixth Congressional District. As a veteran, Hvasta was entitled to educational benefits under the G.I. Bill, and he chose to pursue his studies at a university in Bratislava, where his girlfriend and future wife resided. Unluckily, his arrival coincided with the communist takeover of the country, and in August 1948 he was arrested for taking photographs in a restricted area. Hvasta was convicted in a secret trial on the trumped-up charge of spying, and he was sentenced to ten years in prison. Officials from the American consulate, initially granted limited visiting privileges, were denied any access after Hvasta was jailed at the Leopoldov Fortress north of the city. His frantic parents contacted their congressman and the State Department hoping to secure information about their son's fate. When they received a perfunctory reply, the Hvastas followed the advice of their local priest and called Peter Rodino.[49]

The standard protocol most members of Congress followed when they received a request from someone outside their district was to immediately refer it to the appropriate office. After Rodino met with Hvasta's family, he did the opposite and offered to help someone who was not his constituent. From the beginning, Rodino believed the State Department was treating John Hvasta as a second-class citizen because he had not been born in the United States, and his immigrant parents spoke with an accent. This injustice aroused his sense of fairness, and he took up their cause with the same zealousness he had exhibited in fighting the mistreatment of Italian Americans in the First Ward. Rodino's relentless phone calls and letters succeeded in stirring a complacent State Department to lodge a new protest with the Czech government over Hvasta's arrest. Advised by diplomatic officials that publicity might jeopardize the outcome, Rodino initially worked behind the scenes to monitor developments and serve as the Washington liaison for the family.[50]

Frustrated at not seeing any tangible progress in the case for several months, an impatient Rodino decided to change tactics. In April 1951, American journalist William N. Oatis was arrested in Prague and charged with spying. The front-page news story brought a quick response from the State Department, which suspended all travel to Czechoslovakia. President Truman and senior members of Congress followed with public threats to end bilateral trade unless Oatis was released.[51] This swift reaction confirmed Rodino's suspicions that Hvasta's background affected his importance to the State Department, and he decided to raise awareness of this overlooked imprisonment. In a handwritten memo to his aide Jack Bendit, Rodino outlined a multipronged strategy that was bold and ambitious, particularly for a junior member of Congress with a small staff. His plan called for leveraging the arrest of Oatis to publicize Hvasta's similar plight and to build support for his release. Rodino embarked on an intense one-man crusade, enlisting veterans' organizations to pass resolutions on behalf of their fellow veteran, providing members of Congress with background information on the case, and stoking press interest in the story of the *other* American in a Czech prison.

He also brought his campaign to Capitol Hill, where he introduced a resolution imposing a trade embargo on Czechoslovakia unless Hvasta was released. When the House of Representatives fast-tracked a similar resolution for Oatis for consideration, Rodino single-handedly prevented a vote until he was promised prompt committee action on his own resolution. Appreciating his singular effort, Hvasta's brother Steven assured Rodino that "we realize that it is difficult for one person to carry the load as you have so admirably been doing."[52]

Rodino astutely decided to start referring to John Hvasta as the "forgotten man," and he used this attention-grabbing sobriquet in all his subsequent presentations. Writing to President Truman following the administration's public comments in support of Oatis, Rodino informed the president that "you will be interested to know that for quite some time I have been pressing for the release of the 'forgotten man' John Hvasta...you will agree with me that as an American citizen he is entitled to the same rights and privileges and protection," a point he repeated when he met with Truman the following month at the White House.[53] The nationally circulated *REAL Magazine* invited Rodino to contribute his own version of the story, and it published it under the melodramatic title, "The Forgotten Man Who Defies the Reds."[54] Drew Pearson wrote several columns about Hvasta; he also used the "forgotten" tagline and included a nod to his congressional champion. Frank Edwards of the Mutual Broadcasting System echoed this sentiment, reporting that John Hvasta was forgotten "except for Congressman Peter Rodino of New Jersey, who has fought tirelessly to free [him]."[55] Increasingly, Rodino was recognized at home and in Washington for his tireless work on behalf of John Hvasta, and the chairman of the House Foreign Affairs Committee spoke for many of his colleagues when he said on the House floor, "I want to compliment a member who works so hard for a man who does not live in his district."[56]

The one tangible result of all this attention was that American embassy officials did get to visit Hvasta in August for the first time in more than a year and reported he was in good health. Rodino continued the drumbeat, testifying before the House Committee on Foreign Affairs. He found an unlikely ally in Wisconsin Senator Joseph McCarthy, who joined the call for harsher penalties against the Czechoslovakian government. In June 1952, the State Department informed Rodino of a confidential report that Hvasta was part of a prison break earlier in the year and was missing, which the Czech government publicly confirmed two months later. With the case back in the news, Rodino invited the family to Washington for another round of meetings at the department; officials were pessimistic about the possibility that Hvasta had survived. Afterward, Rodino held a press conference in his Capitol Hill office and called on the United Nations to review the case.[57]

The start of the Eisenhower administration a few months later meant that Rodino had to begin all over again, educating the new political appointees at the State Department and refocusing attention on the case. When William Oatis was released in May, the ban on travel to Czechoslovakia was immediately lifted, and a furious Rodino told the press, "I do not intend that the book be closed on John Hvasta or that he remain a forgotten man."[58] In letters to Secretary of State John Foster Dulles and President Eisenhower, he complained that the United States had forfeited an important lever in the effort to free Hvasta. Eisenhower agreed to meet with him, and, after Rodino made his plea at a White House meeting, the new president shrugged and responded, "well congressman, what do you want me to do, start a war?"[59]

Happily, armed conflict was not necessary, and the Hvasta case reached its own relatively peaceful conclusion. The real-life adventure the *Washington Post* described as "a saga rivaling anything between the covers of a suspense thriller" came to an end on October 2, when John Hvasta arrived at the doorstep of the American embassy in Prague.[60] Finally safe, he told officials of his escape from prison and his almost two-year journey traveling across the countryside and "playing hide and seek" with the police. His arrival triggered months of intense negotiations between the two governments over his ultimate freedom. The signed agreement involved a complicated face-saving maneuver that required Hvasta to be rearrested, before the Czech government pardoned and then expelled him from the country.[61]

On the morning of February 6, 1954, Peter Rodino's five-year crusade ended when John Hvasta arrived at New York's Idlewild Airport. The announcement of his release was major news, and a large throng of reporters and cameramen jammed into the airport terminal. Standing next to the family, Rodino fielded questions from reporters. Two weeks later, he accompanied John Hvasta to a meeting with Secretary of State Dulles.[62] Rodino's zealous pursuit of Hvasta's release garnered accolades and expressions of appreciation from across the country. Of all the tributes he received, the one Rodino most cherished was a citation from the Italian American service organization UNICO National, which applauded his perseverance "when hope seemed dim" and declared him "a congressional representative of the people."[63]

The Hvasta case further raised Rodino's political profile back home, fueling speculation he might enter the race in 1954 for the state's open Senate seat, and this helped him to defeat his Republican opponent in November by a two-to-one margin. Nationally, the results of the election brought the Democrats back to power in the House of Representatives, where they would remain for the next four decades. Rodino was appointed to serve on the new Subcommittee 5 that Celler created to oversee antitrust issues and his other legislative priorities.[64] However, two years later, the extremely popular Dwight Eisenhower was heading the Republican ticket in his quest for a second term, and Democrats were back on the defensive. Since losing the Tenth District, the local Republican party had adopted a variety of different strategies in a futile effort to unseat Rodino, including nominating two Italian Americans from Newark—a county office holder from the suburbs and a political novice from Democratic Hudson County. In 1956, they decided on a political gimmick and selected G. George Addonizio, who was a distant cousin of Rodino's friend and colleague *Hugh* Addonizio. Dismissing Republican disclaimers that this was simply a coincidence, a furious Congressman Addonizio condemned what he considered a blatant attempt to use his recognizable surname to confuse voters. Rodino decided not to focus on this contrivance and instead conducted his usual vigorous campaign, touting his recent efforts to lower the social security age for women and highlighting examples of his support for the president's legislative agenda.[65] On election day, President Eisenhower carried all of New Jersey's twenty-one counties, and three of the state's congressional Democrats lost their seats. Though Rodino experienced a decline in his plurality, he still carried the district by an impressive 15,000 votes. Two years later, he faced George Addonizio in an uneventful rematch, and he rebounded back to secure his previous margin of victory.[66]

While Rodino had succeeded in avoiding any serious pitfalls since arriving in Washington, he unexpectedly stumbled at the end of his first decade on Capitol Hill. The cause of the trouble was his involvement in a business venture with entrepreneur Frank Smith, who Rodino had befriended several years earlier. Smith offered him an opportunity to invest alongside other colleagues in a new company called Capital Cities, created to acquire local radio and television outlets. Using a small amount of his own money, Rodino expanded his stock purchase by accepting Smith's offer to cosign a loan for $20,000, which would be repaid from future profits. At a time when there was no congressional code of ethics, this generous offer did not violate any rules.[67]

The involvement of members of Congress in the venture became public in June 1960, when the Federal Communications Commission (FCC) awarded the company a television license on the basis of the superior "civic participation" provided by having five congressional shareholders. This revelation set off a storm of negative press over this potential conflict of interest, and Wisconsin Senator William Proxmire called the FCC's action "political payola at its worst."[68] Rodino's Republican opponent Alphonse Miele made this the centerpiece of the fall campaign and placed ads using Proxmire's quote in all the local newspapers. At every joint appearance, he demanded that Rodino answer questions about the stock purchase and his relationship with officials at the FCC. Fortunately for Rodino, the details of his loan were never revealed, and he attempted to counter Miele's relentless attacks by releasing a letter of endorsement from Proxmire and a statement from the FCC confirming that he had never contacted the agency. At the end of the difficult campaign, an anxious Rodino was relieved to find both his reputation and political standing in the Tenth District largely unchanged. He was easily reelected, and it was the last time he faced a serious threat from a Republican challenger.[69]

The positive results of the November election were a fitting end to Rodino's apprenticeship years in Congress during which he worked to build the firm foundation he would need to sustain a long-term career. He had established an effective constituent outreach program and nimble campaign operation to help transform a safe Republican district into a reliably Democratic one and secure his political future. He distinguished himself in Washington from the other members of his freshman class by challenging an autocratic chairman, participating in a high-profile investigation, and raising his profile in the national press. No longer lost in the crowded shadows of the backbench and secure at home, he was ready to move up the ladder.

CHAPTER SIX

CLIMBING THE LADDER

After a decade on Capitol Hill, Peter Rodino had mastered the folkways of what was essentially a company town. Recognizing the importance of establishing a public profile, he no longer spent nights alone working in his office. Instead he willingly participated in the ritualistic activities that could help him develop the patina he needed to be considered a part of the Washington establishment. His name was frequently listed in the guest lists at embassy receptions and high-profile dinner parties organized for social and political interaction. Rodino rarely refused a request to support a local charity or join a delegation welcoming a foreign dignitary to the city. His seniority meant that he regularly traveled the short distance down Pennsylvania Avenue to the White House for meetings, bill signings, or evening functions. While still faithfully returning to Newark most weekends, he was a more noticeable presence in the nation's capital during the week, and he confidently embraced his elevated position.[1]

Rodino was also ready to flex his muscles as a seasoned legislator serving on a major congressional committee, and the election of Massachusetts Senator John F. Kennedy as president offered just such an opportunity. Rodino first met the new president in 1946 when they both attended the DNC briefings for congressional candidates, and Kennedy had enlisted Rodino's help during the campaign.[2] Rodino's top priority was the issue he had worked on since he arrived on Capitol Hill: immigration reform. The Immigration Act of 1924 enacted on a wave of American nativism and anti-immigrant sentiment following World War I had dramatically reduced the total number of immigrants entering the United States and erected barriers for certain "undesirable" nationalities through the establishment of annual quotas for individual countries. This national origins system, using a baseline that predated the great migration, intentionally set aside most of the limited entry slots for Protestant Anglo-Saxons in northern Europe rather than the Catholics and Jews in the south, who were no longer welcome.[3]

The impact of this change on Italians was immediate; the largest ethnic group traveling to the United States was now allotted a very small number of annual admissions. Many who had saved for years to make the journey and reunite with family members faced an uncertain delay in their departure or an indefinite postponement. It was estimated that within a few years of the law's implementation, the number of Italian migrants making the transatlantic crossing declined by almost 90 percent.[4] The national quota system also affected Italians living in the United States by stigmatizing them as a group considered "unworthy" or "less desirable," which only compounded the stereotyping and discrimination they already encountered. The Italian American community deeply resented the law for these tangible and intangible harms, and Rodino had pledged during his first campaign that reforming this unfair system would be his top priority.[5]

Rodino's appointment to the House Judiciary Committee in 1950 coincided with the beginning of the first major revision of the law. Because of modifications and technical corrections since its enactment, the immigration system was a myriad of bureaucratic rules and inconsistent regulations in need of simplification. Rodino and other opponents of the national origin quotas hoped the effort to streamline the statute might provide an opportunity to press for more sweeping changes. Considering who the two members of

Congress piloting the review of immigration policy were, this was wishful thinking. Senate Judiciary Committee Chairman Pat McCarran was a conservative Democrat from Nevada known for his fervent anti-communism and determination to prevent those he regarded as "unsavory" from entering the United States. His House counterpart in this undertaking was fellow cold warrior Francis "Tad" Walter of Pennsylvania who had chaired the formerly independent immigration panel before it was absorbed into the Judiciary Committee. Walter was the chairman of the House Democratic Caucus, and he used this position to prevent any interference from his ideological opposite and frequent nemesis, Emanuel Celler.[6]

After several years of study and extensive oversight hearings, McCarran and Walter finally introduced their legislation in early 1952. Although the measure finally ended the long-standing racist ban on all Asian immigration, it did not increase the total number of admissions allowed each year or abolish the national origin system. Rodino testified before a joint hearing held on the bill, urging the sponsors to reconsider eliminating the quotas. "I think it is time to call the law for what it is—an attempt to set out a theory of racial superiority," he bluntly told the members of the panel.[7] Rodino buttressed his emotional arguments with the statistical evidence that only a quarter of the quota went to southern European countries, which resulted in a six-year wait for any Italian hoping to migrate to the United States. Recognizing that this major change was unlikely to be adopted, he joined with Chairman Celler in pushing to at least redistribute any unused quota slots to Italy, Greece, and other underserved countries. But they were fighting against a strong political tide, and this modification along with several amendments Rodino offered on the House floor were all rejected. Both chambers overwhelmingly approved the McCarran-Walter Act, and the sponsors rallied congressional supporters to override President Truman's veto at the end of June.[8]

While this initial effort at comprehensive reform was not successful, it helped to establish Rodino as one of the leading pro-immigration voices in the House of Representatives, alongside Chairman Celler, a significant achievement for a backbencher who was not a member of the subcommittee.

He continued to propose measures to modify or broaden admissions policies, which were all blocked by Francis Walter as he refused to consider any changes to his law.

President Eisenhower entered the debate in 1956 when he proposed redistributing the unused quota and called on Congress to develop a plan to replace the national origins system. The following year, the reformers in the House introduced legislation that raised the annual immigration ceiling and established five new categories for determining eligibility that were not based on place of birth or origin. Walter never followed through on his promise to hold hearings on the proposal, and Rodino continued to press for change.[9]

The inauguration of John F. Kennedy, the great-grandson of Irish Catholic immigrants, offered some hope that the political stalemate over immigration policy might end. Kennedy was actively engaged in the immigration issue during his time in Congress, opposing the McCarran-Walter Act and advocating for fair immigration laws in his book *A Nation of Immigrants*. At the end of his first month in office, Attorney General Robert F. Kennedy instructed the Justice Department staff to begin drafting immigration legislation, and comprehensive reform bills were introduced in the House and the Senate. But the election had not diminished Chairman Walter's opposition, and for the next two years the subcommittee did not take any action on these measures.[10]

In May 1963, Walter died after a long illness. His likely successor to lead the immigration panel was his fellow anti-reformer, Michael A. Feighan of Ohio. Hoping to reclaim the issue, Chairman Celler attempted to seize direct control of the subcommittee, and, when this failed, he proposed expanding its size, which was also rejected. His only remaining avenue for influencing the work of the subcommittee was his authority to fill Walter's vacant slot, and he chose his trusted lieutenant, Peter Rodino. This was not a surprise; the month before he had bypassed subcommittee members and appointed Rodino to replace the ailing Walter as a delegate to the Intergovernmental Committee for European Migration (ICEM), created to address the postwar refugee crisis. By further elevating Rodino's status as an immigration policymaker, Celler was hoping to increase the prospects for revising the McCarran-Walter Act.[11]

Two weeks after Rodino officially joined the immigration subcommittee, President Kennedy finally unveiled the administration's plan for reforming immigration policy and called on Congress to abolish the quota system. The president's proposal followed the basic outline of the reform bill that Celler and Rodino had introduced with skills, family relationships, and date of application designated as the new criteria for admission. To address the current backlog, parents of American citizens would receive immediate nonquota status, a provision benefiting many Italians. Chairman Celler introduced the president's legislation, and Rodino was the first cosponsor in the House. While Walter was gone and Feighan did not have the same clout, it was not going to be easy to pass a reform bill. "No one need repeat to you the complications of immigration legislation," White House Deputy Counsel Myer Feldman wrote to Celler. "It is both an emotional and a technical issue. This makes the drafting of a program very complicated and very difficult."[12]

As Congress prepared to begin consideration of the legislation, President Kennedy was assassinated, and future prospects for any action on immigration reform seemed less certain. In January 1964, his successor Lyndon B. Johnson announced his support for continuing the effort. This important boost forced a reluctant Feighan to begin hearings on the legislation. Although he was the junior member of the subcommittee, Rodino was the most vocal supporter of abolishing the national origins system, and throughout months of hearings he actively encouraged pro-reform witnesses and challenged the arguments of opponents.[13] He provided the White House with regular insights on the progress of the subcommittee's work and helped identify potential supporters in the House. This role became more important as the Johnson administration's relationship with Feighan deteriorated after he threatened to halt consideration of the bill unless the president supported the creation of a House and Senate joint committee on immigration, which he wanted to lead. His political blackmail infuriated presidential aide Jack Valenti, who noted that everyone is "sick and tired of Feighan and his tactics."[14] The impasse ended when the House adjourned early for the upcoming election.

When the new Congress convened, President Johnson formally unveiled his proposal for a new immigration system and urged quick passage of what was largely the original Kennedy plan. Unlike his three predecessors, Johnson's call for reform followed a historic mandate from the electorate, and both chambers of Congress were now filled with members swept into office on his coattails. Feighan insisted on holding a second round of hearings, resulting in the subcommittee not beginning to mark up the president's immigration bill until June.

Meeting in closed executive sessions over the next few weeks, the nine members of the panel tackled complex technical issues and worked diligently to end more than three years of deadlock. Surprisingly, agreement on abolishing the national origins system was reached early in the deliberations and without much rancor. Whether Feighan recognized that quota-based admissions were an increasingly smaller portion of annual immigration totals or succumbed to the hard push from the White House, he gave up the fight and accepted this dramatic change in policy. The most contentious issue was whether or not to place limits on immigration from the Western Hemisphere, which was a radical departure from the historic practice that the State Department strongly opposed. Except for the occasional disruption caused by flare-ups between Feighan and Celler, who attended the meetings, the subcommittee made steady progress.[15] Jack Valenti kept tabs on the closed-door meetings by engaging in "interminable conversations with Pete Rodino and Mike Feighan" and reported to Johnson that the subcommittee was making significant progress.[16]

The subcommittee finally completed its work in late July and favorably reported out the bill by an 8-to-0 vote, with one Republican abstaining. In a rare moment of bipartisan congeniality, most of the members of the full committee endorsed the measure. When the House considered the bill the following month, Rodino told his colleagues that "this is a day I have looked forward to for 17 years. This is legislation I have worked for since I first entered Congress in 1949."[17] With a large Democratic majority and President Johnson's political leverage, the two days of debate were relatively uneventful, and the final vote was a lopsided 318 to 95. The only dramatic moment came when an amendment to place a limit on immigration from the Western Hemisphere almost passed with surprisingly strong bipartisan support, an early sign of the future geographic shift in the immigration debate. When the Senate took up the measure in September, proponents of establishing a hemisphere ceiling were in the majority, forcing the president and House conferees, including Celler and Rodino, to accept this unwanted amendment.[18]

The long battle over the national origins quota system finally ended on Sunday, October 3 when Lyndon Johnson signed the Immigration and Nationality Act Amendments of 1965. In a setting uniquely appropriate to the occasion, Johnson sat at a table beneath the Statue of Liberty, with the recently created Ellis Island national historic site looming in the distance. This legislation, Johnson told the capacity crowd of dignitaries, "repairs deep and painful flaws in the fabric of American justice, it corrects a cruel and enduring wrong in the conduct of the American nation."[19] Peter Rodino was not at the bill signing; he opted not to attend the ceremony when he was unable to bring his son Peter, who was celebrating his birthday. Regardless of his physical absence from the formal event, Rodino had earned the right to savor this moment of triumph. He achieved the goal he set for himself in 1949: to remove a long-resented stigma placed on his fellow Italian Americans. He was now respected in Washington and at home as an authoritative voice on immigration policy. "Of all the people in America that should have been there Pete Rodino should have been at the head of the line," Vice President Hubert H. Humphrey wrote to Rodino when he learned his friend had missed the bill signing. "As long as I've known you, you have fought for a humane and compassionate immigration policy."[20]

Immigration continued to be an important part of Rodino's legislative agenda and focus. Within a year, he had moved up the seniority ladder to become the ranking Democrat on the immigration subcommittee, and he was appointed to the House-Senate Joint Committee on Immigration and Nationality Policy and the Select Commission on Western Hemisphere Immigration established by the 1965 act. Along with his continuing work on the ICEM, he was now a member of the four major bodies responsible for helping to frame

America's immigration policy. He would spend the rest of the decade overseeing the implementation of the law he helped create and seeking solutions to the emerging problem of illegal entry into the United States.[21]

Championing immigration reform was an obvious and natural choice for Rodino. He was the son of an immigrant, he lived his entire life in an Italian-American community, and he witnessed firsthand the need for change. It was what propelled him into the public arena and helped him to remain there with broad support. In contrast, the fight for racial equality in the United States had none of these personal connections for Rodino. He confronted few overt examples of racial discrimination in a city that was not legally segregated and where evidence of prejudice was often masked or hidden. Rodino had little interaction with African Americans in his daily life; not many people of color lived in the First Ward or attended its neighborhood schools. There were few black voters in the Tenth District during the early years of Rodino's career and fewer still in the party hierarchy.

Consequently, tackling the problem of racial inequity was not a priority for most of his constituents. Endorsing the movement for change was more likely to be a political liability rather than an asset. Yet the discrimination and injustice Italian Americans suffered had sparked in Rodino a deeper understanding that transcended the limitations of his own history, instilling in him an empathy for the challenges confronting African Americans. Regardless of the political consequences, he embraced the cause of civil rights with his usual enthusiasm and energy, devoting considerable time and attention to the issue. "There were not many whites who had the courage to do this," Congressional Black Caucus member Parren Mitchell recalled twenty years later. "Peter Rodino was one of them."[22] This involvement would sharpen Rodino's legislative skills, enhance his reputation, and provide unexpected benefits in the future.

Candidate Rodino had always underscored his strong support for a progressive policy agenda that included ending segregation and racial violence. Once in Congress, he followed through on this pledge by regularly introducing measures to remedy these injustices, arguing that "we cannot weaken our democratic society by tolerating mob violence against the safety and security of person, or by denying access to the rights of citizenship because of race or color."[23] His ability to participate in this fight was greatly enhanced when he was selected by Chairman Celler to serve on Subcommittee 5. As one of the leading civil rights advocates in Congress, Celler ensured that any bills on this topic were referred to his panel, and Rodino's appointment coincided with a renewed attempt to pass civil rights legislation.

In the years immediately following the end of World War II, the long simmering effort to end the unequal status of African Americans was gaining momentum, and President Truman called on Congress to end segregation in interstate travel, outlaw lynching, and ban the use of poll taxes used to discourage black voters. His proposal immediately hit an unyielding brick wall of implacable opposition from southern Democrats. Signaling the inherent difficulties of passing any civil rights legislation, it was derailed by a filibuster in the Senate.[24] With the legislative and executive branches at an impasse over the issue of racial equality, the debate shifted to the Supreme Court, which declared in 1954 that segregated schools were unconstitutional. The court's *Brown v. Board of Education* decision reversed a sixty-year-old precedent used to justify discrimination and concluded that separate facilities were inherently unequal. By overturning this principle, the landmark ruling opened the door for broader challenges to all segregation practices.[25]

The court's intervention increased pressure on the relatively silent Eisenhower administration to take some action to address this explosive national issue. Preparing to begin his reelection campaign in the spring of 1956, President Eisenhower unveiled a civil rights proposal. The administration's recommendations, modest in comparison to Truman's effort, included the establishment of a bipartisan commission to study the civil rights problem, creation of a civil rights division at the Justice Department, and an expansion of the attorney general's authority to intervene on behalf of individuals whose civil or voting rights were violated. Chairman Celler agreed to introduce the measure, and the Judiciary Committee approved it a few weeks later. But the segregationist chairman of the House Rules Committee, Howard W. Smith of

Virginia, delayed consideration. An early election year adjournment forced a postponement until the next Congress.[26]

In January 1957, Subcommittee 5 began eight days of frequently contentious hearings before the full committee met in executive session to mark up the bill. A coalition of liberal Democrats and a majority of the Republicans on the panel worked together to prevent southern members from further weakening the proposed Civil Rights Act of 1957. The report Rodino filed on behalf of the committee noted that it was approved without amendment. Rodino was not personally enthusiastic about this "limited" proposal. He acknowledged prior to House passage that "I would prefer to have seen a more comprehensive measure that would have recognized that discrimination takes many and unintended forms and that would have attempted to check economic pressures as well as purely political ones."[27] While he wanted a tougher civil rights bill, Senate approval hinged on making it weaker to avoid a filibuster. Majority Leader Lyndon Johnson agreed to the demand of southern Democrats that the provision expanding the attorney general's power be eliminated, and, when civil rights advocates reluctantly accepted this compromise, the bill was approved.[28]

Beyond its symbolism as the first civil rights law enacted since the end of the Civil War, the new statute had no immediate tangible impact and did little to alter racial tension in the country. Organized protests and boycotts challenging racial barriers in the South multiplied and were met with escalating violence. African American students attempting to enter recently integrated schools were subjected to ugly confrontations, and the government sent federal troops into southern states to enforce the Supreme Court's ruling.[29] Both Celler and Rodino reintroduced comprehensive civil rights proposals in early 1959 to address many of these shortcomings, but most of the tougher provisions were removed by southerners when the committee approved the chairman's bill after several months of hearings. "The pending bill is a lean shadow of the legislation the Congress should enact and is far from what is required in the circumstances," the National Association for the Advancement of Colored People's (NAACP's) Roy Wilkins complained to Celler. "Under the clear notification that they are being abandoned by the Congress Negro citizens have grown cynical and are more restive than at any time in the past decade."[30]

This frustration only grew when the House Rules Committee refused for six months to provide a rule to begin floor debate of the weakened bill. Rodino began collecting signatures for a discharge petition to force the legislation out of the committee; he was close to securing the required 219 signatures when Eisenhower's attorney general persuaded Republican members of the committee to break the logjam. The House finally began consideration in March 1960. However, despite the efforts of Celler and Rodino, none of the deleted provisions were restored. Once again, an already weak bill was further diluted in the Senate, and the final version that became the Civil Rights Act of 1960 was dismissed by civil rights advocates as "a pale version of what they hoped for."[31]

The beginning of the Kennedy administration the following year renewed hope that passing comprehensive civil rights legislation might be possible. To help the new president, Speaker Rayburn secured House approval for expanding the membership of the Rules Committee in an effort to dilute Chairman Smith's power.[32] Kennedy had campaigned on a Democratic party platform that included a civil rights plank, and he asked Celler and Senator Joseph S. Clarke of Pennsylvania to prepare a proposal for his consideration. Although the two unveiled an aggressive plan in May for accelerating desegregation and eliminating voting barriers, the president's advisers expressed concern that "his program would be endangered by pressing this year for the enactment of these measures."[33] Despite entreaties from the sponsors and their allies, Kennedy offered no public support for the proposal, and his reticence added to growing anxiety among civil rights supporters.

Regardless of the political consequences, deferring action became increasingly difficult considering the rising tide of protests and violence in the South drawing national attention. In February 1963, the president finally sent a special message to Congress calling for congressional action on civil rights. Celler's subcommittee immediately began a series of hearings on the ninety civil rights bills already introduced in the House, which ran the gamut from narrow solutions for specific problems to the comprehensive measures to eliminate discrimination offered by Rodino and the chairman. In a courageous admission for a congressman from New Jersey, Rodino acknowledged in his opening statement at the first hearing that "no particular states or sections of our country should be singled out for blame. If Negroes are denied the right to vote in some places, they are discriminated against in employment or in housing in other places."[34]

The hearings were transformed when the administration unexpectedly proposed its own expansive civil rights measure in June. Spurred by the brutal police attack on young African American protesters in Birmingham, Alabama, President Kennedy delivered a nationally televised address and called on Congress to pass legislation to ensure African Americans equal access to public facilities, expand the attorney general's power to initiate civil rights suits, end discrimination in all federal government programs, and remove racially based barriers to voting. Celler agreed to introduce the administration's bill, and he invited Attorney General Robert Kennedy to testify before the subcommittee. The public hearings continued throughout the summer.[35]

A week before more than 250,000 civil rights supporters came to the nation's capital on August 28 as part of the "March on Washington for Jobs and Freedom," the members of the subcommittee went behind closed doors to begin marking up the civil rights legislation. Celler reminded members that the proceedings were "confidential," something he regularly chose to ignore, and then followed his usual practice of taking preliminary, nonbinding votes after discussing each section of the legislation to allow flexibility for any changes. Joining with his fellow liberals in an effort to strengthen the president's bill, Rodino successfully offered several amendments favored by civil rights leaders, most notably one to create an equal employment commission to tackle discrimination in the workplace. "Our meetings are cordial," Celler reported in mid-September to John McCormack, who was now the Speaker of the House, "but the discussions are thorough and prolonged covering practically every phrase and comma and thus entail considerable debate."[36] While several highly charged issues still needed resolution, Celler predicted completion of the subcommittee's work in two weeks. On October 2, the panel agreed to Rodino's motion to report out the bill. "I don't believe there has been a piece of legislation in our Committee which has received a similar amount of time and attention," Rodino wrote to his daughter Peggy after the vote. He was very proud that the "long and exhaustive hearings" had produced such a "good, strong and effective bill."[37]

Rodino's positive assessment was not shared by officials at the White House. The amended and expanded measure was considered unpassable and a serious threat to achieving the president's goal of enacting civil rights legislation well before the next presidential election. Behind the scenes, the administration had courted pro-civil-rights Republicans, particularly House Judiciary Committee ranking minority member William M. McCullough, recognizing that their votes were critical in the full committee and on the floor. The president was prepared to compromise to secure this support; now he was saddled with a stronger bill that most Republicans opposed. Furious that Celler had not restrained his fellow liberals, administration officials forged a bipartisan agreement with House leaders to undo the subcommittee's changes. The attorney general was dispatched to Capitol Hill to deliver this new sanitized proposal, and, meeting with committee members in a private executive session, Robert Kennedy urged the adoption of the abridged version of the legislation. Civil rights groups, impatient and tired of compromising, pressured the liberals not to weaken the bill, and the president's advisers began to fear that southerners might join with them in reporting out the stronger subcommittee bill, confident the House would never approve it.[38]

With the panel crippled by stalemate, consideration of the bill was delayed until the end of October. In the interim, President Kennedy had begun a personal lobbying effort, hosting several private meetings at the White House to persuade committee members to endorse the more moderate bipartisan plan. Late in the afternoon on October 28, the liberals were summoned to the Cabinet Room for a final appeal from the president to withdraw their amendments and back the modified bill. As Celler's "right arm" and a recently named assistant party whip, Rodino was a likely persuadable vote. But sitting across from the president of the United States and the leader of his party, he held firm and refused to support the legislation unless it retained a forceful equal employment clause, even threatening to offer his subcommittee amendment on the floor if it was removed. When Speaker McCormack admonished his friend for not yielding, Kennedy interrupted and, in a conciliatory gesture, agreed to keep the provision—Rodino withdrew his opposition. The following day, the Judiciary Committee, in a tightly scripted session with no discussion, approved the revised civil rights bill, and on November 20 Rodino filed the committee's detailed report. Two days later the president was assassinated in Dallas.[39]

The elevation of Lyndon Johnson to the presidency raised serious questions within the civil rights community about the future of the legislation. Pushed into the background as vice president, Johnson's commitment to the cause remained suspect, and disappointment lingered over his maneuvers to weaken the 1957 law. Many of these anxieties were allayed when Johnson addressed Congress five days after becoming president. "No memorial oration or eulogy could more eloquently honor President Kennedy's memory than the earliest passage of the civil rights bill for which he fought so long," he told the packed chamber in a somber voice. Johnson appealed for quick action, expressing the hope "that we can move forward to eliminate from this Nation any trace of discrimination and oppression that is based upon race or color."[40] The president immediately joined the battle and used his political acumen and persuasive skills to energize the lobbying efforts of labor and civil rights groups, cementing the support of House Republican leaders and leaning on undecided legislators.[41]

The last obstacle to moving the civil rights bill forward in the House of Representatives remained the implacable opposition of the chairman of the Rules Committee. When Judge Smith ignored the Judiciary Committee's formal request for a rule, Celler and Rodino began gathering signatures for a discharge petition, an undertaking that immediately received a presidential endorsement. Reflecting how much the political climate had changed, a majority consisting of Republicans and the members added to the panel now opposed their chairman, and Smith was finally forced to schedule a hearing on the legislation. During two days in early January, Smith used every argument and maneuver to prevent House consideration and derail the measure. His strenuous objections went unheeded, and the panel approved a rule and sent the bill to the floor.[42]

Throughout the weeks of delay, the Judiciary Committee had prepared for what was expected to be a demanding, intense debate. Staff attorneys drafted answers for anticipated questions from opponents and fielded unsolicited advice from anxious civil rights groups. Under the supervision of Deputy Attorney General Nicholas Katzenbach, the Justice Department developed detailed background information on each title of the bill for assigned members to use as a reference on the House floor. Rodino volunteered to focus on the provision ending discrimination in federal programs and the fair employment section, which he had fought so hard to retain. On January 29, armed with thick briefing books, the proponents of the retitled Civil Rights Act of 1964 entered the House chamber beneath the packed public galleries to begin this historic battle.[43]

For nine days, the House debated the broad philosophical merits of enacting civil rights legislation along with the often arcane details of the more than 130 amendments that were offered. Most of the proposed changes came from opponents hoping to weaken or fatally cripple the bill and make Senate approval impossible. The remainder of the amendments, largely technical in nature, were intended to improve the measure or clarify the meaning of its provisions. Chairman Celler and ranking Republican William M. McCulloch, often at odds during committee deliberations, worked harmoniously together on the floor in bipartisan tandem. Assisted by an effective whip operation that ensured supporters appeared for the seemingly endless round of votes, Celler and McCulloch succeeded in defeating most of the unfriendly and harmful revisions. One exception was a "poison pill" amendment offered by Judge Smith adding "sex" to the bill's list of race, religion, and national origin as categories protected against discrimination in the workplace, a change he believed would seriously diminish the prospects of passage. When the women members of the House voiced their support, Celler was forced to accept the modification. To his relief and Judge Smith's consternation, the amendment received surprisingly widespread backing, and sex discrimination became part of the civil rights bill for the first time. On February 10, the legislation, a largely unaltered version of the bipartisan proposal reported out of the Judiciary Committee, was approved by the House.[44]

Diligently fulfilling his duties as trusted lieutenant, Rodino spent most of the long civil rights debate at the side of his mentor Emanuel Celler. Often seated next to the chairman at the long table accorded by custom to the legislative sponsors, Rodino helped control the floor time allocated to the Democrats and ensured that designated members were recognized when it was their turn to speak. He frequently participated directly in the discussion, defending the legislation against the onslaught of hostile amendments or challenging the facts and conclusions of opponents. Standing next to Emanuel Celler demanded a high degree of patience and self-effacement; Celler's was an outsized personality that cast a big shadow, and he rarely shared credit for the committee's accomplishments.[45] Rodino had a reservoir of both of these necessary requirements; if he felt any frustration with his adjutant role, he never publicly expressed it.

Fortunately, his work for almost a decade in the congressional trenches fighting to secure racial equality gradually attracted notice, and his yeoman efforts behind the scenes gained him new respect. The protracted battle for enactment of the civil rights law helped to showcase his contributions, and, following the bill's passage, he finally received his share of recognition and accolades. President Johnson, anxious to thank Rodino personally, reached him by telephone that night in his Capitol Hill office. "I want to compliment you on passing that civil rights bill," Johnson told him in a warm and friendly conversation. "I'm real proud of you."[46] Attorney General Kennedy followed up with his own gracious, if more reserved, thank you call. Arnold Aronson of the Leadership Conference on Civil Rights told Rodino, "I have no doubt that our approbation is only the forerunner of the wider approval history will accord you."[47] Among the many letters of appreciation he received from civil rights groups, Rodino particularly cherished the note from the leader of the movement, Dr. Martin Luther King Jr. "The devotees of civil rights in this country and freedom loving people the world over are greatly indebted to you for your help in securing passage in the House of Representatives of H.R. 7152," King wrote. "I add to theirs my sincere and heartfelt gratitude."[48]

The victory celebration ended when the legislation was sent to the Senate, and its forward progress was halted. Opponents immediately began a filibuster, their favorite delaying tactic, and this time Lyndon Johnson was not willing to weaken the bill to dislodge it. For the next three months, the upper chamber was paralyzed as the southern segregationists refused to allow a vote, and proponents were unable to muster the two-thirds of the Senate necessary for cloture, the procedure used to end debate. Johnson, growing more impatient with each passing week, accelerated his aggressive push for action, and civil rights groups intensified their lobbying efforts. With the president's active participation, chief sponsor Hubert Humphrey and Republican leader Everett Dirksen framed a bipartisan agreement that both retained the scope of the House bill and included enough changes to attract additional votes. This partnership ultimately produced a proposal endorsed by a coalition of senators large enough to invoke cloture and end the longest filibuster in history. To avoid a second round of legislative battles, the House of Representatives accepted the Senate-approved version of the bill without any changes on July 2.[49]

An impatient President Johnson was unwilling to wait for an elaborate ceremony and instead decided to sign the bill that evening. Staff members worked frantically over the next few hours to invite key congressional sponsors, civil rights leaders, and other dignitaries to the White House for the nationally televised six o'clock signing. Rodino was part of this auspicious group, and, sitting together in the East Room, they listened to Johnson recall the long struggle leading to the enactment of the legislation. The president lauded the bipartisan support that made passage possible, and he urged the country to "close the springs of racial poison."[50] When the presidential address concluded, the audience moved forward to gather around the table to witness Johnson sign the measure using the more than seventy pens he would later present to Rodino and other participants as mementos of the occasion. Whether by design or accident, Rodino was standing toward the front of the group, directly behind the president and next to Dr. King, at the moment when the White House photographer captured this tableau for posterity. As a result, Peter Rodino was prominently featured in this enduring and iconic image of a transcendent moment in American history.[51]

In the aftermath of this monumental achievement, there was an assumption that the work of Congress was largely completed, and future efforts would primarily focus on fine-tuning the new law. But President Johnson had very different plans for the legislative branch. Following his landslide election in November, Johnson instructed the Justice Department to draft a proposal to remove electoral barriers for African Americans. Though the previous civil rights statutes included some voting rights provisions, these were weak and largely relied on legal challenges in court, a slow and protracted process. The Twenty-Fourth Amendment to the Constitution ratified in 1964 to outlaw the use of poll taxes to prevent African Americans from registering to vote only applied to federal elections. The suppression of voters in the recent election provided evidence that none of these remedies were working. In the wake of the passage of the 1964 act, Martin Luther King and other civil rights advocates focused their attention on the issue of electoral equality.[52]

While the Johnson administration finalized the details of its plan, the voting rights issue was catapulted to the top of the national agenda when violence erupted in Selma, Alabama, where King was spearheading a voter registration drive. Days of brutal police attacks on nonviolent protesters, climaxed by the vicious beatings of hundreds of marchers on the Edmund Pettus Bridge on March 9, gripped the television audience watching the shocking events unfold and sparked bipartisan calls for action. "I am gravely concerned about the tragic situation in Selma, Alabama," Rodino wrote in a telegram to the recently appointed Attorney General Nicholas Katzenbach. "I most strongly urge you to use all the power and resources at your command to stop once and for all the constitutional violations."[53] Johnson responded by addressing a joint session of Congress on March 15 and called for the quick approval of comprehensive legislation to ensure the constitutional right of every citizen to vote. "This time, on this issue, there must be no delay, or no hesitation, or no compromise with our purpose," the president declared. He called on Democrats and Republicans to work long hours, nights, and even weekends if necessary to pass his voting rights bill.[54]

The measure the administration sent to Capitol Hill was a sweeping effort to remove all racially driven obstacles to voter registration and voting in the South. To accomplish this goal, the proposal outlawed literacy tests and other voting requirements based on race empowered federal officials to register voters where discrimination was practiced, and required those discriminating areas to secure preapproval for any changes in electoral procedures. Heeding the president's admonition, Subcommittee 5 immediately began hearings, and the panel favorably reported out the bill the following month. The 1964 election had expanded the liberal wing in Congress and strengthened their ability to challenge southern opposition. It was no longer easy for southerners to sustain a filibuster in the Senate or bottle up legislation indefinitely in the House, and the voting rights bill moved relatively quickly through both chambers.[55]

One of the few points of contention that did emerge during the debate was an effort by liberals and civil rights groups to include a provision outlawing the poll tax in state and local elections. Fearing an outright prohibition was unconstitutional and might jeopardize the entire legislation, Attorney General Katzenbach preferred to let the courts settle the question. But opponents on Subcommittee 5 ignored his objections and added an anti-poll-tax amendment to the voting rights measure, which the House approved and the Senate rejected.[56] When a conference committee met in July, Rodino was one of the six members representing the House, and he refused to compromise, breaking ranks with Chairman Celler. Katzenbach was anxious to prevent any delay and persuaded Martin Luther King to endorse a weaker provision that simply denounced the poll tax and urged legal action to prevent its use. "Dr. King," the attorney general informed Rodino, "strongly expressed to me his desire that the bill promptly be enacted into law and said that he felt this was an overriding consideration." The next day Rodino agreed to accept the modification, and in August President Johnson signed the Voting Rights Act of 1965.[57]

The Johnson administration wasted little time before launching its next offensive against racial injustice: ending discrimination in housing. The sole existing legal restriction on segregated housing that applied uniformly to all fifty states was an executive order prohibiting racial bias in federally funded housing including the Federal Housing Administration (FHA) and VA mortgage programs. This covered less than one-fifth of recently constructed private housing stock. In his 1966 State of the Union address, President Johnson unveiled a fair housing initiative that was at the center of a new, comprehensive civil rights proposal that also contained greater protections for civil rights workers and a ban on discrimination in jury selection. To redress the inequities in housing, the president called on Congress to outlaw discrimination based on race, religion, or national origin in the sale, rental, and financing of all housing, including owner-occupied dwellings. Since New Jersey and many other states exempted these two- and three-family houses from their antidiscrimination laws, this proposed change would bring the civil rights struggle to northern communities for the first time, and it sparked a firestorm of opposition.[58]

Attorney General Katzenbach received an early preview of the congressional headwinds the legislation might face when he briefed the House Judiciary Committee on the president's plan in March. Some members confessed they were simply "weary" of the entire civil rights issue and no longer believed there was a national urgency to act; most focused the bulk of their criticism on fair housing. Rodino spoke for many Democrats when he expressed his serious reservations about the broad sweep of the housing provision and warned of the political fallout in ethnic neighborhoods. William McCullough opposed the proposal as drafted, and many of his fellow Republicans, including the House and Senate minority leaders, were against the inclusion of any fair housing title in the bill. "The Fair Housing proposal is opposed by a majority of the Committee and it is entirely doubtful that enough votes can be shifted to bring this part of the bill out of committee," the attorney general reported to presidential adviser Joseph A. Califano Jr.[59] His pessimistic assessment was shared by others at the White House, and congressional affairs aide Henry Wilson bluntly told the president, "I think it is clear from all the check-outs that the housing proposal will be impossible to enact."[60]

Subcommittee 5 began hearings a few days after the president formally submitted his proposal amidst an already public outcry over what critics were characterizing as "forced housing." A broad-based group of opponents led by the real estate industry launched an intensive lobbying campaign to remove the fair housing requirements from the bill, while civil rights groups organized a counterattack to strengthen this provision. Inundated with a flood of letters and postcards from constituents and unable to reach any consensus on the issue, the subcommittee opted to let the full committee resolve the housing impasse.[61]

After two days of heated discussions behind closed doors, a majority of the members accepted a Republican amendment to exempt owner-occupied dwellings with fewer than four apartments from the proposed law and agreed to compensate for this by adding a tougher antibias enforcement mechanism for larger apartment buildings and new construction. While fair housing was not a popular issue in the Tenth District, Rodino agreed to author the committee's report and publicly defended the compromise. "It was the best we could hammer out and it is a step in the right direction," he told the *Star-Ledger (Newark)*.[62]

The first skirmish on the House floor at the end of July was not encouraging for the bill's sponsors; the vote discharging the bill from the Rules Committee was much closer than expected. Midway through consideration of the bill, Manny Celler was stricken with a severe case of gout and rushed to the hospital, which required Rodino to assume the mantle of floor manager before many of the most contentious issues were settled. For the next six days, he summoned all his characteristic patience and oratorical skills to fend off a seemingly endless barrage of hostile amendments and parliamentary maneuvers from both opponents committed to killing the legislation and supporters determined to strengthen it regardless of the political consequences. Rodino calmly maneuvered through a particularly choppy point in the proceedings when it appeared that the amendment to exempt owner-occupied dwellings from the fair housing provision—critical to ensuring the bill's ultimate passage—was heading to defeat. At the last minute, two dozen additional members appeared on the floor to vote in the affirmative, resulting in a tie that allowed the presiding officer to rule in favor of the sponsors. Asked by a reporter about this "squeaker," Rodino responded that "I was in the Army once and I learned to keep my troops in reserve."[63]

The House of Representatives concluded twelve days of intense debate on August 9 and approved the Civil Rights Act of 1966 by a vote of 259 to 157. It was far from a perfect bill and the housing section exempted more than half of the nation's dwellings from its discrimination restrictions. Yet the measure had at least succeeded in focusing national attention on racial bias in housing. In the Senate, southerners threatened a filibuster, and, with Republicans opposed to the fair housing provision and unwilling to vote for cloture, Democratic leaders withdrew the legislation.[64] The issue languished on the backburner until the spring of 1968, when pressure from the president and the assassination of Martin Luther King finally spurred congressional action. Once again Rodino worked to win approval of the measure; with few hearings and little debate, Congress passed a civil rights bill that included a fair housing section largely reflecting the language adopted by the House two years earlier. In June, the Supreme Court ruled that discrimination was illegal in the sale and rental of *all* housing, making the hard-won compromise moot.[65]

While the long delay in enacting a fair housing law diminished the historical luster of the 1966 fight compared to the earlier legislative victories, it was still an important milestone for Peter Rodino. The debate provided a rare opportunity for him to step into the spotlight and assume the reins of leadership so tightly held by Chairman Celler. He demonstrated that he was up to the task, and his successful stewardship was applauded on both ends of Pennsylvania Avenue. Expressing his deep gratitude, President Johnson praised Rodino for his leadership, and Vice President Humphrey saluted him for managing the civil rights bill "with the professional skill of an artist and a magician."[66] The NAACP's Clarence Mitchell Jr. appreciated Rodino's "abundance of patience and skill" and told him, "you deserve great credit for the way that you used these qualities to win passage of the measure."[67] Many of his House colleagues joined in praising his performance under pressure, including Majority Leader Carl Albert and Chairman Celler who for once publicly shared credit with his lieutenant. Perhaps the most fitting and prescient tribute came from Rodino's colleague from Pennsylvania Elmer J. Holland who told him, "the old military phrase 'bravery and coolness under fire' is the only appropriate phrase I can think of to describe your twelve day ordeal."[68]

Rodino's elevation into the senior ranks of legislators paralleled his burgeoning political clout as an influential Italian American voice in Washington. When he first arrived on Capitol Hill, Rodino had reached out to the other Italian members of Congress to organize an informal caucus to discuss their mutual interests. Under Rodino's leadership, the small group promoted immigration reform, advocated for aid to Italy, and participated with the Italian embassy in a variety of widely publicized charitable and social events. His growing prominence in the Italian American community had attracted the attention of the Kennedy presidential campaign, and campaign members asked for his assistance in connecting with the voters in his own ethnic group. "I think Senator Kennedy needs your help among the citizens of Italian descent," the nominee's brother and campaign manager, Robert Kennedy, wrote in September 1960, requesting a public endorsement from Rodino and inviting him to serve as a campaign surrogate. "I would appreciate any suggestion you might have on how we can better reach the voters of your particular area," he added.[69] In the endorsement statement Rodino sent the next day, he touted Kennedy's work on immigration and his support for Italy. He followed up with a three-page letter outlining his ideas for the campaign and stressing the need to appoint Italian Americans to prominent government positions, an admonition that became his personal mantra for the next eight years.[70]

Following Kennedy's inauguration, White House officials began the challenging process of staffing the new administration. Expressing a "desire to appoint Italo-Americans to responsible positions in the government," they turned to Rodino for guidance.[71] He was happy to help, becoming a de facto congressional clearinghouse for potential Italian American appointees and patronage. He worked closely with the legislative affairs office, promoting candidates he personally knew, including his district director Joe Benucci to be Newark's postmaster, and forwarding names provided by the various Italian fraternal organizations or his House colleagues. But as the months passed with few Italian Americans appointed to high-profile positions, Rodino began to pepper the White House with letters and phone calls complaining about the slow progress and proposing additional nominees. Recognizing the political consequences of this shortfall, White House officials hoped Rodino could help close the gap. "The Italian Americans are very upset over the failure to appoint more Italians to top administrative posts," an internal White House memorandum acknowledged. "There is no doubt that a great deal needs to be done on this score. Close liaison with Rodino on this subject should be very helpful."[72]

Rodino's influence at the White House grew exponentially when Lyndon Johnson became president. Jack Valenti, a prominent advertising executive in Texas, joined the new president's staff as a trusted adviser and close confidant. Shortly after taking up his post, Valenti called Rodino to introduce himself. These two sons of Italian immigrants instantly bonded, beginning what would become a lifelong friendship.[73] Valenti rarely refused Rodino's request for a meeting at the White House or failed to respond to his appeals on behalf of prominent Italian Americans. The two frequently socialized together, and Valenti avidly touted his friend's loyalty to the administration, prompting the president to tell Rodino that his friend Jack was "always bragging on you."[74] When Valenti left to run the movie industry's Washington office in 1966, Joseph Califano, who had worked with Rodino on civil rights legislation, became his new point of contact at the White House. After an initial meeting with Rodino, Califano reported to the president that the congressman was determined to ensure "more Italian-Americans be appointed to high positions in the Government."[75]

Rodino's push to place more Italian Americans in senior administration positions was a part of his longtime effort to use his position as a member of Congress to upend the unfair stereotypes linking Italian surnames with criminality. This was not an easy task and often complicated by events beyond his control. In 1951, Tennessee Senator Estes Kefauver had launched a series of televised hearings on organized crime. More than thirty million Americans watched the colorful parade of primarily Italian American crime bosses testify on the Mafia and its extensive operations in the United States. The hearings sparked a renewed public fascination with organized crime and mobsters, leading to a wave of unflattering and inaccurate representations of Italians in popular culture.[76] Perhaps the most egregious was the television series *The Untouchables*, based on the memoirs of Prohibition agent Eliot Ness, which clearly identified every criminal as Italian. Rodino and several of his colleagues lodged a formal protest and forced the producers to add a tagline at the end of each episode explaining that the show was fiction. Ironically, a few weeks after this agreement, columnist Walter Winchell wrote that the reason there were so few Italian American appointments in the Kennedy administration was that most of the candidates were "characters right out of the 'Untouchables.'"[77]

The next battle over the image of Italian Americans involved the federal government. A second round of congressional hearings on organized crime had transformed mob informant Joseph Valachi into an overnight celebrity. As an insider-turned-government-witness, he provided intimate and graphic details of the activities of the "Cosa Nostra," the term he used to describe the Italian crime families. His negative portrayal outraged many Italian Americans at the time. Following his return to prison, Valachi began writing his memoirs, and, contrary to a prohibition on publications by prisoners, Justice Department officials decided this would help their law enforcement operations and enlisted journalist Peter Maas to help edit the manuscript.[78]

When Rodino learned of this arrangement in late January 1966, he immediately contacted Jack Valenti at the White House to express outrage that the government was helping to resurrect Valachi's salacious story. His was not the only angry call from Capitol Hill, and Valenti warned President Johnson of the impending firestorm. "These Congressmen, led by Pete Rodino, are unable to understand the reasoning behind the decision of the Justice Department to give such unprecedented approval for a gangster to write a book while he is in prison," he told the president. "Their distaste emerges from the fact that this book obviously to be written about unsavory characters of Italian descent will do far more harm than any good that possibly might result."[79] At Valenti's insistence, Attorney General Katzenbach met with Rodino and his colleagues and attempted to defend this decision to allow the book to be published. Under continued pressure from Rodino and Italian American organizations, he was forced to withdraw his permission, which was unsuccessfully challenged by civil liberties groups in federal court. Peter Maas found a legal loophole that allowed him to publish his original interviews under the title *The Valachi Papers*, with the resulting bestseller eventually being adapted into a movie.[80]

Rodino also hoped to fight these negative stereotypes by promoting positive images of Italians, including the forgotten painter of the Capitol's magnificent frescoes, Constantino Brumidi, and the most revered historical figure within the Italian American community, Christopher Columbus.[81] Before scholars exposed the full scope of the Columbus legacy or Native Americans were accorded a platform to challenge the notion of "discovery," Columbus occupied a venerated place in the historic narrative for all Americans regardless of nationality. While honoring his arrival in the Americas on October 12, 1492, was an established tradition prior to the great migration, newly arrived Italian immigrants fully embraced the occasion and broadened the festivities into a celebration of their ethnic heritage and an opportunity to claim a direct connection to the founding of the United States. Thirty-eight states recognized Columbus Day as a holiday, and the day involved a full program of activities from somber church services to grand celebratory parades in cities like Newark, where there was a sizable Italian population.[82]

Arriving on Capitol Hill in 1949, Rodino joined an effort to make Columbus Day a national holiday. Within a few years, he was leading the movement in Congress. The obstacles to achieving this goal were formidable; there were just seven legal federal holidays at the time and only one honoring an individual. Adding a new holiday would incur an economic cost, and businesses strongly opposed it. Rodino was not discouraged, and he introduced legislation to elevate the Columbus holiday early in his freshman term and in every subsequent Congress for the next fifteen years.[83] He agreed to serve as the national chairman of the Columbian Foundation, created to promote the idea, and persuaded President Kennedy to attend Newark's Columbus Day celebration in 1962, though the president did not officially endorse the establishment of a federal holiday.[84] The following year, Rodino was the lead witness at the first congressional hearing on the issue and urged his colleagues to support his bill before leaving Washington to repeat this message as the keynote speaker at the Columbus Day celebration in San Francisco.[85]

For the next four years, Rodino made little headway toward his goal until he was invited to appear at a second hearing on the topic. After Rodino completed his testimony, Republican Robert McClory, the lead sponsor of legislation to shift several national holidays to Mondays, asked him if he would consider celebrating Columbus Day on a day other than October 12. Rodino responded that his main goal was national recognition, so he was willing to consider this possibility. McClory's suggestion was the perfect compromise since he lacked a Democratic ally for his proposal, and Rodino needed the support of the business community who were backing the Monday bill because of its economic benefits. In early 1968, the two jointly introduced legislation transforming Washington's Birthday, Memorial Day, Veterans Day, and a new federal Columbus Day observance into Monday holidays.[86] Their bill was approved with little debate in the Judiciary Committee. Following House and Senate concurrence in the spring, President Johnson signed it into law at a small Oval Office ceremony, marking the successful end to what *Il Progresso Italo-Americano* called "a tenacious campaign."[87]

On Monday, October 11, 1971, the inaugural Columbus Day federal holiday was celebrated, and Rodino led a congressional delegation to Genoa to mark this special occasion. He returned to Europe the next month, where he was elected chairman of the twentieth anniversary session of the Intergovernmental Committee for European Migration making him the first American to hold this position. It was the culmination of a momentous year in his congressional career that began with his ascension to the chairmanship of the immigration subcommittee following the primary defeat of Michael Feighan, which placed him next in seniority to the eighty-two-year-old Emanuel Celler.[88] Rodino's legislative achievements had brought him recognition as a civil rights advocate, authority on immigration policy, and leading voice in the Italian American community. Alongside his membership on two important subcommittees, he was now an assistant Democratic whip and dean of the New Jersey congressional delegation. Beginning his third decade on Capitol Hill, it seemed unlikely that anything could derail Rodino's continued climb up the ladder.

CHAPTER SEVEN

A NEAR-DEATH EXPERIENCE

On a cloudy April morning in 1949, Peter Rodino returned for the first time to the gritty Drift Street apartment where he had spent a good part of his youth and nurtured his dream of becoming a writer. It was not a sentimental journey intended to idealize the past, nor was it a victory lap for the local boy who made good. Rodino was coming back to focus attention on the need for safe and affordable housing, an issue that was a central part of his recent successful campaign for Congress. Accompanied by his new friend and colleague Hugh Addonizio and the leaders of several veterans organizations, he spent more than three hours touring Newark's blighted areas and the tenement buildings of the First Ward. The group found sagging floors, crumbling walls, windows nailed shut, and garbage-strewn courtyards. "Returning shocked me," Rodino admitted to reporters. "I suppose when you live there you get a bit used to it, but when you go away and come back the contrast is even more startling."[1] Meeting with demoralized tenants, he vowed to support efforts to revitalize their neighborhood. It was a promise that would help to dramatically transform the physical landscape of the Tenth Congressional District and unexpectedly impact his own political future.

Rodino's arrival in Washington four months earlier had coincided with a renewed push in Congress to expand government support for housing in response to the postwar shortage created by returning soldiers. The Housing Act of 1949, which President Truman signed in July, authorized the building of almost a million public housing units and expanded the mortgage market to encourage private sector construction. The new law also declared urban renewal a national priority and created a federal program to provide financial assistance to help localities acquire buildings and land for slum clearance.[2] This was welcome news in Newark, where the postwar challenges of suburban flight and a shrinking tax base had sparked considerable interest in redeveloping blighted neighborhoods. Following Rodino's tenement tour, the *Newark Evening News* began a fourteen-part series documenting substandard housing conditions throughout the city, providing stark evidence of the need for collective action to address the problem. The newspaper sponsored citizens' groups and religious organizations at its headquarters to discuss the issue and consider possible remedies. There was little interest or enthusiasm for undertaking basic improvements or rehabilitating tenements; most attendees advocated razing all existing structures and replacing them with new buildings.[3]

This widespread public concern helped ensure that the city was ready to access this new federal aid by preparing a master plan that identified derelict areas and designating the Newark Housing Authority (NHA) as the city's redevelopment agency. As a result, Newark was one of the first municipalities in the country to receive funding from the U.S. Housing and Home Finance Agency's newly created slum clearance and redevelopment program in Washington. Under the plan, the primarily African American and centrally located Third Ward was judged the neediest area. But NHA Executive Director Louis Danzig wanted an early success in the city's redevelopment effort and concluded that the severe poverty and racial composition of the neighborhood would discourage any private sector investment. Instead, he focused on the place Rodino was ardently promoting for renewal: the historic core of the First Ward, where its less impoverished, overwhelmingly white residents were still poor enough to meet the federal definition of a slum.[4]

In 1952, the NHA presented its sweeping proposal for urban renewal containing a mix of private and public housing, office buildings, and retail space on a forty-six-acre parcel of land currently occupied by most of Newark's Little Italy. A new public housing complex, Christopher Columbus Homes, comprised eight high-rise apartment buildings and was slated for the central core. The market-rate rental units anchoring the northern portion overlooked the nearby park. The project would require the demolition of 469 structures and the displacement of almost five thousand residents living in the densely populated area. The blueprint for the site presented to the public erased several streets from the existing map, including the main commercial artery of Eighth Avenue. Only the McKinley Grammar School and St. Lucy's Church were left untouched because federal regulations prohibited their demolition. Rodino and all of Newark's elected officials enthusiastically embraced the project that the *Italian Tribune* declared was "the best thing that could have possibly happened."[5]

This acclaim was not universal for a plan developed without any input from the stunned community. Within days of the announcement, vocal opposition emerged, and a hastily organized public meeting with government officials including Rodino was held at city hall. More than four hundred residents attended the contentious three-hour session where they raised concerns about relocation and future housing in the First Ward. For the first time, Rodino found himself at odds with a majority of his constituents, who felt betrayed by their representative. He staunchly defended the plan against the attacks from the audience and warned opponents not to spread "discontent and bitterness." Forgoing his usual diplomatic tone, Rodino sharply admonished the crowd not to let fear stand in the way of progress.[6]

The opposition was not appeased and formed the Save Our Homes Council to continue what was likely to be a losing battle to reverse the decision. Struggling with few resources and no allies, they prepared petitions, organized protest marches, and filed a lawsuit in a vain attempt to stop the destruction of their neighborhood.[7]

The project encountered a series of unexpected problems, including the discovery of a forgotten ancient creek running through the site. Bureaucratic infighting further added to the delays. The last residents did not finally move out until the spring of 1954, when bulldozers arrived to level all the buildings. "The heart of Newark's First Ward has stopped beating," the *Newark Evening News* declared. "Where people lived and thrived now is a wide expanse of emptiness."[8] To add further insult, the city's recent consolidation of existing wards had replaced the historic name of this now barren landscape with a new "North Ward" designation.

Rodino never wavered in his belief that completely transforming his old neighborhood was the best way to improve the quality of life for his constituents. His conviction was encouraged by the conventional wisdom of postwar urbanism that linked progress with the replacement of old structures. Unfortunately, for those living in these new buildings, adhering to this dictum did not always mean improvement in the quality of their lives. The sheen of modernity surrounding the eight high-rise buildings rapidly faded because of poor management and inadequate maintenance. The lobbies and elevators became places of increasingly violent crimes, and elderly residents rarely ventured outside after dark. As the apartment blocks aged, the deteriorating conditions began to rival the worst tenements of the old Little Italy, and the tenants organized rent strikes. Several of the buildings were finally declared uninhabitable and the entire complex was razed in the 1990s, when history would come full circle.[9]

While Newark's first urban renewal project erased the past, it could not obscure the growing challenge of race relations in the city. The first public housing projects built during the New Deal were segregated through geography and practice, creating long waiting lists for blacks and a surplus of apartments for whites. Spurred by the need to redress this imbalance between supply and demand, in 1950, the NHA ended discrimination in its existing properties and for any future construction. This policy change complicated the authority's plans for the First Ward; Executive Director Louis Danzig believed that too many black tenants would discourage private development in the adjacent areas of the site. At the same time, most neighborhood supporters of the project presumed the intentionally named Christopher Columbus Homes was earmarked for Italian Americans.[10]

These contradictory goals collided as the first high-rise building neared completion in the summer of 1955. NHA officials were finding it difficult to attract tenants who were within the federal government's income cap for public housing, so they launched a campaign to spark interest in the project. A model apartment outfitted with furnishings from the local Goodwill store was available for viewing during extended hours, and a satellite NHA office was opened to allow applicants to submit their paperwork at the site. Perversely, the city's largest pool of qualified renters in need of housing—African Americans—were not included in this outreach effort. Danzig had decided to quietly set aside a small percentage of units in each completed building for black tenants to move into after their white neighbors arrived. His scheme fell apart when African Americans, rebuffed during the intake process and informed of the delay, complained about this clear violation of NHA policy. Several black civic organizations filed a formal protest over this "hypocrisy," and the authority was forced to allow qualified African Americans into the Columbus Homes without delay.[11]

The success in forcing the NHA to follow its own policy was a rare victory for Newark's burgeoning black community. Beginning at the start of the century, the city and its abundance of factory jobs had attracted a steady flow of African Americans leaving the South for better economic opportunities. This pace only accelerated during the postwar boom. Between 1930 and 1950, the number of African Americans living in Newark doubled, a figure that doubled again in the following decade. This increase nearly paralleled the movement of white Newark residents relocating to the nearby suburbs, and the city actually experienced an overall decline in population. As a result of this two-way traffic, the black share of the populace grew exponentially, and the 1960 census would confirm that African Americans now represented 34 percent of all residents.[12]

These numbers did not immediately translate into corresponding political power. Most of Newark's black population resided in the Third Ward, adjacent to the downtown business district, a concentration that was a liability under the citywide commission form of government. But this began to change in 1953, when Newark replaced this structure with a strong independent mayor and a nine-member council composed of representatives from newly drawn wards and four at-large seats. The inaugural contest under this system resulted in the election of African American Irvine I. Turner to represent the Central Ward, formerly the Third, on the council. Turner used his officially nonpartisan office to build a formidable Democratic political machine in the ward, and his endorsement was soon coveted by the party's nominees. Although it would take more than a decade before another person of color joined Turner, his presence on the council ensured that Newark's black community at least had a seat at the table.[13]

From the outset, Turner had a difficult relationship with Mayor Leo P. Carlin, who was reluctant to share power or patronage, and he enthusiastically supported the decision of his political ally Hugh Addonizio to challenge Carlin in the 1961 municipal election. Rodino was less encouraging of his roommate's plans, questioning the wisdom of sacrificing a safe congressional seat to challenge an incumbent. But once Addonizio decided to run, Rodino dispatched Joe Benucci to help with the campaign and focused his personal attention on fundraising.[14] Many of Carlin's traditional Irish American supporters had left Newark for the suburbs, and Italian Americans were now the city's largest ethnic voting bloc, followed closely by African Americans. For black voters in the Central Ward, Addonizio's steadfast support in Congress for civil rights legislation, his promise to integrate city hall, and the endorsement of Councilman Turner proved decisive. Italian Americans in the North Ward embraced Addonizio's candidacy as an overdue acknowledgement of their political power and a source of ethnic pride. On May 8, Addonizio won in a surprising landslide by forging a politically powerful alliance between these two important voting blocs.[15]

For the next four years, Addonizio struggled to bridge the widening gap between his election day supporters. He was criticized for defending the largely white police force against charges of brutality and the fact that most senior patronage jobs went to Italian Americans and high-profile urban renewal projects were given priority over crumbling neighborhood schools. Tensions increased during his second term as serious economic and social problems crowded the municipal docket. At a time of prosperity in New Jersey, Newark's unemployment rate was double the national average. Among major American cities, it had the highest percentage of substandard housing and the highest rate of maternal mortality. Rodino did what he could to help the city, using his clout with the Johnson administration to secure federal resources and the support of government agencies. But there were no easy solutions to Newark's escalating problems.[16]

All of these simmering issues seemed to converge in July of 1967, when Newark experienced several days of unrest that left twenty-six dead, a thousand people injured, a neighborhood destroyed, and a city fundamentally changed forever. The trigger for these cataclysmic events began with the mistreatment of a black taxi driver who was arrested by white police officers in the Central Ward. Beaten and forcibly dragged into the station house, this latest example of physical abuse in the precinct was witnessed by tenants in the public housing project across the street, and protesters began to gather outside. When the police used force to disperse the group, some bystanders began throwing rocks and bottles at officers, and a few nearby businesses were ransacked. The following evening a larger rally against police brutality rapidly escalated into a violent clash with armed police, and looters attacked the nearby white-owned businesses. The looting and the violence quickly spread to surrounding areas and dozens of burning buildings lit up the sky.[17]

Initially downplaying the incident, Mayor Addonizio was forced to request help from his fellow Democrat Governor Richard J. Hughes, who arrived with a large detachment of state police and National Guard troops. After touring the still-smoldering streets, he briefed President Johnson on the situation before declaring a state of emergency in Newark and ordering a nightly curfew. Major intersections were designated as checkpoints, and soldiers cordoned off these areas with barbed wire and armored tanks. State troopers with rifles and bayonets patrolled neighborhoods in response to ongoing reports of snipers randomly firing at police from rooftops. Most offices downtown were closed, and the adjoining suburban towns set up roadblocks on their boundary lines. Notwithstanding the large contingent of police and soldiers on the streets, violent clashes continued, and the number of dead and wounded increased for the next two days before the bulk of the troops were finally withdrawn amid the return of relative calm in the area.[18]

Peter Rodino was in Washington when the violence started and hurried home after hearing the news. Before the National Guard was in control, he drove through the streets of the Central Ward to see the destruction, narrowly escaping injury after his car was pelted with rocks. Commenting to the press, Rodino echoed the governor's strong condemnation of the lawlessness and expressed his dismay over the level of street violence. But unlike most of the other white politicians, he was equally outspoken in his belief that there were legitimate underlying conditions feeding this breakdown in law and order, which needed to be addressed. At the same time that Italian American militants were patrolling the streets of the North Ward and intimidating African Americans, Rodino was calling for a renewed effort to find solutions to the multitude of problems facing the black community and praising civil rights leaders for their efforts to maintain calm. "The first order of business" Rodino argued, "is to restore the peace and then begin to rebuild essential enterprises and services to reconstruct the progressive spirit of Newark." He called on federal anti-poverty officials to assess the damage and report on what could be done "to assure this never happens again."[19] Two days after the National Guard left Newark, Rodino, Addonizio, and the governor's urban affairs director were in Washington to meet with Attorney General Ramsey Clark and other administration officials to discuss possible emergency and long-term assistance.[20]

Rodino's belief that the "progressive spirit" of the city could be quickly restored was overly optimistic; five days of violence had severely strained whatever links remained between black and white Newark. "Riots have set Newark back 10, 15, maybe 20 years in human relations," the dean of the

Rutgers Law School told the *New York Times*.[21] Spurred by fear and racism, white flight to the suburbs dramatically accelerated; a North Ward real estate agent reported receiving fifty calls in one day from residents anxious to sell their homes and relocate. Fighting between black and white students at Barringer High School was so intense that police were called to the campus to separate the warring factions. Anthony M. Imperiale Sr., the flamboyant leader of the North Ward white militants, organized the North Ward Citizens Committee to continue nightly street patrols aimed at discouraging African Americans from entering the neighborhood; in 1968, he won a special election to fill a city council vacancy.[22]

Criticism over Addonizio's handling of the July unrest and the widening racial schism cost the mayor much of his previous support in the black community as he prepared to run for a third term. A broad coalition of black organizations and representatives from the expanding Puerto Rican population organized a convention to nominate a candidate to challenge him. City Engineer Kenneth A. Gibson, who had made a stronger-than-expected showing in the last contest, quickly emerged as the frontrunner and was unanimously chosen by the delegates to be the nominee.[23] Considering that the majority of registered voters were white, and Addonizio could exercise the powers of incumbency, unseating him would be difficult. But six months before the election, the political landscape was transformed when the mayor and a long list of other public officials were indicted on charges of extortion, kickbacks, and tax evasion. Fingerprinted and released on bail, Addonizio refused to resign, and the *New York Times* noted solemnly that there was now a "shadow over Newark."[24]

Whether Rodino was surprised, disappointed, or both when he heard the news of his friend's indictment, he offered no public comments. Addonizio's interest in improving his economic circumstances was not a secret; he had told Rodino he was running for mayor because the job offered greater financial rewards. Along with others in Newark, Rodino had heard rumors of the mayor's excessive gambling and lifestyle, and he recalled raising these concerns directly with Addonizio early in his tenure as mayor. Accepting assurances that there was no problem, Rodino claimed he never broached the subject again. His immediate concern was to avoid getting embroiled in the scandal because of their close association. Fortunately, Rodino was rarely involved in city hall matters, and the investigators never contacted him, though the *New York Times* refused to endorse him in November because of his failure "to speak out against the intolerable corruption in Newark politics."[25]

Sidestepping the issue became more difficult a few weeks later, when the federal judge presiding over the trial of crime boss Angelo "Gyp" DeCarlo released the transcripts of FBI wiretaps recorded at the mobster's New Jersey headquarters over a four-year period. DeCarlo frequently bragged of his relationships with Garden State politicians, both real and embellished. To Rodino's shock, his name was mentioned, making him a part of this major news story. Unlike the detailed accounts of DeCarlo's extensive dealings with Addonizio, Rodino's name only appeared a few times in a twelve-hundred-page transcript and never in connection with any illegal activity. He vehemently denied any interactions with DeCarlo or his associates, telling the *Newark Evening News,* "I am a product of Newark's old First Ward, but I have never in my life had dealings with that kind of people." In fact, Rodino had attended the First Ward wedding of mobster Anthony Boiardo in 1950, along with two thousand other guests, an error in judgment he never repeated but was now being resurrected in the press.[26] For someone who had spent years fighting against ethnic stereotyping, the connection to the DeCarlo tapes, however baseless, was a painful experience.

A few weeks after the transcripts were released, Addonizio made the stunning announcement that he was still running for a third term. Kenneth Gibson and Anthony Imperiale were among the other six contenders, and, while city hall corruption was an important issue, race permeated every aspect of the campaign. After Addonizio was forced into a runoff with Gibson, he abandoned his initial moderate tone and attempted to use racial scare tactics to win votes. Gibson's white supporters were subjected to physical harassment, and Rodino's refusal to endorse Addonizio angered many of his longtime backers, who picketed his house.[27] Addonizio's repeated efforts to postpone his corruption trial were unsuccessful, and he spent the final weeks of the campaign in a Trenton courtroom defending himself against charges of payoffs and corruption. On June 16, Gibson captured 56 percent of the vote to become the first black mayor of a major city in the Northeastern United States. The following month, Addonizio was found guilty of all charges and sentenced to ten years in prison.[28]

The inauguration of Kenneth Gibson as Newark's thirty-sixth mayor did not end the efforts of African Americans to secure a greater share of political power in the city; it simply shifted the focus. Fittingly, the trigger for this next battle was provided by former resident Supreme Court Justice William J. Brennan Jr., who wrote the opinion in the landmark *Baker v. Carr* ruling in 1961. The case involved a lawsuit against the state of Tennessee for failing to redraw legislative boundaries after the recent census and the claim that this violated the Fourteenth Amendment's guarantee of equal protection under the law. The lower court had dismissed the case, citing the long-standing legal precedent that regarded apportionment as a political question not subject to judicial review. Writing for the majority, Brennan nullified this doctrine by concluding that "arbitrary and capricious" districting violated the Constitution, making the judiciary an appropriate source of relief.[29]

Three years later, the Supreme Court specifically addressed the politically charged process of congressional redistricting. Although Congress had frozen the size of the House of Representatives at 435 in 1929 and required a reallocation of these seats every ten years, the states were free to determine the composition of each district, resulting in a hodgepodge of unequal constituencies. In *Wesberry v. Sanders*, the majority affirmed that the court also had a role in this issue and declared that Georgia's congressional districts were unconstitutional. Offering a guidepost for future adjudication, Justice Hugo Black concluded that under the Constitution "as nearly as is practicable one man's vote in a congressional election is to be worth as much as another's."[30] This notion of numerical parity provided a new yardstick for redrawing the political map of the United States, and the court subsequently extended this same principle to state legislatures.

While Justice Black did not suggest a specific timetable for redressing these imbalances, his decision opened the floodgates for legal challenges to existing districts, including those in New Jersey. The state's two previous congressional realignments in 1931 and 1961 were triggered by the gain of an additional House seat, and the incumbents ensured that there were no significant changes in the rest of the map. Consequently, the boundaries of twelve of New Jersey's fifteen congressional districts had not changed for more than a half century during which the state added two million residents and underwent a rapid suburbanization that redistributed this population. The result was a large disparity between districts with several significantly above the average size and others, including the Tenth, falling far below this level. The most egregious example was the First District encompassing the expanding suburbs of Philadelphia in the southern part of the state, which at the time of the *Wesberry* decision contained as many people as the two northern Hudson County districts *combined*.[31]

The need to conform to the new "one person, one vote" criteria was accelerated when the New Jersey State Senate's composition of equal representation for each county regardless of population was declared unconstitutional. Faced with the difficult task of redrawing state and congressional districts, the Republican-controlled legislature established a bipartisan commission to formulate a comprehensive reapportionment plan. As the dean of a congressional delegation consisting of eleven Democrats and four Republicans following the recent Johnson landslide, Rodino worked aggressively to protect all of their districts from any significant change. The group sent their own proposals to the commission and traveled to Trenton in January 1965 to plead their case in person. The final plan presented by the commission to the legislature a few weeks later reflected little of this input and eliminated the underpopulated districts of two Democratic incumbents, significantly altered the boundary lines of the other districts, and removed the North Ward from the Tenth District. Democratic opposition was swift, and Governor Hughes proposed that any action be deferred until after the next election since the current legislature was itself unconstitutional. Without enough votes to override a veto, the

Republicans were forced to abandon the commission's recommendations.[32]

The delay proved advantageous for the Democrats, who won control of the legislature in addition to the governor's reelection. Now in complete control of the mapping process, the Democratic majority quickly discovered the difficult challenge of reconciling the competing interests of county party leaders unwilling to surrender any political power, incumbents fiercely determined to preserve the territorial integrity of their old districts, and the court's time-sensitive command to correct all population imbalances. After months of internal wrangling and missed deadlines, legislators finally approved a congressional redistricting plan, which Governor Hughes signed into law in June 1966. Sacrificing the most junior northern Democrat in the delegation, the new boundaries shifted this district to the overpopulated Republican south, limiting the impact of the revisions on the remaining Democrats. The boundaries of the Tenth District were altered for the first time since 1931, replacing the Democratic strongholds of Kearny and Harrison with the marginally more Republican suburban towns of Montclair and Cedar Grove. By retaining all his other constituents and gaining Newark's overwhelmingly Democratic South Ward, Rodino was able to secure his usual comfortable margin of victory in the next three elections.[33]

The next cycle of reapportionment did not begin on such a positive note. The results of the 1970 census confirmed that New Jersey's growing population continued to move from the state's traditional urban centers to the newly developed western and southern counties. Newark, officially certified as a majority black city along with its neighbor East Orange, lost almost 6 percent of its residents over the previous ten years. Cities in adjacent Hudson County suffered an equally sharp decline.[34] Before the process of mapping equal districts even started, Rodino and the three other Democratic incumbents from these areas were at a numerical disadvantage. Compounding this problem was the hostile partisan climate in Trenton, where the Republicans controlling the legislature and the governorship hoped to reduce the nine-to-six Democratic advantage in the state's congressional delegation. Republican State Senator Joseph Maraziti was openly lobbying to create a new district for himself, and other legislators were contemplating a similar post-census career move to Capitol Hill.[35]

In an attempt to secure a bipartisan agreement on strategy, Rodino convened a meeting of the entire delegation to discuss the issue before the legislature began the process. His appeal for unity was ignored, and the session ended on a sour note. "The only subject on which the Jersey congressmen agreed yesterday," the *Evening News (Newark)* reported, "was that there is little chance they will be able to agree on a redistricting plan of their own."[36]

In February 1971, Governor William T. Cahill offered the group a second opportunity to reach a consensus when he promised to stave off any legislative action for six weeks to allow them additional time to develop their own plan. To help with the process, Rodino asked pharmaceutical giant Hoffman-La Roche, which was located in his district, for technical assistance. The company assigned two computer specialists to help evaluate available census tracts, determine population deviations, and prepare choices with detailed maps for the delegation. But technology could not overcome politics, and the incumbents could not reach an agreement. Governor Cahill asked the legislature to proceed with the reapportionment and approve a final plan before they recessed in late spring.[37]

The redrawing of New Jersey's congressional districts offered an unexpected opportunity for African Americans. The increase in the state's black population, particularly in the Newark area, suggested that it might be possible to elect an African American representative if a majority black district was created. The Supreme Court's "one person, one vote" edict had enabled just this possibility, and the New Jersey chapter of the NAACP had urged the reapportionment commission in 1965 to create a "homogenous grouping so to get Negro representation."[38] Following the release of the 1970 census six months after the election of Kenneth Gibson, black leaders began to promote the idea of a new urban district to elect the state's first African American congressmen. This coincided with an announcement by Howard University's Joint Center For Political Studies that it was launching an initiative to increase the number of blacks in Congress; Director Frank Reeves listed Newark as one of the organization's top priorities.[39]

Facing this added challenge to the future of the Tenth District and with delegation unity no longer a possibility, Rodino embarked on his own campaign to protect his seat, contacting legislators and organized labor leaders. News of the redistricting fight elicited an outpouring of support from Italian Americans including his former opponent Al Miele, who offered to reach out to Republicans. Many were motivated by loyalty to Rodino; others were aroused by their fierce opposition to a black congressional district that might include the Italian American North Ward of Newark. Rodino's personal argument was simply that he was next in line to be chairman of the Judiciary Committee, and the entire state benefited from his seniority in Congress. He continued to make this case to legislators after they returned to the statehouse in June for a special weeklong session solely devoted to reapportionment. Even with a sizable majority, the Republicans were no more successful at reconciling the competing political interests surrounding redistricting and adjourned without reaching an agreement.[40]

Even judged against the normal tumult of New Jersey politics, the outcome of the 1971 legislative election was unusual. Although the Republicans retained control of the Senate with a reduced majority, unexpected losses in the Assembly produced a virtual tie, with neither party securing the forty-one seats needed to control the chamber. The key to breaking this impasse rested with the lone Independent elected in November—Anthony Imperiale—and Governor Cahill announced that the Republicans would not make any deals with the controversial white militant. When the Democrats began courting him, African American legislators threatened to quit the party. This stalemate remained unsettled as the new legislature convened at the beginning of 1972.

The rancorous opening-day session was about to end without a resolution when four Hudson County Democrats unexpectedly agreed to vote for Republican control of the Assembly in exchange for key committee assignments and patronage. The renegade assemblymen were immediately expelled from the Democratic caucus, leaving no predictable or controllable majority in the lower house and seriously reducing the chances of cooperation.[41]

As the new legislature began to consider various proposals for redistricting, Rodino's prospects appeared brighter. The plan with the best chance to win approval was one that eliminated a Hudson County district to create a congressional seat in the overpopulated northwest for Senator Maraziti. After considerable pressure from Italian Americans and a meeting with Rodino, Maraziti agreed to minimize any changes to the Tenth "as per our agreement."[42] Assemblyman George C. Richardson, a longtime advocate for expanding the political power of African Americans in Newark, introduced a proposal for a majority black district that included significantly more constituents from the Eleventh District rather than the Tenth, and the press reported that Richardson was preparing to challenge the incumbent Joseph Minish, not Rodino.[43] But whatever their individual merits, neither of these proposals were likely to find a clear path forward in a polarized legislature where every vested party had enough leverage to block any plan.

Considering all of these impediments, it was inevitable that the courts would be drawn into the reapportionment fight. Raymond W. Brown, the former director of New Jersey's chapter of the NAACP and a prominent attorney, had filed a lawsuit challenging the legality of New Jersey's congressional districts. He requested an injunction to prevent the use of the current districts in the primary and general elections. A panel of three federal judges heard the complaint, and the Democratic and Republican incumbents hired separate attorneys to represent them in the case. Citing the *Wesberry* precedent, the court ruled on February 29 that New Jersey's unequal congressional districts were unconstitutional and must be redrawn before the filing deadline for the June primary. The judges warned that, in the absence of a new map, they would consider abolishing all districts and ordering at-large statewide elections. They invited defendants, plaintiffs, and other interested parties to submit redistricting plans for consideration before the next hearing on April 3.[44]

The imposition of a hard deadline and the threat of at-large elections were powerful incentives for action, triggering a flurry of activity in Trenton. As expected, the Maraziti plan won Senate approval and attention swung to the unpredictable majority in the Assembly. Writer and activist Amiri Baraka organized a trip to the capital for several busloads of grassroots lobbyists from Newark to intensify the campaign for a black district. At a morning press conference before the group departed, Mayor Gibson told the volunteers that "what we are asking for is political equity."[45] On the other side of the issue, Citizens Against Racial (Congressional) Districts (CARD), a group created by Al Miele with a membership drawn largely from the Tenth District, argued against what it labeled as "racial gerrymandering."[46] As Congress was in session, Rodino closely monitored events from Washington and dispatched Merle Baumgard, his administrative assistant, to Trenton to lobby for the preservation of the Tenth District. On March 21, Rodino and several colleagues participated in a private strategy meeting with the Assembly's Democratic leaders at an off-site location. Two days later, he was at the statehouse testifying before the lower chamber's conference committee in support of a redistricting proposal favoring Democrats—it failed to win enough votes to pass.[47]

While the intensive political wrangling continued, the three-judge federal panel reconvened to consider the various redistricting plans submitted before the deadline. Early in the day-long hearing, election officials testified that a districting plan could be implemented in time for the primary, and this persuaded the judges that at-large elections were no longer necessary. Other witnesses highlighted the merits of specific proposals and urged the court to consider factors such as compactness and contiguity in addition to numerical equality. Representing the Democratic incumbents, Joseph Gannon, the Assembly's minority staff director, argued that any redress to population imbalances should adhere as close as possible to the existing congressional district boundaries. Aware that the legislature was still grappling with the issue, the panel agreed to defer their final decision until April 12.[48]

After two years of gridlock, the legislature now rushed to the finish line in a frenetic attempt to adopt a new congressional map before the court could impose one. A plan favorable to the Democratic incumbents passed the Assembly with the help of Anthony Imperiale only to fail in the Senate. A compromise between Republicans and Essex County Democrats, strongly endorsed by Governor Cahill, passed the Senate and was on the brink of Assembly approval. But African American members, ignoring the entreaties of the county's Democratic party chairman, refused to agree to any plan that did not unify Newark in a single district. Four days later in an act of betrayal Rodino would never forgive, Senator Maraziti reneged on his promise and made a deal with the renegade Hudson Democrats to preserve their two House seats by combining the Tenth and Eleventh districts. Last-minute snags prevented a vote before the court-imposed deadline, and this final attempt at a legislative solution collapsed.[49]

On April 12, the federal panel issued its ruling on reapportionment. Without enough time or the expertise to create their own map, the judges focused on the five plans submitted in evidence. The paramount determinant used by the court in their selection process was numerical equality between districts, with the preservation of municipal boundaries and minimum fragmentation of counties secondary factors. Rejecting the two proposals that won approval in at least one chamber of the legislature, the majority of the court instead embraced an obscure plan introduced by Republican Senator James Turner that was never reported out of committee or debated. According to the majority's written opinion, this plan was selected because it had the lowest population deviation, kept most core constituencies intact, combined just two districts, and allowed every incumbent to remain at their current address. These were not Turner's objectives; he was solely interested in protecting the two Republican incumbent congressmen representing his southern region of the state. To attract Republican support, he had shifted a Hudson County seat to the west for Maraziti and redrawn the boundaries of the Eleventh District to make it less urban. The last component of his plan was a modified Tenth District, primarily crafted to minimize other population deviations, that included all of Newark, East Orange, Glen Ridge, and Harrison. Unintentionally, this final change created New Jersey's first majority black congressional district, and its adoption by the court was an ironic ending for Rodino. After two years of vigilant efforts to safeguard his political future, it was chance, not design, that had determined his fate.[50]

A stunned Rodino now confronted two of the most important decisions of his public career, both of which needed resolution before the April 27 primary filing deadline. The first was whether he should appeal the redistricting decision. Judge Clarkson Fisher, a member of the panel, had filed a strongly worded dissent expressing his belief that the court should have deferred to the "legislative will" and selected a proposal approved by the Senate. His specific objection to the Turner plan was the restructuring of the Tenth and Eleventh districts on "racial grounds." Fisher argued that "any purposeful attempt to maintain a majority of persons of one race within a given district would, in fact, raise grave constitutional questions."[51] Under the court-imposed map, the non-white population of the Tenth District increased from 31 to 52 percent, and the number of non-whites in the Eleventh District dropped from 37 to 7 percent. Rodino asked the Judiciary Committee staff in Washington to research legal precedents, and they advised him that there was a basis for an appeal if reconfiguring the racial composition was intentional, a difficult charge to prove. Rodino recognized that a court challenge could tarnish his reputation with African Americans and place him in an untenable position if he lost. Appreciating the risks, he decided not to pursue the matter.[52]

The second question Rodino faced was whether he should switch districts and challenge Joe Minish for the Democratic nomination in the Eleventh District. Under the redrawn boundaries, there were more former Rodino constituents in this district, more than 180,000, than former Minish constituents. Additionally, the towns of Belleville, Nutley, and Bloomfield, which Rodino had represented since 1949, were part of the modified Eleventh District. Many of his supporters, contributors, and campaign volunteers lived in these communities where he had close relationships with elected officials, newspaper editors, and business leaders. In stark contrast, the revised Tenth District contained a majority of constituents Rodino had never represented, requiring a major rebuilding of his political organization outside the North Ward. Comparing past voting patterns with the racial composition of the new Tenth, Rodino concluded that his long-term prospects were not promising.

The key electoral threshold in this overwhelmingly Democratic district was the party's nominating primary. Rodino believed he could probably win the first contest, particularly in a crowded field, but would be defeated in the following election if the African American community unified around a single opponent. As a longtime champion of civil rights, he also had mixed feelings about running in a majority black district. Expressing this uneasiness to the press, Rodino confessed, "I'm not interested in blocking the legitimate aspirations of black people."[53]

While Rodino weighed his options, the court's action was already changing New Jersey's political landscape. Privately, Republicans gloated that they were likely to capture two seats in November and become the delegation's majority party. Senator Maraziti announced his candidacy for the congressional district he created for himself, incumbent Republican Florence Dwyer decided to retire rather than run in an altered district, and the two representatives from Hudson County, one now under indictment, prepared for a nasty face-off to win the nomination for the county's sole congressional seat. Italian Americans throughout the state were outraged over what happened to Rodino and aimed their wrath at Governor Cahill. Deluged with telegrams unfairly blaming him and calling the ruling "disgusting," a "crime," and "Rodino rape," Cahill defended his efforts to prod the legislature to act and highlighted his support for the Senate bill, "which was quite favorable to Congressman Rodino."[54]

In Newark, George Richardson announced his expected candidacy the day after the court created the urban congressional district he had vigorously promoted in Trenton. Long estranged from Amiri Baraka and Mayor Gibson, Richardson planned to rely on support from the city's black clergymen and labor unions. The following week, Baraka and Gibson organized a meeting of African American political leaders and selected William S. Hart, the first black mayor of East Orange, to be their candidate in the Tenth District contest. Hart was considered the frontrunner, and they urged Richardson to withdraw and not split the black vote—a request he refused. The final African American to enter the race was Newark food store manager Wilbur Kornegay, an unknown political novice. Baraka told reporters that the effort to elect an African American congressman was not directed personally at the incumbent, and he called Rodino "estimable," encouraging him to run against Joe Minish.[55]

Sensing a potential fight with his roommate, Minish had moved out of their apartment and quickly staked out his own position by declaring his intention to run for reelection in the Eleventh District no matter what his colleague decided. Rodino, factoring in the altered makeup of the district and his own stature and public profile, justifiably believed that he would beat Minish in a primary. But his discussions with his allies in organized labor and the Democratic party showed there was little appetite for a nasty intraparty fight. Some supporters were willing to endorse a Rodino switch to protect the benefits of his seniority, and others suggested he run for governor in 1973. Essex County Democratic Chairman Harry Lerner and the United Auto Workers state leader Joel R. Jacobson, along with many of the people Rodino consulted, were unwilling to abandon Minish and told Rodino he was the only white candidate who had a chance of winning in the redrawn Tenth. In the end, Rodino did what he had done so many times in the past and accepted the challenge even if the odds were against him. "I had made up my mind," he recalled, "and I knew it was going to be a real fight." He held a press conference in his Capitol Hill office on April 24 to announce his decision to run for reelection in the Tenth District, underscoring the benefits of his seniority and position as the ranking Democrat on the House Judiciary Committee.[56]

Facing the twin obstacles of unfavorable demographics and African American political aspirations, Rodino was considered the underdog at the start of the concentrated forty-three day campaign leading up to the June 6 primary election. Mayor Hart already had an established grassroots political organization in East Orange, and Gibson and Baraka provided a parallel operation for him in the predominantly African American wards in Newark. Rodino needed to create a ground operation in many black neighborhoods under a tight time frame, made harder because Congress was in session, and he was forced to spend weekdays in Washington. Rodino was also constrained by New Jersey's closed primary system, which only allowed previously declared Democrats to vote in a primary. This requirement eliminated any registered Republicans or independents, including many of Rodino's North Ward constituents, from the pool of potential voters in a presidential primary year that was expected to encourage a larger turnout of black voters.[57]

This discouraging prognosis did not deter Rodino, and he immediately started planning for an intensive contest at an accelerated pace. He was a seasoned and masterful campaigner and personally managed all aspects of the operation, issuing daily detailed instructions to his staff. Six weeks shy of his sixty-third birthday, Rodino embarked on an exhausting and demanding schedule, leaving Washington to return home whenever possible and boarding a plane several times in a single week if necessary. When he was in the district, his day began with shaking hands with the early shift at a factory at sunrise, and his last appointment was often late in the evening at a house party or social gathering. His long days were filled with stops at supermarkets and other retail stores, visits to schools and churches, public events sponsored by civic organizations, lunches and dinners, and an endless lineup of phone calls. Replicating this regimen in black and white neighborhoods, Rodino traveled throughout the district propelled by his tireless energy, greeting old constituents and hoping to enlist new supporters.[58]

The one clear advantage Rodino had over his opponents was the power of incumbency. At a time when the rules establishing the lines between official and campaign activities were lax, he relied heavily on his staff in Newark and on Capitol Hill for help with speechwriting, scheduling, and mailings that could be legally sent to constituents for free using the congressional franking privilege. Being an incumbent on an important committee also gave Rodino access to political contributors in Washington, especially labor organizations, and they willingly provided the $100,000 he needed for an aggressive campaign. These funds, five times more than Rodino had spent in 1970, were earmarked for extensive radio and newspaper advertising, billboards, direct mail, brochures, and volunteers.[59] His legislative accomplishment from more than two decades in office, most notably the landmark civil rights laws he helped enact, provided an abundance of rich source material, something his opponents could not match. Shaping his message around the value of incumbency, Rodino made his case for reelection in the campaign's most pointed and widely distributed publication declaring that:

> This Election Is Not As Simple as Black and White
> The only thing that counts in Congress is power.
> And the only way you get power is by being around awhile.
> Peter Rodino has power.[60]

Both Hart and Richardson countered the incumbent's arguments with a singular response: it was time to elect an African American to represent the people of the Tenth District. Substantively, they had few disagreements with Rodino's progressive record and instead criticized him for being out of touch with the new urban district and for failing to prevent Newark's steep decline. "*Get Rid of Rats, Racism and Rodino*" proclaimed a Richardson campaign poster plastered all over the Central and South Wards in defiance of Rodino's strenuous objections. Mayor Hart called Rodino an "absentee congressman" and accused him of illegally using public funds to mail letters to voters in East Orange, a baseless charge under the prevailing congressional rules. However, the challengers reserved most of their sharpest attacks for each other, with Hart calling Richardson a "spoiler" funded by Rodino, a charge he repeated when all the candidates appeared together in two live debates sponsored by New York television stations.[61]

Although Rodino attempted to stay above the fray, he was forced to confront Hart directly in a dispute over endorsements. A key focus of Hart's campaign advertising was his support from nationally prominent black political leaders, with several traveling to New Jersey to appear with the candidate at campaign rallies, including California Congressman Ron Dellums, Gary Indiana Mayor Richard G. Hatcher, and Georgia State Senator Julian Bond. Listed among Hart's supporters were four other African American members of Congress, who thought Rodino was running in a different district until alerted that Hart was actually his opponent. Representative Augustus F. Hawkins assured Rodino that "I consider your reelection to the Congress vital and essential," and all the members withdrew from scheduled events for the Hart campaign.[62] Rodino countered with his own endorsement coup when he won the backing of A. Philip Randolph, the founder of the Brotherhood of Sleeping Car Porters and a civil rights icon. After Rodino visited him at his New York City apartment in early May, Randolph issued a widely publicized statement endorsing Rodino's reelection bid and calling him "a permanent ally in the struggle for economic and social justice."[63]

At a time when it was difficult to conduct an accurate poll within the confines of a single congressional district, there was no reliable gauge to judge the standing of each candidate during the primary contest. But most observers agreed that the tide seemed to shift in Rodino's favor in late May when a federal court in Newark overturned a forty-year-old election law. Since 1930, New Jersey had required a voter to abstain from participating in two consecutive primary elections before they were eligible to switch political parties. This restriction was implemented in response to the practice of "raiding," used to skewer the general election results by instructing party loyalists to vote for the weakest candidate in the opposition's primary. Following the Supreme Court's "one person, one vote ruling," this limitation imposed to prevent an archaic tactic was now considered an obstacle to a voter's full participation in the electoral process. Ruling on a challenge brought by the American Civil Liberties Union, the three-judge federal panel concluded that this requirement was "unreasonable and excessive" and declared the law unconstitutional. Until an acceptable alternative was enacted by the legislature, the court imposed an open primary system on the state and instructed election officials to permit voting on June 6 without regard to any prior partisan affiliation.[64]

The most significant impact of the court's decision was in the Tenth District, where Republicans and independents could now vote in the Democratic primary. Amiri Baraka's Committee For A Unified Newark called the ruling "one of the most racist decisions concerning electoral politics in New Jersey" and blasted the American Civil Liberties Union (ACLU) for initiating the lawsuit.[65] Mayor Hart recruited the help of redistricting lawyer Raymond

A. Brown and the local NAACP to appeal the case to the Supreme Court. Arguing that an open system would allow Republicans to "raid" the Democratic primary and dilute the party's non-white vote, Brown requested a stay of the court's ruling. Three days before the primary, Justice William Brennan rejected the appeal and refused to stop the enforcement of the new requirements. For the Rodino campaign, this was a surprising last-minute boost, and the campaign recruited volunteers to make telephone calls to potential crossover voters. Hastily rewritten advertisements in the *Italian Tribune* informed readers, "You Can Vote for Peter Rodino in the June 6 Primary Election if you are a registered Republican, Independent or a Democrat."[66]

Twenty-four years after Peter Rodino's congressional career began in a small Newark storefront, hundreds of campaign volunteers, supporters, and friends gathered in an elegant ballroom at the downtown Robert Treat Hotel hoping they were not about to witness its finale. An unusually large number of reporters and cameramen from New York television stations, many of them covering a Rodino campaign for the first time in anticipation of his possible defeat, added to the drama and tension in the room. Ninety minutes after the polls closed, it was all over—Rodino was the Democratic party's nominee, winning 57 percent of the 65,000 votes cast and outpolling Mayor Hart by nearly 14,000 votes. Of greater long-term significance, Rodino received 10,000 more votes than his three opponents combined, which suggested a reassuring electoral strength if he faced a single black opponent in the future. His decision to campaign in all the neighborhoods of the district, regardless of the demographics, proved to be an effective strategy thanks to his long-standing commitment to civil rights and the Randolph endorsement. Though the crossover voting and higher turnout of white voters was a critical factor in his success, he performed better than expected in the largely African American South Ward and won a sizable number of votes in majority black East Orange. Rodino stressed this fact when he addressed the crowd at the Robert Treat hotel, telling them, "I hope and trust the nation looks upon the Tenth Congressional District as a testing ground where blacks and whites can work together." An exhausted Rodino spent the next day celebrating his victory and his birthday.[67]

Two weeks after the primary, Rodino received unexpected news that would change his life. Emanuel Celler, the eighty-four-year-old chairman of the House Judiciary Committee, had consistently rebuffed any suggestions that he retire, telling the *New York Times* he planned "to go on and on." This seemed to be the likely scenario when Celler announced in March that he was running for reelection in his safe Brooklyn district.[68] Although he gained the New York Liberal Party's backing, Celler was increasingly at odds with many of his fellow progressives because of his opposition to the rights for eighteen-year-olds to vote, the Equal Rights Amendment, and his unwillingness to bow to public pressure and give up his private law practice. These disagreements and his advanced age prompted Elizabeth Holtzman to challenge Celler in the Democratic primary. The thirty-year-old attorney and former mayoral aide argued that the district needed a more vigorous representative, and she strongly condemned Celler's legal representation of defense contractors and other special interests.[69]

Despite running an aggressive campaign and receiving the endorsement of the *New York Times,* Holtzman was not regarded as a serious threat to the entrenched and popular incumbent. Consequently, the contest received little press attention in contrast to the coverage accorded the ongoing battle in New Jersey's Tenth District. Stunning reporters and pundits on June 21, Holtzman scored an upset and defeated Celler by the slimmest of margins, a mere 562 votes out of the nearly 35,000 ballots cast. Celler refused to concede, first calling for a recount and then filing a lawsuit demanding a new election because of alleged voting irregularities. When the courts refused in late September to order a new primary, Celler decided not to go forward as the Liberal Party's nominee, convinced that his Democratic colleagues would not allow him to continue to serve as chairman.[70]

Emanuel Celler's defeat was a final and fateful surprise in a year filled with unforeseen and momentous twists for Peter Rodino. Just months after the near death of his own political career, he was about to reap the rewards of a steady and patient climb up the ladder of congressional seniority. Rodino was unwilling to engage in any premature speculation about his elevation to the committee's top slot out of respect for the current chairman and the formal selection process that still needed to unfold. In October, he did accept an invitation to meet with editors and reporters at the *New York Times* to discuss his plans for the committee in the next Congress. Reluctant to appear presumptuous, he characterized his comments as simply "suggestions" and indicated a desire to focus the panel's attention on the right of privacy, which he believed was under attack. Citing the recent controversy over the electronic eavesdropping at the Democratic National Committee's headquarters in Washington, Rodino told the group, "It's something we must get into."[71]

CHAPTER EIGHT

MR. CHAIRMAN

Peter Rodino was the last Democratic member of the 1948 freshman class to assume the chairmanship of a committee in the House of Representatives. For more than two decades, he was the patient protégé, standing loyally at the side of Emanuel Celler, the longest serving chairman of the House Judiciary Committee and someone who completely dominated every aspect of its operations. Now that the wait was almost over, Rodino began to prepare for his new position by soliciting advice from a wide range of sources. He consulted with his friends Jack Valenti and Joseph Califano, seasoned Washington operatives, for guidance on how best to proceed once he was formally chosen to lead the panel. Sensitive to Celler's lame-duck status, he quietly organized a meeting of the subcommittee chairmen to listen to their ideas for the legislative agenda in the next congressional session. At home, he reached out to civic and religious leaders for suggestions on "urban friendly" legislation he could introduce and met with the faculty at Rutgers University Law School to discuss a host of current constitutional issues. Working through the items on his preparatory checklist, Rodino requested his campaign consultants to prepare a strategic plan for the first year of his chairmanship. The document they presented two weeks before Christmas included a long list of recommended actions and one clear warning: proceed cautiously and avoid any high-profile issues. It was advice he would find impossible to follow in the months ahead.[1]

Rodino's elevation to the committee's top position coincided with a major revision in the process for selecting chairmen. The reform movement in the House of Representatives had succeeded over the past two years in weakening the grip of the seniority system by shifting more power to the Democratic Caucus. In 1973, the reformers won approval to allow a secret ballot, placing a potential check on any autocratic leader. An early supporter of these reform efforts, Rodino welcomed the changes and the overwhelming endorsement from his peers that certified his chairmanship. His first objective was to diversify the all-male, largely white committee, and he successfully campaigned to add Celler's opponent Elizabeth Holtzman and Texan Barbara Jordan, the first African American woman elected to Congress from the South, to the roster.[2] His second goal was to decentralize power; presiding over his first committee meeting on February 6, he proposed the appointment of an ad hoc bipartisan subcommittee to prepare a reorganization plan. The proposal adopted in June followed Rodino's outline and established seven permanent and clearly identifiable subcommittees reflecting legislative responsibilities. The most dramatic change was the replacement of Celler's all-powerful Subcommittee 5, with a new panel focusing solely on monopolies and commercial law. Only six months after becoming chairman, Rodino had already demonstrated his willingness to break with the past and exercise a new style of leadership.[3]

All of this preparatory work proved invaluable when the committee found itself shouldering the twin burdens of a vice presidential nomination and a presidential impeachment in October. The day after Speaker Albert assigned the panel the responsibility for determining if President Nixon's actions in the Watergate scandal warranted his removal from office, Rodino announced plans to "proceed full steam ahead."[4] The initial reaction to Rodino's appointment to lead the impeachment inquiry was not encouraging; few of the news stories provided details of his long career particularly his work on the Chelf committee or handling of the contentious fair housing bill, both of which demonstrated the skills needed for the task he was about to undertake. Instead, he was frequently labeled as "obscure" or "untested" and inaccurately portrayed as an anonymous congressman content to remain out of the limelight. Rodino himself contributed to this underestimation by lacking the bravado that was a Capitol Hill mainstay. His humble admission that he spent sleepless nights worrying about his awesome responsibility, one that no one had faced for a century, was interpreted as evidence that he was a reluctant recruit and ill-prepared for the job. Several of Rodino's House colleagues helped stoke these doubts in the press by unfavorably comparing Rodino to his predecessor.[5]

Although Rodino discounted most of these barbs, he could not ignore the rumors that his connection to Newark might link him to organized crime. The day after Albert's appointment, the *New York Times* published a profile intimating that Rodino had ties to mobsters. "He is a man who has been persistently linked to members of organized crime and who just as persistently has denied these ties," reporter Martin Tolchin wrote. The evidence he cited to support this claim was the long-debunked Gyp DeCarlo wiretap recordings from a decade earlier. New Jersey's US Attorney Herbert J. Stern, a member of the original DeCarlo investigative team and a Nixon appointee, told Tolchin the tapes were "unreliable" and assured him that Rodino "is an honest man and a fine public servant."[6] Stern was furious when the story still included references from the tapes and misquoted him, prompting a complaint to the reporter. Rodino had known Tolchin for years and demanded a retraction, which the newspaper declined, and the salacious suggestion of mob connections was repeated in other publications. Rodino and Stern shared the belief that someone in the Nixon White House started the rumors to discredit the chairman and derail the inquiry.[7]

When Chairman Rodino entered the Judiciary Committee's hearing room on October 30 to begin the first presidential impeachment inquiry in 105 years, he had already made several important decisions. The first was to avoid the pervasive partisanship and political maneuverings that tainted the outcome of the 1868 impeachment of Andrew Johnson. In place of this discredited example, he intended to emulate the bipartisan spirit he experienced as a member of the Chelf Committee two decades earlier, which had resulted in the unanimous approval of a widely praised final report. To foster this spirit of cooperation, he decided to follow another aspect of the Chelf model and hire a special counsel from outside the regular committee staff to manage the inquiry.[8] When Rodino became chairman, he placed his close confidant Garner J. "Jim" Cline in charge of the committee's administrative operations and selected subcommittee counsel Jerome "Jerry" Zeifman as the new general counsel. Zeifman had undertaken some preliminary work on impeachment and expected to direct the inquiry. But Rodino was uncomfortable with the chief counsel's close relationship with the panel's most vocal Nixon critics. Fearing this might alienate Republicans and undermine the credibility of the proceedings, he informed Zeifman that he was initiating a search for an outside special counsel. The chief counsel was bitterly disappointed, later channeling much of his resentment toward undermining the decision.[9]

Rodino also resolved beforehand not to embrace the reflexive presumption of guilt embodied in many of the impeachment resolutions and floor speeches offered by Democrats in the wake of the Saturday Night Massacre. The notion of removing a president of the United States from office, especially one recently reelected in a landslide, filled him with dread, and he was not willing to conclude at the commencement of the inquiry that impeachment was either the certain or even likely outcome. Rodino's research into British and American legal precedents and knowledge of constitutional law persuaded him that there should be a very high bar for defining what might warrant impeachment. He believed this necessitated a sober and deliberative process that provided for the careful presentation and examination of all the relevant information before reaching any final judgment. Regardless of any external criticism or pressure, he would spend the time he needed to consider these questions carefully.[10]

The representatives gathered in the hearing room that day reflected a mix of geography, ideology, and personality that was far more complex than suggested by the simple ratio of the twenty-one Democrats to seventeen

Republicans dividing the committee. A third of the members were freshmen. Adding the sophomores to this total meant that close to half of the panel had served fewer than four years in Congress. The Democrats included many of the chamber's leading liberal activists who were ready to declare the president guilty at the outset. Sitting amidst this faction of self-proclaimed Nixon haters were three southern conservatives, Walter W. Flowers Jr. from Alabama, Arkansan Ray H. Thornton Jr., and James R. Mann of South Carolina, representing districts that voted overwhelmingly for Richard Nixon in 1972. Regardless of any unanimity among the liberals, the support of these three was critical to the majority in a close vote.[11]

On the other side of the committee's dais, the Republicans were led by the low-key J. Edward Hutchinson of Michigan, new to his role as ranking minority member after winning a coin toss against equally senior Robert McClory of Illinois. The bulk of the Republicans on the committee were firmly entrenched in the party's conservative wing with a few moderate exceptions, including Thomas Railsback of Illinois, Hamilton Fish Jr. of New York, and freshman William Cohen of Maine. Regardless of ideology, party loyalty remained a compelling force difficult to ignore, and most of the Republicans were predisposed to accept President Nixon's denial of any direct involvement in the Watergate cover-up. Some members like Charles E. Wiggins of California and New Jersey's Joseph Maraziti, the state senator who had betrayed Rodino during the recent redistricting fight, were prepared to go further and assume the role of vigorous presidential defender.[12]

The difficulty of preserving a spirit of bipartisanship within such a fractious group quickly became apparent. Under the existing rules, all subpoenas for witnesses or evidence needed the approval of the full committee. To expedite the inquiry, Rodino proposed that the members grant him the power to issue subpoenas similar to the authority exercised by most other chairmen. This change was endorsed at a caucus of the panel's Democrats, and Hutchinson raised no objections. When other Republicans learned of the proposal, they quickly condemned it as "a partisan power grab," and Hutchinson was forced to withdraw his support. Thomas Railsback complained to reporters that "the chairman is under fire from some of the real wild-eyed liberals on the committee and he's capitulated."[13]

Distressed by this reaction, Rodino was prepared to modify his proposal to include Hutchinson as a cosigner in the approval process. But Jack Brooks, the prickly Texas Democrat and surreptitious Rodino critic, along with several other majority members strenuously objected, arguing that the Republicans would use this to delay the process. Rodino reluctantly dropped his conciliatory gesture. Gaveling the committee to order, he attempted to assure the Republicans that he would use his subpoena power sparingly and consult with them whenever possible. This did not persuade any of them to break ranks, and the 21-to-17 vote providing the chairman with sole subpoena authority followed party lines. As a result of this initial decision, the template for the committee's actions seemed to be partisanship, not the cooperation Rodino envisioned. Reflecting on this unwelcomed outcome many years later, Rodino expressed regret for what he considered his most serious error in judgment during the impeachment inquiry.[14]

The chairman attempted to restore a sense of comity to the committee by meeting regularly with an ad hoc group consisting of the chairmen and ranking members of the seven subcommittees, plus Brooks, who did not chair a subcommittee because of his seniority on the House Committee on Government Operations. Rodino also reached out to individual Republican members like Thomas Railsback to seek their input and address their concerns.[15] Despite these efforts, the partisan bickering erupted again two weeks later over the approval of a special supplemental appropriations measure to fund the impeachment inquiry. When the resolution appropriating the money was debated, Republicans complained about the treatment of the Judiciary Committee's minority members and demanded a clearly designated portion of the funding. Although several Republicans voted with the majority to approve the funding without this restriction, the contentious debate added to a growing perception that the impeachment inquiry was mired in partisanship after less than a month, renewing concerns about the chairman's ability to manage this challenging assignment.[16]

The one thing both sides agreed on for different reasons was that with the approval of the supplemental funding measure the inquiry needed to begin. Republicans wanted to move quickly to remove this cloud hanging over the president. House Democrats were besieged on a daily basis with volumes of anti-Nixon mail from constituents and pleaded for some action on impeachment. Majority Leader O'Neill urged Rodino to at least hire a special counsel and sent him a list of names, which Rodin promptly rejected as too partisan.[17] Rodino was still negotiating to obtain the voluminous material amassed by the Senate Watergate committee, and this made it difficult to address questions about the precise timing for launching the inquiry. Responding to this impatience, Rodino asked his administrative assistant Francis O'Brien to begin the search for a special counsel. He personally reached out to friends for suggestions. Until this key personnel decision was made, he was reluctant to hire any other staff except for a few clerks to answer the increasing amount of mail.[18]

The committee also needed to focus its full attention on confirming a new vice president. Rodino had overestimated the committee's capacity to handle more than one high-profile event at a time, and he was forced to give priority to the more pressing need to act on Gerald Ford's pending nomination.[19] But moving expeditiously was now complicated by opposition from his fellow Democrats and lack of cooperation from the FBI. At a preliminary meeting to discuss the confirmation, several committee Democrats argued for first moving forward on impeaching the president and elevating Speaker Albert, who was next in the succession line, so he could select the new vice president—a suggestion that both Rodino and Albert strongly opposed. To prevent this strategy from gaining traction, Rodino appealed to all the members of the House Democratic Caucus on October 17 and won their unqualified endorsement to proceed with the Ford nomination as planned. When the Saturday Night Massacre sparked the formal launching of the impeachment inquiry the following week, Speaker Albert reaffirmed the leadership's support for proceeding with the Ford confirmation.[20]

While Rodino hoped to begin the hearings following this endorsement, he felt a special obligation to conduct a thorough investigation to ensure that there were no future revelations like those that had forced Spiro Agnew to resign. The committee staff began compiling detailed briefing books for members, and Rodino requested access to Ford's personal and public records. Recapping his own conversations with a long list of political and civic leaders in Michigan, Rodino noted that there was "nothing derogatory" uncovered about Ford.[21] However, these efforts could not match the depth and scope of the background investigation conducted by the FBI, and Rodino wanted all the members of the committee to have access to this valuable information. Acting Attorney General Robert Bork refused, insisting that only the chairman and the ranking member receive the FBI's report, which contained sensitive personal information. Rodino refused to schedule a hearing until everyone had access. After several weeks of negotiations, they finally agreed to a compromise that added six members to the distribution list.[22]

For the members of the Judiciary Committee, the vice presidential confirmation unintentionally proved to be a dress rehearsal for the impeachment inquiry that was looming on the horizon. The televised hearings introduced them to a national audience and revealed the collective challenges as well as the individual opportunities of conducting legislative business in the midst of a media frenzy. Rodino was committed to ensuring that all the members had an ample opportunity to be heard, and he was prepared to hold evening sessions rather than curtail debate. Aiming to avoid duplication, he proposed to his Democratic colleagues that they coordinate their questions, a suggestion that was largely ignored. He was more successful in ensuring that all members followed the protocol for safeguarding highly confidential information that required them to sign out and return briefing books, and he boasted that there were no leaks during the month-long investigation.[23]

The hearing that began shortly after ten in the morning on November 15 embraced a historic trifecta: the first selection of a vice president outside the electoral process, the first implementation of the Twenty-Fifth Amendment, and the first time the House of Representatives considered any executive branch nomination. After recognizing the significance of the meeting, Rodino focused his opening remarks on two key issues that placed him at odds with his fellow liberals on the committee: his opposition to delaying the confirmation process and his belief that, under the amendment, "the President has the right to nominate a man with whom he can work in concert, ideologically and politically."[24] Ford acknowledged his many friends and colleagues on the dais, including his freshman classmate Peter Rodino; he assured the panel that he expected no special favors. Most of the Republicans chose to ignore this request and were very deferential, asking few difficult questions during the two days of his appearance before the committee.[25]

The Democrats compensated for this generosity by repeatedly pressing the nominee on a variety of issues ranging from his record on civil rights to his relationship with Richard Nixon. Ford retained his genial demeanor under often intensive grilling until the hearing focused on his unsuccessful effort in 1970 to impeach Supreme Court Justice William O. Douglas for allegedly accepting payment for writing a magazine article. Ford's uncharacteristically personal campaign to oust the liberal jurist had engendered much criticism at the time and provoked tough questioning from committee members, requiring him to make additional appearances before the panel. With a final vote on the nomination scheduled in the Senate and Speaker Albert anxious for a resolution, Rodino decided he needed to end debate and bring the proceedings to a close. On November 29, the chairman and twenty-eight members of the House Judiciary Committee approved Ford's nomination. The eight liberal Democrats, who were his harshest interrogators, did not join them.[26]

When the House began six hours of debate the following week, Rodino served as floor manager, recounting the details of the investigation and providing an overview of the hearings. This exhaustive process, he told his colleagues, had only deepened his admiration for the nominee. Then to the surprise of those in the chamber and the press gallery, Rodino announced he was going to oppose the nomination. "I vote, not against Gerald Ford's worth as a man of great integrity," he explained, "but in dissent with the present administration's indifference to the plight of so many Americans."[27] Clearly at odds with his own stated belief that a president had the right to select a compatible nominee, Rodino was responding to the criticism of Nixon and

Ford that was pervasive throughout the Tenth District. He was one of only thirty-five House Democrats to vote against Ford. At a moment when he was trying to establish his bipartisan credentials on impeachment, he was criticized by Republicans and the press. The new vice president was considerably more understanding of the political crosswinds that had influenced Rodino's decision, reassuring him, "that last vote was fully understood by me."[28]

The successful completion of the confirmation hearings prompted renewed calls for the Judiciary Committee to begin the impeachment inquiry. Rodino's Democratic colleagues regularly complained at caucus meetings about the delay, Tip O'Neill repeatedly badgered him on the House floor to take some action, and Republicans on the committee proposed the creation of a small ad hoc group to begin the preliminary phase of the inquiry behind closed doors. Feeling this pressure, Rodino held an informal meeting of the panel on December 10. The ninety-minute session offered little new information except the rising tally of largely pro-impeachment mail.[29] Frustrated, a dozen minority members of the committee participated in a special order on the House floor the following week to criticize Rodino's inaction. All of the speakers demanded that the chairman establish a clear timetable indicating when he planned to begin the impeachment process and a date for its expected conclusion.[30]

At the moment when patience seemed to be evaporating on both sides of the aisle, Rodino was finally ready to hire a special counsel and move forward. He had struggled to define the specific criteria for a position he considered critically important to the success of the inquiry, which had slowed the selection process. The three hundred names collected from a variety of sources were eventually winnowed down to a short list of a dozen serious contenders Rodino personally interviewed. Among these finalists was John Doar, director of an anti-poverty program in New York City and a former senior official at the civil rights division of the Justice Department. Not closely following the Watergate scandal and unwilling to campaign for the post, Doar agreed to have his name added to the list and traveled to Washington to meet with Rodino. Doar assured him that he had no predetermined opinion on

President Nixon's innocence or guilt and fully supported the goal of conducting a nonpartisan inquiry, the threshold qualification for the job. Rodino was impressed with Doar's experience and methodical approach to building a case, which created an immediate rapport between the two. In addition to his impressive credentials, Rodino was thrilled to learn that Doar had started his government career as a Republican appointee in the Eisenhower administration. Offering him the position, Rodino cemented the most consequential relationship of the impeachment inquiry and sent a clear signal of how he intended to conduct it.[31]

Two days before the start of the Christmas recess, the chairman held a press conference to announce the appointment of John Doar as the committee's special impeachment counsel "to ensure that the committee will have the benefit of a full, thorough, fair and objective presentation of the law and the facts."[32] Hoping to reclaim some of his bipartisan sheen, he stressed Doar's Republican affiliation and interrupted his remarks to read a congratulatory message from Melvin R. Laird, the outgoing domestic policy adviser to President Nixon who sponsored Doar for his first government job. Although Edward Hutchinson complained that he was not consulted in advance of this "bipartisan" decision, most of the press coverage highlighted Doar's party affiliation and commended Rodino for making the choice. The following morning, the two appeared together on NBC's *Today* program and assured a national television audience that the impeachment inquiry was finally underway and would be conducted in a spirit of bipartisanship.[33]

Doar went to work immediately to create the physical structure needed to house such a sensitive operation. The House of Representatives had recently purchased the old Hotel Congressional, the place where Rodino celebrated his first day as a congressman in 1949, to serve as an annex and provide additional office space in close proximity to the existing congressional buildings on Capitol Hill. Rodino requested that Speaker Albert allocate the entire second floor for the impeachment inquiry, and Doar took possession of this unrenovated and oddly configured collection of former hotel rooms. Among the first things he did was to install a variety of security measures to protect the confidential and classified information he expected to gather. A guard in the lobby controlled strict access to the second floor where another guard ensured that only approved staff and committee members could enter.[34]

Doar's greatest challenge was to assemble a team of highly qualified and skillful individuals willing to relocate immediately for an indeterminate period, at a comparatively modest salary, to do a highly demanding job. He inherited a preexisting core staff that included several attorneys already designated as majority or minority counsels, partisan designations Rodino had hoped to avoid. Reluctantly, the chairman agreed acceded to a Republican request for comity by approving the appointment of Illinois attorney Albert E. "Bert" Jenner to serve as minority special counsel.[35] Rodino instructed Doar to ignore these distinctions and maintain a nonpartisan operation at the annex. Doar strictly followed this guidance, quickly establishing a close relationship with Jenner and never asking any prospective job candidates about their political affiliation.[36] Future senator and presidential nominee Hillary Rodham Clinton, hired by Doar to join the impeachment unit shortly after she received her Yale law degree and before her marriage, confirmed that there was little distinction between minority and majority staff. "We worked very hard to overcome any sense of separation," she recollected, a view shared by her minority counterpart William Weld, also destined for a career in politics as the Republican governor of Massachusetts.[37] Doar moved quickly to expand this work force, recruiting a mixture of senior attorneys, seasoned prosecutors, and recent law school graduates. They were divided into a group responsible for legal research and the larger division handling the factual investigation. Within six weeks, almost ninety people were assembled on the second floor of the congressional annex, and many were already working fifteen hours a day, seven days a week.[38]

Doar's herculean task was made more difficult by the opposition of Jerry Zeifman and his new political patron, Jack Brooks. Although Zeifman was still in charge of overseeing the committee's non-impeachment staff and legislative agenda, he focused much of his energy on sabotaging Doar. Democrat Walter Flowers witnessed many instances of Zeifman "sowing discontent" or "back biting," which he attributed to "sour grapes."[39] When Doar first arrived, Zeifman attempted to inject himself into decisions about staff, budget, and planning for the impeachment inquiry, creating immediate tension between the two counsels. Doar was promised complete autonomy, and he complained to Rodino, who strongly reprimanded Zeifman for this unauthorized interference. A thwarted Zeifman found a willing supporter in Brooks; they shared an animus toward Doar and a frustration with Rodino's management style. Brooks, resenting the selection of a Republican and finding Doar's manner irritating, rarely missed an opportunity to criticize or snipe at him. Attacking Doar provided the added benefit of indirectly criticizing Rodino, which neither Brooks nor Zeifman were willing to do directly in public. The two continued to stoke an undertow of dissent throughout the impeachment proceedings and further added to the myriad of challenges already confronting Doar and Rodino.[40]

While Doar toiled to set up his operation, Rodino had spent most of the congressional recess in Washington working on impeachment. He had reassembled the ad hoc subcommittee group, now formally known as the Advisory Committee to the Impeachment Inquiry of the House Judiciary Committee, and they met several times in January.[41] Among the important decisions Rodino faced was whether the inquiry should be conducted in public. The good government nonprofit Common Cause was pressing for transparent proceedings, and pro-impeachment Democrats wanted nationally televised hearings to make the case against Nixon. But Rodino considered the showmanship of the Senate Watergate hearings to be an inappropriate model for a solemn constitutional undertaking. He decided that the best way to ensure fairness and nonpartisanship was for Doar and his staff to present evidentiary briefings to the committee in executive session until the investigation was completed and ready for a public presentation. He planned to brief the press after every private session, and the committee's business meetings would remain open as required by the rules of the House.[42]

To strengthen the committee's ability to obtain material from other sources, including the White House, Rodino concluded that the entire House of Representatives, not just the speaker, should empower the panel to issue subpoenas and conduct the impeachment inquiry. He raised this idea at the January 24 meeting of the advisory group and, learning from his past mistake, proposed that the ranking minority member share the subpoena authority. Rodino presciently argued that it was vital to establish the committee's unassailable jurisdiction against any future challenge from the White House, and he secured the backing of the Democratic leadership to proceed.[43] While the pro-impeachment Democrats objected to sharing the subpoena power, some Republicans wanted to add a fixed termination date to the resolution, which both the chairman and Doar opposed as impractical. Wisely, Rodino had secured the endorsement of House Minority Leader John J. Rhodes before floor consideration, and Rhodes argued that Rodino's demonstrated commitment to nonpartisanship made it unnecessary to include a deadline. The resolution was approved 410 to 4, finally providing the Judiciary Committee with a solid bipartisan foundation for its proceedings.[44]

Impeachment now occupied all of Rodino's time in Washington, and he adhered to a hectic schedule that began earlier and ended later. He was forced to give up his weekly paddleball games in the gym; the combination of no physical exercise and irregular meals added several pounds to his short frame, not a healthy development for someone a few months away from his sixty-fifth birthday. When he flew home to New Jersey on the weekend, he always carried a briefcase filled with documents to read and study before he returned to Capitol Hill. Shouldering these burdens remained a daunting task, and he recalled that "I would always have terrible nightmares."[45] In February, he experienced severe chest pains after leaving a committee meeting and was admitted to Bethesda Naval Hospital that afternoon. After a series of tests, the doctors concluded he was suffering from exhaustion and recommended he remain in the hospital for several days of bedrest. Rodino believed that this brief hospital respite, which went largely unnoticed, was invaluable and helped reinvigorate him physically and mentally just as the impeachment pressure was escalating.[46]

Following the passage of the impeachment resolution, Rodino and Doar accelerated their ongoing effort to acquire the materials they needed, particularly the vast array of testimony and other evidence collected by the Senate Watergate committee. When the Senate panel lost its legal battle to obtain the secret White House tape recordings in early February, Chairman Sam Ervin canceled plans for further hearings and was finally ready to share their extensive archive that included ten thousand pages of testimony and volumes of supporting documents. By the end of the month, this extensive collection was added to the material from the first Watergate investigation by the House Banking Committee, safely stored on the second floor of the congressional annex and ready for review.[47]

Obtaining the large trove of information in the possession of Special Prosecutor Leon Jaworski was considerably more complicated. Since congressional pressure had forced the Justice Department to replace Archibald Cox, his successor had resumed gathering evidence for presentation in Judge Sirica's courtroom to the grand jury that was still empaneled to hear the Watergate cases. Beyond the first group of tapes that Cox requested and that the appeals court forced Nixon to surrender, Jaworski had secured an additional inventory of White House recordings before the president refused any further cooperation. Despite their poor audio quality and multiple defects of mysterious origin, including the infamous eighteen-minute gap, the tapes were a valuable resource that Rodino wanted to examine. The chairman believed the committee had a right to this material because the Constitution gave the House the sole power to impeach. He argued, "If we can't do the things necessary to exercise this responsibility, where are we?" Dispatching Doar to meet with Jaworski to negotiate an arrangement for viewing the relevant files, he personally followed up with a phone call and letter.[48]

Regardless of Rodino's arguments, Jaworski refused his request because he believed that the rules governing secret grand jury testimony prohibited him from sharing evidence without the direct authorization of the presiding judge. He also expressed serious concerns to Doar about the security of any transferred material and recommended the committee wait until the pending Watergate trials were completed in the spring. Frustrated with this politically impossible suggestion, Rodino decided to move forward anyway with preparations for the future arrival of confidential material.[49] Under unanimously approved procedures, the chairman, ranking minority member, and the two special counsels were given responsibility for screening and determining the distribution of impeachment-related materials sent to the committee. All files and recordings they decided to make available to the members would have to be viewed in a secure examination room at the annex.[50]

The decision to prepare for receiving documents was timely; the special prosecutor was proceeding with his own plan to facilitate the delivery of the information the committee requested. The Watergate grand jury had expressed a desire to include Richard Nixon in the list of indictments it was preparing, an action Jaworski believed would prompt a legal challenge. Seeking an alternative, he proposed that the jurors name the president as an unindicted coconspirator in a sealed decision and then call on the judge to transfer this finding and the supporting evidence to the House Judiciary Committee. On March 1, the grand jury handed down indictments of seven prominent former Nixon administration and reelection campaign officials on multiple counts of conspiracy, bribery, and perjury. The jury foreman then silently presented Judge Sirica with two locked briefcases filled with evidence and two large, sealed envelopes. The first missive contained a fifty-page fact-finding memorandum outlining the grand jury's reasons for adding the president as an unindicted coconspirator; the other enclosed a letter asking that this information and the accompanying material be delivered to the committee. The unexpected presentation sparked considerable speculation, and the judge announced plans to hold a hearing on the grand jury's publicly undisclosed request.[51]

In considering the grand jury's request, Judge Sirica's primary concern was to ensure that any referral of material did not compromise the ability of the plaintiffs to receive a fair trial, and he invited their attorneys to a hearing in his courtroom. He also extended an invitation to John Doar, which posed a dilemma for the committee. While anxious to receive the two briefcases, members were reluctant to take any action that might breach the separation of powers between the two branches, and Rodino convened a meeting to decide whether or not to participate. Jack Brooks and others opposed any cooperation and wanted to issue an immediate subpoena for the grand jury's evidence. As a longtime proponent of the belief that the courts had no role in the impeachment process, Rodino had added credibility when he reminded the impatient Brooks that securing the material voluntarily was faster than a protracted legal confrontation. The committee agreed to send Doar and Jenner to the courthouse as observers.[52]

Following the hearing, Rodino sent a formal request for the material, and Sirica ruled that there was a "compelling need" for the Judiciary Committee to examine this evidence, a decision upheld a few days later on appeal. He requested that the panel prevent any inappropriate disclosure of the confidential material, and Rodino instructed the impeachment staff to decline all future interview requests from the press.[53] Doar and Jenner appeared in Judge Sirica's chambers on March 26, where a clerk from the special prosecutor's office inventoried each document, transcript, and tape before returning them to the briefcases. Accompanied by a police escort and a group of reporters, the two counsels made the return trip to Capitol Hill. The next day, Rodino and Hutchinson spent several hours at the impeachment office beginning the process of examining this latest addition to their evidentiary inventory and listening for the first time to secret recordings of presidential conversations in the White House.[54]

The last remaining holder of information vital to the committee's inquiry was the most uncooperative. Although President Nixon had promised in his State of the Union address to cooperate with the impeachment inquiry, he added that he was not willing to do anything that weakened the presidency.[55] Determining exactly what this caveat meant triggered the start of a contentious and protracted battle between the committee and the White House. The president's representative in this dispute was James D. St. Clair, a prominent Boston trial lawyer appointed in late January to direct the dozen lawyers at the White House responsible for all Watergate-related matters. Following the approval of the impeachment resolution and prior to Judge Sirica's ruling, the president had instructed his new counsel to begin discussions with the committee. The cordial tone of the first meeting encouraged John Doar's hope that they could establish a positive working relationship. He requested that the White House provide the material already submitted to the special prosecutor's office and followed this with a request for additional tape recordings and a detailed explanation of the White House indexing system to help the committee identify other relevant material. Responding to St. Clair's concerns about security protocol, he sent him a copy of the recently adopted rules.[56]

Doar's optimism was quickly dashed following the grand jury's indictments and request to send their evidence to Capitol Hill. The Nixon White House now launched an offensive to stonewall and attack the committee. At a televised press conference on March 6 largely focused on Watergate, Nixon announced that he was prepared to send the committee the same information he previously sent to the special prosecutor, which Judge Sirica was likely to transfer anyway, and then questioned the need for supplying any additional information. This suggestion of legislative overreach was echoed a few days later, when an unnamed White House source leaked Doar's letter to the *New York Times* and claimed his broad request for more than forty additional tapes was a "fishing expedition." Echoing this same inaccurate exaggeration, Nixon's press secretary Ron Zeigler attacked the committee and asserted that "the mere fact of an impeachment inquiry does not give Congress the right to back up a truck and haul off White House files."[57]

If the goal of this aggressive tone was to goad the committee into taking some hasty or careless action as several press reports indicated, the White House seriously underestimated Peter Rodino's patience. He convened a Democratic caucus to defuse the angry demand for an aggressive response to the leaking of Doar's letter and the president's apparent unwillingness to provide the requested information. Several members were prepared to introduce subpoena resolutions immediately, and Rodino spent much of the two-hour meeting attempting to discourage what he considered a premature escalation. The chairman reminded the group that neither Nixon nor St. Clair had explicitly refused the request, and he argued for an interim step to resolve the dispute that might win Republican support. Securing their backing for a calibrated response, he held a press conference with Edward Hutchinson to refute the White House charges of legislative excess and announce that the committee would not issue a subpoena for documents that they still hoped to obtain voluntarily. His reasonable approach to this initial rebuff from the executive branch helped prevent an overreaction and, for the moment, bolstered his efforts to preserve the committee's fragile unity.[58]

Rodino's ability to forge a consensus was put to a greater test over the thorny question of allowing St. Clair to participate in the committee's proceedings. Determined to create a framework encouraging bipartisanship, Rodino and Doar envisioned a process similar to a grand jury where evidence was presented in a nonconfrontational manner before jurors who would then decide whether or not to go forward with an indictment, or, in this case, articles of impeachment. St. Clair did not share this view and wanted to participate fully in the inquiry, presenting his own evidence and witnesses. This proposal threatened to reignite a partisan dispute with Republicans supporting the request, and Democrats opposing it. Usually the bridge between these two factions, Rodino strongly believed that St. Clair's participation would alter both the focus and tone of the inquiry. He was surprised to discover that all the Republicans disagreed with him. "Pete shook his head," Tom Railsback recounted of their conversation in the House gym, "and acted as though he thought we were opening a can of worms."[59] At the committee's briefing session on March 20, members began two days of heated debate over the issue. Anticipating a straight party-line tally, Rodino postponed the vote. Unable to move forward with the presentation of evidence until this was settled, Rodino finally capitulated and asked Doar to include St. Clair's participation in the proposed rules for the presentation of evidence, which the committee approved a few weeks later.[60]

At this same meeting, the committee voted to approve the first congressional subpoena ever issued to a president of the United States to secure the White House tape recordings requested in February. The arrival at the annex a few weeks earlier of the tapes and transcripts from the Watergate grand jury was a transformational occasion. Compared to the static nature of the paper documents from the Ervin committee, hearing Nixon's actual voice engaged in conversations others had previously described was revelatory and at times shocking. Under the procedures the committee established, Rodino and Hutchinson were responsible for screening the tapes to exclude any material not germane to the inquiry. This arduous job was further complicated because of the poor audio quality of the recordings, a problem the committee would partially mitigate with the assistance of technical experts, and this required frequent reliance on the written transcripts prepared by the White House. Rodino and Hutchinson spent several mornings sitting in a small room within the inquiry's second floor office suite listening to these absorbing and convoluted discussions through bulky headphones. Early in this process, Rodino was stunned to hear Nixon "using language like you think you'd hear in the bar room."[61] The president's conversations were not only punctuated with expletives, they were heavily sprinkled with ethnic slurs including demeaning characterizations of Italian Americans. Although Rodino was deeply offended, he believed Nixon's comments were irrelevant to the committee's investigation. Concerned that any disclosure might prejudice members or raise questions about his own objectivity, he proposed deleting these portions of the tapes to maintain the fairness of the proceedings. Hutchinson, anxious to avoid embarrassing the president, readily agreed to keep this secret.[62]

For John Doar and his staff feverishly evaluating and preparing the evidentiary material for presentation to the committee, the tapes were proving to be invaluable; obtaining the additional requested tapes was a top priority. Rodino issued a warning to the president when the committee met on April 4 that "there comes a time when patience and accommodation can begin to undermine the process in which we are engaged" and instructed Doar to send a letter to St. Clair demanding the requested conversations within five days.[63] When the president's counsel responded on the eve of the deadline to ask for more time, Rodino was unwilling to wait any longer and decided he must finally act. While Rodino and Hutchinson were empowered to issue subpoenas, they had agreed to seek the committee's approval for any action involving the president. After slightly narrowing the request, the committee voted 33 to 3 to authorize the issuance of a subpoena directing the president to produce forty-two recorded conversations no later than April 25. Sending an accompanying letter to Nixon, Rodino informed the president that the committee intended to request additional recordings, which Doar did the following week. The day before the subpoenaed tapes were due on Capitol Hill, St. Clair asked for an additional five days to comply because he was having trouble assembling all the material. Several Democrats were ready to charge the president with contempt of Congress, and Rodino, regarding this as an unhelpful distraction from the impeachment inquiry, persuaded most of them to join the Republicans, albeit reluctantly, in granting the extension.[64]

Richard Nixon was the one person who knew for certain what these tape recordings contained, knowledge that fueled his determination not to share them. Since the existence of the White House recording system was first disclosed in the summer of 1973, he had taken extraordinary steps to prevent public exposure of his private conversations. On the evening of April 29, the president delivered his formal answer to the Judiciary Committee in a nationally televised address from the White House. Dramatically positioned next to a large pile of official looking blue notebooks, Nixon announced that he was publicly releasing and sending to the committee detailed transcripts he had prepared of all the subpoenaed conversations and the recordings relinquished to the grand jury. He invited Rodino and Hutchinson to certify the accuracy of the documents by listening to the original tapes at the White House, a task he knew was laborious and impossible without technical support from the impeachment inquiry staff, who he had purposely not invited. Nixon bragged that his decision to waive executive privilege over such an extensive amount of confidential information was unprecedented and demonstrated that he had nothing to hide.[65]

Nixon's gambit to bolster his political standing and shift the burden of proof back to Capitol Hill posed a dilemma for Peter Rodino. While pro-impeachment Democrats immediately rejected the president's response and were eager to proceed with contempt charges, most Republicans accepted the transcript offer, and Hutchinson told reporters that he considered the president to be in full compliance with the subpoena. Nixon's ambiguous message, intentionally crafted to create a split along party lines, made it difficult to forge a bipartisan response, and Rodino struggled to find a consensus among the members.[66]

This task was made significantly harder when he began examining the contents of the boxes delivered to the congressional annex the next morning. The thirteen hundred pages of transcripts were not an equivalent substitute for the requested audio tapes; tone and inflection were key indicators of a speaker's intent, which were missing in the written documents. In addition, all of the supporting material listed in the subpoena and many of the requested conversations was missing. Most of the blue notebooks featured on the broadcast proved to be half empty props, and the remaining transcripts were heavily edited, replete with redacted sentences or paragraphs that produced incomplete and unintelligible narratives. Equally disturbing, there were serious discrepancies between the transcripts the inquiry staff had prepared for the tapes already in their possession and the versions produced at the White House for the same recordings. Whether this was the result of the superior audio quality the committee's technicians produced, the president's intentional tampering, or both, it called into question the reliability of all the newly arrived documents.[67]

These revelations persuaded Rodino to abandon his search for a bipartisan consensus and instead ask the committee to reject Nixon's response. Convening an evening meeting on May 1, the chairman outlined his concerns and asked John Doar to present a detailed report on the omitted material and flawed text. Rodino explained his refusal to accept the president's offer to verify the transcripts, highlighting the enormous practical difficulties, and reminded his colleagues that they did not subpoena transcripts. Accepting them "would only raise questions about the committee's inquiry."[68] Except for a few members who persisted in their efforts to declare Nixon in contempt of Congress, all the Democrats supported a resolution to send a nonthreatening one-sentence letter informing the president that he had failed to comply with the committee's subpoena, which Rodino hoped would persuade Nixon to reconsider his decision. On the Republican side of the room, only William Cohen was unwilling to accept the president's response to the subpoena and his courageous decision was decisive in the narrow 20-to-18 vote.[69]

Before the committee's letter arrived at the White House, the newly released transcripts ignited a firestorm that helped to heal the partisan divide within the committee. The president had expected to receive a positive boost from his "selfless" gesture and in anticipation ordered widespread distribution of the text, instructing the US Government Printing Office to publish all the transcripts as a single volume. The morning following his televised address, most major newspapers began featuring daily excerpts of the conversations. The government's paperback edition sold out in a few hours. But Nixon had seriously miscalculated; the widespread public scrutiny of these secret discussions generated almost universal condemnation, not praise. Although Nixon personally edited and approved the transcripts, the final adulterated version still contained crude language, shadowy discussions, and multiple instances of words replaced with new catchphrases: "inaudible," "unintelligible," and the ridiculed "expletive deleted." Capitol Hill offices were besieged with calls and telegrams from outraged constituents protesting this defilement of the presidency and demanding either that Nixon surrender all the actual tape recordings or resign. Republican newspapers like the *Los Angeles Times* ran editorials demanding Nixon's removal from office—his already anemic popularity further plummeted. Members of Congress, including the Republican leaders in both chambers who had praised the president a week earlier, now condemned him or called for his resignation.[70]

At the Judiciary Committee, where only Rodino and Hutchinson had listened to the tape recordings, the transcript revelations engendered bipartisan shock. A number of Republicans began to reconsider their opposition to requesting additional tape recordings from the White House. Only two weeks after the committee barely mustered a majority for a simple one-line response to Nixon, Rodino's proposal to issue a new subpoena for previously requested recordings that the White House never delivered was approved by a lopsided 37-to-1 vote. Subsequent action over the next month to issue additional subpoenas received strong bipartisan support, reflecting a new collective recognition among members, regardless of their views on impeachment, that the tape recordings of the president's conversations were a critical part of the inquiry.[71]

Nixon's reaction to this public furor was to abandon any pretense of cooperation. Dismissing the committee's second subpoena, he served notice that he would refuse all future requests for information. While this preemptive declaration did not deter the committee, it did help Rodino secure bipartisan backing for a strongly worded final warning he sent to the president on May 30, declaring that his refusal to comply with lawful subpoenas was "a grave matter" that "in and of themselves might constitute a ground for impeachment."[72] Nixon's unilateral decision to stop sharing any information also prompted Judge Sirica to issue a subpoena for the tapes the White House was refusing to relinquish to the special prosecutor. When James St. Clair moved to quash this order on appeal, Leon Jaworski responded by successfully petitioning the United States Supreme Court to hear the case under an expedited process.[73]

Constantly pressured to complete the inquiry, Rodino had decided not to wait for the subpoenaed material. On May 9, the committee began a series of briefings on the evidence acquired and evaluated for the past five months by John Doar and his staff. After brief introductory remarks, the chairman announced plans for a rigorous schedule of long and intensive sessions in the upcoming weeks, with brief interruptions only for lunch and roll call votes. The audience was then asked to leave, and, except for the occasional open business meeting, the doors remained shut. The exiled press contingent huddled outside the hearing room in the first floor corridor of the Rayburn House Office Building. This stakeout, dubbed "the spectacle" by *Newsday's* Myron S. "Mike" Waldman, became a regular feature of the proceedings. Whenever the committee was in session, eager reporters patiently waited to besiege exiting members and receive a sanitized summary of the day's events from Rodino and Hutchinson.[74]

Inside the committee's hearing room, attendance was limited to members, selected inquiry and committee staff, and the president's legal representatives led by James St. Clair, who was not permitted to ask questions. John Doar sat at a table facing the members organized along the two-tiered dais, according to their party affiliation and seniority. From this vantage point, the special counsel shouldered the daily burdens of leading this arduous undertaking. Months earlier, Rodino and Doar had settled on a format and structure that simply presented "statements of information" without interpretation and allowed members to reach their own conclusions. Working without any respite since January, the impeachment staff had developed more than six hundred statements that were placed in thirty-six notebooks and cross-referenced to all the supporting evidence in the committee's possession. The material was organized to reflect the specific areas of possible impeachable offenses that the committee had identified. The inquiry staff was also instructed to prepare separate written reports on Nixon's personal finances, impoundment of appropriated funds, and the secret bombing of Cambodia.[75]

Rodino had ordered the wiring of the Judiciary Committee's hearing room to allow each member to listen to tape-recorded conversations through individual headphones. Doar started his briefings with Watergate, the broadest subject area and one that required four notebooks to contain all the evidentiary material. He carefully recounted the events leading to the burglary and the cover-up, relying heavily on testimony from the grand jury and the Ervin committee. To establish the president's involvement in these activities, he then asked the committee for the first time to put on their headphones and listen to a tape-recorded conversation. While the transcripts released two weeks earlier were disturbing, the impact of finally hearing Nixon's voice, greatly enhanced by the panel's technical experts, was overpowering and stunned many of the president's strongest defenders. Edward Mezvinsky, a freshman Democrat from Iowa, was not expecting members to be shocked after reading the transcripts. But he recalled that "most of my colleagues seemed to be subdued...some looked upset, and a few seemed to be flushed with either embarrassment or anger."[76]

As the sessions began, Rodino was particularly worried about protecting the confidentiality of all the materials included in the notebooks and scheduled for presentation. He appreciated that a security breach would provide White House officials with a new opportunity to claim that the proceedings were unfair, and he repeatedly urged his colleagues to obey these restrictions. Despite his admonitions, a week after the initial briefing, the *Washington Post* ran a story referencing details from one of Doar's information statements. The story extensively quoted from an unreleased transcript, all provided to the newspaper by an anonymous source. James St. Clair immediately lodged a protest with the chairman as did Railsback and several other Republican members. Some Democrats exploited this opportunity to renew their call for ending the closed sessions. But Rodino was not swayed, and, expressing dismay over the leaks, he ordered the numbering of the notebooks and their collection at the end of each session for safekeeping at the annex.[77]

For the next six weeks, the special partnership between Peter Rodino and John Doar was on full display as they carefully guided the committee through a critical phase of the inquiry where previously unsettled views began to crystallize into firm opinions. The two met early every morning to prepare for the upcoming session, spent the day together inside the hearing room, stood side by side at the regular press briefings, and regrouped at night in the chairman's office to assess their progress. Rodino's confidence in Doar was unwavering, and he considered it an important part of his job to serve as a buffer for his special counsel, shielding him from anything that might distract or interfere with moving the process forward. To accomplish this, Rodino was often forced to act like a schoolmaster in charge of a class of unruly students. At every session he constantly requested that his colleagues follow the procedures they had previously approved and regularly ignored. The most egregious violations were the constant interruptions before a presentation was completed that often sparked a protracted debate between the members, further slowing the pace of the deliberations, which was a favorite topic of complaint by these same offenders. Rodino did his best to keep the committee on course, tapping into his deep reservoir of patience to avoid alienating anyone, and he rarely showed his justified exasperation with the undisciplined behavior of his colleagues. While some Democrats privately complained that the Republicans were exploiting the chairman's genial nature to delay the inquiry, Rodino was convinced that whatever the frustrations, taking the required time to present all the facts and ensuring that every member of the committee heard them was essential.[78]

Sitting across from the chairman, John Doar's daily responsibility was to either present information or coordinate presentations he had delegated to his staff. His normally somber persona and colorless speaking voice helped to emphasize the dispassionate and factual nature of his briefings. He usually initiated a presentation by reading the statement of information being considered and followed this with a monotone recitation of all the supporting evidence, an undertaking that could last for hours. The reaction from the members was mixed, ranging from intense interest and appreciation to boredom and restlessness. For Republican Hamilton Fish, the sessions were invaluable, and he thought Doar "did a tremendous job, terribly painstaking." Across the aisle, his fellow New Yorker Elizabeth Holtzman found the scope and detail of the information overwhelming and recalled that it was "like being in quicksand."[79] The pro-impeachment hardliners chafed at the low-key, nonjudgmental character of Doar's performance, and others complained that the presentations were too fragmented. General Counsel Jerry Zeifman, who never missed a chance to undermine his nemesis, was glad to help circulate this criticism within the committee room and outside to the press.[80]

As the sessions continued, several of Doar's liberal critics asked William Dixon, an attorney on the regular committee staff supervised by Zeifman, to prepare a series of background papers to summarize the evidence and frame the unfolding case against the president. Without the knowledge of Rodino or Doar, Dixon produced fourteen memoranda on likely impeachable offenses relying on the confidential material in the statement of information notebooks. Several of these documents were leaked to the *Washington Post*. The revelations brought a quick denunciation from the White House, and Rodino scrambled to reassure the Republicans that he did not authorize this inappropriate use of staff.[81] The leaks triggered renewed criticism of the impeachment inquiry, and some questioned whether the committee was up to the task. Senate Majority Leader Mike Mansfield condemned the leaks and suggested that the committee's lack of progress was jeopardizing the possibility of conducting an impeachment trial before the November election. A month earlier, the release of the transcripts had eroded Nixon's support. Now the press was reporting that "the discipline and coherence which Rodino has sought to maintain in the impeachment inquiry have been seriously eroded."[82]

At this low point, Rodino found himself entangled in his own press imbroglio. Regularly shadowed by a band of reporters, he let his guard down in late June and speculated that, with John Doar's statement of information presentations finally completed, he expected all the Democrats and a handful of Republicans were likely to vote for impeachment in light of the overwhelming evidence. Jack Nelson of the *Los Angeles Times* considered this a major scoop; the chairman had never opined on the impeachment views of committee members, including his own. Rodino later disputed Nelson's account, and other reporters regarded the comments as "off the record." When he saw Nelson's article the next day, a horrified Rodino rushed to the House floor to contain any fallout, declaring the story was inaccurate and recruiting several of the committee's southern Democrats to confirm he never asked them about their vote. Republican Robert McClory joined in defending Rodino. Thanks to the reservoir of goodwill he had built up over the preceding months, the episode did little permanent damage.[83]

Following the Fourth of July recess, the committee's fortunes began to improve. Rodino had finally ended a lingering dispute with the Republicans when he agreed to accept their proposed list of witnesses to appear before the panel, and he announced that the committee would begin the impeachment debate the week of July 22.[84] Rodino also embarked on a strategic effort to enhance the committee's profile and inform the public of the growing evidence against the president by releasing the statements of information before the start of the debate. With bipartisan backing, he instructed Doar to delete any classified information and prepare the remaining materials for dissemination.

During the first three weeks of July, the committee published thousands of pages of material thematically organized and deliberately timed to avoid overwhelming the press and the public. Many details from this material were excerpted in newspapers or reported on television, and a chart comparing the committee's transcripts of eight recorded conversations to the White House's original flawed version was widely reproduced. Publicizing all this material was a master stroke; it offered tangible proof of what the committee was actually doing behind those closed doors. The members were praised for their hard work and diligence, providing an important boost as the panel was preparing to begin the final phase of the impeachment inquiry.[85]

The challenge now facing the committee was to cull and shape this mountain of information into a framework to serve as the basis for impeaching the president of the United States. With the start of the debate now firmly set for July 24, Rodino organized informal study groups within the committee's Democratic caucus to begin the task of dividing the evidence and identifying its significance, an action Hutchinson quickly mirrored on the minority side. At the request of several Democrats, Doar's deputy, Dick Cates, offered a series of briefings where he attempted to connect and weave the evidentiary material into a cohesive narrative making the case against Richard Nixon. Because the committee was hearing from witnesses during the day, these tutorials were scheduled early in the morning, at night, or on weekends. The personally popular Cates attracted a loyal following, including a few Republicans.[86]

Recognizing that many committee members still needed further guidance for the deliberations ahead, Rodino decided it was time to abandon neutrality. He instructed Doar to prepare a case for impeachment in the closing summation he was scheduled to present when the witness hearings were finished. Not comfortable assuming the role of advocate, Doar balked at the directive and only reluctantly deferred to Rodino's judgment that this change in tone was both appropriate and essential. Overcoming his private reservations, the special counsel delivered a forceful and surprisingly emotional presentation to the committee beginning on July 19 that cogently outlined the five fundamental allegations against the president. It offered draft articles of impeachment for each: abuse of power, obstruction of justice, contempt of Congress, failure to faithfully execute the laws, and denigration of the presidency.[87] The Republicans presented a rebuttal maintaining that there was no clear case for impeachment, and White House press secretary Ron Zeigler dismissed the entire committee as "a kangaroo court."[88]

The response Rodino most cared about was from the group he had considered critically important from the outset: southern Democrats and moderate Republicans. These members of the panel, publicly undecided and falling between the hardline pro-impeachers and stalwart Nixon apologists, would determine the ultimate fate of the president in both the hearing room and on the House floor. Although the testimony from the witnesses who appeared before the committee throughout July was not revelatory, it helped these four Republicans (Tom Railsback, William Cohen, Hamilton Fish, and Caldwell Butler) and three Democrats (James Mann, Ray Thornton, and Walter Flowers) each reach the difficult personal decision that Richard Nixon's actions warranted impeachment. Dubbed the "fragile coalition" by Railsback, they gradually drifted together to share their mutual concerns, and the seven began secretly meeting prior to the opening of debate.[89] With Rodino's encouragement, they worked diligently to refine, rewrite, and transform Doar's drafts into articles of impeachment that they could support. Simultaneously, a Democratic task force created earlier in the month began narrowing and prioritizing a long list of possible impeachment articles proposed by their majority colleagues. Rodino closely monitored the progress of both groups, offering input and joining the drafting sessions that continued at a feverish pace as the deadline neared.[90]

The committee was scheduled to begin the impeachment debate at seven thirty the night of Wednesday, July 24. The unusual evening opening was the result of a waiver in the House rules that allowed live television coverage of a committee's legislative deliberations for the first time.[91] That morning, the Supreme Court issued its ruling in the dispute over the special prosecutor's request for presidential tape recordings. A unanimous court dismissed Nixon's claims of broad executive privilege and ordered him to surrender the disputed tapes. Rodino ignored suggestions that he consider delaying the proceedings pending the review of this new evidence. Maryland Republican Lawrence J. Hogan's announced support for impeachment helped bolster Rodino's confidence that he had the bipartisan support he needed, and he spent the day working on the most consequential speech of his congressional career.[92]

Banging his gavel several times for the benefit of the photographers, Rodino called the committee to order and began to deliver his opening statement in a raspier than usual voice, strained by the ongoing negotiating sessions. It was a simple, yet powerful, speech, one that set the appropriate tone for such a momentous occasion with its emphasis on his favorite themes of patriotism, bipartisanship, and the sanctity of the Constitution. He outlined the committee's diligent efforts to pursue a thorough and fair investigation. Recognizing the gravity of what was ahead, he told his colleagues: "Make no mistake about it. This is a turning point, whatever we decide…we must have the integrity and the decency, the will and the courage to decide rightly. Let us leave the Constitution as unimpaired for our children as our predecessors left it to us."[93]

With the exact wording of the proposed impeachment articles still being finalized, a placeholder resolution was introduced to commence the debate. Under the procedures adopted by the committee, each member was allowed a fifteen-minute opening statement starting with the most senior members and alternating between Democrats and Republicans. Midway through these initial presentations, there was a bomb threat. The room was cleared to allow police to sweep for explosives before the statements continued. When a caller later phoned in another false alarm, the chairman recessed the committee for the night. The next day he was assigned two bodyguards for protection.[94]

When the committee reconvened, Rodino pressed forward for the next twelve hours to complete all the opening statements. The fragile coalition members used this opportunity to begin laying the groundwork for their support of impeachment, and both Caldwell Butler and Ray Thornton announced that they were firmly in the "aye" column. The president's defenders had launched their offensive during the opening session, when hardliner

Charles Sandman delivered an angry harangue that personally attacked John Doar, who was seated a few feet away at the staff table. Less strident, Charles Wiggins followed this the next day with a detailed criticism of the evidentiary material and what he considered the weakness of the specific charges against the president. But most members primarily utilized their limited time to speak in broader terms and offered thoughtful and frequently emotional comments that were generally well received. The standout in this crowded field of noteworthy remarks was Barbara Jordan, who was relatively unknown outside of her home state until her spellbinding performance as one of the last speakers of the night. Rodino ended the session by announcing that, with a "heavy heart," he would vote for impeachment.[95]

The next day a harsher political tone emerged as the committee began considering the articles of impeachment. Working behind the scenes, the fragile coalition, Democrats, and Rodino had agreed on revised text for the first article, which charged the president with obstruction of justice. The final draft was more precisely worded than the original placeholder and declared that Richard Nixon had "prevented, obstructed and impeded the administration of justice," listing nine separate subparagraphs describing instances of this conduct. The rules allowed members to speak for five minutes on each motion, and Maryland's Paul Sarbanes, who Rodino tasked with introducing the substitute, commenced by explaining the meaning of the article.[96] Because the proposal did not offer detailed underlying evidence for each allegation, Charles W. Sandman Jr. claimed in a sarcastic, sneering tone that the absence of "specifics" was denying the president due process. This became the rallying cry for the Nixon defenders. Although Sarbanes and John Doar insisted that this material would be included in any report the committee filed, the supporters of impeachment were clearly placed on the defensive by the attacks. As the partisan rhetoric escalated throughout the afternoon, Rodino grew concerned that the television audience was receiving an inaccurate impression of the committee's fair treatment of Nixon. During the dinner break, he asked Barbara Jordan to speak on the issue in prime time, and she delivered a persuasive explanation of the committee's actions, describing in detail the latitude and courtesy extended to the president. But her compelling words were unable to gloss over the fact that it was not a good day for the advocates of impeachment.[97]

Learning from their mistake, the Democrats and fragile coalition members came prepared to reclaim control of the debate on Saturday, and Sandman unintentionally provided the opportunity. The previous day he had introduced a series of amendments to the Sarbanes substitute proposal, primarily to embarrass his opponents and delay the proceedings. The first of these was soundly defeated Friday night, and the remaining amendments were the pending business before the committee, each entitled to a full round of debate. The pro-impeachment forces had spent the intervening hours strategically dividing up the amendments and preparing talking points based on background material from the inquiry staff. Individually using their allotted five minutes, they offered the "specifics" Sandman claimed were missing. Addressing his criticisms with great "specificity," they recounted for the television audience in detail the evidence compiled against Richard Nixon.[98] This was not what Sandman wanted, and, recognizing his error, he withdrew the amendments. But Walter Flowers immediately offered them in his place, voting "present" on each one. To Sandman's increasingly vocal frustration, his opponents were unrelenting in their determination to present this damaging material, and the debate continued throughout the afternoon and into the early evening. When the speakers were finally exhausted, Rodino bent the rules and recognized Walter Flowers and Hamilton Fish, who both announced their support for impeachment.[99]

The committee then proceeded to consider a motion to adopt the changes proposed by Paul Sarbanes to the article on obstruction of justice. With mounting tension and a palpable stillness enveloping the hearing room, Jim Cline, serving as the clerk of the committee, began to read the roster of thirty-eight names for the roll call vote shortly before seven that evening. All the members of the fragile coalition, every Democrat, Lawrence Hogan and Republican Harold Froehlich of Wisconsin, a surprising new addition to the group, voted in favor of the substitute. As the chairman, Rodino voted last and quietly responded "aye" before announcing the motion was carried by a vote of 27 to 11. A second vote was needed to approve the article as amended, and the outcome was the same, making it the first article of impeachment against a president of the United States reported to the House of Representatives in 106 years.[100] Recessing the committee until Monday, a somber Rodino turned away from the handshakes and a mob of reporters to retire alone to his small office behind the hearing room. Closing the door, he picked up the phone and called Ann at the Grafton Avenue house to tell her it was over. She was watching television and already knew; she told her husband how proud she was of him. That seemed to pierce his numbness—the full significance of what had just happened finally registered. "I started to sob," he recalled, "and I'm not at all embarrassed to say it."[101]

If Saturday night's outcome was not entirely unanticipated, it was nonetheless momentous news that rippled across the country in banner headlines and Sunday broadcasts. A majority of the public supported the committee's action, and many journalists noted that the panel had been paralyzed by partisan infighting and the president had appeared ascendant only a month earlier. "Here as elsewhere," R.W. Apple Jr. wrote in the *New York Times*, the White House seriously underestimated Rodino, who "rather than buckling when polarization set in, he persevered in patience and flexibility."[102] Whatever vindication or relief an exhausted Rodino might have felt, he understood the committee's work was not finished. He convened a caucus meeting Sunday morning, and his fellow Democrats loudly applauded their leader when he entered the room. Only briefly smiling, the chairman solemnly commented that the mournful voices of Saturday's roll call vote had reminded him of a funeral. "As usual," Ed Mezvinsky recalled, "it was Rodino who brought us back to the terrible seriousness of what we were about."[103]

The focus of attention on this day of rest was the proposed second article charging the president with abuse of power. Republican Robert McClory, prepared to vote for this article, assumed the lead in rewriting the existing placeholder text to satisfy Democrats and members of the fragile coalition. The abuse of power article covered a broad range of Nixon's misdeeds, including misuse of federal agencies, his reelection campaign's dirty tricks unit, and the illegal surveillance of private citizens.[104] When the committee reconvened at eleven thirty in the morning on Monday, Democrat William L. Hungate of Missouri introduced the second article substitute. Charles Wiggins led the attack and introduced a long list of amendments to weaken the article, which were all defeated and resulted in extending the debate late into the evening. More than twelve hours after Rodino called the committee to order, he announced that the second article was approved 28 to 10.[105]

The committee had now adopted two articles of impeachment incorporating most of the allegations made against Richard Nixon since the Watergate break-in, and they were both likely to win approval from the full House of Representatives and trigger a Senate trial. But there were three more pending articles, and Rodino worried this might be overkill, a concern some of the members of the fragile coalition shared. "I think we could all agree," Rodino recalled, "that you do reach a point where it certainly is not wise to employ unnecessaries which could only result frankly in weakening your case."[106] Confirmation of this came when the committee met on Tuesday, July 30, and began debating a proposed article charging the president with failing to respond to multiple subpoenas to produce materials essential to the inquiry. Only two members of the fragile coalition supported this article, and it was adopted by a narrower 21-to-17 vote. Rodino attempted to persuade his fellow Democrats not to offer a fourth article based on Nixon's secret bombing of Cambodia, which 26 members including Rodino voted against. A final article addressing the president's misuse of government funds, which Rodino did support, was also defeated. At 11:05 in the evening, after nine months of investigation and six long days of televised debate, Peter Rodino banged his gavel and ended the proceedings.[107]

Rodino and Doar immediately began preparing for the next phase in the impeachment process. Rodino met with Speaker Albert and Tip O'Neill on July 31 to discuss scheduling the floor debate of the impeachment resolution. Both were anxious to move expeditiously so members could return home to campaign for the midterm elections. They reached an agreement the following day with the Republicans to begin fifty-five hours of debate on Monday, August 19, under a closed rule that prohibited any amendments, and they all agreed to allow television coverage of the proceedings. To ensure members were briefed in advance, Rodino distributed copies of all the statements of information and set up listening stations in the Rayburn and Cannon office buildings, where members could hear the recorded presidential conversations. He carefully assembled a balanced and bipartisan group of floor managers from the committee to help him secure approval of the three impeachment articles. At the same time, Speaker Albert created an ad hoc committee to oversee the security and logistical arrangements for this historic proceeding.[108]

All of these plans were ultimately upended by events unfolding at the White House. Complying with the Supreme Court's ruling on his tapes, Nixon was forced to surrender a previously withheld recording of a conversation six days after the Watergate break-in, during which he authorized H.R. Haldeman to use the CIA to derail the FBI's investigation, a clear obstruction of justice. James St. Clair, who was unaware of the secret conversation, threatened to resign unless the president publicly released the transcript. On August 5, White House officials met with House Republican leaders and minority members of the committee to warn them of the explosive contents of this recording, ironically providing the president's supporters with the "smoking gun" they had long complained was missing from John Doar's evidentiary presentations. Following the publication of the damaging transcript, Nixon's allies quickly abandoned him. Starting with Charles Wiggins, every Republican on the committee announced that they now planned to vote for impeachment. Rodino recalled feeling "a sense of relief, knowing that what we had done was just, knowing that what we had done was right."[109]

With Nixon's prospects rapidly sinking, and rumors of his imminent resignation circulating on Capitol Hill, not many representatives wanted to defend the president in the upcoming debate, and the original time allocation was reduced by half. Rodino and O'Neill suggested that there might not even be an impeachment debate, telling reporters that if the president resigned they were unlikely to proceed. This possibility increased after a delegation of senior congressional Republicans, led by Arizona's Barry Goldwater, went to the White House to inform the president that he was unlikely to get more than a handful of votes in the Senate for acquittal. The evening of August 8 in a televised address from the Oval Office, Richard Nixon announced that he was resigning from the presidency effective noon the next day. Rodino watched the speech in his office and issued a brief statement acknowledging that "it has been an ordeal for President Nixon and for all our people."[110]

Not surprisingly, few members of Congress expressed any interest in continuing the impeachment process, recognizing that most of their constituents were ready to leave the long Watergate saga behind and move forward under the leadership of the new president Gerald Ford. Rodino agreed and consulted with the House parliamentarian to determine an acceptable avenue for memorializing the committee's work and the case against the president, without having an actual debate and vote on the articles. Twelve days after the resignation announcement, the chairman stood in the House chamber and asked his colleagues to accept the committee's report on the impeachment of Richard Nixon, approve its printing, and agree to place the entire contents in the *Congressional Record,* which they did by a vote of 412 to 3. The highlight of this detailed 528-page document was the unanimous support of all thirty-eight members for the first article on obstruction of justice, enshrining forever Rodino's objective of securing bipartisan unity.[111]

The publication of the report brought a formal close to the impeachment inquiry. The second floor office in the annex was emptied of furniture and equipment, documents were boxed and sent to the National Archives, and John Doar and his team returned to their previous lives. After months of long workdays and stress, Rodino headed home to rest and reflect on the events of the past tumultuous year. He left Washington a more seasoned and confident leader, one who could take great personal satisfaction in having followed his own unique path and one who had exceeded everyone's expectations. Working methodically and cooperatively with both Democrats and Republicans on a committee he had made more diverse and democratic, he confirmed a vice president and impeached a president in a single Congress, an achievement that was unlikely to be repeated. Once dismissed as simply a machine politician despite more than two decades of legislative accomplishments, he was now the subject of flattering profiles in major publications and laudatory editorials that praised his caution and modesty.

Beyond these affirmations, his public profile had grown exponentially, and his anonymity was gone forever. Ninety million television viewers had watched him chair the impeachment hearings, and many sent letters of support and appreciation. Americans had discovered Peter Rodino, if somewhat belatedly, and many deeply admired what the First Ward, World War II, and a political career that did not always follow the easiest path had produced. Perhaps the most satisfying aspect of this new reality for Rodino was that he had finally stepped out of the shadow cast by Emanuel Celler. Whatever future challenges might await him, there was no longer any doubt inside the Judiciary Committee that the title "Mr. Chairman" rightfully belonged to the gentleman from New Jersey.

CHAPTER NINE

AFTERGLOW

When Peter Rodino left Capitol Hill after filing the committee's impeachment report, his immediate concern was rest. Months of extended workdays, skipped meals, and unrelenting stress had taken a toll on the sixty-five-year-old grandfather, taxing the limits of his physical endurance. He needed to recharge and retreated to West Long Branch, New Jersey, where he had purchased a second home a few years earlier. With their children grown and close friends moving out of Newark, the Rodinos had started spending less time at their house on Grafton Avenue, which became primarily a base for weekend events in the Tenth District, and more time in this seashore community. It provided a nurturing refuge for the exhausted congressman. Thanks to his safe Democratic seat and an unknown challenger, he had the luxury of devoting most of the remaining summer congressional recess to relaxation rather than campaigning like many of his colleagues.

But Rodino could not completely escape the demands of his new public profile, and he spent some of this quiet time pondering the future. In the aftermath of the impeachment inquiry, his office was inundated with requests for him to speak, accept an award, or endorse a candidate in the upcoming election, all appeals that required a timely response. Three publishers had contacted him about writing a book, hinting at a sizable advance, and two lecture bureaus were ready to send him out on the paid circuit. If impeachment fame came too late in Rodino's life to alter his fundamentally low-key persona, it did boost his ego and whet his appetite for the spotlight. Now that this unexpected shining moment had arrived, he was eager to prolong it. His past modesty receded in the wake of a justifiable pride in an achievement he never tired of recalling. His one proviso was that nothing he did should give the appearance that he was profiting from impeachment, and, consequently, he never joined the lecture circuit or signed a book contract. In lieu of reaping financial rewards, he decided to spend his time speaking to universities or civic organizations and using his newfound celebrity status to help elect Democrats. With this question resolved and feeling reenergized, he began preparing for an ambitious campaign schedule in the fall.[1]

Before he left for Washington, Rodino was abruptly jolted back to reality when he returned a missed call from the White House on September 8 and spoke to senior aide William Timmons. Timmons informed him that President Ford planned to issue an unconditional pardon to Richard Nixon that provided immunity from prosecution for all federal crimes he committed or might have committed during his presidency. Even before Nixon left the capital in disgrace, there was speculation about the possibility of granting him some type of amnesty because, as an unindicted coconspirator, he was subject to prosecution once he left office. The Senate Committee on Rules and Administration had asked Gerald Ford at his vice presidential confirmation hearings whether he believed someone succeeding to the presidency had the power to terminate the prosecution of their predecessor. Not willing to address the broader constitutional issue, Ford focused on the political consequences and answered, "I do not think the public would stand for it." Two hours after Nixon resigned, the new White House press secretary Jerald terHorst assured reporters that it was highly unlikely that Nixon would ever be pardoned, and Ford declared at his first presidential press conference that he intended to let the legal process unfold before making any decisions on this question.[2]

Considering these previous comments, Rodino was stunned by Ford's sudden action. As the chairman of the committee that approved three articles of impeachment against Nixon, he was expecting some discussion or prior consultation, taking the new president at his word, when he wrote on August 21 that "I have always valued your counsel and I want to reaffirm my pledge to you and my other former colleagues that I intend to continue to listen to you, who are the representatives of the people." Rodino asked Timmons if Ford wanted "to talk with me first, or did he just want to tell me," and the response left no doubt that it was simply a courtesy call.[3] Unbeknownst to the chairman, Ford had already signed the pardon in front of a small press contingent gathered in the Oval Office. Reading a brief statement, the president maintained that he acted to prevent a long divisive legal proceeding against a former president who was in poor health.[4] Regardless of the reasons for his decision, Rodino considered it premature and a serious mistake that undercut the notion that no one is above the law. Although he did not want to see Nixon sent to prison, he believed a pardon should only be issued after an indictment and a trial. It was an opinion shared by many members of Congress on both sides of the aisle, a majority of the public, and Ford's own press secretary, who resigned in protest.[5]

When Rodino arrived back in Washington two days later, Capitol Hill was once again besieged with letters and telegrams from outraged constituents condemning an action involving Richard Nixon. The negative reaction to the pardon was further fueled by the secrecy of the negotiations and the former president's failure to acknowledge guilt when he accepted it. Rodino's immediate challenge was an effort by several Democrats on the House Judiciary Committee to pressure Speaker Albert to bring the panel's report on the three previously approved articles of impeachment to the floor for a formal vote. Senate Majority Leader Mike Mansfield, who believed the impeachment process should have continued after Nixon's resignation, agreed and hinted at the possibility of Senate action if the House moved forward. Rodino firmly opposed the idea, repeating the arguments he had made the previous month that the purpose of impeachment was removal from office and this was accomplished. Responding to the concern that Ford's action muddied the historical record, he expressed confidence that Nixon's grave misconduct was indisputably established and told Albert, "I see a danger to the integrity of government if we were to suggest now to the American public that something more needs to be developed."[6] Once again, the Speaker accepted the advice of his chairman, and the impeachment question was not reopened.

This did not end the furor on Capitol Hill over the pardon, and two members of the House introduced resolutions of inquiry seeking details about the Ford administration's pardon negotiations. These were referred to the Judiciary Committee's Subcommittee on Criminal Justice, and chairman William Hungate sent a letter to the White House requesting answers to a long list of questions.[7] Hoping to refute the charges of a secret deal with Nixon, President Ford offered to appear personally before the subcommittee to explain his action. It was an unprecedented proposal, and his advisers asked for Rodino's help in forging the appropriate ground rules for the president's appearance. Meeting with Ford's senior aide, former Congressman John O. Marsh Jr., Rodino offered to attend the session to ensure that the president was treated with appropriate courtesy. The final guidelines provided for the president's appearance at a two-hour morning session limited questions to the subject of the pardon and allowed for the broadcasting of the hearing. To underscore the voluntary nature of Ford's participation, the subcommittee agreed not to require him to testify under oath.[8]

The hearing convened on October 17 in the Rayburn building appeared eerily familiar at first glance. Usually relegated to a smaller space, the subcommittee was meeting in the main hearing room where the recently concluded impeachment inquiry had been held. The nine members of the subcommittee were joined on the dais by Chairman Rodino, ranking Republican Edward Hutchinson, and a majority of their colleagues from the full committee. The three major television networks, rarely interested in the work of a House subcommittee, were providing live coverage of the proceedings, and a large contingent of reporters huddled in the areas designated for the press. Outside the room, a long line had started forming early in the morning for the limited seats available to the public. Those lucky few allowed inside joined a group of special guests in reserved seating, including John Doar, returning for the first time to his former workplace.[9]

But beyond these cursory similarities, this historic event was starkly different from the previous one that had unfolded in this room; sitting at the witness table in place of the special counsel and his staff was the solitary figure of the president of the United States. Gerald Ford's extraordinary decision to appear in person to defend his pardon of Richard Nixon was welcomed by those who supported his action and many who did not. As much as Peter Rodino deplored the timing of the pardon, he believed his classmate and former colleague was an honorable person and not capable of making a Faustian bargain with his predecessor. He appreciated the special significance of Ford's gesture, especially after battling for months with the Nixon White House to obtain any information, and he wanted to ensure this accommodation was respected and that the committee's reputation for fairness was not diminished. Under generally polite questioning, Ford calmly deflected criticism, and his two-hour appearance provided a mostly positive opportunity to explain his actions directly to a television audience of millions. Whether or not he changed many opinions about the sagacity of pardoning the former president, Ford succeeded in lowering political tensions and repaired some of the damage to his credibility. Rodino rejected the efforts of some members to expand the investigation, and there were no additional hearings.[10]

A few weeks before he issued the Nixon pardon, President Ford had announced the nomination of Nelson Rockefeller to fill his vice presidential vacancy, and the House Judiciary Committee was again required to implement the provisions of the Twenty-Fifth Amendment. Rodino assigned the Subcommittee on Civil and Constitutional Rights the task of evaluating the investigative material collected by the FBI, and a special team of lawyers and investigators was quickly assembled by the committee to assist in this effort. As a member of the wealthiest family in the United States, Rockefeller's financial holdings were vast and complicated; even with additional help from the staff of the congressional Joint Committee on Internal Revenue Taxation, the undertaking was still a formidable challenge. Although the Senate Committee on Rules and Administration was ready to question Rockefeller, Rodino informed members that Judiciary Committee hearings would not begin until after the midterm election.[11]

Not surprisingly, aspects of the investigation began to leak to the press during this waiting period. The most damaging disclosure was that Rockefeller had provided substantial monetary gifts and loans to associates who were former or current public officials, a practice not uncovered by Senate investigators. Rodino called members back to Washington for a closed-door briefing on October 30 to discuss the revelations. He decided to delay the start of the hearings to allow for a further investigation of the matter.[12] Concerned that the confirmation process might not be completed before the end of the year, Ford wrote to Rodino to express his frustration, reminding the chairman that "the national interest is not well served by a continued vacancy in the vice presidency." Rodino reassured the president that the committee was prepared to move expeditiously, and he promised John Marsh in a follow-up conversation that the House would vote on the nomination before adjournment.[13]

While the Rockefeller nomination hearings that began on November 21 could not match the historic drama of the first vice presidential confirmation, it was an equally unique occasion. "At no time in our history," Rodino observed in his opening remarks, "prior to the submission of this nomination, had any Congress, acting alone as surrogates for the people, been called upon to pass judgment on the nomination of a designated Vice President submitted by an unelected President."[14] Rockefeller spent two full days before the panel answering questions largely focused on his expansive wealth and potential conflicts of interest, the previously disclosed gifts, and his more contentious actions as governor of New York. His offer to place his financial portfolio in a blind trust won over some skeptical members. Following a week of testimony from more than two dozen friends and critics, Rockefeller returned on the final day to answer lingering questions about his controversial gifting practices.[15] The committee followed the Senate in giving its overwhelming consent to the nomination, and the House of Representatives began six hours of floor debate on December 19. This time, Rodino was leading the supporters, and Rockefeller won approval just hours before the Ninety-Third Congress ended two momentous years of legislative business. Rockefeller was sworn in that night as the second unelected vice president of the United States.[16]

Despite the demands of confirming a new vice president and addressing other legislative issues, Rodino had maintained a full schedule of campaign appearances in the months prior to the midterm. His inaugural political outing, organized by the Democratic Congressional Campaign Committee, was to New Mexico and South Dakota, where he helped raise money for local candidates, rallied party activists, and met with the local press. At the New Mexico Democratic party's major fundraiser, Rodino addressed more than five hundred attendees, recounting the challenges of impeachment and sharing his personal optimism. "If we proceed with care, decency, thoroughness and honor," he told the crowd, "our Constitution, our system of government will continue to have the overwhelming confidence and support of the people."[17] In Madison, South Dakota, the lifelong Newark native addressed a large group of farmers and urged them to reelect his Democratic colleague Frank E. Denholm and Senator George McGovern. They gave him a standing ovation and a new gavel cut from a century-old black walnut tree. Prior to leaving the next day, he met with party leaders and was the main attraction at two fundraisers in Sioux Falls. "They love him out here," South Dakota's Lieutenant Governor William J. "Bill" Dougherty enthused, crediting the televised impeachment hearings for making Rodino "an instant national hero."[18]

Requests for Rodino to appear at campaign events for candidates or provide a letter of endorsement continued to arrive at his Rayburn office throughout the fall, reflecting what *Washington Post* reporter William Greider identified as the growing belief among Democrats that, in the aftermath of political scandals, "Rodino's blessing has become a sort of Good Housekeeping Seal of Approval in politics."[19] Political consultant David Garth concurred, finding in his own polling of New York voters that Rodino's favorability rating was significantly higher than any other politician and just slightly below that of trusted television anchorman Walter Cronkite, an extraordinary response from a population that rarely looked across the Hudson River. Garth's client was Brooklyn congressman Hugh Carey, who was challenging the party establishment's candidate for the Democratic gubernatorial nomination. As the acknowledged underdog in the race, he needed help and asked Rodino for an endorsement. The chairman, usually hesitant to interfere in a nomination fight, found it difficult to say no to a colleague and agreed to tape a television ad. "It was a very quiet spot, no gimmicks," Garth recalled, "he was very, very effective, amazingly so." Rodino also agreed to campaign in New York City, helping Carey to score a decisive upset win in the primary on September 10.[20]

When the brief congressional election recess began in mid-October, Rodino accelerated his outreach, hoping to counterbalance President Ford's aggressive campaigning for Republicans and to respond directly to his charge that a large veto-proof Democratic majority would be dangerous. Rodino accepted invitations from twenty-four candidates, declining an equal number of requests because of scheduling limitations, and left Capitol Hill immediately to fulfill his transcontinental obligations. In one particularly whirlwind trip, Rodino and his wife Ann visited Denver, Seattle, Portland, and three cities in Iowa during a brief forty-eight hour period. The *Seattle Post-Intelligencer* dubbed Rodino a "Democratic Superstar" after his visit to the city and noted that "Democrats are using his fame on behalf of their candidates across the country in the first post-Watergate election."[21] Along the campaign trail, he met students, reporters, party leaders, and devoted fans eager to get his autograph. He told his impeachment story to countless audiences of various sizes, from an overflow crowd in the cavernous Portland Civic Auditorium to a small gathering of Italian American donors at a dinner in an intimate Des Moines restaurant. He recorded radio and television ads for colleagues running for reelection and novice challengers he did not know. He was the center of attention wherever he appeared and was regularly greeted with cheers and ovations. It was an intense, exhausting, and very heady experience—one that he embraced with relish and thoroughly enjoyed.[22]

Rodino's efforts were rewarded on election day, when nineteen of the twenty-four candidates he supported won as part of a Democratic electoral sweep. Aided by the backlash against Watergate, the Ford pardon, and an economic slowdown, the party increased its support in every region of the country. At the state level, the Democrats captured a majority of legislatures and prevailed in most of the gubernatorial contests, including Hugh Carey's victory in New York, which ended sixteen years of Republican rule. The New Jersey results transformed the congressional delegation's slight 8-to-7 Democratic edge into an unprecedented 12-to-3 dominance. Nationally, thirty-six incumbent Republican House members were defeated, guaranteeing a two-thirds veto proof majority for the Democrats when the next Congress convened. It was "not just a victory," Speaker Albert declared, "it was a mandate."[23]

The seventy-five new Democrats that were members of 1974's "Watergate class" were young, liberal, independent, and determined to bring sweeping change to Capitol Hill. They launched their first assault against the lingering remnants of the seniority system during freshman orientation in early December, when they forced their party to transfer responsibility for committee assignments from the entrenched Ways and Means Committee, led by the autocratic Wilbur Mills, to the more representative Steering and Policy Committee, controlled by Speaker Albert.[24] The next freshman focus was on the upcoming vote for committee leaders in the new Congress, and they summoned all the current sitting chairmen back to the capital to plead their case for reselection. Rodino was one of the first to accept the extraordinary invitation, and on January 9 he answered generally friendly questions from the freshmen, many of whom had praised Rodino's impeachment leadership in their electoral campaigns. A few days before the final vote, the influential citizens' lobby Common Cause released a study rating the committee leadership on the basis of fairness, appropriate exercise of power, and compliance with rules. Although fourteen chairmen failed the test, Rodino received the highest rating and was judged "the model chairman of the House."[25] At the Democratic Caucus meeting, three of the lowest ranked chairmen were replaced; Rodino was overwhelmingly approved to continue in his position.

When the Ninety-Fourth Congress convened in January 1975, thirteen of the thirty-eight members who had participated in the impeachment inquiry were no longer there. Of the missing, five members were not reelected, including Nixon defenders Sandman, Maraziti, Dennis, and Mayne; three voluntarily left to run unsuccessfully for higher office; Donohue and Smith retired; and Rodino's friend Charles Rangel and two others moved to different committees. The substantial increase in the total number of Democrats in the House of Representatives necessitated the modification of the panel's partisan ratio, which was recalibrated to a wider 23 to 11 in favor of the majority, providing the chairman with a much larger cushion in any close vote. Rodino was now joined on the dais by several more liberals representing districts in the Northeast. The addition of four Democratic freshmen elevated committee sophomores Barbara Jordan and Elizabeth Holtzman to higher places on the seating chart.

For the returning members, the biggest difference was that the public spotlight was no longer shining intensely on Rayburn 2141, and the daily retinue of reporters clogging the corridor outside the hearing room had scattered in different directions to cover other news stories. After a presidential impeachment and two vice presidential confirmations, whatever assignment the committee tackled next was likely to seem anticlimactic and pedestrian in comparison. Republican Tom Railsback confessed to finding it difficult to focus his attention on "some of the mundane affairs" of the panel's work that he had previously enjoyed. Sharing many of these same concerns, Rodino admitted asking himself, "after a period like that, a height, a golden moment, you know, what is there left?"[26]

He found the answer in the full roster of legislative issues the committee had either ignored or postponed as a result of the crowded schedule and pressing demands of the past year. The first item on the agenda was one that the chairman had a strong personal connection to: the extension of the provisions of the Voting Rights Act of 1965, which were scheduled to expire. As Manny Celler's lieutenant and a senior member of his Subcommittee 5, Rodino had contributed to the drafting of the legislation and actively participated in the often-challenging political battle to win congressional approval of the law enacted to eliminate the array of barriers used to prevent African

Americans from voting or running for public office. The original proposal was authorized for ten years, which was later reduced by half to overcome a Senate filibuster. When this additional time frame proved inadequate, Congress was forced to extend the act for what was regarded as a final five years ending on August 6, 1975.[27]

Anticipating this deadline, the US Commission on Civil Rights released the first in-depth analysis of the electoral changes in the southern states covered under the law and concluded that the process was not completed and recommended another extension. With civil rights groups, non-southern Democrats, many Republicans, and President Ford supporting this recommendation, the focus of the debate was on the specific details of a reauthorization. Rodino proposed legislation on the first day of the session to extend the law for ten years without any new provisions, a position supported by the major civil rights groups. The version the committee approved in May that passed the House the following month included an amendment proposed by Barbara Jordan to add "language minorities" to the existing list of those protected under the law. As the August deadline neared, Senate Democrats were forced to accept a compromise that reduced the extension to seven years, placing Rodino in a difficult position because there was no time for protracted negotiations between the two chambers. Reluctantly, he accepted the compromise and expressed his frustration during the final debate over being forced to make "practical choices" so the president could sign the bill before the law expired.[28]

While the voting rights extension was awaiting final approval, Rodino and the Judiciary Committee were forced to direct their attention to an unexpected and urgent problem caused by the abrupt end of the long-running war in Southeast Asia. In 1969, the Nixon administration began to shift the burden of the conflict to South Vietnam's military, allowing for the gradual withdrawal of American ground forces from the region. Congressional opposition to any additional funding and a cease fire agreement after years of stalled peace talks in Paris further accelerated this shift in policy and helped to expedite the ongoing process of sending the remaining troops home. When the North

Vietnamese violated the truce and launched a major offensive in March 1975, there was little resistance from an opponent no longer supported by its American allies; within weeks, the first communist soldiers reached the outskirts of the south's capital city of Saigon. Shocked by the surprising swiftness of this military collapse, the Ford administration and officials scrambled to redirect naval vessels to the area to help evacuate the thousands of South Vietnamese desperately rushing to leave their country. These evacuees, fearing retribution for their role in the war effort and connection to the United States, gathered along the coastline and crowded into ports searching for any way to reach safety. By the time the South Vietnamese government unconditionally surrendered on April 30, a flotilla of ships teeming with refugees and helicopters removing the remaining Americans from the US embassy were the indelible images that signaled the end of two decades of conflict.[29]

To meet this emerging humanitarian crisis, the Ford administration relied on the provisions of the 1952 McCarran-Walter Act that authorized the attorney general to grant permission in an emergency for an individual to enter and remain temporarily in the United States. Following the influx of refugees after the unsuccessful 1956 uprising against the communist regime in Hungary, this parole authority was increasingly used to facilitate the entry of large groups and individuals, and Congress affirmed its willingness to accept this expanded definition if there was appropriate consultation between the two branches.[30] Early estimates suggested that as many as two million refugees might flee Vietnam and Cambodia, and the State Department urged Attorney General Edward H. Levi to consider exercising his parole authority. President Ford agreed to a proposal to accept 150,000 refugees at greatest risk, including former employees of the US government and those with knowledge of sensitive intelligence operations. Rodino assured his colleagues on April 22 that his committee was in close contact with Justice Department officials and regularly consulted on their plans to address the refugee crisis.[31]

Rodino's support was invaluable to the Ford administration; persuading the public and Congress to support the admission of tens of thousands of evacuees from Southeast Asia was going to be a formidable challenge. The country was experiencing the highest unemployment rate in three decades, and this further inflamed existing hostility toward immigrants and Asians. The evacuations prompted a flood of angry calls to the White House and Capitol Hill, where several members immediately announced their opposition to funding this resettlement operation.[32] Rodino agreed to introduce the legislation to authorize the administration's refugee assistance program. When members of the immigration subcommittee expressed reservations, he appeared before the panel to urge them to act immediately. "When this country forgets its immigrant heritage and turns it back on the homeless of the world," he exhorted his colleagues, "it will have written 'finis' to the American dream." His inspiring words and private political pressure resulted in unanimous approval, a turnaround the press and the White House officials credited to Rodino. He held a full committee meeting that night and sent the bill to the House floor in less than twenty-four hours.[33]

Televised images of throngs of fleeing refugees on ships and reports of extreme overcrowding in the emergency evacuation areas set up in the Pacific region helped to soften some of the earlier hostility, which helped expedite passage of the refugee assistance bill by the end of May. The funding supported the establishment of four resettlement centers at military bases in the United States to temporarily house refugees and facilitate their permanent relocation into local communities. With the active participation of a wide range of churches and civic groups serving as sponsors, more than 130,000 Vietnamese and Cambodians were processed and relocated throughout the country. On Christmas Eve, President Ford proudly announced the settlement of the last refugee and the closing of the centers. Considering the limited time frame and early opposition, the admission and resettlement of so many refugees from Southeast Asia was an impressive accomplishment and an exemplary model of an effective partnership between the executive and legislative branches. Reflecting decades later on the reasons for this success, Rodino attributed it to the simple fact that "we made a good case."[34]

The issue Rodino was most eager to return to after the impeachment inquiry concluded was antitrust policy, which was a core part of the portfolio under the jurisdiction of his Subcommittee on Monopolies and Commercial Law. A dry and highly technical subject, he always viewed it through the lens of his liberal philosophy, regarding fair competition to be an essential weapon in the effort to improve economic conditions for all Americans. The challenge he faced was that Congress had not passed any major antitrust legislation in more than two decades, stymied by the opposition of the powerful business lobby. Recognizing this political reality, the panel focused its energies on exposing monopolistic practices in specific business sectors through a series of high-profile hearings similar to the ones Chairman Celler held when Rodino first joined the committee.[35] However, with runaway inflation gripping the US economy, the idea of beefing up antitrust laws to encourage competition became part of the policy debate over finding effective tools to lower prices. In October 1974, President Ford called on Congress to strengthen the enforcement provisions of current antitrust laws, and Rodino offered his support for what he considered a long overdue effort. He introduced the administration's proposal to make an antitrust violation a felony and increase the maximum corporate fine to one million dollars and shepherded it to an easy victory in the House and subsequent conference with the Senate.[36]

Rodino's next effort to strengthen antitrust enforcement was more difficult. Under the existing provisions of the law, state attorneys general were not allowed to take legal action in federal court on behalf of citizens economically hurt by monopolistic practices. Because consumers were unlikely to pursue a small individual claim, the absence of this collective power at the state level meant that financial punishment for anticompetitive behavior was often minimal and consequently an ineffective deterrent against future abuse. Rodino proposed legislation to remove this restriction and authorize attorneys general to seek treble damages from those causing harm to the economy of their state by violating antitrust laws. The proposal received broad support from state officials, labor organizations, and the Ford Justice Department and won committee approval on a voice vote.[37]

But the prospects for what initially appeared to be easy passage dimmed when the Business Roundtable began to lobby against the measure and persuaded the House Rules Committee to shelve the bill, forcing Rodino to appeal directly to Speaker Albert to get the measure on the legislative calendar.[38] Undeterred, the business community enlisted the House Republican Policy Conference to lead the opposition to the bill when the debate began in March 1976, placing the Ford administration in a difficult position. Minority Leader John Rhodes and major corporate executives privately demanded the president withdraw his support. The previously supportive White House, now claiming that the legislation was flawed, threatened that the president might veto it. A furious Rodino immediately responded to Ford in a letter he released to the press warning that "the considered pronouncements of your administration on pending legislation will lose credibility if the rug is to be pulled out repeatedly by last-minute presidential action."[39] Ford did not respond, and the legislation was approved largely along party lines.

A less controversial measure involved the problem caused by the absence of a requirement that companies provide advance notice to the federal government before completing a corporate merger. This posed a major challenge for officials who were forced to evaluate the impact of this marketplace concentration and its legality after the new entity was already created and in full operation. If the merger was subsequently deemed unlawful, a divestiture requiring the separation of these blended assets was in Rodino's words "like trying to unscramble an omelet" and likely to result in years of protracted litigation.[40] His legislation required companies with assets of more than $100 million to give the Justice Department and the Federal Trade Commission a thirty-day notice of any anticipated merger. All the Republicans on the monopolies subcommittee cosponsored the legislation. It was brought to the House floor under the suspension calendar, which was only used for noncontroversial measures, and approved in August.[41]

On the other side of Capitol Hill, the Senate had taken a different approach to antitrust reform and the chairman of the monopolies panel, Michigan Democrat Philip Hart, and his cosponsor, Minority Leader Hugh Scott, had introduced a single comprehensive bill. Business allies in the chamber launched a filibuster. When this failed, they began a series of parliamentary maneuvers to derail the bill. Faced with the prospect of a protracted delay, Hart and Scott were forced to remove or alter several of the tougher provisions in their bill, and this weaker substitute was approved.[42] With opponents threatening to filibuster again over the appointment of conferees, the sponsors from both chambers decided to meet unofficially to resolve their differences. Rodino agreed to combine his proposals into a single measure under the title "Hart-Scott-Rodino Antitrust Improvements Act of 1976," and the senators accepted a majority of the legislative language in the House bills. A week after the Senate passed the revised bill on September 9, Rodino persuaded his House colleagues to accept this final version without amendment, assuring them that 90 percent of the original House content remained. President Ford abandoned his earlier veto threat and signed the measure.[43] Although a Supreme Court ruling the following year effectively neutralized the impact of the hard-won provision expanding the authority of state attorneys general, the enactment and implementation of the Hart-Scott-Rodino Act was an important landmark in the history of antitrust law. Rodino often joked that considering the number of citations in legal briefs and court rulings, it was probably his greatest legacy.[44]

Alongside this burst of legislative activity, Rodino managed to find the time to fulfill an extensive list of speaking commitments, regularly leaving Capitol Hill when there were no scheduled votes and frequently missing weekends at home in New Jersey. His post-impeachment luster remained bright; he was receiving more than two hundred invitations a month and delivered more than fifty speeches in 1975, primarily outside of Washington. During this same whirlwind period, he was honored by the NAACP, awarded five honorary degrees, received the prestigious Jefferson Award for Public Service from the American Institute for Public Service, named the National Italian American of the Year by the Greater New Orleans Italian Cultural Society, and narrated a PBS documentary.[45]

The first anniversary of the Nixon impeachment vote in July brought a new round of attention and sparked the publication of several books on Watergate. Jimmy Breslin's *How The Good Guys Finally Won* and *Breach of*

Faith by Theodore White were both bestsellers and highly complimentary of Rodino's leadership.[46] The chairman willingly sat through hours of interviews for the opportunity to retell his favorite stories from the long impeachment saga and reminisce with many of the same reporters who had covered the hearings. Freed of the previous year's responsibilities, he was far more candid in these exchanges and revealed formerly withheld details or personal opinions, including his belief that Richard Nixon knew in advance about the illegal activities connected to Watergate.[47]

With Democrats worried about retaining the large number of Republican seats they captured in 1974, Rodino directed much of his off-year travels to the districts of the Watergate class he had helped elect. "His benediction has come to count for something in American politics," the *Boston Globe* observed. As a result, he received far more requests than he could accept within the limitations imposed by his legislative schedule.[48] His multistate visits primarily focused on bolstering the fundraising efforts of these potentially vulnerable freshmen, who were facing their inaugural reelection campaign. One member who benefited from Rodino's assistance was Michigan's James J. Blanchard, the state's future two-term governor, who asked Rodino to be the guest of honor at his first postelection fundraiser. Rodino attracted so many attendees that they were forced to have two separate seatings for dinner. "We never had a better turnout in all my years in politics," Blanchard recalled. "Peter Rodino was the most popular public figure in America at the time...he did me a huge favor."[49]

Rodino's political value was also recognized by the Democratic National Committee, and he was invited by chairman Robert S. Strauss to participate in the fourth fundraising telethon organized to help erase the party's lingering debt. Televised live from Los Angeles, this twenty-two-hour broadcast presented a combination of entertainment, policy discussions, and celebrities appealing for contributions. Rodino was allotted two segments during prime time hours, the first involved answering questions from viewers and the second was a conversation on criminal justice with noted attorney Edward Bennett Williams. The event was held the same weekend as the Nixon impeachment anniversary.[50]

Overhanging all of these activities was a growing speculation about Rodino's own political future and his possible entry into the upcoming presidential contest. Throughout the impeachment inquiry, he had received a steady stream of fan mail asking him to consider running for president. With a crowded field and no clear frontrunner for the 1976 Democratic nomination, there was a renewed effort to promote a Rodino candidacy. From Sacramento to Peoria, supporters wrote urging the chairman to seek the nomination. Many of his friends in Washington and New Jersey offered the same encouragement. However flattering the suggestions, Rodino had no real aspirations for national office and never seriously contemplated running for president. He was certainly not willing at this point in his political career to undertake the intensive fundraising and arduous effort needed to secure the nomination. "I really don't have any ambition for running for the presidency," he told the *North Dade Journal* during a fundraising event in Florida and continued to deny the rumors of a presidential run to the disappointment of his boosters.[51]

The start of the 1976 primary season quickly ended this speculation, and by June former Georgia governor Jimmy Carter had secured enough delegates to win the party's nomination. With that secured, attention swung to the selection of a vice presidential candidate. At Carter's campaign headquarters in Plains, Georgia, planning was already underway for an intensive vetting process. Rodino's name was among a long list of potential choices mentioned in the press. The *Boston Globe* argued that Rodino offered Carter "a number of pluses" as a potential running mate, particularly as an ideological and geographic counterbalance. *Newsday* concluded "on paper at least, he was the perfect Veep."[52] Acting on these positive assessments, fifty of Rodino's colleagues held a press conference on Capitol Hill and, sporting newly minted "Rodino For Veep" buttons, announced they were launching a major push for his selection. Their effort was given a strong boost from Majority Leader Tip O'Neill, who informed Charles H. Kirbo, the Georgia attorney leading Carter's vice presidential search team, that Rodino was his first choice for the nomination. Poised to be the next Speaker of the House following Carl Albert's announced retirement, O'Neill's backing was politically significant, and he enthusiastically repeated these words of support when he met with Carter in Georgia the following week.[53] Rodino regarded all of this activity with mixed emotions; flattered by the vote of confidence from his peers and genuinely uncomfortable to be the object of a public campaign for a job he was unlikely to get and not sure he wanted. Neither encouraging nor discouraging his colleagues, he released a statement thanking them and making it clear he was not seeking the vice presidency.[54]

Operating out of an office in Washington, Charles Kirbo began conducting preliminary screenings of possible running mates before they were invited to Georgia for a personal interview with the presidential nominee. The initial short list drawn up by Carter and his advisers comprised a half dozen senators and did not include Rodino. But O'Neill's strong endorsement was not something an incoming Democratic president could simply ignore, and Rodino's name was added to the roster as a political courtesy.[55] Carter phoned him at home on July 4 to share this news, and Kirbo arranged a meeting to discuss the vice presidency three days later. At the conclusion of their hour-long session, Rodino was asked to fill out a detailed questionnaire and provide extensive background information for campaign officials to review. To avoid the appearance of an eager supplicant, Rodino requested that his follow-up personal interview with Carter take place in New York before the opening of the Democratic convention instead of in Plains. His congressional office and committee staff worked frantically over the next few days to collect and prepare all the requested tax, medical, and legislative records.[56]

When Rodino walked into the lobby of the Americana Hotel on Sunday, July 11, for his meeting with Jimmy Carter, he had already decided to withdraw his name from consideration. Feeling an obligation to his patron Tip O'Neill and his other congressional champions, he was willing to allow the vetting process to run its course. But the recognition that he was unlikely to be chosen and his sense of pride now convinced him to bow out gracefully before Carter made his final decision. Rodino recalled that he began their private session by immediately informing Carter that he would not accept the vice presidency if it was offered because of his responsibilities as chairman and the need to continue work on the committee's legislative agenda. With that topic settled, Rodino spent the rest of the hour offering his assessment of the six other potential nominees and urging Carter to soften his anti-Washington rhetoric during the general election campaign. The two met briefly with reporters afterward so that Carter could declare that Rodino was "qualified in every respect" to be his running mate and neither offered any further details of their discussion.[57]

Following the meeting, Rodino and campaign officials began formulating a plan to announce his withdrawal. Carter wanted it to be clear that he had not preemptively rejected Rodino. To underscore that point, he invited him to deliver the main nominating speech later in the week. Rodino's chronic glaucoma and the possibility of a flare-up during the rigors of the campaign, regardless of the fact that it had not previously interrupted his hectic travel schedule, provided a convenient and believable reason for his decision. Press Secretary Jody Powell made this announcement the next day, and Rodino did a few follow-up interviews to explain his recurring eye problems and assure reporters that his overall health was good.[58]

The speech Rodino delivered the evening of July 14 before a packed Madison Square Garden and a nationwide television audience was a blend of his personal story as the son of an immigrant, a reflection on the tribulations the country had suffered during the past two years, and an optimistic guide for the future. Extending his own impeachment halo to Jimmy Carter, he portrayed the nominee as the ideal post-Watergate candidate to challenge President Ford. "With honest talk and plain truth," Rodino told the crowd, "Jimmy Carter has appealed to the American people. His heart is honest, and the people will believe him. His purpose is right, and the people will follow him." The speech was widely praised, and the following morning Jimmy Carter announced his selection of Walter Mondale as his running mate before they were both nominated by acclamation that night.[59]

With his own reelection assured, Rodino offered to do whatever he could to help the new Democratic ticket. He became an important conduit to the Italian American community, where Carter's pronunciation of Italian as

"Eyetalian" in his convention speech continued to rankle many potential voters. To help repair this damage, Rodino persuaded the former governor to attend the inaugural event of the newly formed National Italian American Foundation, where Rodino and Judge Sirica were being honored, and he used this opportunity to introduce Carter to many of the prominent Italian Americans in attendance. A few days later, the two appeared together at several campaign events in Italian neighborhoods in New York City and then boarded a train for a whistle stop tour across New Jersey. Continuing to promote the Democratic ticket to his fellow Italian Americans, Rodino hosted Walter Mondale at Newark's Columbus Day celebration and then flew to Chicago to walk alongside Jimmy Carter in a return appearance at that city's annual parade.[60]

In a closer-than-expected outcome, Carter defeated Gerald Ford on November 2, and the Democrats retained their post-Watergate gains in both chambers of Congress. The president-elect called Rodino that night to thank him personally for all his help in the campaign.[61]

As the Carter presidential transition began, Rodino was in an enviable position. For the first time since he became chairman of the Judiciary Committee, the Democrats were poised to control both the legislative and executive branches of government and reap the benefits of one-party rule. Rodino now had the cachet of being a former contender for the vice presidential nomination and the political leverage he earned campaigning hard to elect the winning ticket. A few weeks after the election, he was among a small group of senior Democrats invited to a private lunch on Capitol Hill to meet with the president-elect and discuss plans for his incoming administration. Carter spoke of a new spirit of cooperation and promised to work closely with Congress.

This honeymoon was short-lived, however, and tensions between the two branches appeared shortly after inauguration day. The initial spark was dissatisfaction with the White House congressional liaison office and its director Frank Moore, who was criticized for not returning phone calls and ignoring the advice of members of Congress, two cardinal sins in Washington. This was compounded by the lack of coordination from a largely inexperienced White House staff that often failed to inform members before the administration made a public announcement involving their district.[62]

All of this contributed to an emerging schism between the new president and Democrats on Capitol Hill that was further fueled by differences in style and ideology. Carter had won the Democratic nomination running as an outsider without the backing of the party establishment, and he promised in his campaign to bring a new politics to post-Watergate Washington. The reserved Georgian rarely engaged in the clubby backslapping that was a mainstay on Capitol Hill. To the dismay of many members, he refused to fill positions in his administration through the traditional reliance on political patronage. Unlike much of the congressional leadership, the president was not a liberal, and his moderate legislative agenda focused on issues like government reorganization and tax cuts, not the big federal programs of the Great Society. Frequently at odds with the president, Speaker O'Neill complained in his memoirs that "during the Carter years, congressional Democrats often had the feeling that the White House was actually working against us."[63]

Rodino shared many of these same frustrations, as well as additional concerns specifically related to the Judiciary Committee's legislative responsibilities. His first disappointment was the selection of former federal judge Griffin Bell to be attorney general. Rodino had urged Carter to pick Joseph Califano. After he was chosen to head the Department of Health, Education, and Welfare, his second choices were either John Doar or Barbara Jordan. Rodino considered the selection of Carter's longtime friend a setback in reestablishing the Justice Department's independence following the Watergate scandal, and he thought Bell was too conservative. He was not alone in these concerns, and Bell's nomination provoked opposition from liberal groups upset over his past record on civil rights and continued membership in several segregated country clubs.[64] Equally unsettling for Rodino were Bell's views on a variety of issues he considered important, particularly the nominee's belief that there was no need for additional antitrust reforms. The two never really developed a close working relationship, and Rodino was often offended by what he considered a lack of deference from Bell and his staff. Consequently, they usually pursued their own individual policy goals, and, except for the enactment of a long postponed measure to enlarge the federal judiciary, the two achieved few significant legislative successes together.[65]

While Rodino complained privately about the difficulties of working with the Carter administration, he never expressed this publicly and was regarded as one of the president's most loyal supporters. Even as relations between the White House and Congress continued to deteriorate, he staunchly defended the administration. The *Star-Ledger* called him "one of Carter's best allies on Capitol Hill." He often made reference to his personal friendship with the president and frequent conversations and private Oval Office meetings, a claim not reflected in the daily logs of presidential activities.[66] If Rodino overstated their closeness, Carter did seek his counsel on multiple occasions and always treated Rodino with a genuine respect, which fostered a similar deference among the White House staff. The president seemed to look for opportunities to lavish praise on Rodino and highlight his leadership in the impeachment crisis; during a state dinner for the visiting president of Italy, Carter deviated from the usual protocol to include a tribute to Rodino in his official toast.[67] As evidenced by a noticeable increase in their interactions, the connection between the two grew stronger when Senator Edward M. "Ted" Kennedy indicated he might launch a bid for the 1980 Democratic nomination. The White House staff recommended that the president schedule a meeting "to solicit Rodino's counsel, views and suggestions on the Presidency, the political scene and the general mood of the country." After they met, Carter thanked Rodino for the frank discussion because "I continue to benefit from your political and personal wisdom."[68]

One of the best demonstrations of the president's regard came early in his presidency when he dispatched a large delegation consisting of his wife Rosalynn, Vice President Mondale, and two members of his cabinet to Capitol Hill to represent the administration at a special event honoring Rodino. It was a long-standing tradition to commission an artist to paint a portrait of the chairman of the House Judiciary Committee to hang on the walls of the main hearing room, and Rodino's portrait, begun the previous year, was scheduled for public presentation in May 1977. In addition to the contingent from the executive branch and Chief Justice Warren E. Burger, an impressive array of other Washington luminaries attended the ceremony in the now historic and familiar Rayburn 2141. Rodino's wife, Ann, officially unveiled the portrait, and Speaker O'Neill offered the first of several heartfelt tributes calling his friend "a truly international hero." Sitting in the audience alongside the invited dignitaries were the members of the Ladies Auxiliary, who had traveled to Washington to witness this important event in a career they helped launch. Rodino arranged for them to have tea with the First Lady at the White House the next day.[69]

The following year, Rodino received an equally enduring honor in New Jersey, and Vice President Mondale was sent to represent the president. Prior to the construction of Newark's federal building, the local offices of agencies, ranging from the Social Security Administration to the Immigration and Naturalization Service, were located at various sites throughout the city. This made it difficult for the residents of the Tenth District to access these services. Rodino initiated the effort to win approval and funding for a single federal building. The sixteen-story structure that opened in 1968 near city hall housed all these agencies and Rodino's relocated district office.[70] When he reached the requisite twenty-five years of service needed to name a federal building after a sitting member of Congress, his New Jersey colleague James J. Howard secured the passage of legislation to designate the "Peter W. Rodino Jr. Federal Building," and President Carter signed the executive order formalizing the designation. On November 3, 1978, most of the state's elected officials and several hundred attendees listened to the vice president deliver the keynote address and witnessed the unveiling of a plaque with the new designation.[71]

Sadly, the federal building naming ceremony was the last public appearance of Rodino's wife. Ann had been experiencing frequent blackouts earlier in the year, and a series of tests revealed that she had a malignant brain tumor. Doctors concluded that it was inoperable and recommended radiation treatments to delay the inevitable physical impairment. The brief period of remission that this bought made it possible for her to attend the event. For one of the few times in his long career, Rodino's personal responsibilities took precedence over his public duties, and he accompanied Ann to all her treatments and focused his efforts on refitting their Long Branch house with wheelchair ramps and a chair lift in preparation for what was ahead. He spent most of his time in New Jersey, making less frequent and shorter trips to Washington. "I just went when it was necessary to really vote on something," he recollected, "otherwise I just wouldn't."[72]

Rodino's initial plan to keep this family crisis confidential was not practicable; his disappearance from Capitol Hill soon attracted attention. In May, his office released a press statement announcing that Ann was "seriously ill" and explaining that Rodino was at her bedside. The news triggered a rush of get well wishes, including a note and later call from President Carter.[73] Although Rodino never publicly acknowledged the terminal nature of her illness, her condition continued to worsen. He was forced to spend more time at home, generally attending Judiciary Committee meetings on Tuesdays and only staying longer if necessary. His committee colleagues were very supportive, and he conducted an impressive amount of legislative business by telephone. He also relied heavily on his staff. As Press Secretary John Russonello recalled, "We covered for him." In addition to Russonello, Rodino was fortunate to have three longtime staff members to help manage his congressional operations in Washington and Newark: the seasoned staff director of the Judiciary Committee, Jim Cline, tireless district administrator, Anthony "Tony" Suriano, and his gifted legislative director, Eva J. Denev, who had single-handedly managed his non-judiciary portfolio since 1965. Together, these four helped to ease the burdens of their overwhelmed boss and maintained a level of activity that provided the outward appearance of normality.[74]

Despite Rodino's herculean efforts to fulfill his duties and remain engaged in important issues, he could not completely mask his nonattendance or the mounting tally of missed votes. Rumors began circulating in the Tenth District that he was planning to retire, and former freeholder Donald M. Payne Jr. and municipal judge Golden E. Johnson, both African Americans, announced in February 1980 that they were running for Congress.[75] The speculation over his possible departure forced Rodino to declare his own intentions to seek reelection and to begin preparations for a campaign. He accelerated efforts to raise money and hired pollster Peter D. Hart to assess the attitude of voters in the district. The good news from Hart's survey was that a majority continued to rate Rodino's job performance very positively, giving him the highest marks for honest leadership and having influence in Congress.[76] While his opponents criticized his absenteeism, Rodino touted his record and showcased a long list of endorsements from prominent African Americans. Because of Ann's illness, he largely conducted the campaign through radio and print ads rather than personally appearing at events. He did participate in one debate and accompanied Rosalynn Carter when she visited Newark to rally support for her husband who was fighting a challenge from Senator Kennedy in the New Jersey primary. While Carter lost in the Tenth District by a 2-to-1 margin on June 3, Rodino won more than 60 percent of the vote.[77]

With only token Republican opposition in the fall, Rodino devoted some of his limited time away from Ann to campaign for the national ticket. After winning the nomination, President Carter emerged from the Democratic convention in August politically wounded and began the presidential campaign with the twin burdens of a faltering economy and the recent seizure of American hostages in Iran. New Jersey was an important swing state in his expected close race against the Republican nominee Ronald Reagan, the conservative former governor of California, and Carter and his surrogates made several visits to the state. Their efforts had little effect on the outcome; Carter lost New Jersey for the second time and suffered a crushing defeat nationally in a Reagan political tidal wave. On Capitol Hill, Republicans captured nine Senate seats and won control of the chamber for the first time since 1955, replacing many of Rodino's longtime liberal allies with stalwart conservatives. The Democratic majority in the House was reduced by thirty-four seats and the once lopsided New Jersey delegation returned to a slight Democratic edge of 8 to 7. Judged in terms of partisanship and ideology, it was the most fundamental change in the political landscape since Rodino came to Congress.[78]

One month later, Marianna Stango Rodino died at the age of 70 after an almost two-year battle with cancer. "Without Ann's support and love and understanding, I would not have been able to serve the people of Newark or the nation as I have done," Rodino told the *Star-Ledger*.[79] Learning of Ann's death, President Carter telephoned the chairman and sent a handwritten note that same day expressing his "deep feeling of friendship and the sense of personal loss which Rosalynn and I share with you." Vice President Mondale and a delegation of House members traveled to New Jersey to pay their respects and offer comfort to the bereft Rodino and his family. Fittingly, Ann's funeral mass was held at St. Lucy's Church, the place where the two met on a Sunday morning more than a half century earlier.[80]

As Rodino began the difficult adjustment to life without Ann and the reality of being alone for the first time, he was also forced to prepare for the anticipated transformation that awaited him in Washington. For six years, he had basked in the aura from the Nixon impeachment and relished the attention and the accolades. He used this unexpected fame to help elect more Democrats to promote the liberal agenda he embraced. But the results of the 1980 election now cast a shadow over this afterglow. Facing a new political dynamic, he needed to recalibrate his expectations and prepare for a decidedly different chapter in his long public career.

CHAPTER TEN

A FITTING CONCLUSION

"AT MY AGE, I SHOULD BE SITTING in the sun and writing my memoirs," Peter Rodino lamented to *Los Angeles Times* reporter Robert Shogan in late September of 1982. The Ninety-Seventh Congress, the first since the political landslide that brought Republicans control of both the Senate and the White House, was preparing to adjourn so members could return home to campaign before the midterm elections; the seventy-three-year-old chairman was exhausted. It had been a taxing and challenging session for Rodino, who was constantly pushing back against the ascendant "New Right" and their tidal wave of conservative proposals on school prayer, busing, abortion, and other equally contentious issues. According to Shogan, Rodino had emerged as "the self-appointed commander of a liberal roadblock that is attempting to halt a fundamental shift in the ideological initiative from left to right." Rodino and his allies adopted the obstructionist tactics of his adversaries, stalling and sidetracking measures they opposed by scheduling endless rounds of hearings, declining to hold any hearings at all, or calling for detailed studies to bury objectionable legislation. The House Judiciary Committee was a critical bulwark for progressives on Capitol Hill, and a watchful Rodino was compelled to spend much of his time and energy fighting the conservative onslaught. "I saw when this Administration took office," he acknowledged, "that I was going to have to be the guy with his finger in the dike."[1]

Two years earlier, Rodino had returned to Washington eager to resume his congressional duties following the prolonged absences caused by Ann's long illness. He hoped that work could help fill the large void in his personal life, and he recollected that he returned to his office shortly after the funeral so "I couldn't think of things."[2] Unfortunately, the desire to find refuge from grief in his work coincided with a fundamental change in the political landscape. Ronald Reagan was the new president, and, unlike his fellow Republican predecessors, he was a hard-core conservative determined to abandon the consensus politics that had previously dominated the postwar capital. On the other side of Capitol Hill, South Carolina's Strom Thurmond, a segregationist Dixiecrat turned Republican, was the new chairman of the Senate Judiciary Committee. For the first time, Rodino would have to negotiate with a chamber controlled by the other party and work with a person who vigorously opposed every civil rights bill he had championed. Publicly, he expressed a willingness to try and work with Thurmond; privately, he was getting ready for a long siege and recruited three new liberal allies to serve on his committee.[3]

The first major skirmish involved the long simmering debate over court-ordered busing to promote racial integration in public schools. During the Carter administration, Rodino fought efforts in Congress to prohibit the Department of Justice from supporting this remedy, and the president had vetoed a measure that the sponsors forced out of the committee. Regardless of the Reagan administration's declaration that it would no longer pursue these cases, congressional proponents added a prohibition to the department's authorization bill in 1981 and pressed for a constitutional amendment banning busing. The following year, the Senate passed a restrictive measure prohibiting federal courts from using busing to desegregate, an incursion into the judiciary that Rodino condemned as "without precedent." He requested that Attorney General William French Smith offer an opinion on the constitutionality of this action.[4] Considering he was President Reagan's former personal attorney and had appointed legal conservatives hostile to vigorous enforcement to run the civil rights division, it was not surprising that in his response he sided with the Senate sponsors and endorsed the validity of their proposal. Rodino immediately consigned the antibusing measure to a subcommittee, where it joined constitutional amendments on school prayer and abortion to languish in a legislative graveyard for the remainder of the session.[5]

Alongside these social issues, the chairman faced a reinvigorated campaign for a constitutional amendment requiring a balanced federal budget. For the past three years, Rodino had successfully maneuvered to prevent any House consideration of what he dismissed as a gimmick. With mounting deficits, budgetary gridlock, and a still struggling economy, emboldened conservatives reintroduced an amendment that was attracting support from Democrats and placing the committee under considerable political pressure to act. Rodino no longer had an ally in the White House; President Reagan wholeheartedly endorsed the amendment and personally worked for its passage. The Senate's overwhelming approval of a balanced budget amendment in July 1982 prompted the chairman to begin a new round of hearings in an attempt to slow momentum and sidetrack the issue until after the midterm election.[6]

But the popularity of this economic panacea among members was difficult to counteract. On September 30, balanced budget proponents secured the 218 signatures needed for a discharge petition to force the amendment out of the committee. Fearing Republicans would use any further delay as an issue in the upcoming campaign, Rodino and Speaker O'Neill decided to begin the debate immediately and deny supporters the ability to launch a major lobbying push. The wisdom of this decision was confirmed the next day when the balanced budget amendment failed to win the required two-thirds vote in the House. As a result of the chairman's steadfast patience and skillful deflections, all the proposals he considered unworthy additions to the Constitution were either defeated or derailed. "The New Right took its best shot and missed," the *Trenton Times* sardonically observed.[7]

In addition to assuming the role of constitutional gatekeeper, Rodino joined with fellow liberals to defend vulnerable progressive policies from conservative attacks. He was particularly vigilant about protecting the civil rights programs that were now the responsibility of an administration publicly opposed to affirmative action, busing, and many of the other enforcement remedies previously used by the federal government. An unusually pessimistic Rodino told the members of the Leadership Conference on Civil Rights in late April 1981 that "we face a difficult task in attempting to resist these efforts to turn back the calendar."[8] His top priority was to safeguard the future of the Voting Rights Act, which was scheduled to expire in August 1982. While Strom Thurmond opposed another extension, Rodino won bipartisan approval in the House for an additional ten years.[9] The Reagan administration agreed not to oppose an extension if the House bill was significantly weakened. When a conservative filibuster to block consideration failed, and the Senate approved a ten-year extension, President Reagan reluctantly bowed to Republican pressure and signed a bill that largely mirrored Rodino's original proposal.[10]

The chairman was less successful at thwarting conservative efforts to limit existing gun control requirements. As a longtime advocate of stricter regulations, Rodino had either authored or sponsored proposals to impose a waiting period for gun sales and ban the interstate transport of all firearms. Following the attempted assassination of President Reagan in March 1981, he introduced a bill outlawing the manufacture, assembly, and sale of handguns known as "Saturday night specials," the weapon John Hinckley Jr. used to shoot the president, hoping this event might alter the political climate. But the president and the National Rifle Association's allies in the Senate were moving in the opposite direction and planning a major push to end the current federal prohibition of the mail-order sale of guns and broaden eligibility for gun ownership. Rodino vehemently opposed these proposed changes and managed to postpone debate in the House until early 1986, when gun advocates were able to secure a discharge petition forcing the measure out of the committee. Losing control of the legislative calendar, he could do little to stop the passage of what was the first weakening of the Gun Control Act of 1968, which had passed following the assassinations of Martin Luther King and Robert Kennedy.[11]

While fighting against the adoption and implementation of conservative policies, Rodino was equally concerned about any possible political interference from the White House that might undermine the independence of the Justice Department, a fear that was heightened when Edwin Meese, Reagan's senior adviser, was selected to succeed Smith as the attorney general. This oversight responsibility compelled Rodino to get involved in the investigation of a major political scandal that first erupted publicly at the beginning of 1982. Amid allegations that officials at the Environmental Protection Agency (EPA) were strategically directing toxic waste cleanup funds to help Republicans, several House subcommittees launched probes into potential malfeasance at the agency. When they were forced to issue subpoenas for the release of the relevant internal documents, President Reagan followed Attorney General Smith's guidance to claim executive privilege and refused to release the documents. The result was that EPA Administrator Anne Gorsuch Burford, who privately disagreed with this decision, became the first executive branch official to be cited by the House of Representatives for contempt of Congress. Consequently, the Justice Department was now simultaneously responsible for prosecuting the contempt case against Burford and defending the president's executive privilege claim that placed her in this legal jeopardy.[12]

This confusing quagmire raised serious doubts about the appropriateness of the department's actions, and, fearing it might threaten the ongoing congressional inquiries, House leaders asked Rodino for help in resolving this stalemate. The chairman sent a sharply worded letter to the attorney general in February 1983 demanding he provide timely answers to a long list of questions regarding "the apparent conflicts of interest in the numerous roles the Department has played."[13]

Before Rodino received an answer, the public disclosure of potential criminal activity at the EPA compelled President Reagan to release the contested documents to avoid charges of a cover-up, and Burford's resignation allowed the congressional inquiries to move forward. Rodino did not stop his own review of the Justice Department's actions. For the next eighteen months, members of a small special staff he created interviewed more than one hundred government officials, largely succeeding in avoiding any public attention. The result of this hidden diligence was a thirteen-hundred-page report released in December 1985 that was highly critical of the Justice Department for providing "false and misleading" testimony to Congress, misusing the claim of executive privilege, and obstructing the committee's own probe. Two Republicans joined all the Democrats in requesting that Attorney General Edwin Meese appoint an independent counsel to pursue possible criminal prosecutions. Meese's delayed response and his unwillingness to authorize a broader legal review of official misconduct frustrated Rodino and further soured their strained relationship. Almost three years later, the independent counsel's inquiry ended without any indictments.[14]

The one issue that did bring Rodino and the Reagan administration together was immigration reform. Since the passage of the 1965 act, which for the first time placed a limit on immigration from the Western Hemisphere, illegal immigration into the United States had mushroomed. Seeking economic opportunities, a large influx of undocumented workers from Mexico and Central America were entering the United States in record numbers, creating a burgeoning shadow economy where they were often exploited by unscrupulous employers. When he became chairman of the immigration subcommittee in 1971, Rodino conducted extensive field hearings on the border problem and introduced legislation to prevent the mistreatment of this vulnerable population. His innovative proposal addressed the immediate need by granting amnesty and a path to citizenship for those who were already illegally in the United States and discouraged future economic flight by punishing any employers who hired undocumented workers. After his elevation to the leadership of the full committee, he made this a priority and succeeded in winning House approval for his immigration reform bill in two consecutive congressional sessions before the business lobby derailed it in the Senate. Rodino's measure was revived by the Carter administration in 1977 only to suffer a similar political fate.[15]

Unable to break the impasse over immigration reform, Congress agreed to create the Select Commission on Immigration and Refugee Policy the following year to evaluate the laws, regulations, and procedures governing immigration and to determine what changes were needed. Rodino was appointed to serve as one of the congressional members on the panel alongside several cabinet secretaries, academics, and local government officials. In the months that followed the opening session, this eclectic group heard presentations from experts, held numerous hearings, and engaged in sometimes acrimonious policy debates. Their final report issued in March 1981 outlined a long list of recommendations, including Rodino's proposals for legalization and employer sanctions.[16]

As governor of California, Ronald Reagan had experienced the difficulties of stemming the flow of illegal immigration into the United States, and he signed the first state law imposing penalties on employers. Receiving the commission's report two months after his inauguration, the president asked Attorney General Smith to review the findings and prepare draft legislation to revamp immigration policy, which the cabinet approved in July.[17] The administration's plan, introduced by Wyoming Republican Senator Alan K. Simpson, called for limited amnesty, employer sanctions, a temporary farmworkers program, and stricter border enforcement. Because of Simpson's leadership and Reagan's influence with conservatives, this time the Senate acted first and overwhelmingly approved the measure in August 1982, shifting the burden to the House where Rodino's past success raised expectations for passage.[18]

Even with the strong bipartisan vote in the Senate and the president's endorsement, assembling a majority in the House of Representatives to support immigration reform remained a formidable challenge. The business lobby continued to oppose any burdens on its members, western agricultural interests feared the loss of essential migrant workers, organized labor was against any expansion of the legal job market at a time of high unemployment, and many Hispanics believed that employer sanctions would lead to widespread discrimination. This loose confederation of opponents straddled partisan, ideological, and geographic boundaries, making it hard to counter their lobbying efforts on Capitol Hill. During an intense week of deliberations in the Judiciary Committee, Rodino managed to forge a compromise measure and win a narrow victory for his bill on the eve of the scheduled October recess.[19] The delay in floor action until the House returned for a lame duck session after the midterm election allowed opponents to undermine the already fragile coalition supporting reform, and Congress adjourned without taking a final vote on the legislation. Lamenting this "lost opportunity," Rodino warned his colleagues that the problem "will not go away, but will continue to grow and grow."[20]

When the new Congress convened the following month, supporters of reform urged the chairman to try again. But after repeated unsuccessful attempts, he was unenthusiastic and pessimistic about the prospects for passing any measure that incorporated the necessary balance he believed was essential to transform immigration policy. His uneasy alliance with the Reagan administration was seriously frayed, and he blamed weak support from the White House for the defeat of the legislation. He was also under enormous pressure, as was Speaker O'Neill, from Hispanic members of the Democratic caucus who opposed the employer sanctions, many of whom were his fellow progressives and personal friends. Consequently, Rodino decided to step back and allow the chairman of the immigration subcommittee, Kentucky representative Romano L. Mazzoli, take the lead in working with Senator Simpson to reintroduce the legislation. The amended bill that the House finally approved in June 1984 contained many provisions the Reagan administration opposed, and the issue was embroiled in presidential politics when Democratic nominee Walter Mondale denounced the legislation as anti-Hispanic. A few months later, Rodino led the House conferees in difficult negotiations with the Senate, which ended in failure when the president threatened to veto the bill unless the funding for the amnesty program was capped at a level the Democrats considered unacceptable.[21]

With the election over and Hispanic opposition appearing to soften, Rodino decided to make one last attempt to rewrite immigration policy. Although Alan Simpson had already offered a modest reform proposal in the Senate, he could not find a cosponsor in the House. Rodino's announcement in July 1985 that he was introducing his own comprehensive legislation was greeted with great applause and heightened expectations. "A thunderbolt has just plunged down out of the cloud that darkens immigration reform," a *New York Times* editorial proclaimed. "Representative Peter Rodino says he'll champion it in the House...it's hard to imagine a more dramatic development in the long struggle to persuade America to take control of its borders."[22] The measure the chairman introduced incorporated many of the provisions fashioned in previous efforts to address specific concerns and attract necessary support, including granting legal status to those who came to the United States before 1982, imposing civil and criminal penalties on employers for hiring workers without proper documentation, enhancing protections against discrimination in the workplace, and expediting the process for issuing visas for temporary workers. Acknowledging this was still "an uphill climb," Rodino maintained that the fate of immigration reform legislation depended upon the Reagan administration's willingness to make this a top priority and lobby hard for its passage, an admonition he later made directly to the president at a White House meeting.[23]

While the long battle over immigration reform encompassed an array of contentious and complex issues, each iteration of the fight seemed to flounder on a uniquely irreconcilable disagreement. By the spring of 1986, the major roadblock to congressional action was the unresolved dispute regarding the future status of illegal immigrants who came from Mexico every year to pick the fruits and vegetables growing in the western United States. Employed to supplement American farmworkers, these seasonal migrants were considered an essential part of a labor force operating under the time constraints imposed by a perishable commodity. Both Rodino and Simpson recognized this unique situation and attempted to address it in their respective bills, providing a three-year transition period before imposing employer sanctions on farmers and allowing the Labor Department to issue emergency visas if more temporary workers were needed during harvest time. The growers, openly acknowledging their dependency on illegal workers, dismissed these provisions as inadequate and instead lobbied Congress and the White House to allow up to 350,000 undocumented guest workers to spend nine months every year picking crops in the western United States. Most supporters of immigration reform regarded this as an unacceptably broad exemption that essentially maintained the status quo and provided a large loophole for a special interest group. Offering no effective mechanism to ensure that these "temporary" workers returned home, it did little to protect the interests of American farmworkers or prevent the exploitation of the undocumented. Disregarding Alan Simpson's vigorous opposition to what he considered "not simply survival but greed," the Senate added the growers' plan to Simpson's bill before approving it, and a "deeply disappointed" Rodino warned that the House would not accept this proposal.[24]

At the request of a group of Judiciary Committee Democrats led by Representative Charles Schumer of New York, Rodino agreed to delay consideration of his bill so they could quietly pursue a resolution of the impasse over the farmworker issue. By the time the panel began marking up the immigration reform measure in late June 1986, Schumer had succeeded in forging a compromise that attempted to address many of the concerns of agricultural interests, organized labor, and the Hispanic community. With the chairman's blessing, he offered an amendment that granted legal status to any foreign farmworker employed in the United States for at least sixty days during a one-year period beginning in 1985. Schumer argued that this would ensure an adequate pool of farmworkers who enjoyed the protections of legalization, and, anticipating the possibility of an unexpected demand for more workers in the future, he provided a mechanism for raising this cap if needed. The Reagan administration and critics of amnesty dismissed this as too expansive, and most growers continued to prefer the less constraining Senate provision. Following a heated debate, the committee narrowly agreed to the proposal and accepted additional modifications before a bipartisan majority approved the amended bill.[25]

Confident that the major obstacle to passage was now removed, Rodino brought the legislation to the House floor, where he suffered an unexpected defeat over the adoption of the rule for debate. To protect the carefully crafted farmworker compromise, no amendments were allowed on this issue.

Opponents were furious and joined together to defeat the rule, sending the measure back to the committee. A stunned Rodino blamed President Reagan for failing to rally Republicans. With only a few weeks remaining before adjournment, he declared, "this bill is dead."[26]

In a surprising turnaround, the House of Representatives began floor debate two weeks later on Rodino's legislation. Hours after the rules defeat, supporters of immigration reform from both sides of the aisle had gathered in the chairman's Rayburn office to reassess and consider their next step. There was general agreement that this was probably the last opportunity to pass a balanced proposal that included the politically charged amnesty program. Working with opponents and Senator Simpson, they revised the Judiciary Committee's farmworkers' provision to make it less generous by extending the time required for a migrant to gain legal status and by capping the total number of participants in the legalization program at a fixed level that could be raised if there was a shortage of workers. This defused the issue, and, except for a close vote that defeated a motion to remove the entire amnesty program, the day-long debate went as expected—the bill passed by a vote of 230 to 166.

Throughout this process, Rodino and Simpson were in constant discussions to reconcile many of the other differences between their two bills, making it possible for the conference committee to complete its work in a few days. Simpson secured President Reagan's backing for the final agreement, which included the House's farmworker provision and more liberal amnesty program, and both chambers approved it before Congress adjourned.[27]

On November 6, Rodino traveled to the White House for a bill signing ceremony, an event he had waited fifteen years to witness. Leaving the ceremony, he expressed the hope that the new law would provide "the opportunity for people who have been long in this shadow society to come forward, live as decent human beings and be given an opportunity to join the mainstream." Those gaining legal status under the amnesty program would become known in Mexico as "los rodinos."[28]

A few weeks before the enactment of immigration reform, Rodino stood on the floor of the Senate to address another topic he was closely identified with: impeachment. If memories of the Nixon impeachment inquiry were beginning to fade, it remained an important touchstone for many Americans, one that was inextricably linked to Peter Rodino and his public persona. To his great satisfaction, tourists still recognized him when he walked through the Rayburn building, and reporters routinely sought his views on Richard Nixon's latest attempt to burnish his reputation. Rodino welcomed the attention, and, when he was bumped from his usual second row seat on the Washington shuttle by the former president and his security detail, the chairman made sure the press was informed; the press widely reported on the incident. The tenth anniversary of the impeachment deliberations had provided Rodino with a timely opportunity during the summer of 1984 to revisit this seminal event in his congressional career and revel in the national spotlight. He gladly accepted all requests for interviews and was prominently featured in the documentary *Summer of Judgment*, which PBS aired to mark the occasion. Although no longer as enthusiastic about traveling across the country to participate in campaign events, Rodino remained committed to using his post-impeachment fame to help elect Democrats. He continued to serve as a potent symbol for the party faithful—only Tip O'Neill's signature on a fundraising letter raised more money. Asked to explain the reason for Rodino's enduring appeal, the head of the Democratic Congressional Campaign Committee attributed it to the fact that "he has done nothing to destroy his credibility."[29]

But Rodino's appearance on the other side of Capitol Hill was not a nostalgic occasion; he was there as the House of Representatives' chief prosecutor for the first impeachment in fifty years. Judge Harry E. Claiborne, a Carter appointee serving on the United States district court in Nevada, was convicted of filing false income tax returns and sentenced to two years in prison. After several rounds of unsuccessful appeals, he finally entered a minimum security prison in May 1986, becoming the first sitting federal judge to be incarcerated. Claiborne refused to resign from his lifetime position, claiming he was the victim of retribution from an overzealous US attorney for what were simply accounting errors. Consequently, the judge continued to collect his salary, accrue pension benefits, and was automatically eligible to return to the bench upon release, unless he was removed from office.[30]

When the scandal of having a prisoner on the federal government's payroll became a national news story, the House Judiciary Committee was compelled to consider the possibility of initiating impeachment proceedings, and Rodino introduced a resolution to begin the process. As he did in 1974, he hired a special counsel rather than rely on the regular staff to manage this undertaking. This time, he tasked a subcommittee to do the preliminary work of examining the evidence and drafting articles of impeachment. With this completed, the committee moved expeditiously to adopt articles that cited Claiborne's false tax returns, criminal conviction, and disgraceful conduct. The House of Representatives unanimously approved the articles in July 1986 and sent them to the Senate.[31] Rodino was appointed to lead the nine House managers from the Judiciary Committee who presented evidence to a special Senate committee holding pretrial hearings, where Judge Claiborne and other witnesses also testified. On October 7, the managers began their formal defense of the impeachment articles before the full Senate. Delivering the closing argument for the House, Rodino focused on the larger impact of this "sad day for our nation" and maintained that to preserve the integrity of the judiciary, "Judge Claiborne must be removed from office." Following presentations from the judge and his attorney, two-thirds of the Senate accepted this admonition and approved three articles of impeachment.[32]

In a surprising coincidence, Rodino and his Judiciary Committee colleagues soon found themselves burdened with two additional judicial impeachments after a half century of inactivity. The first was similar to the Claiborne case and involved Walter L. Nixon Jr., a district court judge in Mississippi who was convicted of perjury and refused to resign. When the Supreme Court denied his appeal, the Judicial Conference recommended his impeachment. Rodino requested funding to hire an outside counsel. Following a review of the evidence and several days of hearings, the committee approved three articles of impeachment in July 1988. The Nixon case generated less public outcry; without the same pressure on the House, the matter was not a priority for Democratic leaders anxious to complete other items on the legislative agenda before the election. They postponed action until the next Congress, and the Senate trial and final vote to remove Judge Nixon was held in November 1989.[33]

The second impeachment posed a unique and complicated challenge for Rodino and the committee, starkly highlighting the differences between the impeachment process and a criminal prosecution. Alcee Hastings, the first African American appointed to the federal bench in Florida, had been acquitted in 1982 on charges that he accepted bribes to reduce the sentences of criminal defendants. Disregarding the jury's verdict after a long trial, several of his fellow jurists in the Eleventh Circuit filed a complaint against Hastings for what they maintained was his repeated contravention of the code of judicial conduct. John Doar, now in private practice, was hired to conduct an investigation, and the methodical lawyer spent three years and $2 million accumulating evidence and receiving testimony from witnesses. Ignoring repeated objections from Hastings that this violated the Constitution's ban on double jeopardy and was racially motivated, a panel of all white judges concluded that he had taken a bribe, lied at his trial, and should be removed from office. The Judicial Conference of the United States, without conducting its own investigation, sent this recommendation for impeachment to the House of Representatives in March 1987.[34]

Rodino recognized that the ongoing controversy surrounding the Hastings case demanded a more vigorous process than the one the panel followed with Judge Claiborne. "There are no precedents to guide us in this type of impeachment inquiry," he wrote in requesting supplemental appropriations, "so we are clearly entering into uncharted waters."[35] He proposed funding a temporary staff of six, including attorneys and investigators, along with the resources needed for expected travel and hearings. In addition, Rodino decided to bypass the usual subcommittees and instead referred the impeachment resolution to the Subcommittee on Criminal Justice chaired by John Conyers Jr., a senior member of the Congressional Black Caucus and veteran of the Nixon inquiry. Conyers had expressed a profound skepticism over the validity of the charges leveled by white conservative judges against one of the few African Americans on the federal bench, a view the National Bar Association and other black organizations shared. Whatever the subcommittee decided, Rodino concluded that Conyers's stewardship of this racially charged undertaking was the best way to ensure public confidence in the fairness of the outcome.

Following months of investigation and a week of hearings, Conyers and the other members of the subcommittee voted in July 1988 to adopt seventeen articles of impeachment charging Hastings with soliciting bribes and lying about it at his trial. Conyers acknowledged the difficulty of his decision in an emotional speech during the House debate the next month, explaining that the overwhelming evidence convinced him that Hastings was guilty.[36] On August 9, Rodino read the articles of impeachment on the floor of the Senate to initiate the trial phase of the process, which ended with the removal of Hastings from office three weeks before Judge Nixon met a similar fate. Seeking vindication from what he continued to denounce as unfair treatment, Alcee Hastings was elected to the House of Representatives in 1992, where he worked alongside many of his former impeachers and served until his death twenty-nine years later.[37]

During the time that Rodino was managing impeachments and pushing immigration reform in Washington, he was also facing political developments at home that would culminate in his most serious electoral battle since 1972. The results of the 1980 census triggered a new round of congressional apportionment. With New Jersey losing a seat, creating a new map was even thornier and more protracted than it had been a decade earlier. Although the difficult process was entangled in legislative and legal battles for eighteen months, the political pressure to preserve the Tenth District as a majority black district limited Rodino's options to maneuver, and the relatively unchanged final boundaries finally established in 1984 boosted the number of black voters to nearly 60 percent.[38] His pollster, Peter Hart, warned him that civil rights activist Jesse Jackson, seeking the Democratic presidential nomination, was planning a major campaign drive in New Jersey, which was likely to increase the turnout of African American voters. "Jesse Jackson's presidential candidacy," he warned, "could change Tenth District electing dynamics in the primary from an appreciation of congressional abilities and stature to a crusade for a black candidate." Such a warning bore no fruit however; while Jackson swept Newark and Essex County, Rodino won 75 percent of the vote to easily defeat his unknown opponent.[39]

One of the reasons for Rodino's continued success in fending off primary challenges was his strategic alliances with key African American leaders in the district, particularly Newark mayor Kenneth Gibson. Although Gibson opposed him in the pivotal 1972 race, the two soon developed a close and mutually beneficial relationship. Rodino's clout in Washington brought much needed federal dollars to the struggling city and helped the mayor win reelection three times; Gibson's disinterest in running for Congress eliminated a formidable opponent, and his endorsement discouraged other challengers. The mayor did launch two unsuccessful bids to win the Democratic nomination for governor, and Rodino gave these efforts a significant boost when he abandoned his long-standing primary neutrality to support Gibson.[40] The mayor returned the favor after Jesse Jackson told reporters during an appearance at a Newark fundraiser in the fall of 1984 that the ten white members of Congress representing black districts should be replaced. Promising to support any African American who challenged Rodino at the next election, Jackson declared, "it's time for blacks to have adequate representation in the Congress."[41] Gibson immediately dismissed the idea, and as New Jersey's most prominent African American elected official, his rebuff helped to quash any further public discussion of the issue. As a *New York Times* article published the same week confirmed, "the leading black officials in the district say Mr. Rodino can hold the seat as long as he wants."[42]

But this willingness to wait indefinitely to have an African American in New Jersey's congressional delegation was not shared by everyone in the Tenth District. At the start of the 1986 election cycle, a group of black political leaders agreed to work together and develop their own slate of candidates to run for countywide offices and Congress in the upcoming primary. On March 8, several hundred party activists gathered at Rutgers University's Paul Robeson Hall in Newark to participate in the first Essex County Black Democrats Convention. Following presentations from all the potential nominees, the delegates selected the finalists; former Rodino rival and now South Ward Councilman Donald Payne was chosen over six other contenders as their candidate to run against Rodino. Mayor Gibson attended and announced to the press that he would not make any endorsements until after the mayoral election in May.[43]

Closely monitoring these developments from Washington, Rodino decided to begin his reelection drive earlier than usual, and he asked civil rights icon Bayard Rustin to send a letter of support to leading black officials in the district. Rodino formally announced his candidacy the day before the Rutgers convention to remove any lingering doubts about his future plans and provide a response to the gathering.[44] With Payne largely focused on winning reelection to the council, Rodino initially encountered little opposition, and the early weeks of the campaign were relatively uneventful. This tranquility abruptly ended on May 13, when Mayor Gibson was unexpectedly defeated in the first round of the municipal election. Councilman Sharpe James, tapping into anger over rising crime and higher taxes, scored a stunning upset by promising to bring sweeping changes to the city. The surprising result was both unwelcomed and ill-timed news for Rodino; less than a month before the June 3 primary, he lost a valuable ally who had provided an important political safety net in the past. The impact of this loss was underscored a week later when mayor-elect James announced that he was endorsing Donald Payne for Congress, the first time since 1972 that a Rodino challenger received any significant support from an elected official. The reelected councilman was now free to devote his full attention to the congressional race, and, hoping to capitalize on the momentum for change, he adopted the campaign slogan "Our time has come."[45]

Rodino's response to this new political climate was to fortify his regular campaign playbook with additional fundraising, more frequent radio advertisements, and accelerated activity in the district. He recruited the assistance of the Congressional Black Caucus, which had granted him honorary membership earlier in the year, and longtime colleague Charlie Rangel made several visits to Newark. Wherever Rodino appeared, he talked about his efforts to block the Reagan agenda and stressed the importance of his seniority to the Tenth District, highlighting in one radio ad that his opponent would not attain the same status on Capitol Hill until 2024.[46]

A week before the primary, Rodino received another jolting reminder of the consequences of Gibson's defeat when Jesse Jackson came to Newark to endorse Donald Payne. Fulfilling the promise he had made two years earlier, Jackson appeared alongside the councilman at a press conference and declared, "Mr. Rodino has had his day."[47] He told the audience that electing New Jersey's first African American congressman far outweighed any other consideration, and he returned three more times to campaign for Payne and increase the turnout of black voters. Jackson's decision to join the effort to oust Rodino attracted national press attention and sparked criticism for what many considered a reversal of his previous position that a candidate's race should not matter. "If Jesse Jackson could construct a congressman from scratch," the *Washington Post*'s Richard Cohen wrote, "he would build a Peter Rodino. But he wouldn't color him white."[48] Attempting to downplay the importance of Jackson's visit, Rodino issued a statement expressing confidence that his constituents would make their own decision based on his long record of service and noted that "Jesse Jackson and I have been on the same side for over 30 years fighting against the forces of reaction and racism." Privately, Rodino was deeply hurt by Jackson's personal attacks and seriously worried they might influence voters during the critical closing days of the contest.[49]

On June 3, a noticeably relieved Rodino declared victory two hours after the polls closed, proclaiming that the voters had rejected Jackson's appeal and "put aside any thoughts of race."[50] Thanks to his large war chest, low voter turnout, and an opponent who only campaigned for three weeks, Rodino was able to win a larger-than-predicted 60 percent of the vote. But the results provided little long-term reassurance; Donald Payne captured a higher percentage of the vote than any previous challenger and demonstrated the political potential of African American unity. Payne emerged from the race with a higher public profile and announced in his concession speech that he planned to run again in 1988. Less certain on primary night was whether or not Peter Rodino would be his opponent. For six years, the chairman had cited the need to thwart Ronald Reagan as the reason he was seeking reelection. Now that he was assured another term and the administration was nearing its end, there was growing speculation and even anticipation that this might finally be Rodino's last campaign. Considering his repeated promise that "as long as Reagan is around I'll be around," it was not unreasonable to expect that when the president left Washington, the chairman would follow.[51]

Facing only token opposition and easily reelected in November, Rodino returned to Capitol Hill to participate in the congressional investigation of a scandal that was already being compared to Watergate. A year earlier, the Reagan administration had launched a secret operation to sell arms to Iran in exchange for assistance in securing the release of American hostages held in Lebanon. This violation of long-standing policy, initiated by officials at the National Security Council (NSC) without congressional approval, was unexpectedly exposed in a series of press accounts that appeared shortly after the midterm elections, setting off a firestorm in Washington. President Reagan's initial response was to deny the reports until additional revelations finally forced him to acknowledge and defend these covert activities in a nationally televised address. With the administration under considerable pressure to provide more details to Congress, Attorney General Meese offered to conduct an informal inquiry and collect the relevant facts needed for preparing a credible chronology. His review uncovered a parallel enterprise managed by the same NSC officials using the profits from the arm sales to help the contras, the counterrevolutionaries fighting the Marxist government in Nicaragua. Although supporting these rebels was an important part of Reagan's anti-communist foreign policy agenda, Congress had prohibited the US government from providing direct aid to the group, making this diversion of funds potentially illegal. Meese disclosed his surprising discovery at a White House press briefing a few days later, where he assured reporters that no senior officials, including the president, were involved. He announced that the Justice Department was launching a formal investigation into what the press was beginning to call the "Iran-Contra" affair.[52]

While the intelligence committees in both chambers began a review of the arms deal, Rodino used the Judiciary Committee's oversight authority to scrutinize the role of the attorney general and the Justice Department in the unfolding controversy. From the beginning of their uneasy relationship, the chairman had criticized Meese for placing loyalty to the president above his duty to be the nation's chief law enforcement officer. Rodino's first action was to call for the appointment of an independent counsel to replace the Justice Department in any criminal investigation. He followed this with a request that the attorney general provide a detailed narrative of his actions and respond to a series of specific questions regarding his NSC investigation, past legal advice to the administration, and premature exoneration of the president. Rodino also requested that the committee receive all the relevant documents connected to these events. The Justice Department's response was to ignore the questions and refuse to send any documents because they were "highly classified." An irate Rodino reminded Meese that as the chairman of a committee that frequently handled confidential material he was not a security risk and noted his astonishment "that you, as Attorney General and chief legal adviser, have failed to respond to the many questions that are central to the legal implications of the Iran/contra controversy."[53]

Rodino was given another opportunity to challenge Meese's decisions when the House of Representatives joined the Senate in creating a select committee to investigate the Iran-Contra affair. Appointed by the new Speaker Jim Wright, Rodino was the most senior member of a panel that included several other committee chairmen and a contingent of staunch Reagan defenders. The two select committees, agreeing to complete their work by the August recess, started meeting separately behind closed doors before coming together in May 1987 to begin televised hearings.[54] With President Reagan's personal connection to the diversion of funds still unclear, memories of Watergate inevitably cast a shadow over the proceedings and gave a special relevance to Rodino's presence on the dais. In his opening statement, he acknowledged this connection, noting that "the question which has been asked most frequently since the November disclosures of the Iran/Contra affairs has been is this another Watergate?" Unwilling to offer an answer until all the evidence was presented, Rodino did admit to reporters afterward that even if they found a "smoking gun," it was unlikely that the Judiciary Committee would undertake impeachment proceedings against a popular president in the final year of his term.[55]

Rodino maintained a hectic schedule throughout the summer, fulfilling his duties as chairman and spending four days a week at the Iran-Contra hearings. Freed from the responsibility and constraints he felt during impeachment, he savored being back in the national spotlight and frequently stopped to chat with reporters and offer surprisingly candid observations about the ongoing proceedings. Rodino regularly participated in the cross-examination of witnesses. His finest moment as congressional interrogator came in late July, when Attorney General Meese spent two days in front of the panel. Initially praised for uncovering the channeling of aid to the contras, Meese was increasingly under attack for not taking swifter action to prevent NSC officials from destroying evidence, which raised suspicions he was involved in a possible cover-up. Rodino was the first member to grill the attorney general and spent a frustrating hour attempting to get the answers he requested six months earlier with what the *New York Times* called "hard, skeptical questioning."[56] Their tense, often testy exchanges enlivened the session, but yielded no new information. The hearings concluded the following week.

The final report of the select committee was released in November and strongly criticized President Reagan for his poor management and lack of oversight, holding him ultimately responsible for the illicit actions of his subordinates. Rodino believed the committee's strict deadline was a serious mistake and allowed the White House to delay providing evidence that might have revealed the president's direct involvement in the diversion of funds. Authoring two supplemental statements highlighting this obstructionism, he focused his harshest judgment on the inappropriate role Ed Meese had played in this entire process. "When one reviews the Attorney General's conduct during the Iran-Contra episode," he wrote, "it is impossible to avoid questions about his actions."[57]

Rodino did manage to take a break from the demands of the Iran-Contra inquiry to do something he had never done before: endorse a presidential candidate prior to the Democratic party's nominating convention. The decision to deviate from his long-standing posture of neutrality was the result of a burgeoning friendship with Joseph R. Biden, the junior senator from Delaware. Rodino had known Biden for several years, and they had worked closely together on a variety of issues after Biden succeeded Ted Kennedy as the ranking member of the Senate Judiciary Committee. When the Democrats regained control of the chamber at the start of 1987, Biden became chairman, and he regularly consulted with Rodino on pending legislative business. Around the same time, Biden decided to run for president. One of his early exploratory visits was to Rodino's Rayburn office to share the news and ask for his support. Always impressed by Biden's passion and flattered to be courted, Rodino agreed to serve as the national cochairman of the campaign. On June 9, Biden formally launched his presidential bid in Wilmington, Delaware, and Rodino cohosted a companion event in Washington with Biden's sister Valerie, introducing the candidate's congressional supporters and reminding the gathered crowd that Biden "can bring to the presidency those qualities of leadership that our country needs and that our people expect in a president." Unfortunately, Biden was forced to withdraw from the race a few months later amid charges of plagiarism, and the chairman never had the opportunity to campaign for his friend and colleague.[58]

Relishing the public attention from the Biden campaign and the Iran-Contra hearings, Rodino began hinting that he might run for reelection. "I knew I was really at a peak at the time," he recalled and deeply regretted his election-night comments implying he would retire at the end of the Reagan administration.[59] The reports of his likely departure had reverberated on Capitol Hill, and he quickly discovered that being considered a lame duck complicated his ability to lead the committee. To signal a possible change of plans and remove this stigma, Rodino decided to hold a Washington fundraiser in late July to replenish his depleted campaign coffers and keep his options open. "There is still time before I make up my mind," he told reporters, "but based on everything at this moment, I am making preparations to run."[60]

If this was a trial balloon as some suggested, it did not produce the desired result, and there was no overwhelming outpouring from constituents demanding he seek another term. On the contrary, the reaction in the Tenth District was largely negative, and he was criticized for reneging on what many regarded as a promise to retire. Rodino claimed that his remarks were misunderstood, and he had never ruled out the possibility of staying longer than Reagan, a technically accurate parsing of his words that few accepted. Many of his past supporters in the black community were opposed to his reelection, and Democratic chairman Raymond M. "Ray" Durkin indicated that Rodino was unlikely to receive the party's official endorsement, a rebuff that would force the incumbent into the difficult position of running as a challenger.[61]

The pressure on Rodino only intensified after Donald Payne formally launched his campaign for Congress in early 1988. Payne's initial fundraiser produced three times more money than his total expenditures in the last race and attracted many current officeholders, including several previous Rodino backers. With the April filing deadline for the primary approaching, press interest in the contest increased, and once friendly journalists now joined the growing chorus of those urging Rodino to bow out.[62] Privately, he remained convinced he could win renomination even without the Democratic party's endorsement, an overly optimistic view few shared. But he also recognized this scenario would require intensive fundraising and vigorous campaigning, a demanding assignment for a seventy-eight-year-old and one that was unlikely to get any easier in the future.

On March 9, he informed his senior staff in Washington that he had decided to retire, and they met the next day to finalize the mechanics of the actual announcement. Press Secretary Lawrence Spinelli was tasked with transforming Rodino's broadly outlined thoughts into a one-page statement, which they would release to the press at the end of the following week. During the intervening weekend, Rodino shared his plans with close friends in the district, and someone leaked the news to the *Star-Ledger*. Before Rodino returned to Washington on Monday, reporters began calling the office to confirm the rumor, and he decided to scrap the original timetable and make his retirement announcement that day.[63] The six-paragraph statement released to the press in the late afternoon on March 14 summarized the high points of his time on Capitol Hill and incorporated many of the same themes Rodino had referenced on previous occasions. Wanting to emphasize the difficulty of the decision, he expressed a "sense of sadness" at ending his "long and fulfilling" journey: "One cannot have served in this great body for forty years without some mixed emotions at the thought of leaving it. Nevertheless, I believe that my part of the journey in this great American experiment is at its end. I feel I have served my time and a purpose."[64]

Rodino's retirement was a major news story that night and for the next two days on television, radio, and newspapers throughout the country. Not surprisingly, the laudatory accounts of his four decades in Congress focused primarily on his chairmanship of the Nixon impeachment inquiry and recognition of his work on immigration and civil rights. Rodino's decision not to seek reelection, however reluctant or protracted, was widely praised as "gracious" for preventing an unpleasant political fight and "honorable" for clearing the path to electing New Jersey's first African American congressman. "There are two ways to retire from Congress," a *New York Times* editorial declared. "Some stay on until they are over the hill and have begun to embarrass themselves; some leave while they are on top and still appreciated. Typically, Peter Rodino took the noble way."[65] The day after the announcement, Rodino was besieged by a group of reporters writing follow-up stories. At the regular weekly meeting of the Judiciary Committee, he received tributes from members on both sides of the aisle before gaveling the panel to order. It was a bittersweet moment, and he spent the next several days reading the glowing news stories and responding to congratulatory messages from colleagues and friends. One particularly meaningful note was from a fellow graduate of Barringer High School. "It's been one of my truly great delights to read the magnificent editorials recognizing your extraordinary accomplishments in the House and as the Chairman of the Judiciary Committee," Justice William Brennan wrote. "All of us from New Jersey take enormous pride in you and none more so than I."[66]

Throughout the months that followed his retirement announcement, Rodino kept busy attending a whirlwind of dinners and receptions in his honor, most notably one at the Supreme Court hosted by Chief Justice Warren Burger. Widely diverse organizations like the Police Foundation and the ACLU were anxious to express their appreciation for his support, and he gladly accepted their awards and accolades. Although officially a lame duck, Rodino was not willing to coast for the rest of the congressional session. He remained actively engaged in the work of the committee, continuing his robust schedule of oversight hearings to focus attention on his policy priorities and participating in the preparations for the upcoming impeachment proceedings against Judge Hastings. He also agreed to serve as a congressional superdelegate to the Democratic National Convention in July, traveling to Atlanta, where the New Jersey delegation hosted a lunch in his honor. There, he met with his expected successor Donald Payne for the first time since the June primary.[67] As the scheduled fall adjournment of Congress neared, the number of tributes and interview requests increased. New Jersey public television began filming a documentary about his life, and many of the New York television stations sent reporters to Washington to capture Rodino's last days as a member of the House of Representatives. He cast his final vote on October 21, admitting to a reporter that "after 40 years of having answered the roll call, it's going to be rather extraordinary to know there will not be such calls anymore."[68] He spent the remainder of his time on Capitol Hill packing up four decades of memories and preparing for the future.

Rodino's plans for the next chapter of his life did not include a quiet retirement. Returning to New Jersey, he immediately launched several new ventures. The first was to resume his legal career after a long hiatus. Eschewing lucrative offers from major law firms, he decided to open his own practice in partnership with his son Peter where he could be more than a name on a masthead. He regularly spent several days a week at their office helping to manage the business and advising clients on government relations and a variety of other issues. At the same time, Rodino decided to revisit the idea of writing his memoirs now that he was no longer a public official. Contacted by several prospective book agents following his retirement announcement, he selected one who scheduled a series of meetings with the major publishers in New York. Although there was some interest in publishing a Rodino autobiography, no one was prepared to match the large advances offered in 1974. He spent several months searching for an acceptable ghostwriter willing to work for this lower fee until he abandoned the project in frustration; a second attempt a decade later did not result in a finished manuscript or a book contract.[69]

A far more fulfilling undertaking was the close and enduring relationship he established with Seton Hall University School of Law, which was located in Newark. Rodino had selected Seton Hall to serve as the repository for his papers and memorabilia, which would be housed in a new law library named in his honor. In addition, he joined the faculty as a "Distinguished Visiting Professor," and the law school agreed to provide him with office space, staff, and transportation to replace the congressional support network he could no longer access. A month after leaving Washington, Peter Rodino entered a classroom for the first time and recited from memory the Constitution's preamble before expounding on its meaning for the next hour to a group of enthralled law students. The *New York Times* reporter covering this high-profile career transition concluded that the former chairman had found his second calling, and, for the next fifteen years, Rodino would offer his personal insights in weekly lectures that were part of the Constitutional law courses he taught alongside a full-time faculty member.[70]

The biggest change in Rodino's post-congressional life was his marriage to Joy Judelson in 1989. Judelson, a public interest attorney living in New York, had worked in his Washington office in the late 1960s. Twenty years later, they reconnected and began a relationship that culminated in their marriage in September. The couple moved into a condominium in West Orange following the sale of Rodino's Grafton Avenue house and Judelson's relocation to New Jersey, where she continued her legal career. The two maintained an active schedule, frequently participating in events at the law school, where Rodino was accorded celebrity status and he occasionally accepted other speaking invitations. The twentieth anniversary of Watergate brought an uptick in interview requests, which the Seton Hall press office helped to coordinate, and he was featured in a BBC documentary that aired in the United States.[71]

In 1998, Rodino was unexpectedly thrust back into the national spotlight when Independent Counsel Kenneth Starr submitted his report on the Monica Lewinsky scandal and recommended that the House Judiciary Committee consider impeaching President Bill Clinton. Several committee members traveled to Newark to seek Rodino's confidential advice, including Republican Deputy Whip James E. Rogan, sent by Speaker Newt Gingrich, who confessed he was "spellbound" during his three-hour meeting with the former chairman. Initially reluctant to offer any public comments, Rodino agreed to do an interview in September with ABC correspondent Cokie Roberts, daughter of his old friends Hale and Lindy Boggs, and he expressed his concern about a rush to judgment before carefully determining whether or not the allegations against the president were impeachable offenses.[72] During the Judiciary Committee's efforts to answer this increasingly contentious question, Rodino became a frequent point of reference for both sides in the acrimonious debate. Chairman Henry J. Hyde, who had served and traveled with Rodino, claimed that the scope and deliberative process his predecessor had established, which he called "Rodino rules," provided the basis for a broad and unrestricted inquiry into Clinton's actions. Democrats disagreed and instead recalled Rodino's fairness and bipartisanship in their criticism of Hyde's leadership style. "The name falls from their lips with uncharacteristic reverence, like ball players conjuring up Joe DiMaggio in Yankee Stadium," the *New York Times* wryly observed of the repeated Rodino citations. With his portrait looming over the committee room, it was hard to ignore his shadow.[73]

Rodino was furious at Hyde's hijacking of his legacy and dismayed by the Republican efforts to compare Clinton's actions to the illegal activities of Nixon. When the committee approved articles of impeachment in December on a strict party-line vote, he abandoned any restraint and openly criticized the committee's decision, process, and leadership. Six months after the Senate acquitted President Clinton on all charges, Rodino revisited the issue in an op-ed he wrote for the *New York Times* on the twenty-fifth anniversary of the Judiciary Committee's bipartisan vote to impeach Richard Nixon. Unfavorably comparing the recent proceedings with the one he led, Rodino warned that "the House Republicans who drove the Clinton impeachment have cast down a gauntlet of partisanship that future majorities will feel inspired, if not obligated, to pick up."[74]

Except for chronic eye problems and a blocked artery corrected by surgery, Rodino remained in generally good health after he left Congress. He started using a cane to help him walk because of his impaired vision. Though moving a little slower, he continued to fulfill all his teaching duties and never lost his ability to recall the vivid details of his career, which he once again demonstrated in several press interviews marking the thirtieth anniversary of the Nixon impeachment.[75] This was the last time Rodino publicly discussed the event that changed his life.

In the spring of 2005, Peter Rodino died at home after a brief illness, a month before his ninety-sixth birthday. Reporting on his death, the *New York Times* echoed the tone of many of the obituaries that appeared across the country, observing that Rodino had "impressed the nation by the dignity, fairness and firmness he showed as chairman of the impeachment hearings."[76] The governor of New Jersey ordered a thirty-day period of mourning and Rodino would lie in state at the law school the following weekend to allow a steady stream of mourners to pay their final respects. Among those traveling to Newark was former representative and current Transportation Secretary Norman Mineta, who came in gratitude for Rodino's help in enacting legislation officially apologizing to all the Japanese Americans interned by the government during World War II, including Mineta and his family. In Washington, the House Judiciary Committee honored their former chairman with testimonials and a moment of silence.[77]

On Monday, May 16, family, friends, and former constituents gathered for his funeral mass at St. Lucy's Church, a lonely survivor of the once vibrant neighborhood that played such an important role in Rodino's political career. Sitting in the crowded church were past and present elected officials, three members of the 1974 Judiciary Committee, and the surviving supporters from the Ladies Auxiliary. Seton Hall law professor Paula Franzese delivered the eulogy, recounting Rodino's final words to her to "keep that good heart" and his legacy as "a champion of the underdog and a spokesman for those without a voice" before his interment at Gate of Heaven Cemetery.[78] Among the many tributes and expressions of sympathy that followed Rodino's death was a particularly meaningful one from his friend and former colleague Ted Kennedy. "Many of us felt we were seeing a founding father in action, living the highest ideals of the Constitution," he wrote of Rodino's leadership during the Nixon impeachment. "I am sure my brother would have called him a profile in courage. I feel the same way, and I'll never forget him."[79] Kennedy was not alone in concluding that Peter Rodino had served his time and a purpose.

BIBLIOGRAPHY

INTERVIEWS

James "Jim" Blanchard

Arthur P. "Skip" Endres Jr.

Ronna Freiberg

Frank Gerard Godlewski

Edward E. "Ted" Kaufman

Joy Rodino

John Russonello

Sandra Sincavitz

Charles Stanziale

MANUSCRIPT COLLECTIONS

Annapolis, Maryland, Maryland State Archives, Department of Health Bureau of Vital Statistics, Marriage Certificates.

Ann Arbor, Michigan, National Archives, Gerald R. Ford Presidential Library and Museum, Benton L. Becker Papers.

Ann Arbor, Michigan, National Archives, Gerald R. Ford Presidential Library and Museum, Edward Hutchinson Papers.

Ann Arbor, Michigan, National Archives, Gerald R. Ford Presidential Library and Museum, Gerald R. Ford Presidential Papers.

Ann Arbor, Michigan, National Archives, Gerald R. Ford Presidential Library and Museum, Betty and Gerald R. Ford Special Materials Collection.

Atlanta, Georgia, National Archives, Jimmy Carter Presidential Library and Museum, Jimmy Carter Presidential Papers.

Atlanta, Georgia, National Archives, Jimmy Carter Presidential Library and Museum, Oral History Exit Interview Project.

Austin, Texas, National Archives, Lyndon B. Johnson Library and Museum, Lyndon Baines Johnson Presidential Papers.

Austin, Texas, National Archives, Lyndon B. Johnson Library and Museum, Oral Histories.

Boston, Massachusetts, National Archives, John F. Kennedy Presidential Library and Museum, John F. Kennedy Pre-Presidential and Presidential Papers.

Boston, Massachusetts, Howard Gotlieb Archival Research Center, Boston University, John W. McCormack Papers.

Boston, Massachusetts, John J. Burns Library, Boston College, Tip O'Neill Congressional Papers.

Charlottesville, Virginia, Miller Center, University of Virginia, Jimmy Carter Presidential Oral History.

College Park, Maryland, National Archives, Records of the Bureau of Naval Personnel, Record Group 24.

Lexington, Virginia, Lewis F. Powell Jr. Archives, Washington and Lee University, School of Law, M. Caldwell Butler Papers.

Macomb, Illinois, Malpass Library, Western Illinois University, Thomas F. Railsback Collection.

Newark, New Jersey, Rodino Law Library Center for Information and Technology, Seton Hall University School of Law, Peter W. Rodino Jr. Archives.

Newark, New Jersey, New Jersey Historical Society, Kenneth Gibson Papers.

Newark, New Jersey, Newark Public Library, Charles F. Cummings New Jersey Information Center, Barbara J. Kukla Papers.

__________Angelo DeCarlo: Transcripts.

New York City, New York, Columbia Oral History Archives, Rare Book & Manuscript Library, Columbia University.

Norman, Oklahoma, Carl Albert Research and Studies Center, University of Oklahoma, Carl Albert Collection.

__________Joe Foote Collection.

Simi Valley, California, National Archives, Ronald Reagan Library, Presidential Papers of Ronald Reagan.

Saint Louis, Missouri, Selective Service System Records, National Personnel Records Center, National Archives.

Trenton, New Jersey, New Jersey State Archives, Essex County Court of Common Pleas, Naturalization Records, 1792–1931.

__________New Jersey Marriage Index, 1901–1914.

__________New Jersey Birth Index, 1901–1914.

__________Papers of Richard J. Hughes.

__________Papers of William T. Cahill.

__________Papers of Brendan T. Byrne.

__________Records of Dr. Ernest C. Reock

Washington, DC, Emanuel Celler Papers, Library of Congress, Manuscript Division.

Washington, DC, General Records of the Immigration and Naturalization Service, 1891–1957, Record Group 85, National Archives, Washington Building.

__________General Records of the Committee on the Judiciary, Record Group 233, National Archives, Washington Building.

__________World War I Selective Service System, Draft Registration Cards, Microfilm Edition, MI509, National Archives, Washington Building.

Yorba Linda, California, National Archives, Richard Nixon Presidential Library and Museum, Richard Nixon Presidential Papers.

Yorba Linda, California, National Archives, Richard Nixon Presidential Library and Museum, Richard Nixon Oral History Project.

OTHER UNPUBLISHED SOURCES

Bennett, Hugh Francis. "A History of the University of Newark 1908–1946." Doctoral dissertation, New York University, 1956.

Corbo, Robert. "Italian Settlements in Newark New Jersey." Master's thesis, Georgetown University, 1975.

Frascella, Thomas. "Commune di San Fele." San Felese Society of New Jersey, www.sanfelesesocietynj.org.

New Jersey Network. *Rodino: An Ordinary Guy*, 1989.

Public Broadcasting Service, *Summer of Judgment*, 1984.

Stellhorn, Paul Anthony. "Depression and Decline: Newark, New Jersey 1929–1941." Doctoral dissertation, Rutgers University, 1982.

NEWSPAPERS AND PERIODICALS

Belleville Times

Belleville Times-News

Belleville Telegraph

Chicago Tribune

Christian Science Monitor

Congressional Quarterly

East Orange Record

Easton Express

Essex Inquirer

Evening News (Newark)

Fort Monmouth News

Glen Ridge Paper

The Home News

Il Progresso Italo-Americano

Independent Press

Italian American Tribune

Italian Tribune

Jersey Journal

Jersey Press

The Jersey Review

Labor News

Labor Weekly

Los Angeles Times

Miami Herald

Montclair Times

Newark Evening News (all editions)

Newark Record

Newark Star-Eagle

Newark Star-Ledger

Newark Sunday Call

New Jersey Afro American

New Jersey Democrat

New Jersey Italian American

New York Times

Newsday

Newsweek

Nutley Sun

Political Review of New Jersey

REAL Magazine

The Record (Bergen)

Roll Call

The Spotlight on Essex

Star Ledger (Newark)

Time

U.S. News and World Report

USA Today

Washington Post

Washington Star

Washington Times Herald

GOVERNMENT PUBLICATIONS

Congressional Directory. Eighty-First Congress, First Session, 1949.

Congressional Record. (Bound Volumes)

New Jersey Legislative Reapportionment and Congressional Redistricting Planning

Commission. *Report of the New Jersey Legislative Reapportionment and Congressional Redistricting Planning Commission Established Pursuant to Senate Concurrent Resolution No. 21, 1964; reconstituted by Senate Concurrent Resolution No. 3, 1965* (Trenton, New Jersey: February 5, 1965).

New Jersey State Board of Education. "New Jersey School Laws and Rules and Regulations prescribed by the State Board of Education," 1914.

New Jersey Tenant Housing Commission. "Annual Report," 1904.

US Congress. House of Representatives. Committee on Education and Labor. "National Labor Relations Act of 1949: Hearings Before a Special Subcommittee of the Committee on Education and Labor." Eighty-First Congress, First Session, 1949.

US Congress. House of Representatives. Committee on the Judiciary. "Study of Monopoly Power: Hearings Before the Subcommittee on the Study of Monopoly Power of the Committee on the Judiciary." Eighty-Second Congress, First Session, Parts I–VI, 1951.

______________"Investigation of the Department of Justice: Hearings Before the Special Subcommittee to Investigate the Department of Justice." Eighty-Third Congress, First Session, 1953.

______________"Investigation of the Department of Justice: Report to the Committee on the Judiciary by the Special Subcommittee to Investigate the Department of Justice Pursuant to H.Res. 50." Eighty-Third Congress, First Session, H. Report 1079, 1953.

______________"Problem of Presidential Inability: Hearings Before Special Subcommittee to Study Presidential Inability." Eighty-Fourth Congress, Second Session, 1956.

______________"Presidential Inability: Hearings Before the Special Subcommittee on the Judiciary." Eighty-Fifth Congress, First Session, 1957.

______________"Civil Rights: Hearings Before Subcommittee No. 5." Eighty-Sixth Congress, First Session, 1959.

______________"Voting Rights: Hearings Before the Committee on the Judiciary." Eighty-Sixth Congress, Second Session, 1960.

______________"Civil Rights: Hearings Before Subcommittee No. 5." Eighty-Eighth Congress, First Session, Parts, I, II, III, 1963.

______________"Civil Rights: Hearings Before the Committee on the Judiciary on H.R. 7152 as Amended by Subcommittee No. 5." Eighty-Eighth Congress, First Session, IV, 1963.

______________"Civil Rights Act of 1963: House Report to Accompany H.R. 7152." Eighty-Eighth Congress, First Session, November 20, 1963.

______________"Columbus Day: Hearings Before Subcommittee No. 4." Eighty-Eighth Congress, First Session, December 1963.

______________"Immigration: Hearings Before Subcommittee No. 1." Eighty-Eighth Congress, Second Session, Parts I, II, II, 1964.

______________"Immigration: Hearings Before Subcommittee No. 1." Eighty-Ninth Congress, First Session, 1965.

______________"Civil Rights: Hearings Before Subcommittee No. 5." Eighty-Ninth Congress, Second Session, 1966.

______________"Presidential Inability: Hearings Before the Committee on the Judiciary." Eighty-Ninth Congress, First Session, 1966.

______________"Civil Rights Act of 1966, House Report to Accompany H.R. 14765." Eighty-Ninth Congress, Second Session, June 30, 1966.

______________"Columbus Day: Hearings Before Subcommittee No. 4 on H.R. 2372." Ninetieth Congress, First Session, October 1967.

______________"History of the Committee on the Judiciary of the House of Representatives." Ninety-Second Congress, Second Session, 1972.

______________"Application of the Twenty-Fifth Amendment to Vacancies in the Office of the Vice President: Legislative History." Ninety-Third Congress, First Session, 1973.

______________"Impeachment: Selected Materials." Ninety-Third Congress, First Session, 1973.

______________"Nomination of Gerald R. Ford to be the Vice President of the United States: Hearings Before the Committee on the Judiciary." Ninety-Third Congress, First Session, 1973.

______________"Constitutional Grounds for Presidential Impeachment." Ninety-Third Congress, Second Session, 1974.

______________"Impeachment Inquiry: Hearings Before the Committee on the

Judiciary." Ninety-Third Congress, Second Session, Books I–III, January–July 1974.

______________"Work of the Impeachment Inquiry Staff As of February 5, 1974." Ninety-Third Congress, Second Session, Committee Print, February 1974.

______________"Work of the Impeachment Inquiry Staff As of March 1, 1974." Ninety-Third Congress, Second Session, Committee Print, March 1974.

______________"Impeachment Inquiry Procedures: Committee on the Judiciary." Ninety-Third Congress, Second Session, May 2, 1974.

______________"Statement of Information: Hearings Before the Committee on the Judiciary." Ninety-Third Congress, Second Session, Volumes I–XII, May–June 1974.

______________"Transcripts of Eight Recorded Presidential Conversations: Hearings Before the Committee on the Judiciary." Ninety-Third Congress, Second Session, May–June 1974.

______________"Testimony of Witnesses: Hearings Before the Committee on the Judiciary," Ninety-Third Congress, Second Session, Books I–III, July 1974.

______________"Summary of Information: Hearings Before the Committee on the Judiciary." Ninety-Third Congress, Second Session, July 19, 1974.

______________"Minority Memorandum on Facts and Law: Hearings Before the Committee on the Judiciary." Ninety-Third Congress, Second Session, July 22, 1974.

______________"Debate on Article of Impeachment: Hearings Before the Committee on the Judiciary." Ninety-Third Congress, Second Session, July 1974.

______________"Impeachment of Richard M. Nixon, President of the United States: Final Report." Ninety-Third Congress, Second Session, August 20, 1974.

______________"Pardon of Richard M. Nixon and Related Matters: Hearings Before the Subcommittee on Criminal Justice." Ninety-Third Congress, Second Session, September, October 1974.

______________"Nomination of Nelson A. Rockefeller to Be Vice President of the United States: Hearings Before the Committee on the Judiciary." Ninety-Third Congress, Second Session, November, December 1974.

______________"Debate on the Nomination of Nelson A. Rockefeller to Be Vice

President of the United States: Meeting Held by the Committee on the Judiciary." Ninety-Third Congress, Second Session, December 1974.

______________"Extension of the Voting Rights Act: Hearings Before the Subcommittee on Civil and Constitutional Rights." Ninety-Fourth Congress, First Session, February, March 1975.

______________"Indochina Refugees: Hearings Before the Subcommittee on Immigration, Citizenship, and International Law." Ninety-Fourth Congress, First Session, May 1975.

______________"Antitrust Civil Process Act Amendments: Hearings Before the Subcommittee on Monopolies and Commercial Law." Ninety-Fourth Congress, First Session, May, July 1975.

______________"Antitrust Parens Patriae Amendments: Hearings Before the Subcommittee on Monopolies and Commercial Law." Ninety-Fourth Congress, First Session, February, March 1975.

______________"Merger Oversight and H.R. 13131, Providing Premerger Notification and Statutory Requirements: Hearings Before the Subcommittee on Monopolies and Commercial Law," Ninety-Fourth Congress, Second Session, March, May 1976.

______________"Additional District and Circuit Court Judges: Hearings Before the Subcommittee on Monopolies and Commercial Law." Ninety-Fifth Congress, First Session, March 1977.

______________"A Ceremony for the Unveiling of the Portrait of the Honorable Peter W. Rodino, Jr.: Proceedings Before the Committee on the Judiciary." Ninety-Fifth Congress, First Session, May 1977.

______________"Constitutional Amendments to Balance the Federal Budget: Hearings Before the Subcommittee on Monopolies and Commercial Law." Ninety-Sixth Congress, First and Second Session, 1979, 1980.

______________"History of the Committee on the Judiciary." Ninety-Seventh Congress, Second Session, Committee Print, February 1982.

______________"Investigation of the Role of the Department of Justice in the Withholding of Environmental Protection Agency Documents from Congress: Report of the Committee on the Judiciary." Volumes I–IV, Ninety-Ninth Congress, First

Session, December 1985.

______________"Conduct of Harry E. Claiborne, U.S. District Judge, District of Nevada: Hearings Before the Subcommittee on Courts, Civil Liberties and the Administration of Justice." Ninety-Ninth Congress, Second Session, June 1986.

______________"Iran-Contra Investigation: Joint Hearings Before the Senate Select Committee on Secret Military Assistance to Iran and the Nicaraguan Opposition and the House Select Committee to Investigate Covert Arms Transactions with Iran." 100th Congress, First Session, 1987.

______________"Report of the Congressional Committee Investigating the Iran Contra Affair." 100th Congress, First Session, 1987.

US Department of Commerce. Bureau of the Census. *Census of Population 1890.*

______________*Census of Population 1900–1970.*

______________*Statistical Abstract of the United States 1946.*

PUBLISHED SOURCES

Blueprint for Neighborhood Conservation. National Association of Real Estate Boards, 1963.

Campaign Issues, 1946: A Handbook for Candidates, Speakers and Workers of the Democratic Party. Washington, DC: Democratic National Committee, 1946.

Congressional Quarterly Almanac. Washington, DC: CQ Politics, 1949–60.

New Jersey Congressional Districts: A Plan for the Sixties. Bureau of Government Research. Rutgers University, November 1960.

Newark City Directories, 1900–1910.

Report for Action: Governor's Select Commission on Civil Disorder. Trenton, NJ: State of New Jersey, 1968.

Report of the National Advisory Commission on Civil Disorders. Washington, DC: Government Printing Office, 1968.

Semi-Annual Report to Congress: The Select Commission on Immigration and Refugee Policy, March 1980.

Statistics of the Presidential and Congressional Election of November 4, 1952. Washington, DC: Government Printing Office, 1975.

Statistics of the Congressional Election of November 4, 1974. Washington, DC:

Government Printing Office, 1953.

U.S. Immigration Policy and the National Interest: The Final Report and Recommendations of the Select Commission on Immigration and Refugee Policy to the Congress and the President of the United States. US Congress, March 1, 1981.

The Voting Rights Act: Ten Years After: A Report of the United States Commission on Civil Rights. United States Commission on Civil Rights, January 1975.

Whom We Shall Welcome: Report of the President's Commission on Immigration and Naturalization. Washington, DC: Government Printing Office, 1953.

Alter, Jonathan. *His Very Best: Jimmy Carter, A Life.* New York: Simon & Schuster, 2020.

Archdeacon, Thomas. *Becoming American: An Ethnic History.* New York: The Free Press, 1983.

Atkinson, Rick. *An Army at Dawn: The War in North Africa, 1942–1943.* New York: Henry Holt and Company, 2002.

____________*The Day of Battle: The War in Sicily and Italy 1943–1944.* New York: Henry Holt and Company, 2007.

Baedeker, Karl. *Italy Handbook for Travellers, Third Part: Southern Italy, Sicily.* Leipzig, Germany: Karl Baedeker, 1875.

Ballard, Jack Stokes. *The Shock of Peace: Military and Economic Demobilization after World War II.* Washington, DC: University Press of America, 1983.

Baraka, Amiri. *The Autobiography of LeRoi Jones.* Chicago: Lawrence Hill Books, 1997.

Battisti, Danielle. *Whom We Shall Welcome: Italian Americans and Immigration Reform, 1945–1965.* New York: Fordham University Press, 2019.

Bayor, Ronald H. *Encountering Ellis Island: How European Immigrants Entered America.* Baltimore, MD: Johns Hopkins University Press, 2014.

Bebout, John E. and Ronald J. Grele. *Where Cities Meet: The Urbanization of New Jersey.* The New Jersey Historic Series, Vol. 22., Princeton, New Jersey: D. Van Nostrand Co., 1964.

Bell, Griffin B. *Taking Care of the Law.* New York: William Morrow and Company, 1982.

Bernstein, Carl and Bob Woodward. *All the President's Men.* New York: Simon & Schuster, 1974.

Bird, Kai. *The Outlier: The Unfinished Presidency of Jimmy Carter.* New York: Crown, 2021.

Bishop, Gordon B. *Greater Newark: A Microcosm of America*. Chatsworth, CA: Windsor Publications, 1989.

Blum, John Morton. *V Was for Victory: Politics and American Culture During World War II*. New York: Harcourt Brace Jovanovich, 1976.

Bockley, Kathryn M. "A Historical Overview of Refugee Legislation: The Deception of Foreign Policy in the Land of Promise." *North Carolina Journal of International Law and Commercial Regulation* 21, no. 1 (1995).

Borsella, Cristogianni. *On Persecution, Identity & Activism: Aspects of the Italian American Experience from the Late 19th Century to Today*. Boston: Dante University Press, 2005.

Boylan, James R. *The New Deal Coalition and the Election of 1946*. New York: Garland Publishing, 1981.

Breslin, Jimmy. *How the Good Guys Finally Won: Notes From an Impeachment Summer*. New York: Ballantine Books, 1975.

Brown, Lawrence Guy. *Immigration: Cultural Conflicts and Social Adjustments*. New York: Arno Press and the *New York Times*, 1969.

Burns, James McGregor. *Congress On Trial: The Legislative Process and The Administrative State*. New York: Harper and Brothers, 1949.

Byrne, Malcolm. *Iran-Contra: Reagan's Scandal and the Unchecked Abuse of Presidential Power*. Lawrence, KS: University Press of Kansas, 2014.

Calabro, Marian. *Making Things Work: PSEG's First Century*. Lyme Connecticut: Greenwich Publishing Group, 2003.

Califano Jr., Joseph A. *The Triumph and Tragedy of Lyndon Johnson: The White House Years*. New York: Touchstone, 1991.

__________________*Inside: A Public and Private Life*. New York: Public Affairs, 2004.

Cannato, Vincent J. *American Passage: The History of Ellis Island*. New York: Harper Collins, 2009.

Cannon, James. *Time and Chance: Gerald Ford's Appointment with History*. New York: HarperCollins, 1994.

Cannon, James. *Gerald R. Ford: An Honorable Life*. Ann Arbor, MI: University of Michigan Press, 2013.

Carnevale, Nancy C. *A New Language, a New World: Italian Immigrants in the United*

States, 1890–1945. Urbana, IL: University of Illinois Press, 2009.

Caro, Robert A. *The Years of Lyndon Johnson: Master of the Senate*. New York: Alfred A. Knopf, 2002.

____________*The Years of Lyndon Johnson: The Passage of Power*. New York: Alfred A. Knopf, 2012.

Carola, Robert and Ben Morreale. *Italian Americans: The Immigrant Experience*. New York: Metro Books, 2008.

Carter, Jimmy. *Keeping Faith: Memoirs of a President*. New York: Bantam Books, 1982.

Celler, Emanuel. *You Never Leave Brooklyn: The Autobiography of Emanuel Celler*. New York: John Day Company, 1953.

Chermayeff, Ivan, Wasserman, Fred, and Mary J. Shapiro. *Ellis Island: An Illustrated History of the Immigrant Experience*. New York: Macmillan Publishing Company, 1991.

Churchill, Charles W. *The Italians of Newark: A Community Study*. New York: Arno Press, 1975.

Clarke, Thurston. *JFK's Last Hundred Days: The Transformation of A Man and The Emergence of A Great President*. New York: Penguin Press, 2013.

Clifford, J. Garry and Samuel R. Spencer Jr. *The First Peacetime Draft*. Lawrence, KS: University Press of Kansas, 1986.

Cohen, William S. and George J. Mitchell. *Men of Zeal: A Candid Inside Story of the Irán Contra Hearings*. New York: Viking Penguin, 1988.

Connors, Richard J. *A Cycle of Power: The Career of Jersey City Mayor Frank Hague*. Metuchen, NJ: Scarecrow Press, 1971.

Crea, Robert M. "Racial Discrimination and Baker v. Carr; Note." *Notre Dame Journal of Legislation* 30 (2004).

Cummings, Urban K. *Ronson: The World's Greatest Lighter*. Palo Alto, CA: Bird Dog Books, 1992.

Cunningham, John T. *Newark. Revised edition*. Newark, NJ: New Jersey Historical Society, 1988.

________________*Railroads in New Jersey: The Formative Years*. Andover, NJ: Afton Publishing, 1997.

Curvin, Robert. *Inside Newark: Decline, Rebellion, and the Search for Transformation*.

New Brunswick, NJ: Rutgers University Press, 2014.

Dallek, Robert. *Franklin D. Roosevelt and American Foreign Policy, 1932–1945*. New York: Oxford University Press, 1979.

___________*Flawed Giant: Lyndon Johnson and His Times 1961–1973*. New York: Oxford University Press, 1998.

___________*Franklin D. Roosevelt: A Political Life*. New York: Viking, 2013.

Dash, Samuel. *Chief Counsel: Inside the Ervin Committee—The Untold Story of Watergate*. New York: Random House, 1976.

Dawkins, Wayne. *Emanuel Celler: Immigration and Civil Rights Champion*. Jackson, MS: University Press of Mississippi, 2020.

Deering, Christopher J. and Steven S. Smith. *Committees in Congress*. Washington, DC: Congressional Quarterly, 1997.

Deitche, Scott M. *Garden State Gangland: The Rise of the Mob in New Jersey*. Lanham, MD: Rowman and Littlefield, 2018.

Delozier, Alan Bernard. *Images of America: Roman Catholic Archdiocese of Newark*. Charleston, SC: Arcadia Publishing, 2011.

De Stefano, George. *An Offer We Can't Refuse: The Mafia in the Mind of America*. (New York: Faber and Faber, 2006).

Dobbs, Michael. *King Richard: Nixon and Watergate: An American Tragedy*. New York: Alfred A. Knopf, 2021.

Drew, Elizabeth. *Washington Journal: Reporting Watergate and Richard Nixon's Downfall*. New York: Overlook Duckworth, 2014.

Duggan, Christopher. *The Force of Destiny: A History of Italy Since 1796*. New York: Houghton Mifflin Company, 2008.

Dunn, Susan. *1940: FDR, Wilkie, Lindbergh, Hitler: The Election Amid the Storm*. New Haven, CT: Yale University Press, 2013.

Eizenstat, Stuart E. *President Carter: The White House Years*. New York: Thomas Dunne Books, 2018.

Eliseo, Maurizio and Paolo Piccione. *Transatlantici: The History of the Great Italian Liners in the Atlantic*. Genoa, Italy: Tormena Editore, 2001.

Ellis, John. *The Sharp Edge: The Fighting Man in World War II*. London: Aurum Press, 2009.

Engel, Jeffrey A., Meacham, Jon, Naftali, Timothy, and Peter Baker. *Impeachment: An American History*. New York: Modern Library, 2018.

Engelmayer, Sheldon D. and Robert J. Wagman. *Hubert Humphrey: The Man and His Dream 1911–1978*. New York: Methuen, 1978.

Eula, Michael J. *Between Peasant and Urban Village: Italian-Americans of New Jersey and New York, 1880–1980*. New York: Peter Lang, 1993.

Farrell, John A. *Tip O'Neill and the Democratic Century: A Biography*. New York: Little, Brown and Company, 2001.

____________*Richard Nixon: The Life*. New York: Doubleday, 2017.

Feerick, John D. *The Twenty-Fifth Amendment: Its Complete History and Application*. New York: Fordham University Press, 2014.

Fields, Howard. *High Crimes and Misdemeanors*. New York: W.W. Norton & Company, 1978.

Fitzgerald, Keith. *The Face of the Nation: Immigration, the State, and the National Identity*. Stanford, CA: Stanford University Press, 1996.

Foerster, Robert F. *The Italian Emigration of Our Times*. Cambridge, MA: Harvard University Press, 1919.

Ford, Aaron L. "The Legislative Reorganization Act of 1946." *American Bar Association Journal* 32, no. 11 (November 1946).

Freeman, Daniel M. *The House Was My Home: My Life on Capitol Hill and Other Tales*. Port Angeles, WA: Cadmus Press, 2020.

Galishoff, Stuart. *Newark: The Nation's Unhealthiest City: 1832–1895*. New Brunswick, NJ: Rutgers University Press, 1988.

Galloway, George B. "The Operation of the Legislative Reorganization Act of 1946." *The American Political Science Review* 45, no. 1 (March 1951).

______________*History of the United States House of Representatives*. Washington, DC: Government Printing Office, 1965.

Gardiner, Juliet. *'Over Here': The GIs in Wartime Britain*. London: Collins and Brown, 1992.

Gillon, Steven M. *Separate and Unequal: The Kerner Commission and the Unraveling of American Liberalism*. New York: Basic Books, 2018.

Ginsborg, Paul. *A History of Contemporary Italy: Society and Politics 1943–1988*.

London: Penguin Books, 1990.

Goodwin, Doris Kearns. *Lyndon Johnson and the American Dream*. New York: St. Martin's Griffin, 1991.

Goodwin, George Jr. "The Seniority System in Congress." *American Political Science Review* 53, no. 2 (June 1959).

Graham, Hugh Davis. *The Civil Rights Era: Origins and Development of National Policy 1960–1972*. New York: Oxford University Press, 1990.

Green, Matthew N. *The Speaker of the House*. New Haven, CT: Yale University Press, 2010.

Greene, John R. *The Presidency of Gerald R. Ford*. Lawrence, KS: University Press of Kansas, 1995.

Groseclose, Tim and Charles Stewart III. "The Value of Committee Seats in the House, 1947–91." *American Journal of Political Science* 42, no. 2 (April 1998).

Hamilton, Nigel. *The Mantle of Command: FDR at War 1941–1942*. New York: Houghton Mifflin Harcourt, 2014.

Hart, Steven. *American Dictators: Frank Hague, Nucky Johnson, and the Perfection of the Urban Political Machine*. New Brunswick, NJ: Rutgers University Press, 2013.

Hasen, Richard L. *The Supreme Court and Election Law*. New York: New York University Press, 2003.

Hill, Philip H. "Housing-Legislative Proposals," *Law and Contemporary Problems* 12, no. 1 (Winter 1947).

Hiltzik, Michael. *The New Deal: A Modern History*. New York: The Free Press, 2011.

Hinckley, Barbara. *Seniority System in Congress*. Bloomington, IN: Indiana University Press, 1971.

Hitchcock, William L. *The Age of Eisenhower: America and the World in the 1950s*. New York: Simon & Schuster, 2018.

Holland, James. *The Allies Strike Back 1941–1943: The War in the West, Volume I*. New York: Atlantic Monthly Press, 2017.

Holmes, Robert C. and Richard W. Roper, eds. *A Mayor for All the People: Kenneth Gibson's Newark*. New Brunswick, NJ: Rutgers University Press, 2020.

Holtzman, Elizabeth. *Who Said It Would Be Easy? One Woman's Life in the Political Arena*. New York: Arcade Publishing, 1966.

Howe, George F. *The Battle History of the 1st Armored Division*. Washington, DC: Combat Forces Press, 1954.

Humphrey, Hubert H. *The Education of A Public Man: My Life and Politics*. New York: Doubleday and Company, 1976.

Hutchinson, E.P. *Legislative History of American Immigration Policy, 1798–1965*. Philadelphia, PA: University of Pennsylvania Press, 1981.

Iacocca, Lee. *Iacocca: An Autobiography*. New York: Bantam Books, 1984.

Immerso, Michael. *Newark's Little Italy: The Vanished First Ward*. Newark, NJ: Newark Public Library and Rutgers University Press, 1997.

Iorizzo, Luciano J. and Salvatore Mondello. *The Italian Americans*. Boston: Twayne Publishers, 1980.

Iorizzo, Luciano J. "The Padrone and Immigrant Distribution" in *The Italian Experience in the United States*, edited by Silvano M. Tomasi and Madeline H. Engel. New York: Center for Migration Studies, 1970.

Jackson, Kenneth T. *Crabgrass Frontier: The Suburbanization of the United States*. New York: Oxford University Press, 1985.

Jaworski, Leon. *The Right and the Power: The Prosecution of Watergate*. New York: Reader's Digest Press, 1976.

Jennings, Christian. *At War on the Gothic Line: Fighting in Italy, 1944–45*. New York: St. Martin's Press, 2016.

Johnson, James P. *New Jersey: History of Ingenuity and Industry*. California: Windsor Publications, 1987.

Kamasaki, Charles. *Immigration Reform: The Corpse That Will Not Die*. Simsbury, CT: Mandel Vilar Press, 2019.

Kaplan, Harold. *Urban Renewal Politics: Slum Clearance in Newark*. New York: Columbia University Press, 1963.

Katz, Robert. *The Battle for Rome: The Germans, the Allies, the Partisans, and the Pope September 1943–June 1944*. New York: Simon & Schuster, 2003.

Katzenbach, Nicholas deB. *Some of It Was Fun: Working with RFK and LBJ*. New York: W.W. Norton & Company, 2008.

Kennedy, David M. *Freedom from Fear: The American People in Depression and War, 1929–1945*. New York: Oxford University Press, 1999.

Kennedy, John F. *A Nation of Immigrants*. New York: Anti-Defamation League of B'nai B'rith, 1959.

Klein, Maury. *A Call to Arms: Mobilizing America for World War II*. New York: Bloomsbury Press, 2013.

Klurfeld, Herman. *Behind the Lines: The World of Drew Pearson*. Englewood Cliffs, NJ: Prentice-Hall, 1968.

Krasovic, Mark. *The Newark Frontier: Community Action in the Great Society*. Chicago: University of Chicago Press, 2016.

Kutler, Stanley I. *The Wars of Watergate: The Last Crisis of Richard Nixon*. New York: Alfred A. Knopf, 1990.

Kyvig, David E. *The Age of Impeachment: American Constitutional Culture Since 1960*. Lawrence, KS: University Press of Kansas, 2008.

LaGumina, Salvatore J. *WOP!: A Documentary History of Anti-Italian Discrimination in the United States*. Toronto: Guernica Editions, 1973.

LaGumina, Salvatore J. "Prejudice and Discrimination: The Italian American Experience Yesterday and Today." In *Anti-Italianism: Essays on a Prejudice*, edited by William J. Connell and Fred Gardaphé. New York: Palgrave Macmillan, 2010.

Lash, Joseph P. *Eleanor: The Years Alone*. New York: W.W. Norton & Company, 1972.

Laurino, Maria. *The Italian Americans*. New York: W.W. Norton & Company, 2015.

Lee, Sandra S. *Images of America: Italian Americans of Newark, Belleville, and Nutley*. Charleston, SC: Arcadia Publishing, 2008.

Linky, Donald. *New Jersey Governor Brendan Byrne: The Man Who Couldn't Be Bought*. Madison, NJ: Fairleigh Dickinson University Press, 2014.

Linnett, Richard. *In the Godfather Garden: The Long Life and Times of Richie "The Boot" Boiardo*. New Brunswick, NJ: Rutgers University Press, 2013.

Longendyck, Catherine and Kathleen P. Galop. *Images of America: Forest Hill*. Charleston, SC: Arcadia Publishing, 2014.

Lopreato, Joseph. *Italian Americans*. New York: Random House, 1970.

Lowe, Keith. *Savage Continent: Europe in the Aftermath of World War II*. New York: St. Martin's Press, 2012.

Maas, Peter. *The Valachi Papers*. New York: G.P. Putnam's Sons, 1968.

Maddow, Rachel and Michael Yarvitz. *Bag Man*. New York: Crown Publishing Group, 2020.

Mangione, Jerre and Ben Morreale. *La Storia: Five Centuries of the Italian American Experience*. New York: HarperCollins, 1992.

Martis, Kenneth C. *The Historical Atlas of Political Parties in the United States 1789–1989*. New York: Macmillan, 1989.

________________*The Historical Atlas of United States Congressional Districts 1789–1983*. New York: The Free Press, 1982.

Matthews, Chris. *Tip and the Gipper: When Politics Worked*. New York: Simon & Schuster, 2013.

Mattia, Peter B. *The Recollections of Peter B. Mattia*, edited by Kenneth J. Rosa. Nutley, NJ: K.J. Rosa, 1985.

McCracken, Alison. *Real Men Don't Sing: Crooning in American Culture*. Durham, NC: Duke University Press, 2015.

McCullough, David. *Truman*. New York: Simon & Schuster, 1992.

McNulty, Brendan and Tim McNulty. *The Meanest Man in Congress: Jack Brooks and the Making of an American Century*. Montgomery, AL: New South Books, 2019.

McPherson, Milton M. *The Ninety-Day Wonders: OCS and the Modern American Army*. Columbus, GA: Army Officer Candidate School Alumni Association, 2001.

Mezvinsky, Edward. *A Term to Remember*. New York: Coward, McCann & Geoghegan, 1977.

Mistry, Kaeten. *The United States, Italy and the Origins of Cold War: Waging Political Warfare 1945–1950*. Cambridge, UK: Cambridge University Press, 2014.

Moe, Richard. *Roosevelt's Second Act: The Election of 1940 and the Politics of War*. New York: Oxford University Press, 2013.

Morrow, William L. *Congressional Committees*. New York: Charles Scribner's & Sons, 1969.

Mumford, Kevin. *Newark: A History of Race, Rights, and Riots in America*. New York: New York University Press, 2007.

Murphy, Reg. *Uncommon Sense: The Achievement of Griffin Bell*. Atlanta, GA: Longstreet, 1999.

Nelli, Humbert S. "Italians in Urban America," in *The Italian Experience in the United*

States, edited by Silvano M. Tomasi and Madeline H. Engel. New York: Center for Migration Studies, 1970.

Nelson, Garrison. "Committees in the U.S. Congress: 1947–1992 Committee Histories and Member Assignments." Washington, DC: *Congressional Quarterly*, 1994.

______________ *John William McCormack: A Political Biography*. New York: Bloomsbury, 2017.

Nichols, David A. *A Matter of Justice: Eisenhower and the Beginning of the Civil Rights Revolution.* New York: Simon & Schuster, 2007.

Norris, John. *Mary McGrory: The First Queen of Journalism*. New York: Viking, 2015.

O'Brien, Lawrence F. *No Final Victories: A Life in Politics—from John F. Kennedy to Watergate*. Garden City, NY: Doubleday and Company, 1974.

Offner, Arnold A. *Hubert Humphrey: The Conscience of A Country*. New Haven, CT: Yale University Press, 2018.

Okrent, Daniel. *The Guarded Gate: Bigotry, Eugenics, and the Law That Kept Two Generations of Jews, Italians, and Other European Immigrants Out of America.* New York: Scribner, 2019.

Olsen, Kevin K. *A Great Conveniency: A Maritime History of the Passaic River, Hackensack River, and Newark Bay*. Franklin, TN: American History Imprints, 2008.

Olson, Lynne. *Citizens of London: The Americans Who Stood with Britain in its Darkest, Finest Hour*. New York: Random House, 2010.

O'Neill, Thomas P. *Man of the House: The Life and Political Memoirs of Speaker Tip O'Neill.* New York: Random House, 1987.

O'Neill, William L. *A Democracy At War: America's Fight at Home and Abroad in World War II.* New York: Free Press, 1993.

Pearson, Drew and Jack Anderson. *The Case Against Congress: A Compelling Indictment of Corruption on Capitol Hill.* New York: Simon & Schuster, 1968.

Perkins, Lynette P. "Member Recruitment to a Mixed Goal Committee: The House Judiciary Committee." *Journal of Politics* 43, no. 2 (May 1981).

Petriello, David. *Military History of New Jersey*. Charleston, SC: History Press, 2014.

Pierson, David L. *Narratives of Newark (in New Jersey) from the Days of its Founding.* Newark, NJ: Pierson Publishing Company, 1917.

Pietrusza, David. *1948: Harry Truman's Improbable Victory and the Year That*

Transformed America's Role in the World. New York: Union Square Press, 2011.

Pitkin, Thomas M. *Keepers of the Gate: A History of Ellis Island*. New York: New York University Press, 1975.

Pomper, Gerald M. *Ordinary Heroes and American Democracy*. New Haven, CT: Yale University Press, 2004.

Porambo, Ron. *No Cause for Indictment: An Autopsy of Newark*. New York: Holt, Rinehart and Winston, 1971.

Purdum, Todd S. *An Idea Whose Time Has Come: Two Presidents, Two Parties, and the Battle for the Civil Rights Act of 1964*. New York: Henry Holt and Company, 2014.

Reiman, Richard A. *The New Deal and American Youth: Ideas and Ideals in a Depression Decade*. Athens, GA: University of Georgia Press, 1992.

Remini, Robert V. *The House: The History of the House of Representatives*. Washington, DC: Smithsonian Books, 2006.

Reston, James Jr. *The Impeachment Diary: Eyewitness To The Removal of a President*. New York: Arcade Publishing, 2019.

Reynolds, David. *Rich Relations: The American Occupation of Britain, 1942–1945*. New York: Random House, 1995.

Ritchie, Donald A. *Electing FDR: The New Deal Campaign of 1932*. Lawrence, KS: University Press of Kansas, 2007.

______________*The Columnist: Leaks, Lies, and Libel in Drew Pearson's Washington*. New York: Oxford University Press, 2021.

Roberts, Andrew. *The Storm of War: A New History of the Second World War*. New York: HarperCollins, 2011.

Rodino, Joy. *Fifty-Two Words My Husband Taught Me: Love, Inspiration and the Constitution*. West Orange, NJ: DRJ Publishing, 2007.

Rodino, Peter W. Jr. "Forgotten Man Who Defies the Reds." *REAL Magazine* 2, no. 5 (August 1953).

Rogers, Mary Beth. *Barbara Jordan: American Hero*. New York: Bantam Books, 1998.

Severn, Bill. *Ellis Island: The Immigrant Years*. New York: Julian Messner, 1971.

Shales, Ezra. *Made in Newark: Cultivating Industrial Arts and Civic Identity in the Progressive Era*. New Brunswick, NJ: Rivergate Books, 2010

Shank, Alan. *New Jersey Reapportionment Politics: Strategies and Tactics in the Legislative*

Process. Madison, NJ: Fairleigh Dickinson University Press, 1969.

Shanks, Cheryl. *Immigration and the Politics of American Sovereignty, 1890–1990*. Ann Arbor, MI: University of Michigan Press, 2001.

Sirica, John J. *To Set the Record Straight: The Break-In, the Tapes, the Conspirators, the Pardon*. New York: W.W. Norton & Company, 1979.

Smith, Denis Mack. *Modern Italy: A Political History*. Ann Arbor, MI: University of Michigan Press, 1997.

Smith, J. Douglas. *On Democracy's Doorstep: The Inside Story of How The Supreme Court Brought "One Person, One Vote" To The United States*. New York: Hill and Wang, 2014.

Smith, Robert C. "The Changing Shape of Urban Black Politics: 1960–1970." *The Annals of the American Academy of Political Science and Social Science* 439 (September 1978).

Spinelli, Lawrence. *Dry Diplomacy: The United States, Great Britain and Prohibition*. Lanham, MD: Rowman & Littlefield, 2007.

Starr, Dennis J. *The Italians of New Jersey: A Historical Introduction and Bibliography*. Newark, NJ: New Jersey Historical Society, 1985.

Stein, Eric. "War, Politics, Law-And Love: Italy 1943–1946." *Michigan Journal of International Law* 32, issue 3 (2011).

Stein, Jeff. *A Murder in Wartime: The Untold Spy Story that Changed the Course of the Vietnam War*. New York: St. Martin's Paperbacks, 1993.

Stern, Herbert J. *Diary of a DA: The True Story of the Prosecutor Who Took on the Mob, Fought Corruption, and Won*. New York: Skyhorse Publishing, 2012.

Stern, Seth and Stephen Wermiel. *Justice Brennan: Liberal Champion*. Lawrence, KS: University Press of Kansas, 2010.

Svejda, George J. *Castle Garden as an Immigrant Depot, 1855–1890*. Washington, DC: Office of Archaeology and Historic Preservation, National Park Service, 1968.

Thowless, Herbert. *Historical Sketch of the City of Newark, New Jersey*. Newark, NJ: Holbrook's Newark City Directory, 1902.

Tobin, Maurice B. *Hidden Power: The Seniority System and Other Customs of Congress*. Westport, CT: Greenwood Press, 1986.

Tractenberg, Paul. *A Centennial History of Rutgers Law School in Newark: Opening a*

Thousand Doors. Charleston, SC: The History Press, 2010.

Truman, Harry S. *Memoirs: Years of Trial and Hope*. Volume II. New York: Doubleday and Company, 1956.

Turner, Jean-Rae and Richard T. Koles. *Images of America: Newark*. Charleston, SC: Arcadia Publishing, 2001.

Tuttle, Brad R. *How Newark Became Newark: The Rise, Fall and Rebirth of an American City*. New Brunswick, NJ: Rivergate Books, 2011.

Valenti, Jack. *A Very Human President*. (New York: W.W. Norton & Company, 1975).

___________*This Time, This Place: My Life in War, the White House, and Hollywood*. New York: Harmony Books, 2007.

Vecoli, Rudolph J. "The Italian People of New Jersey," in *The New Jersey Ethnic Experience,* edited by Barbara Cunningham, 275. Union City, NJ: William H. Wise and Company, 1977.

Ventresca, Robert A. *From Fascism to Democracy: Culture and Politics in the Italian Election of 1948*. Toronto: University of Toronto Press, 2004.

Waldman, Myron S. *Forgive Us Our Press Passes: The Memoirs of a Veteran Washington Reporter*. New York: St. Martin's Press, 1991.

Ward, David. *Cities and Immigrants*. New York: Oxford University Press, 1971.

Weand, A.E. "The Short Life of Shrivenham American University." *The Journal of the Royal Military College of Science* 8, no. 7 (1995).

Wefing, John B. *The Life and Times of Richard J. Hughes: The Politics of Civility*. New Brunswick, NJ: Rutgers University Press, 2009.

Whalen, Charles and Barbara Whalen. *The Longest Debate: A Legislative History of the 1964 Civil Rights Act*. Cabin John, MD: Seven Locks Press, 1985.

White, Theodore H. *Breach of Faith: The Fall of Richard Nixon*. New York: Atheneum Publishers, 1975.

Wilentz, Sean. *The Age of Reagan: A History 1974–2008*. New York: HarperCollins, 2008.

Williams, Andrew. *The Battle of the Atlantic: Hitler's Gray Wolves of the Seas and the Allies' Desperate Struggle to Defeat Them*. New York: Basic Books, 2003.

Williams, Isobel. *Allies and Italians Under Occupation: Sicily and Southern Italy 1943–45*. London: Palgrave MacMillan, 2013.

Williams, Junius. *Unfinished Agenda: Urban Politics in the Era of Black Power*. Berkeley, CA: North Atlantic Books, 2014.

Winters, Stanley B., ed. *From Riot To Recovery: Newark After Ten Years*. Lanham, MD: University Press of America, 1979.

Wofford, Harris. *Of Kennedys and Kings: Making Sense of the Sixties*. Pittsburgh, PA: University of Pittsburgh Press, 1980.

Woodward, Bob and Carl Bernstein. *The Final Days*. New York: Simon & Schuster Paperbacks, 1976.

Yang, Jia Lynn. *One Mighty and Irresistible Tide: The Epic Struggle Over American Immigration, 1924–1965*. New York: W.W. Norton & Company, 2020.

Zeifman, Jerry. *Without Honor: Crimes of Camelot and the Impeachment of President Nixon*. New York: Thunder's Mouth Press, 1995.

Zeitz, Joshua. *Building The Great Society: Inside Lyndon Johnson's White House*. New York: Viking, 2018.

ENDNOTES

INTRODUCTION

1 "Secaucus' Summer Intern Once Served For Rep. Rodino," *Jersey Journal*, July 30, 1974.

2 Thomas P. O'Neill and William Novak, *Man of the House: The Life and Political Memoirs of Speaker Tip O'Neill* (New York: Random House, 1987), 242.

CHAPTER ONE

1 William Vance, "Watergate, Ford Confirmation Put Him in Spotlight," *Miami Herald*, October 28, 1973; Yale University Oral History Transcript, Peter W. Rodino Jr. Archives (RA), Rodino Law Library Center for Information and Technology, Seton Hall University School of Law, Newark, New Jersey, April 22, 1975, 9–10; Maurice Carroll, "Public Reacts Strongly to Cox Ouster," *New York Times*, October 22, 1973; Stanley I. Kutler, *The Wars of Watergate: The Last Crisis of Richard Nixon* (New York: Alfred A. Knopf, 1970), 399–411.

2 Bob Woodward and Carl Bernstein, "GOP Security Aide Among 5 Arrested in Bugging Affair," *Washington Post*, June 19, 1972; Joseph Kraft, "The Watergate Caper," *Washington Post*, June 25, 1972; Carl Bernstein and Bob Woodward, *All the President's Men* (New York: Simon & Schuster, 1974), 13–26, 45–48.

3 Bob Woodward and E.J. Buchinski, "White House Consultant Tied to Burglary," *Washington Post*, June 20, 1972.

4 "Transcript of News Conference by the President," *New York Times*, August 30, 1972; Jim Mann and Bob Woodward, "Watergate Questions Abound," *Washington Post*, September 3, 1972.

5 Bob Woodward and Carl Bernstein, "Jury Bares New Detail of Break In," *Washington Post*, September 16, 1972; John J. Sirica, *To Set the Record Straight: The Break-In, the Tapes, the Conspirators, the Pardon* (New York: W.W. Norton & Company, 1979), 49–59.

6 "House Banking Committee to Study Watergate Case," *New York Times*, August 20, 1972; "House Unit Scans Fund Given G.O.P.," *New York Times*, September 13, 1972; Democratic Study Group, "The Most Corrupt Administration in History," 1972 Issue, Report No. 13, Box 282, Folder 9, Tip O'Neill Congressional Papers, John J. Burns Library, Boston College, Boston, Massachusetts.

7 E.W. Kenworthy, "$30,000 Donation Traced," *New York Times*, November 1, 1972; Lillian Levenson to Carl Albert, October 9, 1972, Legislative (LEG), Box 131, Folder 27, Carl Albert Collection, Carl Albert Congressional Research and Studies Center, University of Oklahoma, Norman, Oklahoma.

8 Carl Bernstein and Bob Woodward, "Testimony Ties Top Nixon Aide to Secret Fund," *Washington Post*, October 25, 1972; Lawrence Meyer, "McCord Ties Others to Plot," *Washington Post*, March 24, 1973; Sirica, *Set the Record Straight*, 61–116; Woodward and Bernstein, *All the President's Men*, 228–41.

9 Carl Bernstein and Bob Woodward, "Dean Cites Haldeman and Ehrlichman," *Washington Post*, April 29, 1973; "Nixon Statement on Resignations," *Washington Post*, May 1, 1973; John A. Farrell, *Richard Nixon: The Life* (New York: Doubleday, 2017), 506–14.

10 Bob Woodward and Carl Bernstein, "Senate Votes Watergate Probe," *Washington Post*, February 8, 1973; Edward Walsh, "Senate Sets Rules in Watergate Quiz," *Washington Post*, April 19, 1973; Samuel Dash, *Chief Counsel: Inside the Ervin Committee—The Untold Story of Watergate* (New York: Random House, 1976), 3–124.

11 George Lardner Jr., "Democrat Served Under Kennedy As Solicitor General," *Washington Post*, May 19, 1973; Jules Witcover, "Ervin Unit Wins Reputation

for Fairness," *Washington Post*, June 4, 1973; Woodward and Bernstein, *All the President's Men*, 246–51; Dash, *Chief Counsel*, 44–46, 48–51, 81–86.

12 Jules Witcover, "The First Day of Watergate," *Washington Post*, May 18, 1973; Lawrence Meyer and Peter Osnos, "Dean Firm on Nixon's Cover-Up Knowledge," *Washington Post*, June 30, 1973; Kutler, *Wars of Watergate*, 350–82.

13 Dash, *Chief Counsel*, 176–86; Kutler, *Wars of Watergate*, 367–71.

14 Susanna McBee, "Senate Panel Sues President to Get Tapes," *Washington Post*, August 10, 1973.

15 Yale Oral Transcript, 2, RA; O'Neill and Novak, *Man of the House: The Life and Political Memoirs of Speaker Tip O'Neill* (New York: Random House, 1987), 234–47; "Petition to the House of Representatives to Impeach Richard Nixon," January 1973, LEG, 168, 1, Albert Collection.

16 Carl Albert to Philip Isaacs, May 10, 1973, LEG, 168, 1 and John McLees to Carl Albert, May 1, 1973, 168, 1, Albert Collection; "Democrats Consider Talk of Impeachment Premature," *Washington Post*, May 24, 1973.

17 Representative Peter W. Rodino, introduction of H.R. 7490, on May 3, 1973, Ninety-Third Congress, First Session, *Congressional Record* 119, Pt. 11: 14233; Robert W. Maitlin, "Rodino Panel May Play Guiding Role in Watergate," *Star-Ledger*, May 3, 1973.

18 Yale Oral Transcript, 2, RA.

19 Committee on the Judiciary, House of Representatives, "Impeachment: Selected Materials," Ninety-Third Congress, First Session, October 1973; Committee on the Judiciary, House of Representatives, "Constitutional Grounds For Presidential Impeachment," Ninety-Third Congress, First Session, February 1974; Jeffrey A. Engel and Jon Meacham, Timothy Naftali, and Peter Baker, *Impeachment: An American History* (New York: Modern Library, 2008).

20 Yale Oral Transcript, 2–5, RA.

21 Dash, *Chief Counsel*, 167–68; Jerry Zeifman, *Without Honor: Crimes of Camelot and the Impeachment of President Nixon* (New York: Thunder's Mouth Press, 1995), 38–40.

22 Yale Oral Transcript, 6–7, RA; "Rodino Committee Creates Line to Prosecutor," *Star-Ledger*, July 12, 1973; Zeifman, *Without Honor*, 36–38; Howard Fields, *High*

Crimes and Misdemeanors (New York: W.W. Norton & Company, 1978), 33–34.

23 Representative Robert Drinan, "Introduction of Resolution on Impeachment," on July 31, 1973, Ninety-Third Congress, First Session, *Congressional Record* 119, Pt. 21: 27062; O'Neill and Novak, *Man of the House*, 247–48; John A. Farrell, *Tip O'Neill and the Democratic Century: A Biography* (New York: Little, Brown and Company, 2001), 337–43.

24 "Rodino Statement on the Impeachment Resolution H.Res. 513 Introduced by Representative Robert Drinan," August 1, 1973, Congressional Papers, Impeachment Files (IM), Box 1, Judiciary Committee Action Folder 2 (JCA), Thomas F. Railsback Collection, Malpass Library, Western Illinois University, Macomb, Illinois; Transcript of oral history interview with Peter W. Rodino Jr, Columbia Center for Oral History Archives, Rare Book & Manuscript Library, Columbia University, New York (Columbia Oral Transcript), 72–77, 80–81.

25 *Face the Nation*, transcript, *CBS News*, September 30, 1973, Legislative Files (LEG), Box 165, Folder 6, RA,.

26 Richard M. Cohen and Edward Walsh, "Agnew Investigation Mushrooms," *Washington Post*, August 8, 1973; Rachel Maddow and Michael Yarvitz, *Bag Man* (New York: Crown Publishing Group, 2020), 3–151; Myron S. Waldman, *Forgive Us Our Press Passes: The Memoirs of a Veteran Washington Reporter* (New York: St. Martin's Press, 1991), 53–54.

27 Rowland Evans and Robert Novak, "Agnew Ready to Go It Alone," *Washington Post*, September 7, 1973; Edward Walsh, "Agnew Talks Stalled," *Washington Post*, September 23, 1973; Farrell, *Nixon*, 346–47.

28 Spiro Agnew to Carl Albert, September 25, 1973, LEG165, 6, RA; Yale Oral Transcript, 7–8, RA; Carl Albert, "Interview 1," Joe Foote Collection, audio recordings, Carl Albert Center Congressional and Political Collection, University of Oklahoma, Norman, Oklahoma.

29 Columbia Oral Transcript, 84–86, RA.

30 Carl Albert, "Interview 1," Foote Collection; Fields, *High Crimes*, 39–41.

31 Columbia Oral Transcript, 87–89; Yale Oral Transcript, 7–8, RA; Carl Albert, "Interview 1," Foote Collection; Zeifman, *Without Honor*, 52–55.

32 Laurence Stern, "Vice President Agnew Resigns, Fined for Income Tax Evasion,"

Washington Post, October 11, 1973; Maddow and Yarvitz, *Bag Man*, 152–217.

33 Representative Rodino, speaking on the Twenty-Fifth Amendment, on April 13, 1965, Eighty-Ninth Congress, First Session, *Congressional Record,* 111, Pt. 6: 7954–55; John D. Feerick, *The Twenty-Fifth Amendment: Its Complete History and Application* (New York: Fordham University Press, 2014), 2–48; Committee on the Judiciary, House of Representatives, Ninety-Third Congress, First Session, "Application of the Twenty-Fifth Amendment To Vacancies in the Office of the Vice President: Legislative History," November 1973.

34 Feerick, *Twenty-Fifth Amendment*, 56–78.

35 "Special Subcommittee to Study Presidential Inability of the Committee on the Judiciary," House of Representatives, Eighty-Fourth Congress, Second Session, *Problems of Presidential Inability: Hearings*, April 1956; Kenneth Keating to Peter Rodino, February 21, 1958, LEG161, 2, RA; Emanuel Celler to Peter Rodino, March 3, 1958, LEG161, 2, RA.

36 Committee on the Judiciary, House of Representatives, Eighty-Ninth Congress, First Session, *Presidential Inability: Hearings*, February 1965; Feerick, *Twenty-Fifth Amendment*, 105–107.

37 Columbia Oral Transcript, 94.

38 Carl Albert, "Interview 3," Foote Collection; Columbia Oral Transcript, 101–102; Richard L. Lyons and Spencer Rich, "Hill Vows Thorough Probe of Successor," *Washington Post*, October 12, 1973.

39 Robert W. Maitlin, "Rodino Insisting on Careful Probe of Ford's Records," *Star-Ledger*, October 18, 1973; James Cannon, *Time and Chance: Gerald Ford's Appointment with History* (New York: HarperCollins, 1994), 201–14; Carl Albert, "Interview 3," Foote Collection; Edward Mezvinsky, *A Term to Remember* (New York: Coward, McCann & Geoghegan, 1977), 59–60.

40 "Statement by the President," August 15, 1973, LEG, 184, 2, Albert Collection; "Transcript of President Nixon's Press Conference," *Washington Post*, August 23, 1973; Kutler, *Watergate Wars*, 383–90.

41 "Excerpts From Transcript of Cox's News Conference on Nixon's Decision on Tapes," *New York Times* October 21, 1973; Kutler, *Watergate Wars*, 400–412.

42 Leslie Oelsner, "Cox Office Shut on Nixon's Order," *New York Times*, October

21, 1973; John M. Crewdson, "Richardson Quits Over Order on Cox," *New York Times*, October 21, 1973; "Ziegler Statement and Texts of Letters," *New York Times*, October 21, 1973.

43 Richard L. Madden, "Outcry in House," *New York Times*, October 21, 1973.

44 John Moss to Carl Albert, October 21, 1973, LEG, 182, 4, Albert Collection; Maurice Carroll, "Public Reacts Strongly to Cox Ouster," *New York Times*, October 22, 1973; Elizabeth Drew, *Washington Journal: Reporting Watergate and Richard Nixon's Downfall* (New York: Overlook Duckworth, 2014), 47–62.

45 Yale Oral History, 9–10, RA; Theodore H. White, *Breach of Faith: The Fall of Richard Nixon* (New York: Atheneum Publishers, 1975), 281.

46 Columbia Oral Transcript, 82–83, 97–99; Carl Albert, "Interview 3," Foote Collection; Joseph Califano to Carl Albert, October 22, 1973, LEG, 184, 2, Albert Collection; Mezvinsky, *Term to Remember*, 67–69; O'Neill and Novak, *Man of the House*, 249–50; Francis O'Brien interview by Timothy Naftali, September 29, 2011, Richard Nixon Oral History Project, Richard Nixon Presidential Library and Museum, Yorba Linda, California.

47 "Statement of Carl Albert," October 23, 1973, 282, 9, O'Neill Papers; Fields, *High Crimes*, 48–50.

48 "Majority Leader Thomas P. O'Neill Jr. Says Judiciary Committee to Study Impeachment Question," October 23, 1974, 282, 9, O'Neill Papers; Representative Jerome Waldie et al., on resolutions of impeachment, on October 23, 1973, Ninety-Third Congress, First Session, *Congressional Record*, 119, Pt. 27: 34819–823; Mezvinsky, *Term to Remember*, 69–71.

49 "Rodino's Challenge," *Washington Star*, November 4, 1973.

CHAPTER TWO

1 John T. Cunningham, *Newark*, revised edition (Newark, NJ: New Jersey Historical Society, 1988), 10–42; Frank J. Urquhart, *A History of the City of Newark, New Jersey, Volumes I and II, 1666–1913*, reprint of the 1913 edition (Loschberg, Germany: Jazzybee Verlag, 2017), I, 30–43, 61–64.

2 Kevin K. Olsen, *A Great Conveniency: A Maritime History of the Passaic River, Hackensack River, and Newark Bay* (Franklin, TN: American History Imprints,

2008), 31–33, 90–92; James P. Johnson, *New Jersey: History of Ingenuity and Industry* (California: Windsor Publications, 1987), 71, 113–15; John T. Cunningham, *Railroads in New Jersey: The Formative Years* (Andover, NJ: Afton Publishing, 1997), 48–61.

3 Brad R. Tuttle, *How Newark Became Newark: The Rise, Fall, and Rebirth of the American City* (New Brunswick, NJ: Rivergate Books, 2011), 22–28; Cunningham, *Newark*, 95–101.

4 "Newark Industrial Exposition," *New York Times*, September 21, 1872; Gordon B. Bishop, *Greater Newark: A Microcosm of America* (Chatsworth, CA: Windsor Publications, 1989), 27–35.

5 "Irish Laborers No Longer Available," *Newark Sunday Call,* May 19, 1889; Cunningham, *Newark*, 201–204; David Ward, *Cities and Immigrants* (New York: Oxford University Press, 1971), 71.

6 Jerre Mangione and Ben Morreale, *La Storia: Five Centuries of the Italian American Experience* (New York: HarperCollins, 1992), 31–53; Joseph Lopreato, *Italian Americans* (New York: Random House, 1970), 24–25; Robert Carola and Ben Morreale, *Italian Americans: The Immigrant Experience* (New York: Metro Books, 2008), 11–13.

7 Laurence Guy Brown, *Immigration: Cultural Conflicts and Social Adjustments* (New York: Arno Press and the *New York Times*, 1969), 177–79; Robert Franz Foerster, *The Italian Emigration of Our Times* (Cambridge, MA: Harvard University Press, 1919), 89–99.

8 Foerster, *Italian Emigration*, 51–54; Michael J. Eula, *Between Peasant and Urban Villager: Italian-Americans of New Jersey and New York, 1880–1980* (New York: Peter Lang, 1993), 1–7.

9 Foerster, *Italian Emigration*, 94–98.

10 Foerster, *Italian Emigration*, 59–62; Lopreato, *Italian Americans*, 27–30.

11 Mangione and Morreale, *La Storia*, 71–72, 105–106; Carola and Mangione, *Italian Americans*, 49–53.

12 Maurizio Eliseo and Paolo Piccione, *Transatlantici: The History of the Great Italian Liners on the Atlantic* (Genoa, Italy: Tormena Editore, 2001), 24; Maria Laurino, *The Italian Americans* (New York: W.W. Norton & Company, 2015), 38–39.

13 Ronald H. Bayor, *Encountering Ellis Island: How European Immigrants Entered America* (Baltimore, MD: Johns Hopkins University Press, 2014), 19–21.

14 Carola and Morreale, *Italian Americans*, 66–68; Ivan Chermayeff, Fred Wasserman, and Mary J. Shaprio, *Ellis Island: An Illustrated History of the Immigrant Experience* (New York: Macmillan Publishing Company, 1991), 38–42.

15 Vincent J. Cannato, *American Passage: The History of Ellis Island* (New York: HarperCollins, 2009), 42–54.

16 Bayor, *Encountering Ellis Island*, 38–80; Chermayeff, Wasserman, and Shapiro, *Ellis Island*, 109–23.

17 "Admitted Being Convicts," *New York Times,* May 18, 1893; Maria Laurino, *The Italian Americans*, 39.

18 "Crowded with Immigrants," *New York Times*, April 5, 1896; "Anchor Line Bolivia," *New York Times*, April 14, 1896.

19 He used "Rodini" from 1905 until 1910. "Records of the Immigration and Naturalization Service, 1891–1957," New York, New York, Roll 93, Record Group 85 (RG85), National Archives Building,Washington, D.C. (NAB).

20 Karl Baedeker, *Italy Handbook for Travellers, Third Part: Southern Italy, Sicily* (Leipzig, Germany: Karl Baedeker, 1875), 391. Although Pellegrino provided various birth years on earlier forms, his consistent answer from 1915 until his death was May 30, 1883.

21 "Declaration of Intention of Pellegrino Rodini," July 17, 1915, 44, and "Petition for Naturalization of Pellegrino Rodini," February 21, 1922, 188, Series CESCP005, Essex County Court of Common Pleas, Naturalization Records 1792–1931, New Jersey State Archives, Trenton, New Jersey (NJSA); "Draft Registration Card of Pellegrino Rodino, September 12, 1918," World War I Selective Service System draft registration cards, M1509, Roll NJ77, Selective Service System Records, National Personnel Records Center, National Archives, St. Louis Missouri. (NPRC); "Marriage License of Pellegrino Rodini and Guiseppina Gerardo," May 11, 1905, New Jersey Marriage Index, 1901–1914, NJSA.

22 Roll 70 and 93, RG85, NAB; Eliseo and Piccione, *Transatlantici*, 24; "Biographies," Personal Files (PER), Box 001, Folder 12, RA

23 George J. Svejda, *Castle Garden As American Immigrant Depot, 1855–1890*

(Washington, DC: Office of Archaeology and Historic Preservation, National Park Service, 1968), 105, 145–46.

24 "Abuses at Barge Office," *New York Times,* June 3, 1900.

25 Michael Immerso, *Newark's Little Italy: The Vanished First Ward* (New Brunswick, NJ: Rutgers University Press and the Newark Public Library, 1997), 1–3; Charles Wesley Churchill, *The Italians of Newark: A Community Study* (New York: Arno Press, 1975), 23–26.

26 US Census, 1900; Herbert Thowless, *Historical Sketch of the City of Newark, New Jersey* (Newark, NJ: Holbrook's Newark City Directory, 1902), 3–10; Catherine Longendyck and Kathleen P. Galop, *Images of America: Forest Hill* (Charleston, SC: Arcadia Publishing, 2014), 88–89.

27 "New Jersey Board of Tenement House Supervision," *Annual Report,* 1904, 95–96; Stuart Galishoff, *Newark: The Nation's Unhealthiest City: 1832–95* (New Brunswick, NJ: Rutgers University Press, 1988), 68–69, 203.

28 Cunningham, *Newark,* 201-202; Immerso, *Newark's Little Italy,* 2.

29 Luciano J. Iorizzo, "The Padrone and Immigrant Distribution," in *The Italian Experience in the United States,* eds. Silvano M. Tomasi and Madeline H. Engel (Staten Island, NY: Center For Migration Studies, 1970), 43–75; Rudolph J. Vecoli, "The Italian People in New Jersey," in *The New Jersey Ethnic Experience,* ed. Barbara Cunningham (Union City, NJ: William. H. Wise and Company, 1977), 275; Biographies, PER001, 12, RA.

30 Lopreato, *Italian Americans,* 40–47; Cristogianni Borsella, *On Persecution, Identity and Activism: Aspects of the Italian-American Experience from the Late 19th Century to Today* (Boston, MA: Dante University Press, 2005), 42–46; Mangione and Morreale, *La Storia,* 129–48.

31 Dennis J. Starr, *The Italians of New Jersey: A Historical Introduction and Bibliography* (Newark, NJ: New Jersey Historical Society, 1985), 1–2; Immerso, *Newark's Little Italy,* 2–7, 65–80; Peter B. Mattia, *The Recollections of Peter B. Mattia* (Nutley, NJ: K.J. Rosa, 1985), 15–19, 54–57.

32 Immerso, *Newark's Little Italy,* 15–17.

33 Thomas Frascella, "Commune di San Fele," San Felese Society of New Jersey, www.sanfelesesocietynj.org; interview with Frank Gerard Godlewski, March 30,

2018; "Daniel Gerards Mark Anniversary," *Newark Evening News,* December 6, 1949.

34 "Marriage License of Pellegrino Rodini and Guiseppina Gerardo," May 11, 1905, NJSA; Godlewski interview. Her name was spelled "Girardo" on the marriage license.

35 John M. McDowell, "A Tour of the Slums of Newark," *Newark Star-Ledger*, April 24, 1949; Cunningham, *Newark*, 245–46.

36 "Certificate and Record of Birth of *Pellegrino* Rodini," June 7, 1909, Bureau of Vital Statistics, City of Newark, New Jersey, PER001, 1, RA; *Newark City Directory by the Price and Lee Company* 1909, 1910, 1911, 1916. He also used the Rodino spelling of his name on his draft registration in 1918. "Draft Registration of Pellegrino Rodino," NJSA.

37 Rodino Personal Recordings, Oral Transcripts (Oral Transcripts), Tape 16, 7–10, RA; Oral Transcript, 4/29/99, 7–8, RA; Oral Transcript, 5, 4, RA; PER002, 12, RA.

38 Mangione and Morreale, *La Storia*, 139–40; Churchill, *Italians of Newark*, 130–31; Oral Transcript, 5, 4, RA; Oral Transcript, 16, 9, RA; Luciano J. Iorizzo and Salvatore Mondello, *The Italian Americans* (Boston, MA: Twayne Publishers, 1980), 104–105; Foerster, *Italian Emigration*, 393–94.

39 Oral Transcript, 4/29/99, 7–8, RA; Oral Transcript, 16, 7–9, RA.

40 Columbia Oral Transcript, 7–8; Oral Transcript, 16, 7, RA.

41 "Certificate of Merit," Newark Public Schools, August 15, 1919, PER001, 192V, RA; *The Tattler*, McKinley School, November 1921, PER001, 2, RA.

42 New Jersey State Board of Education, *New Jersey School Laws and Rules and Regulations prescribed by the State Board of Education* (Trenton, 1914).

43 Urquhart, *History of Newark*, II, 116–22; Cunningham, *Newark*, 213–17.

44 Oral Transcript, 5, 1–3, RA.

45 Johnson, *New Jersey*, 255–56; "Peter Rodino Sr. Dead," *Newark Evening News*, May 10, 1957; Oral Transcript, 5, 3–4, RA.

46 *The Acropolis*, Barringer High School, January 1927, PER001, 3, RA; Oral Transcript, 5, 3, RA.

47 Oral Transcript, 5, 5–6, RA; Cunningham, *Newark*, 217–20.

48 Oral Transcript, 6, 10, RA; Starr, *Italians of New Jersey*, 17, 25.

49 Oral Transcript, 6, 1–10, RA; Seth Stern and Stephen Wermiel, *Justice Brennan: Liberal Champion* (Lawrence, KS: University Press of Kansas, 2010), 3–13.

50 Columbia Oral Transcript, 1–9; Oral Transcript, 5, 5–8, RA; Barringer High School, *The Acropolis*, January 1927.

51 Scott M. Deitche, *Garden State Gangland: The Rise of the Mob in New Jersey* (Lanham, MD: Rowman and Littlefield, 2018), 2–3; Laurino, *Italian Americans*, 50–56.

52 Lawrence Spinelli, *Dry Diplomacy: The United States, Great Britain and Prohibition* (Lanham, MD: Rowman & Littlefield, 2008), 1–30; Richard Linnett, *In the Godfather Garden: The Long Life and Times of Richie "The Boot" Boiardo* (New Brunswick, NJ: Rutgers University Press, 2013), 15.

53 Linnett, *In the Godfather Garden*, 15–21, 34–40; Deitche, *Garden State Gangland*, 40–41.

54 Columbia Oral Transcript, 13.

55 Oral Transcript, 5, 7–10, RA; Oral Transcript, 21, 1–2, RA; Immerso, *Newark's Little Italy*, 109–13.

56 Oral Transcript, 7, 8–10, RA; Owen Clayton to Peter Rodino, April 4, 1946, PER001, 5, RA; Marian Calabro, *Making Things Work: PSEG's First Century* (Lyme, CT: Greenwich Publishing Group, 2003), 22–41.

57 Hugh Francis Bennett, "A History of the University of Newark 1908–1946," (PhD diss., New York University, 1956), 31–69; Paul Tractenberg, *A Centennial History of Rutgers Law School in Newark: Opening a Thousand Doors* (Charleston, SC: The History Press, 2010), 21, 29.

58 New Jersey Law School, Pre-Legal Department, "Certificate of Completion," June 12, 1930, PER001, 192, Oversized Volumes (OV), RA; Oral Transcript, Tape 7, 8–8, RA.

59 Paul Anthony Stellhorn, "Depression and Decline: Newark, New Jersey, 1929–1941," (Doctoral dissertation, Rutgers University, 1982), 66–94.

60 David M. Kennedy, *Freedom from Fear: The American People in Depression and War, 1929–1945* (New York: Oxford University Press, 1999), 58–68; Cunningham, *Newark*, 280–82.

61 Columbia Oral Transcript, 3–4, RA; Oral Transcript, 7, 9–10, RA.

62 Oral Transcript, 21, 1, RA; Oral Transcript, 7, 9, RA.

63 Oral Transcript, 7, 3–8, RA; "Mrs. Rodino Dies at 70," *Star-Ledger*, December 4, 1980.

64 Oral Transcript, 7, 3–11, RA.

65 Columbia Oral Transcript, 4–6, 9; Oral Transcript, 7, 7, RA; Oral Transcript, 5, 8, RA.

66 Columbia Oral Transcript, 4–5; Alison McCracken, *Real Men Don't Sing: Crooning in American Culture* (Durham, NC: Duke University Press, 2015), 84–88, 276–78.

67 Oral Transcript, 3, 1–2, RA.

68 Urban K. Cummings, *Ronson: The World's Greatest Lighter* (Palo Alto, CA: Bird Dog Books, 1992), 21–50; Oral Transcript, 7, 10–11, RA.

69 Columbia Oral Transcript, 10; Oral Transcript, 7, 12, RA.

70 School of Law of the University of Newark, *Legacy*, 1937, PER001, 4, RA; Peter Rodino to Vince Biunni, May 21, 1942, PER002, 7, RA.

71 *Legacy*, PER001, 4, RA; Owen Clayton to Peter Rodino, April 4, 1946, PER001, 5, RA; Oral Transcript, 5, 6–7, RA.

72 Columbia Oral Transcript, 13; "Who's Who in Campaign for City Commission," *Newark Star-Eagle*, May 18, 1933; "Obituary of Judge Albano," *Newark Star-Eagle*, April 13, 1939.

73 "Young Republicans from First Unite to Promote Harmony," *Newark Evening News*, March 3, 1926; Churchill, *Italians of Newark*, 115–21.

74 Churchill, *Italians of Newark*, 122–24; Starr, *Italians of New Jersey*, 41.

75 Columbia Oral Transcript, 13–16; Oral Transcript, 7, 8, RA; Thomas J. Archdeacon, *Becoming American: An Ethnic History* (New York: The Free Press, 1983), 192; Richard A. Reiman, *The New Deal and American Youth: Ideas and Ideals in a Depression Decade* (Athens, GA: University of Georgia Press, 1992), 97–140.

76 *Legacy*, PER001, 4, RA; University of Newark; "Bachelor of Laws Diploma," June 10, 1937, PER192OV, RA; "177 Newark U Pupils Will Get Degree Tonight," *Newark Star-Eagle*, June 10, 1937; Office of the Clerk of the Supreme Court of New Jersey to Peter Rodino, June 27, 1938, PER001, 1, RA. Prior to his graduation, the school became part of the recently established University of Newark.

77 "Friends to Fete Peter Rodino," *Italian Tribune*, October 8, 1938; "Peter Rodino to

be Honored," *Jersey Press*, October 11, 1938; "Roaming the Town," *Essex Enquirer*, October 19, 1938; "Testimonial Dinner Tendered in Honor of Peter Rodino Jr., Vittorio Castle, Program," November 17, 1938, Scrapbook 01 (SCR), RA.

78 Columbia Oral Transcript, 10–13.

79 "Newark's Own Jimmy Walker," *Italian Tribune*, May 17, 1940; "Democratic Voters Will Have Little to Stir Them," *Newark Sunday Call*, May 19, 1940.

80 "Essex Ticket Asks 'Hague Lie' Defeat," *Newark Sunday Call*, September 28, 1940; "First Ward Dem Club to Hold Benefit Dance," *Italian Tribune*, September 26, 1940; "Roosevelt Night at the Mosque," *Newark Evening News*, October 23, 1940.

81 Mangione and Morreale, *La Storia*, 318–22; Doris Kearns Goodwin, *No Ordinary Time: Franklin and Eleanor Roosevelt: The Home Front in World War II* (New York: Simon & Schuster, 1994), 67–69.

82 "Vote for Giffoniello and Bozza Also Cavicchia and Rodino," *Italian Tribune*, November 1, 1940; "Assembly," *Newark Evening News*, November 6, 1940; "Election Results," *Italian Tribune*, November 8, 1940.

83 *Legacy*, PER001, 4, RA.

CHAPTER THREE

1 "Peace in Strength," *New York Times*, October 30, 1940; J. Garry Clifford and Samuel R. Spencer Jr. *The First Peacetime Draft* (Lawrence, KS: University Press of Kansas, 1986), 1–3.

2 Robert Dallek, *Franklin D. Roosevelt and American Foreign Policy, 1932–1945* (New York: Oxford University Press, 1979), 102–108, 187–91; Maury Klein, *A Call to Arms: Mobilizing America for World War II* (New York: Bloomsburg Press, 2014), 13–39.

3 Susan Dunn, *1940: FDR, Willkie, Lindbergh, Hitler—The Election Amid the Storm* (New Haven: Yale University Press, 2013), 167–88; Richard Moe, *Roosevelt's Second Act: The Election of 1940 and the Politics of War* (New York: Oxford University Press, 2013), 251–54.

4 Klein, *Call to Arms*, 118–20; Clifford and Spencer Jr., *Peacetime Draft*, 119–53.

5 "Registration for Draft Presents Varied Scenes," *Newark Evening News*, October 16, 1940; "Its R-Day for Men 21-36: Board Sit Until 9PM," *Newark Star-Ledger*, October

16, 1940; "Records of Peter Wallace Rodino," Selective Service System, NPRC.

6 "Draft Board Names Sifted," *Newark Evening News*, September 18, 1940; "Essex Cards Go to Draft Boards," *Newark Star-Ledger*, October 18, 1940; "N.J. Draft Quota Set at 32, 170," *Newark Sunday Call*, October 20, 1940.

7 "Certificate of Appointment," November 6, 1940, State of New Jersey Selective Service System, PER002, 1, RA; "Draft Boards and Appeals Agents," *Newark Sunday Call*, October 13, 1940; Klein, *Call To Arms*, 342.

8 Oral Transcript, 3, 4–5, RA;

9 Office of the Director of Selective Service, "Appointment of Leader of Assistant Leader," March 10, 1941, SCR01, RA; Columbia Oral Transcript, 19–22; "Drafter Drafted," *Newark Evening News,* March 7, 1941; "Loizeaux's Kin and Lawyer Off to Fort Dix as Draftees," *Newark Star-Ledger,* March 11, 1941.

10 "Fort Dix Growing Into Military City," *New York Times*, September 22, 1940; Marshall Newton, "Fort Dix Capacity to be 40,000," *New York Times*, December 10, 1940.

11 "71st Fights 'War' Amid Wintry Blasts," *New York Times*, March 18, 1941; "Induction Center at Fort Dix Ready," *New York Times*, November 17, 1940; "Fort Dix Trainees Hold First Review," *New York Times*, April 18, 1941.

12 Meyer Bergercamp Dix, "Trainee: Four Months Later," *New York Times*, April 6, 1940; John Ellis, *The Sharp Edge: The Fighting Man in World War II* (London: Aurum Press, 2009), 13.

13 US Army, Temporary Warrant, December 11, 1941, SCR01, RA; Oral Transcript, 2/2/99, 1–2, RA; Oral Transcript, 11, 4–5, RA; Goodwin, *No Ordinary Time*, 267–69.

14 "Text of Proclamation," *New York Times*, May 28, 1941.

15 Dallek, *Roosevelt*, 239–42. In March, the State Department requested that the Italian government close its consulate in Newark. "Italian Consulate Closing," *Newark Star-Ledger*, March 7, 1941; Frederick R. Barkley, "House for 2 1/2 Years Army Service by One Vote," *New York Times*, August 13, 1941; "FDR Signing Draft Bill," *Newark Star-Ledger*, September 16, 1941.

16 Oral Transcript, 7, 8, RA; Oral Transcript, 11, 4, RA.

17 Oral Transcript, 11, 3–5, RA; Klein, *Call to Arms*, 281–85.

18 Oral Transcript, 11, 3–6, RA; "Marriage License of Peter W. Rodino Jr. and

Marianna Stango," December 27, 1941, Department of Health, Bureau of Vital Statistics, State of Maryland; "Announcement of the Marriage of Marianna Stango and Peter W. Rodino on December 27, 1941," dated February 28, 1942, PER001, 1, RA.

19 Peter Rodino to Vince Biunno, May 21, 1942, PER002, 7, RA; Oral Transcript, 11, 4, 6–7.

20 John Morton Blum, *V Was for Victory: Politics and American Culture During WWII* (New York: Harcourt Brace Jovanovich, 1976), 147–55; Peter Rodino to Vince Biunno, May 21, 1942, PER002, 7, RA.

21 Daniel Henkin to Peter Rodino, June 15, 1942, PER002, 7, RA; Mark Clark to William Smathers, August 21, 1942, SCR01, RA.

22 Writings From Florida, PER002, 7, RA; Oral Transcripts, 11, 7, RA.

23 Oral Transcript, 11, 2–3, 7–8, RA; Peter Rodino to Vince Biunno, June 4, 1942, PER002, 7, RA; "National Service Life Insurance," Veterans Administration, March 1, 1942, PER002, 1, RA; "Immunization Record," PER002, 1, RA.

24 Nigel Hamilton, *The Mantle of Command: FDR at War 1941–1942* (New York: Houghton Mifflin, 2014), 100–109; James Holland, *The Allies Strike Back 1941–1943: The War in the West, Volume I* (New York: Atlantic Monthly Press, 2017), 120–22, 280–81.

25 James MacDonald, "Secret Trip Made: American Fighting Men Land Unheralded at Beflagged Pier," *New York Times*, January 27, 1942; David Reynolds, *Rich Relations: The American Occupation of Britain, 1942–1945* (New York: Random House, 1995), 90, 99.

26 Oral Transcript, 3, 7, RA; Andrew Williams, *The Battle of the Atlantic: Hitler's Gray Wolves of the Sea and the Allies' Desperate Struggle to Defeat Them* (New York: Basic Books, 2004), 161–88, 242–43.

27 Military Service Record of Peter W. Rodino, US Army, PER002, 1, RA; Reynolds, *Rich Relations*, 112–14; Jim Minnock to Peter Rodino, August 29, 1979, PER002, 11, RA: Salisbury memorabilia, PER001,192OV, RA; Oral Transcript, 3, 7–10, RA.

28 Milton M. McPherson, *The Ninety Day Wonders: OCS and the Modern American Army* (Columbus, GA: United States Army Officer Candidate School Alumni Association, 2001), 80–83; A .E. Weand, "The Short Life of Shrivenham American

University," *The Journal of the Royal Military College of Science* 8, no. 7 (1995): 9–11.

29 American School Center, Officer Candidates School, "Diploma," December 9, 1942, SCR01, RA; "Honorable Discharge," US Army, December 8, 1942, SCR01, RA; Oral Transcript, 3, 8–9, RA. Candidates were honorably discharged so they could return to active duty.

30 "When The Yanks Go Rolling Along," PER002, 6, RA; Oral Transcript, 3, 2–3, 9–10, RA.

31 Rick Atkinson, *An Army at Dawn: The War in North Africa 1942–1943* (New York: Henry Holt and Company, 2002), 10–17; O'Neill, *Democracy at War*, 159–69; Oral Transcript, 3, 7–10, RA.

32 Atkinson, *Army at Dawn*, 366–75, 389–91; George F. Howe, *The Battle History of the 1st Armored Division* (Washington, DC: Combat Forces Press, 1954), 166–98.

33 Peter Rodino to (unaddressed), February 28, 1943, PER002, 8, RA.

34 Oral Transcript, 5, 1–3, RA; Oral Transcript, 5/12/99, 3–4, RA; Jonathan Dimbleby, *Destiny in the Desert: The Road to El Alamein: The Battle That Turned the Tide of World War II* (New York: Pegasus Books, 2012), 440–42; Atkinson, *Army at Dawn*, 513–23.

35 Dallek, *Roosevelt*, 368–71; O'Neill, *Democracy at War*, 177–80.

36 Rick Atkinson, *The Day of Battle: The War in Sicily and Italy 1943–1944* (New York: Henry Holt and Company, 2007), 21, 112–37, 140–42; Christian Jennings, *At War on the Gothic Line: Fighting in Italy, 1944–45* (New York: St. Martin's Press, 2016), 6–11.

37 Atkinson, *Day of Battle*, 203–36, 412–45.

38 "Bronze Star Citation," PER001, 1920V, RA; Oral Transcript, 5/12/99, 3–6, RA; "Officers and Warrant Officer Qualification Card," RA.

39 Jennings, *Gothic Line*, 33–48; Howe, *1st Armored Division*, 331–46; Robert Katz, *The Battle For Rome: The Germans, the Allies, the Partisans and the Pope September 1943–June 1944* (New York: Simon & Schuster, 2003), 312–29; "Bronze Star Citation," PER001, 192OV, RA.

40 Dallek, *Roosevelt*, 412–14; Katz, *Battle for Rome*, 181–83, 294–96; Oral Transcript, 5/12/99, 4–5, RA.

41 Clayton P. Kerr to Peter Rodino, November 2, 1945, PER002, 2, RA; Eric Stein, "War, Politics, Law—and Love: Italy 1943–1946," *Michigan Journal of International Law* 32, no. 3 (2011): 557.

42 Clayton P. Kerr, "Promotion of Officer Peter W. Rodino, Jr," April 19, 1945, PER002A, 2, 3, RA; Oral Transcripts, 5/12/99, 5–6, RA; Oral Transcript, 4/29/99, 1–6, RA.

43 Oral Transcript, 4/29/88, 1–6, RA; Oral Transcript, 5/12/99, 5–7, RA; Peter Rodino to Prince Nicolas Nemagnan Paleologue, September 22, 1945, PER002, 2, RA; Peter Rodino to commanding general, MTUSA, "Request for Authority to Accept Foreign Decorations," September 12, 1945, PER002A, 2, RA. See original Italian honors in PER001, 192OV, RA.

44 "Recommendation for Award," PER002A, 2, RA; William A. Widemeyer, "Award of Bronze Star Medal," July 24, 1945, PER002, 2, RA; "Promotion of Officer Peter Rodino," PER002, 2, RA. The promotion to captain was delayed because army rules changed, and Rodino was required to first agree to serve in the reserves.

45 "Tally Sheet of Lieutenant Rodino," US Army, November 3, 1945, PER002A, 3, RA; "Separation Qualification Record of Peter W. Rodino," US Army, PER002, 2, RA; "Movement Orders to Separation Center for Peter W. Rodino," US Army, December 4 and December 9, 1945, PER002, 2, and PER002A, 3, RA.

CHAPTER FOUR

1 "Throngs Marooned in Yule Travel Jam Across the Nation," *New York Times*, December 23, 1945.

2 "Neither Storm Nor Delay Depresses Arriving GIs," *New York Times*, December 26, 1945; "Military Record and Report of Separation Certificate of Service of Peter W. Rodino," US Army, PER002, 2, RA. There is no passenger list for the USS *Randolph*, but it is the only troopship that conforms to Rodino's orders and timetable. December 15–26, 1945, "Desk Logs of the *USS Randolph*," Records of the Bureau of Naval Personnel, Record Group 24, National Archives at College Park, College Park, Maryland (NACP).

3 "Overseas Vet Meets Child, Now 3, for the First Time," *Fort Monmouth News*, January 4, 1946; Columbia Oral Transcript, 23–24.

4 Jack Stokes Ballard, *The Shock of Peace: Military and Economic Demobilization After World War II* (Washington, DC: University Press of America, 1983), 85–92, 469–70; "Special Orders," Number 11, December 28, 1945, US Army, PER002A, 3, RA; Oral Transcript, 11, 2–3, RA.

5 Oral Transcript, 12, 4, RA; Kenneth C. Martis, *The Historical Atlas of United States Congressional Districts 1789–1983* (New York: The Free Press, 1982), 246–47.

6 "Ex-Rep. Fred Hartley Jr., Co-author of Labor Law," *Evening News*, May 12, 1969; "Hartley 9 votes in Lead," *Newark Evening News*, December 14, 1928; "Eleven States Gain, 21 Lose House Seats," *New York Times*, November 19, 1930. The *Permanent Reapportionment Act of 1929* capped the House of Representatives at 435 members and required an automatic reapportionment after every census.

7 Columbia Oral Transcript, 22–26; Oral Transcript, 11, 9, RA; "Veterans Group to Aid Democrats," *Newark Star-Ledger*, May 23, 1946.

8 "Peter Rodino Returns Honored and Decorated," *Italian Tribune*, March 22, 1946.

9 "Capt. Rodino, War Hero, Will Seek Hartley's Seat in Congress," *Newark Star-Ledger*, April 3, 1946; Owen Clayton to Peter Rodino, April 4, 1946, PER001, 5, RA; George L. Ripley to Peter Rodino, April 17, 1946, PER001, 5, RA.

10 "Campaign Advertisements," 1946 Rodino Campaign, PER002A, 5, RA; SCR02, RA; Oral Transcript, 11, 9–12, RA; Columbia Oral Transcript, 24–25; "Rodino Hits Reds at Kearny Rally," *Newark Evening News*, April 2, 1946.

11 Oral Transcript, 11, 10, RA; Columbia Oral Transcript, 36; "Jersey Campaign," *Newark Star-Ledger*, June 16, 1946. Rodino's labor supporters included the Greater Newark Industrial Council, New Jersey CIO-PAC, Amalgamated Clothing Workers of America, Brotherhood of Railroad Trainmen, Textile Workers Union of America, United Steelworkers, and the state and local teachers' union.

12 Oral Transcript, 11, 18, RA.

13 Oral Transcript, 2/2/99, 2–3, RA; "Rodino Speaks," *Newark Star-Ledger*, October 8, 1946; "Sleuth Helped Rodino Win on a Shoestring," *Newark Star-Ledger*, November 4, 1948; "Joseph Benucci Dies, Newark Postmaster," *Star-Ledger*, May 29, 1990.

14 Sam O'Neal to Peter Rodino, June 15, 1946, PER002A, 4, RA; Columbia Oral Transcript, 38; *Campaign Issues, 1946: A Handbook for Candidates, Speakers and Workers of the Democratic Party* (Washington, DC: Democratic National

Committee, 1946).

15 Ballard, *The Shock of Peace*, 162–170; David McCullough, *Truman* (New York: Simon & Schuster, 1992), 520–22; "Truman Visitors: Jersey Democratic Candidates at Capital," *Newark Star-Ledger*, September 18, 1946.

16 "Nod For Vet," *Newark Star-Ledger*, September 12, 1946; Columbia Oral Transcript, 26; Joseph P. Lash, *Eleanor: The Years Alone* (New York: W.W. Norton & Company, 1972), 138–3;, RA; Oral Transcript, 11, 3, RA.

17 Oral Transcript, 11, 11–12, RA; "Guest of Honor Peter W. Rodino, Jr.," Garibaldi American Fraternal Society, PER002A, Folder 4, RA; "Veterans Canvass Votes, Set Sights on Hartley," *Newark Star-Ledger*, September 26, 1946; "Rodino Campaign Launched at Dinner," *Italian Tribune*, October 18, 1946.

18 "Rodino Compares Party Programs," *Newark Evening News*, October 25, 1946; "Rodino Labels Hartley Lobbyist," *Newark Evening News*, October 29, 1946; "Charges Hartley Leads Reactionaries," *Newark Evening News*, October 25, 1946.

19 "Campaign Advertisements," PER002A, Folder 4, RA.

20 "Flyer for League of Women Voters Forum at Nutley High School," May 3, 1946, SCR01, RA; Columbia Oral Transcript, 36; "Rodino Sees Shifts in House," *Newark Evening News*, October 24, 1946; "Republicans Hit on Vets," *Newark Evening News*, October 18, 1946.

21 "Dr. Mattia Endorses Rodino," *Newark Star-Ledger*, October 19, 1946; "GOP Ward Leader Supports Rodino," *Newark Evening News,* October 19, 1946.

22 "Hartley Rodino Race in Spotlight," *Newark Star-Ledger*, October 21, 1946.

23 "Says GOP Lists Possible Losers," *Newark Evening News*, September 30, 1946; "Jersey Seats Seem Static," *Newark Evening News*, October 2, 1946.

24 "Hartley Charges Strong-Arm Plot," *Newark Sunday Call*, November 3, 1946; "Bilboism Charge Hurled at Hartley by Rodino," *Newark Star-Ledger*, November 3, 1946.

25 "The Senate, Too!" *Newark Star-Ledger*, November 6, 1946; Columbia Oral Transcript, 27–28; Oral Transcript, 18, 2–3, RA.

26 William Graff, compiler, *Statistics of the Presidential and Congressional Election of November 5, 1946* (Washington, DC: Government Printing Office, 1947); "Hartley Wins Hardest Race," *Newark Evening News*, November 6, 1946; "Hartley Reelected

by 6,646 for 10th term in House," *Newark Star-Ledger*, November 6, 1946.

27 Columbia Oral Transcript, 27–28.

28 Oral Transcript, 15, 5–6, RA; Quentin J. DeFazio to Peter Rodino, April 9, 1947, PER001, 5, RA; Robert Meyner to Peter Rodino, July 9, 1947, SCR01, RA; "Rodino Is Appointed AVC Housing Chairmen," *Newark Evening News*, February 23, 1947.

29 Joseph R. Salerno to Peter Rodino, February 21, 1946, PER001, 5, RA; Oral Transcript, 4/29/99, 1–4, RA; Oral Transcript, 11, 1–2, RA; Juvenal Marchiao to Peter Rodino, March 9, 1946, PER001, 5, RA.

30 Kaeten Mistry, *The United States, Italy and the Origins of Cold War: Waging Political Warfare 1945–1950* (Cambridge, UK: Cambridge University Press, 2014), 127–52; "Pearson Broadcast to Italians," *New York Times*, March 25, 1948; "Anti-Red Appeals to Italy Increase," *New York Times*, April 13, 1948.

31 Press statement, March 24, 1948, PER002A, 4, 5, RA.

32 "Centers to Spur Letters to Italy," *Newark Star-Ledger*, March 18, 1948; Columbia Oral Transcript, 40; "Italians Here Hail Victory Over Reds," *Washington Post*, April 24, 1948.

33 "Sleuth Helped Rodino Win on a Shoestring," *Newark Star-Ledger*, November 4, 1948; Oral Transcript, 2/23/99, 1, 7–11, RA.

34 "Giuliano by 5,816 votes," *Newark Evening News*, April 21, 1948; "Hartley Reiterates Intention to Retire," *New York Times*, July 29, 1947; McCullough, *Truman*, 565–66. Hartley implied during the 1946 Republican primary that this would be his last term. "Schaefer Wins More Backing," *Newark Star-Ledger*, May 29, 1946.

35 Oral Transcript, 2/23/99, 3–7, RA; Columbia Oral Transcript, 28–35.

36 "Essex Scrapbook," *Newark Evening News*," April 17, 1948.

37 Peter Rodino, "Mr. Rodino's Candidacy," *Newark Evening News*, April 24, 1948. Rodino claimed the Republicans offered him their nomination, but it seems unlikely this was a serious proposal. Columbia Oral Transcript, 27–29.

38 David Pietrusza, *1948: Harry Truman's Improbable Victory and the Year that Transformed America's Role in the World* (New York: Union Square Press, 2011), 362–64; McCullough, *Truman*, 632–38.

39 Speaking Engagements, October 1948, PER002A, 4, RA; Oral Transcript, 11, 11, RA; Oral Transcript, 15, 2–3, 6, RA; "State CIO Backs Rodino," *Newark*

Star-Ledger, October 5, 1948; "Veterans Organize to Elect Rodino," *Newark Star-Ledger*, October 8, 1948.

40 "Forum Soothes Candidates," *Newark Evening News*, October 29, 1948; "Candidates Give Answers to Questions on Policies," *Newark Evening News*, October 13, 1948; "Rodino Blames 80th Congress for Nation's Housing Shortage," *Italian Tribune*, October 29, 1948.

41 "Jersey Considered Safely Republican," *New York Times*, October 13, 1948; "Scores Giuliano for 'Hartley' Aims," *Newark Evening News*, October 30, 1948; "Defiant Truman Raps Tories," *Newark Star-Ledger*, October 8, 1948.

42 "Rodino, Addonizio Laud Vote Results," *Newark Evening News*, November 3, 1948; "Congress Victories Cheer State CIO," *Newark Star-Ledger*, November 4, 1948; "Election Results," *Newark Star-Ledger*, November 4, 1948.

43 Columbia Oral Transcript, 39; Oral Transcript, 2/23/99, 6–10, RA; "Sleuth Helped Rodino Win on a Shoestring," *Newark Star-Ledger*, November 4, 1948.

44 "Rodino, Addonizio Sweep to Victory," *Newark Star-Ledger*, November 3, 1948; "Democrats in Full Power; Truman and Congress Too," *Newark Star-Ledger*, November 4, 1948.

45 "Rodino is Winner," *Newark Star-Ledger*, November 3, 1948.

46 "Democratic Victors Get Connubial Congratulation," *Newark Evening News*, November 3, 1948; "Rodino Says He's No Professional," *Newark Evening News*, November 3, 1948.

CHAPTER FIVE

1 James McGregor Burns, *Congress on Trial: The Legislative Process and The Administrative State* (New York: Harper and Brothers, 1949).

2 George B. Galloway, "The Operation of the Legislative Reorganization Act of 1946," *American Political Science Review* 45, no. 1 (March 1951): 41–68; Aaron L. Ford, "The Legislative Reorganization Act of 1946," *American Bar Association Journal* 32, no. 11 (November 1946): 741–44, 808–09.

3 Barbara Hinckley, *Seniority System in Congress* (Bloomington, IN: Indiana University Press, 1971), 4–8; George Goodwin Jr., "The Seniority System in Congress," *American Political Science Review* 53, no. 2 (June 1959): 413–18.

4 Garrison Nelson, *Committees in the U.S. Congress: 1947–1992, Committee Histories and Member Assignments Vol. 2* (Washington, DC: Congressional Quarterly, 1994), 411–12, 543.

5 Matthew N. Green, *The Speaker of the House: A Study of Leadership* (New Haven, CT: Yale University Press, 2010), 60–110.

6 Oral Transcript, 2/23/99, 9, RA; interview with Sandra Sincavitz; William Kelly to Peter Rodino, January 3, 1949, "Political and Party Leadership Files IV (POL)," Box 10, Folder 6, RA.

7 Drew Pearson, "Washington Merry Go Round," *Newark Evening News*, January 16, 1949; "New Faces in Congress," *Evening Star*, January 6, 1949; "A Look at Congress Freshmen," *Washington Post*, January 15, 1949. See also Donald A. Ritchie, *The Columnist: Leaks, Lies and Libel in Drew Pearson's Washington* (New York: Oxford University Press), 2021.

8 Columbia Oral Transcript, 39–41; Oral Transcript, 2/2/99, 4, RA.

9 Oral Transcript, 12, 7, RA; "N.J. Solons Get Committee Jobs," *Newark Star-Ledger*, January 18, 1949.

10 Emanuel Celler, *You Never Leave Brooklyn: The Autobiography of Emanuel Celler* (New York: John Day Company, 1953), 177–83; Garrison Nelson, *John William McCormack: A Political Biography* (New York: Bloomsbury, 2017), 265–66, 412.

11 C.P. Trussell, "House Unit at Odds, Votes," *New York Times*, February 16, 1949; Columbia Oral Transcript, 42–43.

12 Representative Rodino speaking on veterans pension bill on February 15, 1949, Eighty-First Congress, First Session, *Congressional Record* 95, Pt. 3: 1213.

13 Columbia Oral Transcript, 45–49; "Rodino Rips Rankin, Wins House Cheers," *Newark Star-Ledger*, February 16, 1949; "Rodino's Revolt," *Newark Star-Ledger*, February 16, 1949.

14 "The Daybook," *Washington Times Herald*, February 16, 1949; Robert C. Albright, "Uproar Reigns as House Group Reports Veterans Pension Bill," *Washington Post*, February 16, 1949; "House Unit at Odds," *New York Times*, February 16, 1949.

15 "Rankin and the Veterans," *Newsweek*, February 28, 1949; Representative Rodino speaking on veterans' pensions on March 23, 1949, Eighty-First Congress, First Session, *Congressional Record* 95, Pt. 3: 3059–60; "Rodino Hails Shelving of

Pension Bill," *Newark Star-Ledger*, March 25, 1949. Rodino was booed at veterans' meetings and events he attended in the weeks following the vote. Oral Transcript, 12, 9–11, RA.

16 Oral Transcript, 12, 2–4, RA; Arthur Sylvester, "Two Freshmen Get Congress Lowdown," *Newark Evening News*, January 5, 1949.

17 Oral Transcript, 2/2/99, 6, RA; "Rep. Rodino Swamped by Sea of Mail," *Newark Star-Ledger*, February 6, 1949; Joseph Benucci to Peter Rodino, April 29, 1949, PER66, 8, RA; Jack Bendit to Peter Rodino, September 11, 1949, and October 26, 1949, PER66, 8, RA.

18 Oral Transcript, 12, 4–6, RA; Oral Transcript, 2/2/99, 3, 6–10, RA; Peter Rodino to Jack Bendit, September 2, 1949, and September 11, 1949, PER66, 8, RA.

19 "New Members Pick Aides at Capitol," *Newark Evening News*, January 5, 1949; Peter Rodino to Joseph Benucci, January 25, 1949, PER66, 8, RA; Oral Transcript, 21, 3–4, RA. Benucci remained on the Newark police force and split his time between the two jobs for the next decade.

20 Peter Rodino to Joseph Benucci, January 24, 1949, PER66, 8, RA.

21 "No Rest for Rodino," *Newark Evening News*, February 27, 1949.

22 Representative Rodino speaking on H.R. 2150 on February 2, 1949, Eighty-First Congress, First Session, *Congressional Record* 95, Pt. 1: 777.

23 Representative Rodino speaking on H.R. 2150, on February 2, 1949, Eighty-First Congress, First Session, *Congressional Record* 95, Pt. 1: 777.

24 US Congress, House of Representatives, Committee on Education and Labor, Special Subcommittee, "National Labor Relations Act of 1949: Hearings Before the Special Subcommittee of the Committee on Education and Labor," Eighty-First Congress, First Session, 1949, 8; "Rodino Leads Attack on Hartley," *Newark Star-Ledger*, March 8, 1949; Louis Stark, "Hartley Assailed at Labor Hearing," *New York Times*, March 8, 1948.

25 Emanuel Celler to Mary T. Norton, December 6, 1948, and Mary T. Norton to Emanuel Celler, December 12, 1948, copies from Mary T. Norton Papers, Rutgers University, New Brunswick, New Jersey in Vertical File, RA.

26 Columbia Oral Transcript, 49; Oral Transcript, 2/2/99, 6, RA; Representative Rodino letter of resignation to Speaker and H. Res. 444, on January 26, 1950,

Eighty-First Congress, Second Session, *Congressional Record* 96, Pt. 1: 95.

27 US Congress, House of Representatives, Committee on the Judiciary, "History of the Committee on the Judiciary of the House of Representatives," Ninety-Second Congress, Second Session, (February 1972), 1–7.

28 Wayne Dawkins, *Emanuel Celler: Immigration and Civil Rights Champion* (Jackson, MS: University Press of Mississippi, 2020), 3–73; William L. Morrow, *Congressional Committees* (New York: Charles Scribner's Sons, 1969), 40–43.

29 Oral Transcript, 2/4/99, 3, RA; Oral Transcript, 5/12/99, 12, RA; Oral Transcript, 3/4/99, 6, RA.

30 "Hard to Unseat Rodino," *Belleville Times*, August 4, 1949.

31 "Driscoll and Top GOP Map Strategy for '50," *Newark Star-Ledger*, November 29, 1949.

32 Daniel E. Durant, "Rodino Piles Up Majority," *Newark Evening News*, November 8, 1950; "Re-Elect Your Congressman" brochure, SCR044, RA; "Service Above Self" 1950 campaign advertisement and flyer, PER80, 2, RA; "Monster Mass Meeting and Rally" flyer, SCR044, RA. The Democrats lost ten seats in the Senate and five in the House.

33 Emanuel Celler, "Extension of Remarks on Monopoly Subcommittee," on January 24, 1950, Eighty-First Congress, Second Session, *Congressional Record* 96, Pt. 13: A530; C. Murray Bernhardt to Emanuel Celler, "Memorandum on Future of Subcommittee on Study of Monopoly," July 28, 1950, Box 53, Folder 4, Emanuel Celler Papers, Manuscript Division, Library of Congress, Washington, DC; "Memorandum Setting Forth a Tentative Program for the Subcommittee on Monopoly Power," November 10, 1950, 53, 1, Celler Papers.

34 US Congress, House of Representatives, Committee on the Judiciary, Subcommittee on the Study of Monopoly Power, "Hearings on the Study of Monopoly Power," 1951, Part 6, 145, 143–46, 33, 66, 74, 116; "Minutes of Meeting of Subcommittee on Study of Monopoly Power," 1951, 52, Celler Papers. In February 1955, Rodino was appointed to Subcommittee 5, which had jurisdiction over antitrust issues. Emanuel Celler to Thomas J. Lane, January 31, 1955, Legislative Files II (LEG), Box 161, Folder 1, RA; Emanuel Celler to Peter Rodino, February 14, 1955, LEG161, 1, RA.

35 US Congress, House of Representatives, Committee on the Judiciary, "Investigation of the Department of Justice: Hearings Before the Special Subcommittee to Investigate the Department of Justice," Eighty-Third Congress, First Session, 1953; McCullough, *Truman*, 870–72.

36 Arthur Sylvester, "Rodino Faces Stiff Job," *Newark Evening News*, February 6, 1952; "Rodino Given A Heavy Charge," *Belleville Times*, February 15, 1952.

37 "Rodino Pledges Probe Won't Be a Witch Hunt," *Newark Star-Ledger*, February 6, 1952; "Chelf to Head House Probe of McGrath," *Washington Post*, February 6, 1952.

38 "Will Check Delays and Failure of Prosecution," *Washington Post*, February 23, 1952; Drew Pearson, "Washington Merry Go Round," *Newark Star-Ledger*, March 9, 1952.

39 "Investigation of the Department of Justice: Hearings Before the Special Subcommittee to Investigate the Department of Justice," 2.

40 Drew Pearson, "Washington Merry Go Round," *Washington Post*, May 25, 1952.

41 Drew Pearson, "Washington Merry Go Round," *Washington Post*, May 31, 1952; "Rodino Autograph Bolsters Probers," *Newark Star-Ledger*, June 30, 1952; Peter Rodino to Patrick Hillings, March 30, 1988, PER65, 2, RA; Oral Transcript, 16, 1–3, RA.

42 US Congress, House of Representatives, House Committee on the Judiciary, "Investigation of the Department of Justice: Report to the Committee on the Judiciary by the Special Subcommittee to Investigate the Department of Justice pursuant to H.Res. 50," Eighty-Third Congress, First Session, H. Report 1,079, 1–3, 1953; "Investigation of the Department of Justice: Hearings Before the Special Subcommittee to Investigate the Department of Justice," 1, 683–85, 1, 743–44.

43 "Rodino Will Open Battle Here on Sunday," *Nutley Sun*, July 11, 1952; Frank L. Chelf to Peter Rodino, September 22, 1952, PER003, 6, RA; Carmine La False to William J. Egan, February 14, 1952, POL10, 5, RA; William J. Egan to Peter Rodino, February 15, 1952, POL10, 5, RA.

44 "On His Record?" Matturi campaign, advertisement, copy in PER80, 4, RA.

45 Drew Pearson to Peter Rodino, November 1, 1952, PER3, 4, RA; Oral Transcript, 15, 9–12, RA.

46 "Matturri's Tactics Attacked By Rodino," *Newark Evening News*, November 2, 1952; "Great Crusader Turns Into Big Smear," "Citizens for Rodino," campaign advertisement, PER80, 4, RA; Patrick J. Hillings to Peter Rodino, July 2, 1952, PER3, 6, RA.

47 "Ike The Winner; N.J. Landslide," *Newark Star-Ledger*, November 5, 1952; "Essex Vote Summary," *Newark Evening News*, November 5, 1952.

48 "Keating Plans Wide Justice Investigation," *Washington Post*, January 28, 1953.

49 John Hvasta to John Almquist, June 29, 1948, POL87, 8, RA; "Prague Release Sought," *New York Times*, June 18, 1949.

50 Oral Transcript, 4/9/03, 2–4, RA; Ben H. Brown to Peter Rodino, November 15, 1949, POL87, 8, RA; Peter W. Rodino to Hvasta family, November 28, 1949, POL87, 8, RA; Peter Rodino, handwritten notes, November 22, 1949, RA; Jack K. McFall to Peter Rodino, December 9, 1949, POL87, 8, RA; Peter Rodino to Hvasta family, May 17, 1950, POL87, 8, RA.

51 "U.S. Halts Travel to Czechoslovakia," *New York Times*, June 3, 1951; "Truman Sharply Tells Envoy Czechs Should Release Oatis," *New York Times*, August 29, 1951.

52 Steven Hvasta to Peter Rodino, June 28, 1952, and July 24, 1951, POL87, 8, RA; Peter Rodino, "Memorandum," August 30, 1951, POL87, 4, RA; Peter Rodino, introduction of H. Res. 345, on July 19, 1951, Eighty-Second Congress, First Session, *Congressional Record* 97, Pt. 6: 8503; Peter Rodino, "Memorandum for Mike Mansfield," August 1, 1951, POL87, 8, RA; Franklin Roosevelt Jr. to Peter Rodino, February 6, 1952, POL87, 8, RA.

53 Peter Rodino to Harry Truman, August 31, 1951, POL87, 8, RA; "Plea Made to Truman," *New York Times*, September 5, 1951; Oral Transcript, 4/9/03, 3–4, RA.

54 "The Forgotten Man Who Defies the Reds," *REAL Magazine*, August 1953; Theodore Edwards to Peter Rodino, August 5, 1953, POL87, 6, RA.

55 Frank Edwards, Mutual Broadcasting System, transcript, February 27, 1952, POL87, 7, RA; Drew Pearson, "Washington Merry Go Round," *Washington Post*, September 20, 1951; "The Forgotten Man Who Defies the Reds," *REAL Magazine*, August 1953; Theodore Edwards to Peter Rodino, August 5, 1953, POL87, 6, RA.

56 J.B. Richardson, speaking on Peter Rodino and the Hvasta case, on August 2,

1951, Eighty-Second Congress, First Session, *Congressional Record* 97, Pt. 6: 9447; Peter Rodino to J.B. Richardson, August 9, 1951, POL87, 8, RA; Oral Transcript, 14, 1–2, RA. See POL87, 8, RA for letters of support from veterans and Slovakian organizations.

57 "McCarthy Asks Senate Action to Free Hvasta," *Newark Star-Ledger*, June 21, 1952; Peter Rodino, "Memorandum Regarding John Hvasta," June 25, 1952, POL87, 8, RA; Peter W. Rodino, "Notes on Hvasta case," August 11, 1952, POL87, 7, RA; State Department, "Information Memorandum on the Case of John Hvasta," September 9, 1952, POL87, 7, RA.

58 Peter Rodino, press release, May 27, 1953, POL87, 7, RA.

59 Oral Transcript, 14, 3, RA; Peter Rodino to John Foster Dulles, June 5, 1953, POL87, 7, RA; Thurston Morton to Peter Rodino, June 12, 1953, and June 26, 1953, POL87, 7, RA; C. Harold Saidt to Peter Rodino, June 10, 1952, POL87, 4, RA; Peter Rodino to C. Harold Saidt, June 12, 1953, POL87, 4, RA.

60 "Czechs Free US Fugitive Who Fled Jail," *Washington Post*, February 5, 1954.

61 Ben H. Brown to Peter W. Rodino, September 4, 1953, POL87, 7, RA; Peter Rodino, "Notes on Hvasta Release Plan," February 3, 1954, POL87, 7, RA.

62 Oral Transcript, 4/9/03, 4–5, RA; Frederick Graham, "Hvasta Greeted, Tells of Ordeals," *New York Times*, February 7, 1954; Peter Rodino to John Hvasta, February 17, 1954, POL87, 2, RA.

63 Harrison A. Williams, speaking about Peter Rodino's receiving the UNICO award, on March 24, 1954, Eighty-Fourth Congress, First Session, *Congressional Record* 100, Pt. 17: A2251. For all the letters of appreciation following Hvasta's release, see POL87, 1, RA. Hvasta pursued a career in business after finishing school and did not return to his native Slovakia until the cold war ended. Yasmine Bahrani, "Slovak Native Comes Full Circle on Visit Home," *Washington Post*, February 3, 1990.

64 Emanuel Celler to Peter Rodino, February 14, 1955, LEG161, 1, RA; Alexander Feinberg, "New Dealer Bidding For His 4th Term in Intensive Campaign," *New York Times*, October 11, 1954; John O. Davies Jr., "Jersey's Congress Lineup Unchanged," *Newark Evening News*, November 3, 1954.

65 George Dixon, "GOP's Fine, Italian Hand," *Washington Post*, June 13, 1956; Drew

Pearson, "Washington Spotlight," *Il Progresso Italo-Americano,* July 29, 1956; Milton Honig, "Rodino Rival in 10th Making First Race for Elective Office," *New York Times,* October 15, 1956.

66 Joseph W. Katz, "Ike Victory in N.J. Biggest in History," *Newark Evening News,* November 7, 1956; Lester Abelman, "Rodino Wins Fifth Term by 15,000 Margin," *Newark Star-Ledger,* November 7, 1956; Peter Rodino to John W. McCormack, November 3, 1956, Folder 20, Box 49, John W. McCormack Collection, Howard Gotlieb Archival Research Center at Boston University, Boston, Massachusetts; Milton Honig, "Aid Given by Rodino Raised as Issue by Addonizio," *New York Times,* October 9, 1958; "Wallhauser, Addonizio and Rodino Win," *Newark Star-Ledger,* November 5, 1958.

67 Oral Transcript, 3/17/99, 2–7, RA; Oral Transcript, 4/14/99, 3–5, RA; Peter Rodino to Frank Smith, February 28, 1963, PER74, 10, RA. The loan was repaid in full within a few years, and Rodino estimated that when he finally sold the stock it was worth more than $2 million.

68 Senator Proxmire, speaking on FCC Award, on June 20, 1960, Eighty-Sixth Congress, Second Session, *Congressional Record* 106, Pt. 10: 13308–09; David Wise, "Firm With 5 Congressmen Wins TV Nod," *Washington Post,* June 19, 1960; "Of Course, You Won't Let My Weight Influence You," *Newark Evening News,* June 22, 1960.

69 "When Is the Republican Candidate for Congress in the 10th District Going to Tell the Truth," campaign ad, October 13, 1960, SCR10, 84;, RA "Congressman Rodino You Cannot Deny a Single One of These Political Facts," campaign brochure, 1960, PER80, 13, RA; Milton Honig, "Conflict of Interest Charges Enliven Race In the 10th," *New York Times,* October 14, 1960; Oral Transcript, 17, 1–7, RA. See the campaign memos in PER80, 12, RA.

CHAPTER SIX

1 Sarah Booth Conroy, "Dessert Pits Yankee Finish to Italian Feast," *Washington Post,* June 1, 1958; "The Mayor's Daughter," *Washington Post,* May 25, 1958; Bill McPherson, "The Eyes of Texas Are on the Sidewalk," *Washington Post,* April 8, 1960.

2 John F. Kennedy to Peter Rodino, August 30, 1958, September 16, 1960, October 19, 1960, PER71, 2, RA; Peter Rodino to John F. Kennedy, July 27, 1960; Robert F. Kennedy to Peter Rodino, August 31, 1960, PER71, 2, RA; Kenneth P. O'Donnell to Peter Rodino, September 12, 1960, PER71, 2, RA; Franklin Gregory, "Kennedy Mobbed in NJ," *Newark Star-Ledger,* November 7, 1960; "Kennedy the Winner," *Newark Star-Ledger,* November 9, 1960.

3 Daniel Okrent, *The Guarded Gate: Bigotry, Eugenics, and the Law That Kept Two Generations of Jews, Italians, and Other European Immigrants Out of America* (New York: Scribner, 2019), 285–88, 326–41.

4 Okrent, *Guarded Gate*, 3, 97–101; Mangione, *La Storia*, 33.

5 David A. Reed, "America of the Melting Pot Comes to End," *New York Times*, April 27, 1924; Okrent, *Guarded Gate*, 97–101; "He United Families in a Lone Crusade," *Italian Tribune News*, February 4, 1972.

6 Jia Lynn Yang, *One Mighty and Irresistible Tide: The Epic Struggle Over American Immigration, 1924–1965* (New York: W.W. Norton & Company, 2020), 156–58, 170–75; Keith Fitzgerald, *The Face of the Nation: Immigration, The State, and National Identity* (Stanford, CA: Stanford University Press, 1996), 200–201; Cheryl Shanks, *Immigration and the Politics of American Sovereignty, 1890–1990* (Ann Arbor, MI: The University of Michigan Press, 2001), 140–46.

7 US Congress, House of Representatives, Committee on the Judiciary, "Revision of Immigration, Naturalization, and Nationality Laws: Joint Hearings Before the Subcommittee of the Committee on the Judiciary," Eighty-Second Congress, First Session, 1951, 728–31.

8 Representative Rodino on H.R. 5678, on April 23 and April 24, 1952, Eighty-Second Congress, Second Session, *Congressional Record* 98, Pt. 4: 4309–11, 4406–07; C.P. Trussell, "Immigration Bill Passed by House Over Truman Veto," *New York Times*, June 27, 1952. Truman appointed a commission that called for the end of the quota system. "Report of the President's Commission on Immigration and Naturalization," *Whom We Shall Welcome* (Washington, DC: Government Printing Office, 1953), 15.

9 "Roundtable on Immigration, Naturalization, and Refugees, Democratic National Committee Congressional Dinner," program, January 28, 1956, 478, 5, Celler

Papers; *Il Progresso Italo-Americano*, "Washington Spotlight," July 29, 1956; Anthony Lewis, "President Urges Wide Law Change to Aid Immigrants," *New York Times*, February 9, 1956; Representative Rodino, on immigration, on February 7, 1957, Eighty-Fifth Congress, First Session, *Congressional Record* 103, Pt. 2: 1776–77. For background on Italian American lobbying for immigration reform, see Danielle Battisti, '*Whom We Shall Welcome': Italian Americans and Immigration Reform, 1945–1965* (New York: Fordham University Press, 2019), 49–83.

10 "Kennedy Record on Immigration," Digital JFKCAMP1960-1061-021-1, Papers of John F. Kennedy, Pre-Presidential Papers, Presidential Campaign Files, 1960, "Speeches and the Press," John F. Kennedy Presidential Library, Boston, Massachusetts (JFK); John F. Kennedy, *A Nation of Immigrants* (New York: Anti-Defamation League of B'nai B'rith, 1959); Frederick G. Dutton to Meyer Feldman, January 31, 1961, Papers of John F. Kennedy, White House Central Subject Files (WHCSF), Legislation: Immigration-Naturalization (LE:IM), Box 482, JFK; Lawrence O'Brien to Peter Rodino, February 18, 1961, Presidential Papers of John F. Kennedy, White House Central Name Files (WHCNF), Box 2364, Peter W. Rodino Folder (PWR), JFK.

11 "Celler Fails In Move To Liberalize His Subcommittee on Immigration," *Washington Post,* June 26, 1963; "Minutes of Immigration Subcommittee," July 11, 1963, "Subcommittee Minutes," Subcommittees 1–5, Box 402, Folder 1, "Records of the House Of Representatives," Eighty-Eighth Congress, Committee on the Judiciary, RG233, NAB; B.W. Haveman to Peter Rodino, August 18, 1963, POL31, 1, RA; Emanuel Celler to Peter Rodino, August 22, 1963, POL31, 1, RA.

12 Myer Feldman to Emanuel Celler, July 23, 1963, WHCNF, Emanuel Celler Folder, Box 452, JFK; John F. Kennedy to John McCormack, July 23, 1963, WHCSF, 482, LE:IM, 482, JFK; Chuck Daley to Lawrence O'Brien, July 27, 1963, WHCSF, LE, 467, JFK; "Dear Colleague," August 5, 1963, 480, 4, Celler Papers.

13 "Test of President Johnson's State of the Union Message," *Washington Post*, January 9, 1964; US Congress, House of Representatives, Eighty-Eighth Congress, Second Session, Committee on the Judiciary, Subcommittee No. 1, "Hearings Before Subcommittee No. 1 on H.R. 7700 a Bill to Amend the Immigration and Nationality

Act," June, August, September 1964, Parts 1–3.

14 Jack Valenti to Lyndon Johnson, July 1, 1964, WHCNF, Box 226, Rodino Folder (PWR), Presidential Papers of Lyndon Baines Johnson (LBJ), Johnson Presidential Library, Austin Texas; Jack Valenti to Lawrence O'Brien, July 24, 1964, Office Files of the White House Aides (WHA), Lawrence O'Brien, Box 20, Rodino Folder (PWR), LBJ; Chuck Daley to Larry O'Brien, July 30, 1964, WHA, O'Brien, 20, PWR, LBJ; Michael Feighan to John McCormack, April 6, 1964, 136, 1, McCormack Papers.

15 "Working Papers," LF, 76, 1,2, RG233, NAB; "89th Congress Rules of Procedure," House of Representatives, Committee on the Judiciary, Subcommittee No. 1, Copy in 97, 1, McCormack Papers; US House of Representatives, Eighty-Ninth Congress, Committee on the Judiciary, Subcommittee No. 1, "Immigration: Hearings Before Subcommittee No. 1 on H.R. 2580," March, April, May, June 1965; "Explanatory Remarks of Mr. Feighan," July 27, 1965, LF, 76, 2, RG233, NAB.

16 Jack Valenti to Lyndon Johnson, July 16, 1965, and July 22, 1965, WHCNF, 226, PWR, LBJ.

17 Representative Rodino on immigration legislation, on August 24, 1965, Eighty-Ninth Congress, First Session, *Congressional Record* 11, Pt. 19: 21593; press release, Committee on the Judiciary, August 3, 1965, LE, 75, 1, RG233, NAB; US House of Representatives, Eighty-Ninth Congress, First Session, Committee on the Judiciary, Report 745, "Amending the Immigration and Nationality Act, and for Other Purposes," August 6, 1965.

18 Michael Feighan to Peter Rodino, September 14, 1965, LE, 76, 1, RG 233, NAB; Garner J.Cline to Emanuel Celler, September 24, 1965, LE, 76, 1, RG 233, NAB; Emanuel Celler, "Conference Notes," undated, 481, 3, Celler Papers.

19 "Text of President's Speech on Immigration," *New York Times*, October 4, 1965.

20 Hubert Humphrey to Peter Rodino, October 8, 1965, PER57, 3, RA; Oral Transcript, 20, 5–6, RA.

21 Peter W. Rodino, "Appraisal of New Immigration Legislation, *The Immigrant* (New Jersey Bar Association, February 1966) 1; Richard Scammon to Peter Rodino June 24, 1966, LEG232, RA; Garner J. Cline to Peter Rodino, August 4, 1966, LEG232, 10, RA and September 26, 1967, LEG232, 7, RA; John McCormack to

Peter Rodino, January 24, 1967, LEG232, 10, RA and February 2, 1967, LEG232, 6, RA.

22 Representative Parren Mitchell, speaking on the twentieth anniversary of the Voting Rights Act, on December 18, 1985, Ninety-Ninth Congress, First Session, *Congressional Record* 131, Pt. 27: 37821; Oral Transcript, 3/4/99a, 9–10, RA.

23 Representative Rodino, speaking on introduction of antidiscrimination bill, on February 2, 1953, Eighty-Third Congress, First Session, *Congressional Record* 99, Pt. 9: A412; Representative Rodino, speaking on introduction of civil rights bill, on January 29, 1952, Eighty-Second Congress, Second Session; *Congressional Record* 98, Pt. 1: 618.

24 McCullough, *Truman*, 586–588, 638–40.

25 Hugh Davis Graham, *The Civil Rights Era: Origins and Development of National Policy 1960–1972* (New York: Oxford University Press, 1990), 366–69.

26 David A. Nichols, *A Matter of Justice: Eisenhower and the Beginning of the Civil Rights Revolution* (New York: Simon & Schuster, 2007), 131–32, 143–68; Murrey Marder, "House Opens Its Debate on Civil Rights," *Washington Post*, July 17, 1956.

27 Representative Rodino, speaking on the Civil Rights Act of 1957, on June 6, 1957, Eighty-Fifth Congress, First Session, *Congressional Record* 101, Pt. 6: 8498–99; "List of Supporters of H.R. 6127," May 30, 1957, 455, 2, Celler Papers; "Committee Balks Moves to 'Weaken' Rights Bill," *Washington Post*, March 13, 1957. Also see Celler's notes and background information for the floor debate in 455, 1, Celler Papers.

28 Clarence Mitchell to Emanuel Celler, July 10, 1957, 455, 4, Celler Papers; Emanuel Celler to Sam Rayburn, August 21, 1957, 455, 5, Celler Papers; Robert A. Caro, *The Years of Lyndon Johnson: Master of the Senate* (New York: Alfred A. Knopf, 2002), 869–702.

29 William L. Hitchcock, *The Age of Eisenhower: America and the World in the 1950's* (New York: Simon and Schuster, 2018), 359–66; Harris Wofford, *Of Kennedy and Kings: Making Sense of the Sixties* (Pittsburgh, PA: University of Pittsburgh Press, 1980), 461–83.

30 Roy Wilkins to Emanuel Celler, August 7, 1959, 458, 1, Celler Papers; Representative Rodino, on the introduction of H.R. 5323, on March 5, 1959, Eighty-Sixth

Congress, First Session, *Congressional Record* 105, Pt. 4: 5323; "Minutes of Subcommittee 5," June 17, 1959, "Subcommittee Minutes," Box 854, "Records of the House Of Representatives," Eighty-Sixth Congress, Committee on the Judiciary (HR86A), RG233, NAB; US Congress, House of Representatives, Committee on the Judiciary, "Civil Rights: Report to Accompany H.R. 8601," Eighty-Sixth Congress, First Session, August 20, 1959.

31 Russell Baker, "Johnson Praised," *New York Times*, April 9, 1960; Representative Rodino, speaking on civil rights legislation, on January 27, 1960, Eighty-Sixth Congress, Second Session, *Congressional Record* 106, Pt. 2: 1436; John McCormack to Emanuel Celler, February 1, 1960, 459, 10, Celler Papers; US Congress, House of Representatives, Committee on the Judiciary, Eighty-Sixth Congress, Second Session, "Discussions on Proposals For Voting Rights," Confidential Committee Print, February 9, 1960; Representative Rodino, speaking on civil rights bill, on March 16, 17, 21, 1960, Eighty-Sixth Congress, Second Session, *Congressional Record* 106, Pt. 5: 5773, 5912, 6171.

32 Green, *Speaker of the House*, 94–98; "Text of the Democratic Rights Plank," *New York Times*, July 13, 1960.

33 Louis Martin to Theodore Sorenson, May 10, 1961, WHCSF, LE, Human Rights (HU), 482, JFK; Harris Wofford to John F. Kennedy, May 22, 1961, WHCSF, HU, 359, JFK; John F. Kennedy to Emanuel Celler, August 7, 1961, WHCNF, Celler, 452, JFK.

34 US Congress, House of Representatives, Committee on the Judiciary, Eighty-Eighth Congress, First Session, "Civil Rights: Hearings Before Subcommittee No. 5, Part II," May 1963, 912–913, 907–908; Theodore Sorenson, "Memorandum," February 5, 1963, WHCSF, LE, 466, JFK; "Special Message on Civil Rights," February 28, 1963, Papers of John F. Kennedy, President's Office Files (POF), Legislative Files (LF), Box 52, JFK.

35 US Congress, House of Representatives, Eighty-Eighth Congress, First Session, "Civil Rights: Message From The President of the United States," June 19, 1963. Kennedy's appearance was considered a disaster and alienated many Republicans. Todd S. Purdum, *An Idea Whose Time Has Come: Two Presidents, Two Parties, and the Battle for the Civil Rights Act of 1964* (New York: Henry Holt and Company,

2014), 78–80, 117–25.

36 Emanuel Celler to John McCormack, September 18, 1963, copy in WHCSF, LE:HU, 82, JFK; "Minutes of Subcommittee 5," September 10, 17, 23, 24, 25 and October 1, 1963, "Subcommittee Minutes," 402, 1, RG233, NAB; Nicholas Katzenbach to Emanuel Celler, August 13, 1963, 465, 1, Celler Papers.

37 Peter Rodino to Margaret (Peggy) Rodino, October 8, 1963, PER74, 1, RA; Emanuel Celler, "Memorandum on H.R. 7152," October 2, 1963, 463, 4, Celler Papers.

38 Oral Transcript, 3/4/99a, 4–6, RA; Drew Pearson, "JFK Wants Rights Legislation Before '64," *Washington Post*, October 29, 1964; Nicholas deB. Katzenbach, *Some of It Was Fun: Working with RFK and LBJ* (New York: W.W. Norton & Company, 2008), 121–24; Lawrence F. O'Brien, *No Final Victories: A Life in Politics: From John F. Kennedy to Watergate* (Garden City, NY: Doubleday and Company, 1974), 144–46.

39 Meeting on Civil Rights, October 1963: 23–24, POF, Tape 116/A52 and Tape 117/A53, JFK; Oral Transcript, 4/09/03, 10, RA; Peter Rodino to Margaret (Peggy) Rodino, October 30, 1963, PER74, 1, RA; Robert F. Kennedy to John F. Kennedy, "Draft Civil Rights Statement," October 29, 1963, WHCSF, LE:HU, 482, JFK; US Congress, House of Representatives, Committee on the Judiciary, Eighty-Eighth Congress, First Session, "Civil Rights Act of 1963," Report 914, November 20, 1963.

40 Tom Wicker, "Johnson Bids Congress Enact Civil Rights Bill With Speed," *New York Times*, November 28, 1963.

41 Robert A. Caro, *The Years of Lyndon Johnson: The Passage of Power* (New York: Alfred A. Knopf, 2012), 484–99, 558–60.

42 Emanuel Celler to Howard Smith, November 21, 1963, Legislative "H.R. 7152," Records of the US House of Representatives, Eighty-Eighth Congress, Committee on the Judiciary, Box 46, Folder 17, Record Group 233, NAB; Nicholas Katzenbach to Emanuel Celler, December 2, 1963, Legislative Files, "H.R. 7152," 46, 1, RG233, NAB; Henry Wilson to Lawrence O'Brien, Office Files of the White House Aides (WHA), Henry Wilson, Box 2, Presidential Papers of Lyndon Baines Johnson (LBJ).

43 "Chairman's Floor Book," 466, Celler Papers; "Floor Amendments to H.R. 7152 Civil Rights Act of 1963," Legislative Files, "H.R. 7152," 49, 23, RG 233, NAB; Clarence Mitchell to Emanuel Celler, January 29, 1964, Legislative Files, "H.R.

7152," 46, 1, RG 233, NAB; William Foley to Emanuel Celler, January 28, 1964, 465, 2, Celler Papers; "Chairman's Notes," 465, 2, Celler Papers.

44 E.W. Kenworthy, "Civil Rights Bill Passed by House in 290–130 Vote," *New York Times*, February 11, 1964; Emma G. Miller to Emanuel Celler, January 28, 1964, Legislative Files, "H.R. 7152," 46, 1, RG 233, NAB; Martin Luther King to John McCormack, February 14, 1964, 43, 1, McCormack Papers; John McCormack to Martin Luther King, February 19, 1964, 43, 1, McCormack Papers.

45 Representative Rodino, speaking on H.R. 7152, on January 31, 1964, Eighty-Eighth Congress, Second Session, *Congressional Record* 110, Pt. 2:1511, 1528, 1538–42; Representative Rodino, speaking on H.R. 7152, on February 1, 1964, Eighty-Eighth Congress, Second Session, *Congressional Record* 110, Pt. 2:1511, 1528, 1613, 1633; Representative Rodino, speaking on H.R. 7152, on February 4, 1964, Eighty-Eighth Congress, Second Session, *Congressional Record* 110, Pt. 2:1511, 1913–1919, 1930.

46 Lyndon Johnson and Peter Rodino, February 10, 1964, "Telephone Conversation No. 2024, Recordings and Transcripts of Telephone Conversations and Meetings (RT)," Presidential Papers of Lyndon Baines Johnson, LBJ; Nicholas Katzenbach to Peter Rodino, February 17, 1964, PER58, 4, RA.

47 Arnold Aronson to Peter Rodino, February 19, 1964, PER58, 4, RA; Leonard Carter to Peter Rodino, February 14, 1964, PER58, 4, RA.

48 Martin Luther King to Peter Rodino, February 14, 1964, PER58, 4, RA.

49 Hubert H. Humphrey, *The Education of a Public Man: My Life and Politics* (New York: Doubleday and Company, 1976), 274–84; Lawrence O'Brien to Lyndon Johnson, June 18, 1964, WHCSF, LE:HU2, 65, LBJ; Emanuel Celler to Howard Smith, June 22, 1964, Legislative Files, "H.R. 7126," 48, 16, RG 233, NAB; E.W. Kenworthy, "Rights Bill Cleared for Final House Vote Tomorrow," *New York Times*, July 1, 1964.

50 "Text of Johnson's Remarks on Signing Civil Rights Bill," *Washington Post*, July 3, 1964; Lawrence O'Brien to Lyndon Johnson, July 2, 1964, WHCSF, LE:HU2, 65, LBJ.

51 Tom Wicker, "Johnson Bestows Pens Used on Bill," *New York Times*, July 3, 1964. The pen Johnson presented to Rodino is on display at the Peter W. Rodino Jr.

Library, Seton Hall University Law School, Newark, New Jersey.

52 Nan Robertson, "Johnson Pressed for a Voting Law," *New York Times*, March 9, 1965; Joseph A. Califano Jr., *The Triumph and Tragedy of Lyndon Johnson: The White House Years* (New York: Touchstone, 1991), 43–47.

53 Peter Rodino to Nicholas Katzenbach, March 10, 1965, LEG221, 1, RA; Representative Rodino, speaking on Selma, on March 10, 1965, Eighty-Ninth Congress, First Session, *Congressional Record* 111, Pt. 4: 4749.

54 "Text of the President's Message to Congress on Voting," *New York Times*, March 16, 1965; Peter Rodino, press release, March 15, 1965, LEG162, 3, RA.

55 "Voting Rights Act of 1965," working papers, Committee on the Judiciary, 472, 1, Celler Papers; Representative Rodino, speaking on the voting rights bill, on July 6, 1965, Eighty-Ninth Congress, First Session, *Congressional Record* 111, Pt. 11: 15660–61; E.W. Kenworthy, "Democratic Bill on Voting Passed by House 333–85," *New York Times*, July 10, 1965.

56 Lawrence O'Brien to Lyndon Johnson, April 26, 1965, WHCSF, LE:HU2, 66, LBJ; Clarence Mitchell to Emanuel Celler, July 14, 1965, 473, 1, Celler Papers.

57 Nicholas Katzenbach to Peter Rodino, July 29, 1965, PER57, 6, RA; E.W. Kenworthy, "Johnson Signs Voting Rights Bill," *New York Times*, August 7, 1965; Arnold Aronson to Peter Rodino, August 13, 1965, PER58, 6, RA.

58 "Transcript of President's State of the Union Message to Joint Session of Congress," *New York Times*, January 13, 1966; Graham, *Civil Rights Era*, 258–60; Arthur J. Sills, "Memorandum to Owners of Residential Property," May 1, 1966, LEG221, 1, RA.

59 Nicholas Katzenbach to Joseph Califano, March 9, 1966, WHA, Henry Wilson, 11, LBJ. The White House scorecard prepared on March 8 listed Rodino as against the fair housing proposal.

60 Henry Wilson to Lyndon Johnson, March 11, 1966, WHA, Henry Wilson, 11, LBJ; Sherwin Mark to Lawrence O'Brien, March 11, 1966, WHA, Henry Wilson, 11, LBJ.

61 Maud-Ellen Zimmerman to Thomas O'Neill, April 14, 1966, 153, 6, O'Neill Papers; "Form Letter on Title IV," undated, Legislative Files, "H.R. 14765," 140, 27, and 141, 29–35, RG 233, NAB; Clarence Mitchell to Emanuel Celler, May 12, 1966, Legislative

Files, "H.R. 14765," 137, 1, RG 233, NAB; "Minutes of Subcommittee 5 Executive Session," June 16, 1966, Legislative Files, "H.R. 14765," 137, 6, RG 233, NAB.

62 "The Best We Could Get," *Star-Ledger*, June 30, 1966; Clarence Mitchell to Emanuel Celler, June 14, 1966, Legislative Files, "H.R. 14765," 143, 45, RG 233, NAB; US House of Representatives, Committee on the Judiciary, Eighty-Ninth Congress, Second Session, "Civil Rights Act of 1966: To Accompany H.R. 14765," June 30, 1966. The *Newark Star-Ledger* became the *Star-Ledger* in May 1964.

63 Michael Mossetig, "Rodino: Closer Than We Thought," *Star-Ledger*, August 4, 1966; Peter Rodino, "Edited Floor Statements," July–August 1966, Staff Files, Box 54, RA; Oral Transcript, 5/12/99, 12 and 3/4/99a, 7, RA; Representative Rodino, speaking on Civil Rights Act of 1966, on July 27, 1966, Eighty-Ninth Congress, Second Session, *Congressional Record* 112, Pt. 13: 117183–95; Nicholas Katzenbach to Lyndon Johnson, July 28, 1966, WHCSF, LE:HU2, 65, LBJ; Henry Wilson to Lyndon Johnson, August 5, 1966, WHCSF, LE:HU2, 65, LBJ; Nicholas Katzenbach to Peter Rodino, August 4, 1966, LEG221, 1, RA.

64 Robert B. Semple Jr., "Rights Bill Dies As Cloture Fails," *New York Times*, September 20, 1966; Emanuel Celler, press release, September 19, 1966, 468, 4, Celler Papers; Clarence Mitchell to Emanuel Celler, October 19, 1966, 468, 4, Celler Papers.

65 Committee on the Judiciary, "Working Paper on H.R. 2516," 475, 2, Celler Papers; Barefoot Sanders to Lyndon Johnson, February 29, March 9, and March 13, 1968, WHCSF, LE:HU2, 66, LBJ; Clarence Mitchell to Peter Rodino, August 16, 1968, PER57, 6, RA; Graham, *Civil Rights Era*, 270–72, 375–76. Joseph Califano, who was the White House aide responsible for the legislation, claimed that Rodino assumed most of the burden in the House for the 1968 act because Celler was worried about the strong opposition to open housing in his district. Joseph A. Califano Jr., *Inside: A Public and Private Life* (New York: Public Affairs, 2004), 298.

66 Hubert Humphrey to Peter Rodino, August 10, 1966, PER57, 3, RA; Lyndon Johnson to Peter Rodino, August 14, 1966, PER57, 5, RA.

67 Clarence Mitchell Jr. to Peter Rodino, August 23, 1966, PER57, 6, RA.

68 Elmer J. Holland to Peter Rodino, August 18, 1966, SCR21, 169, RA; Frank Annunzio to Peter Rodino, August 5, 1966, PER56, 8, RA; Representative Carl Albert,

speaking on Peter Rodino, on August 4 and August 9, 1966, Eighty-Ninth Congress, Second Session, *Congressional Record* 112, Pt. 14: 18210, 18727; Representative Emanuel Celler, speaking on Peter Rodino, on August 9, 1966, Eighty-Ninth Congress, Second Session, *Congressional Record* 112, Pt. 14: 18728.

69 Robert F. Kennedy to Peter Rodino, September 20, 1960, PER71, 2, RA; Oral Transcript, 2/4/99, 5–6, RA; "Italian Descended Legislators To Be Honored by Lido Club," *Washington Post*, June 20, 1954.

70 Peter Rodino to Robert F. Kennedy, September 30, 1960, PER71, 2, RA; Peter Rodino to E. William Henry, October 7, 1960, PER71, 2, RA; E. William Henry to Peter Rodino, October 8, 1960, PER71, 2, RA.

71 Ralph Dugan to James Reynolds, February 25, 1961, WHCNF, 2364, PWR, JFK; "Ralph Dugan Memorandum," February 29, 1961, WHCNF, 2364, PWR, JFK.

72 Profile of Peter W. Rodino, May 23, 1961, Office of Legislative Affairs, WHA, O'Brien, 20, PWR, LBJ; Peter Rodino to Ralph Dugan, February 2, 1961, WHCNF, 2364, PWR, JFK; Ralph Dugan to Peter Rodino, February 4, 1961, WHCNF, 2364, PWR, JFK; Henry H. Wilson to Lawrence O'Brien, February 28, 1961, WHA, 20, PWR, LBJ; Sidney Bishop to Richard Donahue, May 14, 1962, WHCNF, 2364, PWR, JFK; "Jay Helzer, Memorandum," June 24, 1961, POF, 101, Italian Americans Folder, JFK.

73 Oral Transcript, 3/4/99a, 7, RA: Oral Transcript, Tape 20, 5–6, RA; Oral History Transcript, Lawrence F. O'Brien, "Interview 2," October 29, 1985, Lyndon Baines Johnson, Oral Histories, LBJ; Claude Desautels to Lawrence O'Brien, July 13 and 15, 1963, WHA, O'Brien, 20, PWR, LBJ; Lawrence O'Brien to John F. Kennedy, July 15, 1963, POF, 64, O'Brien Folder, JFK. Also see Jack Valenti, *A Very Human President* (New York: W.W. Norton & Company, 1975), 70–71, 177–182.

74 Lyndon Johnson and Peter Rodino, February 10, 1964, 2024, RT, LBJ; Peter Rodino to Jack Valenti, January 9, 1964, WHCNF, 226, PWR, LBJ; Peter Rodino to Jack Valenti, February 25, 2965, WHCNF, 226, PWR, LBJ; Jack Valenti to Cliff Carter, July 24, 1964, WHCNF, 226, PWR, LBJ; Chuck Daley to Lawrence O'Brien, July 30, 1964, WHA, O'Brien, 20, PWR, LBJ; Jack Valenti to John Macy, August 12, 1965, WHA, John Macy, Box 871, Rodino Folder, LBJ; Jack Valenti to Lyndon Johnson, July 13, 1965, WHCNF, 226, PWR, LBJ; Jack Valenti to Lyndon Johnson,

September 8, 1965, WHA, Macy, PWR, LBJ. For the full list of Rodino's visits to the White House, see "Diary Cards," Box 69, LBJ.

75 Joseph Califano to Lyndon Johnson, June 10, 1966, WHCNF, 226, PWR, LBJ; Joseph Califano to Peter Rodino, June 29, 1967, WHA, Califano, 19, Italian American Folder, LBJ; Joseph Califano to Peter Rodino, November 28, 1967, POL22, 1, RA; Peter Rodino to Joseph Califano, August 1, 1967, WHA, Joseph A. Califano, Box 19, Italian American Folder, LBJ; Peter Rodino to Joseph Califano, March 7, 1968, WHA, Macy, 871, PWR, LBJ.

76 George De Stefano, *An Offer We Can't Refuse: The Mafia in the Mind of America* (New York, Faber and Faber: 2006), 40–41; Carola, *Italian Americans*, 224–228.

77 Arnold Orsatti to Pierre Salinger, April 5, 1961, WHCSF, Box 359, Italian American Folder, JFK; Pierre Salinger to Arnold Orsatti, April 7, 1961, WHCSF, 359, Italian American Folder, JFK; Pierre Salinger to Victor Anfuso, April 29, 1961, WHCSF, 359, Italian American Folder, JFK.

78 "Italian Americans' Ire on Valachi Hearings Causing Concern in Capital," *New York Times*, October 13, 1963; Alfred B. Lewis, "Professional Writer Named to Help Joe Valachi Polish Up His Life Story," *Washington Post*, January 26, 1966.

79 Jack Valenti to Lyndon Johnson, January 26, 1966, WHCNF, 226, PWR, LBJ; Oral Transcript, 3/17/99, 1–2, RA.

80 "Italian-Americans Fight Valachi Book," *New York Times*, February 2, 1966; Marvin Watson to Lyndon Johnson, February 3, 1966, WHCNF, 226, PWR, LBJ; "Appeals Court Upholds Ban on Valachi Memoirs," *Washington Post*, November 26, 1966; Peter Maas, "The White House, The Mob and the Book Biz," *New York Times*, October 12, 1986; Peter Maas, *The Valachi Papers* (New York: G.P. Putnam's Sons, 1968).

81 Representative Rodino, appointed to Brumidi Committee, on June 19, 1951, Eighty-Second Congress, First Session, *Congressional Record* 97, Pt. 5: 6775; Representative Rodino, speaking on marking of Brumidi grave, on February 20, 1952, Eighty-Second Congress, Second Session, *Congressional Record* 98, Pt. 8: A1114–15.

82 Battisti, "*Whom We Shall Welcome*," 228–231; "Columbus Day Observance," *Italian Tribune*, October 14, 1949.

83 Representative Rodino, speaking on Columbus Day Holiday, on May 27, 1949, Eighty-First Congress, First Session, *Congressional Record* 95, Pt. 5: 6996.

84 Peter Rodino and Hugh Addonizio to John F. Kennedy, October 5, 1962, WHCSF, 980, Folder Trip 43/State 30, JFK; Kenneth O'Donnell to Peter Rodino, October 9, 1962, WHCNF, 2364, PWR, JFK; Joseph Carragher, "150,000 Turn Out to Salute Kennedy," *Newark Star-Ledger*, October 13, 1962; "Rodino Named Chairman," *Italian Times* (Boston), September 19, 1958.

85 Statement of Peter Rodino, "Columbus Day: Hearings Before Subcommittee No. 4," US House of Representatives, Committee on the Judiciary, Subcommittee No. 4, Eighty-Eighth Congress, First Session, December 1963, 15–19; Joseph Manett to Peter Rodino, September 26, 1964, SCR16, 15–16, RA; "Columbus Day 1964 San Francisco," program, October 10, 1964, POL21, 2, RA.

86 "Columbus Day: Hearings on H.R. 2372 Before Subcommittee No. 4," US House of Representatives, Committee on the Judiciary, Subcommittee No. 4, Ninetieth Congress, First Session, October 1967, 13–15; "Rodino Hails Holiday Plan," *Newark Evening News*, March 28, 1968.

87 "Towards The Crowning of A Tenacious Campaign," *Il Progresso Italo-Americano*, June 29, 1968; Jack Valenti to Charles McGuire, June 26, 1968, WHCNF, 226, PWR, LBJ; James R. Jones to Peter Rodino, July 1, 1968, LEG143, 7, RA; Representative Rodino, speaking on signing of Columbus Day bill, on July 1, 1968, Ninetieth Congress, Second Session, *Congressional Record* 114, Pt. 15: 19436.

88 "Rodino Carries Nixon Columbus Tribute to Italy," *Italian Tribune*, October 1, 1971; "Statement of the Honorable Peter W. Rodino, Jr., USA, Chairman of the Council of the Intergovernmental Committee For European Migration on the Occasion of the Twentieth Anniversary," November 30, 1971, POL35, 2, RA; interview with Arthur P. Endres Jr., July 17, 2019.

CHAPTER SEVEN

1 "Try One Day in Slums," *Newark Evening News*, April 24, 1949; "A Tour of Slums of Newark," *Newark Star-Ledger*, April 24, 1949.

2 Ibid. Representative Rodino, speaking on housing, on August 25, 1949, Eighty-First Congress, First Session, *Congressional Record* 95, Pt. 6: 12267–69; "Roaming

the Town," *Italian Tribune*, November 3, 1950.

3 Max Weiner, "People Live There," *Newark Evening News*, October 10, 16, 19, 21, 1949; "Citizens Launch Campaign to Clear Newark's Slums," *Newark Evening News*, November 22, 1949.

4 "$2 million for Newark Slum Clearance Plans," *Newark Evening News*, February 3, 1950; Harold Kaplan, *Urban Renewal Politics: Slum Clearance in Newark* (New York: Columbia University Press, 1963), 10–17, 39–46; Robert Curvin, *Inside Newark: Decline, Rebellion, and the Search for Transformation* (New Brunswick, NJ: Rutgers University Press, 2014), 19–20.

5 "NHA to Rebuild Newark's First Ward," *Italian Tribune*, January 25, 1952; Immerso, *Newark's Little Italy*, 139–54.

6 "Rodino, Addonizio, Matturi and Villani Support Housing," *Italian Tribune*, February 1, 1952.

7 "Alternative Proposed to Slum Clearance," *Newark Evening News*, February 22, 1952; "City Housing Plan Upheld," *Newark Evening News*, March 7, 1953.

8 Carmine Addonizio, "Death of an Era," *Newark Evening News*, November 24, 1954.

9 Robert C. Ruth, "Columbus Tenants Want to Get Out," *Evening News*, August 30, 1970; Clifford J. Levy, "4 High-Rises Torn Down by Newark," *New York Times*, March 7, 1994. The private sector Colonnade Park apartments fared better and are still standing though isolated on a broad expanse of cleared land because the office buildings and retail space were never built. *Urban Renewal Progress: City of Newark, 1972–73* (Newark Housing Authority, 1973), 4–7.

10 Kaplan, *Urban Renewal*, 151–52; Tuttle, *How Newark Became Newark*, 140–41; *Rebuilding Newark: Report of the Housing Authority of the City of Newark* (Newark, NJ: Newark Housing Authority, 1952), 6–10. The New Jersey legislature amended the law in 1950 to end segregation in public housing.

11 "Tenant Office for Project," *Newark Evening News*, August 20, 1955; "Negroes Now Admitted in North Ward Project," *Newark Evening News*, December 15, 1955; Kevin Mumford, *Newark: A History of Race, Rights, and Riots in America* (New York: New York University Press, 2007), 56–63.

12 Mumford, *History of Race, Rights, and Riots*, 20–23; Cunningham, *Newark*, 312; Anthony Lewis, "Census Portrays Shift of Negroes," *New York Times*, March 8,

1961; "Census in Center for the Study of New Jersey Politics, Eagleton Institute of Politics," "Background Report on Essex County," October 1965, copy in IV/80/6, RA.

13 "Report of Ward Commissioners," 1953, copy in New Jersey State Legislative Apportionment Commission, Records of Dr. Ernest C. Reock (Reock Papers), SZRAP001, Box 1, Folder 1, New Jersey State Archives, Trenton, New Jersey; Cunningham, *Newark*, 305–6; Curvin, *Inside Newark*, 44–64.

14 Oral Transcript, 2/4/99, 6–7, RA; Milton Honig, "Mayoral Battle Opens in Newark," *New York Times*, March 4, 1962.

15 Richard O. Schafer, "Addonizio Landslide," *Newark Star-Ledger*, May 9, 1962; "Dynamism in City Hall," *Newark Star-Ledger*, July 2, 1962; Hugh Addonizio to Peter Rodino, July 11, 1962, PER65, 4, RA.

16 Hugh Addonizio to Peter Rodino, July 11, 1962, and July 24, 1962, PER65, 4, RA; "A Mission of Concern," *Star-Ledger*, September 23, 1966; Douglas Robinson, "Community Leaders in Newark Battle to Improve Negroes' Lot," *New York Times*, May 29, 1967.

17 *Report of the National Advisory Commission on Civil Disorders* (Washington, DC: Government Printing Office, 1968), 30–38; *Report For Action: Governor's Select Commission on Civil Disorder* (Trenton: State of New Jersey, 1968), 105–44; Junius Williams, *Unfinished Agenda: Urban Politics in the Era of Black Power* (Berkeley, CA: North Atlantic Books, 2014), 147–61.

18 "Wouldn't Listen Say Race Leaders," *Newark Evening News*, July 14, 1967; "Brutality Is Laid to Newark Police," *Newark Evening News*, July 15, 1967; Donald Warshaw and James McHugh, "Hughes: A City in Open Rebellion," *Star-Ledger*, July 15, 1967; John B. Wefing, *The Life and Times of Richard J. Hughes: The Politics of Civility* (New Brunswick, NJ: Rutgers University Press, 2009), 168–73; "Guard, Troopers Pull Out as Newark Calms Down," *Star-Ledger*, July 18, 1967.

19 Oral Transcript, 3/4/99A, 11, RA; Representative Rodino, speaking on the Newark riots, on July 20, 1967, Eighty-Eighth Congress, First Session, *Congressional Record* 113, Pt. 15: 19583–85.

20 Joseph Califano to Lyndon Johnson, July 15, 1967, Califano/11/Commission on Civil Disorder, LBJ; Douglas Robinson, "Jersey Will Seek U.S. Funds to Rebuild

Newark," *New York Times*, July 18, 1967; Peter Bernstein, "No Federal Aid Promised for Newark, Other Cities," *Star-Ledger*, July 19, 1967; William T. Cahill to Richard M. Nixon, May 4, 1970, Box 8, Folder 22, S5200004, Subject Files, Papers of William T. Cahill, New Jersey State Archives, Trenton, New Jersey.

21 Richard Reeves, "Hatred and Pity Mix in Views of Whites on Newark Negroes," *New York Times*, July 22, 1967. See also Stanley B. Winters, ed., *From Riot to Recovery: Newark After Ten Years* (Lanham, MD: University Press of America, 1979).

22 Maurice Carroll, "Newark Still Edgy, 3 Months After Riot," *New York Times*, October 14, 1967; Herbert J. Gans, "The White Exodus to Suburbia Steps Up," *New York Times*, January 7, 1968; Paul Goldberger, "Tony Imperiale Stands Vigilant for Law and Order," *New York Times*, September 29, 1968.

23 "CORE'S Plan: Oust Addonizio," *Star-Ledger*, July 22, 1967; Kenneth Gibson, "Concentration Camp Newark," February 1968, Box 6, Folder 2, Kenneth Gibson Papers, MG1684, New Jersey Historical Society, Newark, New Jersey; Tuttle, *How Newark Became Newark*, 173–81, 186–90. See also Amiri Baraka, *The Autobiography of LeRoi Jones* (Chicago, IL: Lawrence Hill Books, 1974), 363–86, 394–402.

24 "Shadow Over Newark," *New York Times*, December 19, 1969; "Officials Face Arraignment," *Evening News*, December 18, 1969; George Hallam, "Addonizio's 21 Year Political Career at New Turning Point in U.S. Probe," *Evening News*, December 18, 1969. Originally launched in response to the allegations in the final report of the governor's civil disorder commission, the investigation into city hall corruption overlapped with the work of the Department of Justice's Organized Crime Strike Force created to dismantle the extensive network of crime families in New Jersey. Herbert J. Stern, *Diary of a DA: The True Story of the Prosecutor Who Took on the Mob, Fought Corruption, and Won* (New York: Skyhorse Publishing, 2012), 228–30, 259–61.

25 "Congressional Choices," *New York Times*, October 19, 1970; Oral Transcript, 2/4/99, 7, 12, RA; Oral Transcript, 3/4/99, 2, RA.

26 Angelo Baglivo, "Top Names Included in New FBI Tapes on Mafia's Influence in NJ Politics," *Evening News*, January 7, 1970; *Angelo DeCarlo: Transcripts*, Charles F. Cummings New Jersey Information Center, Newark Public Library, Newark,

New Jersey; Oral Transcript, 2/4/99, 6–7, RA; Deitche, *Garden State Gangland*, 71–78; Linnett, *In the Godfather Garden*, 63–64.

27 Walter H. Waggoner, "Blacks in Newark Seeking a Winner," *New York Times*, March 15, 1970; Gibson Campaign, "Saving Newark in the Seventies," "This Is Ken Gibson," "Why Ken Gibson Must Be Mayor of Newark," 1970, 1/9, Gibson Papers; Hugh Addonizio, campaign letter, June 1970, (149–001), Barbara J. Kukla Papers, Charles F. Cummings New Jersey Information Center, Newark Public Library, Newark, New Jersey; Ronald Sullivan, "Newark Mayoral Contest Reaches a Bitter Climax," *New York Times*, June 14, 1970.

28 "Delay in Addonizio Trial Is Denied by Court Again," *New York Times*, May 23, 1970; Kenneth Gibson, "Victory Statement," June 16, 1970, 6/2, Gibson Papers; Douglas Eldridge, "Gibson Triumph Was Years in the Making," *Evening News*, June 18, 1970; Thomas F. Brady, "Addonizio and 4 Convicted of Extortion by U.S. Jury," *New York Times*, July 23, 1970. Addonizio was released after serving five years.

29 *Baker v. Carr*, 369 US 186 (1962); Douglas J. Smith, *On Democracy's Doorstep: The Inside Story of How the Supreme Court Brought "One Person, One Vote" to the United States* (New York: Hill and Wang, 2014), 71–93.

30 *Wesberry v. Sanders* 376 US 1 (1964), 7–8; Richard L. Hasen, *The Supreme Court and Election Law* (New York: New York University Press, 2001), 47–56.

31 "Top Court Ruling Points up Disparity in N.J. Districts," *Newark Evening News*, February 18, 1964; John J. Farmer, "District Inequity Severe in Jersey," *Newark Evening News*, February 21, 1964; Peter Rodino to David Furman, April 19, 1960, POL77, 4, RA; Office of Governor Robert Meyner, press release, January 2, 1961, copy in POL, 77, 5, RA.

32 Reapportionment and Redistricting Commission, agenda, December 23, 1965, Reock Papers, 1/1; Samuel A. Alito to Ernst C. Reock, January 18, 1965, Reock Papers, 1/1; Samuel A. Alito to Peter Rodino, January 18, 1965, POL77, 10, RA; Reapportionment and Redistricting Commission to Peter Rodino, January 24, 1965, POL77, 9, RA; *Report of the New Jersey Legislative Reapportionment and Congressional Redistricting Planning Commission Eastablished Pursuant to Senate Concurrent Resolution No. 21, 1964; reconstituted by Senate Concurrent Resolution*

No. 3, 1965 (Trenton, New Jersey: February 5, 1965).

33 David Goldberg to Peter Rodino, August 3, 1965, POL, 78, 3, RA; "15 New N.J. Districts," *Newark Evening News*, June 28, 1966; Peter Rodino to Richard J. Hughes, May 1, 1967, Governor Richard J. Hughes Papers, S510001, Box 201, Rodino Folder, New Jersey State Archives, Trenton, New Jersey. A Republican challenge to the plan was partially upheld by the New Jersey Supreme Court, which ruled that a few districts, not the Tenth, were unequal and needed to be redrawn before the 1968 election. Angelo Baglivo, "Court Upsets Democrats [sic]Plan," *Newark Evening News*, July 24, 1966.

34 Robert W. Maitlin, "Here's a Final Rundown on the Census in New Jersey," *Star-Ledger*, January 6, 1971; *New York Times*, "Census Data Listed For 3-State Region" *New York Times*, September 2, 1970; Fox Butterworth, "Newark Transforms Once White Suburbs," *New York Times*, September 27, 1971,

35 J. Edward Crabiel to Peter Rodino, November 25, 1970, POL79, 1, RA; William T. Dietz to Frank Thompson, December 12, 1970, POL79, 5, RA; Joseph Carragher, "Redistricting Plans Carve Careers," *Star-Ledger*, February 21, 1971.

36 John Farmer, "N.J. House Delegation Split on Redistricting," *Evening News*, December 18, 1970. The *Newark Evening News* became the *Evening News* in December 1968.

37 Merle Baumgard to Robert Gordon, February 12, 1971, POL79, 5, RA; Robert Gordon to Merle Baumgard, February 22, 1971, POL9, 6, RA; Merle Baumgard to Peter Rodino, February 1971, POL, 79, 5, RA; William T. Cahill, "Statement From the Office of the Governor," March 22, 1971, copy in POL79, 5, RA.

38 Legislative Reapportionment and Congressional Redistricting Planning Commission, "Notice of Public Hearing" and "Notes on Witnesses," January 15, 1965, Reock Papers, 1/1.

39 "Study Center Hopes to Add Black Congressman in '72," *Evening News*, December 12, 1970.

40 Citizens Against Racial (Congressional) Districting, fundraising letter, December 12, 1971, PER87, 14, RA; Al Miele to Peter Rodino, May 6, 1971, POL79, 5, RA; Peter Rodino to Al Miele, undated, POL79, 2, RA; David J. Goldberg to Democratic members of the New Jersey Congressional delegation, May 3, 1971, POL79,

5, RA.

41 Ronald Sullivan, "Jersey G.O.P. Bars Aid of Imperiale," *New York Times*, November 4, 1971; Ronald Sullivan, "4 Dems Give G.O.P. Jersey Assembly Control," *New York Times*, January 12, 1972.

42 Joseph Maraziti to Peter Rodino, February 13, 1972, POL81, 1, RA; Oral Transcript, 3/4/99A, 1–2, RA.

43 Lawrence Hall, "Richardson Wants Congress District Tailored to Cities," *Star-Ledger*, January 30, 1972; "Richardson Ready to Reset the 'Wrong' Remap Plan," *Star-Ledger*, February 25, 1972; Arthur P. Endres to Peter Rodino, February 25, 1972, POL80, 1, RA.

44 *David v. Cahill* 342 F. Supp. 463 (1972); David J. Goldberg to Joseph Gannon, February 9, 1972, POL80, 1, RA; David J. Goldberg to clerk, United States District Court, February 18, 1972, IV, 81, 1, RA; Peter Rodino to Congressional delegation, February 29, 1972, POL, 80, 1, RA.

45 Lawrence H. Hall, "Essex Residents Taking Remap Plea to Trenton," *Star-Ledger*, March 23, 1972; Committee for United New Ark, "Let's Put the Pieces Together," POL80, 2, RA.

46 Citizens Against Racial (Congressional) Districts, press release, January 13, 1972, POL, 81, 10, RA; Al Miele to CARD Committee Members, January 11, 1972, POL, 51, 9, RA; Samuel J. Faiello, "Masterplan for Citizens Against Racial Congressional Districts," undated, PER87, 14, RA.

47 Peter Rodino to David Friedland, March 23, 1972, POL81, 1, RA; Joseph Carragher, "Dems Huddle on Remap Alternate," *Star-Ledger*, March 22, 1972; "Jersey Defeats Districting Plans," *New York Times*, March 28, 1972; author's recollection.

48 *David v. Cahill.*

49 Jean Joyce, "Redistricting Cauldron Bubbling," *Evening News*, April 10, 1972; Joseph Carragher, "Hope Dim for Assembly Remap," *Star-Ledger*, April 12, 1972; Oral Transcript, 4/16/99, 6–7, RA.

50 *David v. Cahill*; "U.S. Judge Hands Down Remap Lines," *Star-Ledger*, April 13, 1972.

51 *David v. Cahill.*

52 Congressional Research Service, "Memorandum," April 17, 1972, POL81, 1, RA;

Garner J. Cline to Peter Rodino, April 20, 1972, POL81, 1, RA; Oral Transcript, 3/4/99A, 1, 3, RA.

53 "Rodino Is Said to Weigh House Bid in 11th District," *New York Times*, April 20, 1972; "10th Congressional District Analysis," PER90, 13, RA; Oral Transcript, 4/16/99, 7, RA; Oral Transcript, 2/8/99, 9, RA.

54 Draft letter from William T. Cahill, 59, Rodino Folder, Cahill Papers; Lorenzo Nunez to William Cahill, April 17, 1972, Joseph Volker to William Cahill, April 16, 1972, Bayonne Veterans to William Cahill, April 15, 1972, all in 59, Rodino Folder, Cahill Papers; Ronald Sullivan, "G.O.P. Is Aided by Districting," *New York Times*, April 16, 1972.

55 Lawrence H. Hall, "Hart Declares Candidacy for New 10th District Seat," *Star-Ledger*, April 19, 1972; Jean Joyce, "Hart, Richardson, Vie in 10th District," *Evening News*, April 19, 1972.

56 Oral Transcript, 2/8/99, 9–10, RA; Oral Transcript, 3/4/99, 9–13, RA; Peter Rodino to Harry Lerner, April 24, 1972, PER60, 3, RA; Peter Rodino, "Statement Announcing His Candidacy for Reelection," April 24, 1972, PER87 10, RA.

57 Oral Transcript, 3/4/99A, 10, RA; Merle Baumgard to Peter Rodino, undated, PER90, 13, RA; "New 10th District," memorandum, PER90, 13, RA. Gibson was leading the campaign in New Jersey for George McGovern. Ronald Sullivan, "Gibson Stumps in Newark in Support of McGovern," *New York Times*, June 2, 1972.

58 Rodino campaign, "Schedule," May 1972, PER88, 3, RA; Rodino campaign, "Schedule," June 1972, PER87, 1, and PER88, 3, RA; Rodino campaign, "Black Ministers, Italian American Organizations, Hispanic Groups," May 1972, PER, 91, 1, RA; Rodino campaign, "Contact List at Factories," May 1972, PER93, 6, RA; Rodino campaign, "Supermarket Visits," May 1972, PER93, 7, RA.

59 "Citizens for Rodino, Primary Campaign Budget," May–June 1972, PER90, 13, RA; Ted Nalikowski to Murray W. Miller, May 8, 1972, PER90, 10, RA; "Citizens for Rodino, Itemized Receipts," May 1972, I, 88, 9, RA; Peter Rodino, "List of Possible Donors," undated, PER92, 7, RA; Rodino campaign, "Postal Patron Mailings," PER87, 10, RA.

60 Rodino campaign, brochure, "This Election Is Not As Simple As Black and White,"

PER88, 1, RA; Rodino campaign, brochure, "Peter Rodino a Man for All the People," PER87, 8, RA; Rodino campaign, advertisement, "Rodino's Fight Against Crime," SCR30, 47, RA.

61 Fred Feretti, "3 Blacks Vie for Rodino's Seat in Newark Race," *New York Times*, May 31, 1972; Anonymous brochure, "George Richardson the Spoiler," PER87, 30, RA; WCBS, "Debate Transcript," May 7, 1972, PER87, 4, RA.

62 Augustus Hawkins to Peter Rodino, May 18, 1972, PER90, 10, RA; Walter Fauntroy to Peter Rodino, May 19, 1972, PER56, 19, RA; Peter Rodino to William Hart, May 21, 1972, PER90, 10, RA; Hart Campaign, brochure, "We Got to Have Hart," PER87, 3, RA.

63 "Statement of A. Philip Randolph on the Candidacy of Congressman Peter Rodino," PER87, 10, RA; "Rights Leader Comes Out for Rodino," *Star-Ledger*, May 16, 1972; Oral Transcript, 19, 5–6, RA.

64 *Nagler v. Stiles* 343 F. Supp. 415 (1972); "Court Throws Out Jersey Law Barring Primary Cross-Voting," *New York Times*, May 27, 1972.

65 "Crossover Verdict Labeled Racist," *Star-Ledger*, May 28, 1972.

66 "Attention All Voters," *Italian Tribune*, June 2, 1972; Rodino campaign, brochure, "Court Guarantees Voting Rights," PER87, 5, RA; Rodino campaign, telephone message, PER87, 11, RA; "Crossovers Upheld in Jersey Primary by Justice Brennan," *New York Times*, June 3, 1972.

67 Michael J. Jayes, "Rodino Easily Defeats 10th District Rivals," *Evening News*, June 7, 1972; Robert M. Herbert, "Rodino Beats Three Blacks in the 10th District," *Star-Ledger*, June 7, 1972; Donald Warshaw, "Rodino Win," *Star-Ledger*, June 8, 1972; Fred Feretti, "Cross-Over Republicans Helped Rodino to Win," *New York Times*, June 11, 1972; author's recollection.

68 Richard L. Madden, "Celler, Honored at 83, Hopes 'to go On and On,'" *New York Times*, May 9, 1971; Richard L. Madden, "Celler, Now 83, to Make Race for His 26th Term in the House," *New York Times*," March 18, 1972.

69 William E. Farrell, "Celler Accused by Rival of Conflict," *New York Times*, June 16, 1972; Elizabeth Holtzman, *Who Said it Would Be Easy? One Woman's Life in the Political Arena* (New York: Arcade Publishing, 1996), 25–33.

70 "Time to Retire," *New York Times*, June 15, 1972; Francis X. Clines, "Celler Looking

to a Recount," *New York Times*, June 22, 1972; "Celler to Seek a New Election," *New York Times*, July 6, 1972; Richard L. Madden, "Celler Declines to Seek Re-election to the House," *New York Times*, September 29, 1972.

71 Fred Feretti, "Rodino Would Oversee Crime Inquiry," *New York Times*, October 20, 1972; "Rodino Hopes to Reap Reward of 23 Years in House," *Star-Ledger*, June 23, 1972; Oral Transcript, 19, 4–7, RA.

CHAPTER EIGHT

1 Michael Rowan to Peter Rodino, October 9, 1972, LEG163, 6, RA; Joseph Rothstein and Michael Rowan to Peter Rodino, December 14, 1972, PER91, 4, RA; Peter Rodino to subcommittee chairmen, October 19, 1972, LEG163, 6, RA; Peter Rodino, handwritten notes, December and January 1972, PER91, 4, RA.

2 Peter Rodino to Carl Albert, January 8, 1973, LEG, 181, 55, Albert Collection; Mary Beth Rogers, *Barbara Jordan: American Hero* (New York: Bantam Books, 1998), 178–179; "Rodino Favors Seniority Revision as Aid to Democratic Majority," *Evening News*, November 29, 1970. For background on the reforms, see Robert V. Remini, *The House: The History of the House of Representatives* (Washington, DC: Smithsonian Books, 2006), 427–34.

3 Edward Hutchinson, "Memorandum of Telephone Conversation with Rodino," January 12, 1973, Rodino Folder, Box 87, Edward Hutchinson Papers, Gerald R. Ford Presidential Library, Ann Arbor, Michigan; Peter Rodino, "Proposed Recommendation to Be Submitted to the Democratic Caucus of the House Committee on the Judiciary," June 13, 1973, LEG166, 3, RA.

4 Statement of Peter W. Rodino, October 24, 1973, IM, 1, JCA2, Railsback Collection; James M. Naughton, "Democrats Firm," *New York Times*, October 25, 1973.

5 Richard L. Lyons, "Peter W. Rodino Jr: Little Known N.J. Congressman Finds Himself in Rare Spotlight," *Washington Post*, November 15, 1973; William Vance, "Watergate, Ford Confirmation Put Him in Spotlight," *Miami Herald*, October 28, 1973; John Pierson, "Rep. Peter Rodino Faces a Rough Task," *Wall Street Journal*, November 9, 1973.

6 Martin Tolchin, "Head of House Judiciary Panel," *New York Times*, October 24, 1973; Herbert J. Stern, *Diary of a DA: The True Story of the Prosecutor Who Took*

on the Mob, Fought Corruption, and Won (New York: Skyhouse Publishing, 2012), 514.

7 Herbert Stern to Peter Rodino, October 25, 1973, PER57, 22, RA; Columbia Oral Transcript, 111–14; Thomas Railsback, "Conversation with Congressman Peter Rodino and Bryce Harlow," November 14, 1973, IM, 3, Personal Notes Folder, Railsback Collection.

8 Yale Oral Transcript, 33RA; Oral Transcript, 7/13/99, 1, RA; O'Brien interview, 11–12, Nixon Oral History.

9 Oral Transcript, 7/13/99, 3, RA; Columbia Oral Transcript, 116; interview with Arthur P. Endres, August 13 and 25, 2020. Zeifman continued to express bitterness over the decision two decades later in his score-settling memoir. Zeifman, *Without Honor*, 23–25.

10 Columbia Oral Transcript, 72–77, 169–72; Yale Oral Transcript, 16–20, RA.

11 Walter Flowers, July 11, 1975, Fragile Coalition Interviews (FCI), Group Transcripts (GT), Carton 54, Tape 4, 2, M. Caldwell Butler Papers, Lewis F. Powell Jr. Archives, Washington and Lee University, School of Law, Lexington, Virginia; Charles Rangel interview by Timothy Naftali, June 28, 2007, 9–12, Richard Nixon Oral History Project, Richard Nixon Presidential Library and Museum, Yorba Linda, California.

12 Thomas Railsback, "Memorandum of Telephone Conversation with Charles Wiggins," October 29, 1973, IM, 1, JCA2, Railsback Collection; Columbia Oral Transcript, 145–46; Richard L. Madden, "38 Lawyers Handling 1 Hard Case," *New York Times*, November 4, 1973.

13 Walter Taylor, "House GOP Criticizes Impeachment Inquiry," *Washington Star-News*, October 26, 1973; Jim Mann and Walter Flowers, July 11, 1975, FCI/GT, 54, 4, 2–4, Butler Papers.

14 Peter Rodino, "Opening Statement," October 30, 1973, IM, 1, JCA2, Railsback Collection; Columbia Oral Transcript, 139–40; Thomas Railsback, June 11, 1975, FCI, 54, Butler Papers.

15 Peter Rodino to Committee on the Judiciary, November 1, 1973, IM, 1, JCA2, Railsback Collection; Thomas Railsback, November 14, 1973, IM, 3, Personal Notes Folder, Railsback Collection.

16 Representative Rodino, speaking on impeachment budget, on November 15, 1973, Third Congress, First Session, *Congressional Record* 119, Pt. 28: 37142–46.

17 O'Neill and Novak, *Man of the House*, 251–53; Rangel interview, 8–9, Nixon Oral history; Mezvinsky, *Term to Remember*, 59–60.

18 "Memorandum to the Speaker," October 1973, LEG, 184, 2, Albert Collection; O'Brien interview, 19–21, Nixon Oral History.

19 Columbia Oral Transcript, 91–92; Carl Albert, "Interview 3," Foote Collection.

20 Carl Albert, "Statement," October 23, 1973, IV, 262, 9, O'Neill Papers; Columbia Oral Transcript, 92–94.

21 Gerald R. Ford to Peter Rodino, October 22, 1973, Box 1, Vice Presidential Confirmation Folder, Benton L. Becker Papers, Gerald R. Ford Presidential Library, Ann Arbor, Michigan; Peter Rodino, personal notes, LEG165, 2, RA.

22 Peter Rodino, speaking on Ford nomination, on November 7, 1973, Ninety-Third Congress, First Session, *Congressional Record* 119, Pt. 28: 36202; Committee on the Judiciary, House of Representatives, Ninety-Third Congress, First Session, "Nomination of Gerald R. Ford to Be the Vice President of the United States: Hearings Before the Committee on the Judiciary," November 1973, 91–95.

23 Peter Rodino to Committee on the Judiciary, November 7, 1973, LEG165, 10, November 8, 1973, LEG165, 10 and November 13, 1973, LEG164, 12, RA; Peter Rodino to Gerald Ford, November 12, 1973, 1, Judiciary Committee Correspondence Folder, Becker Papers.

24 "Ford Hearing," 2 –3.

25 "Ford Hearing," 6–9; "Questions Posed By House Judiciary Committee and Talking Points," Box 1, Vice Presidential Questions Folder, Becker Papers. When William Cohen posed some tough questions, Hutchinson reprimanded him. William Cohen, June 17, 1975, FCI, 54, 4–5, Butler Papers, "Ford Hearing," 44–45.

26 "Ford Hearing," 12–65, 149–51, 207–18. For details of Senate action see James Cannon, *Time and Chance: Gerald Ford's Appointment With History* (New York: HarperCollins, 1994), 229–51.

27 Representative Rodino, speaking on confirmation of Gerald Ford, on December 6, 1973, Ninety-Third Congress, First Session, *Congressional Record* 119, Pt. 30: 39807–13; Columbia Oral Transcript, 101–104. See letters from constituents

applauding his vote in LEG165, 9, RA.

28 Gerald Ford to Peter Rodino, December 9, 1973, LEG165, 8, RA; "Small Thinker in a Big Job," *The Record*, (Bergen), December 14, 1973; Elizabeth McGuire to Peter Rodino, December 7, 1973, LEG165, 9, RA.

29 O'Neill and Novak, *Man of the House*, 255–56; Endres interview, August 13, 2020; Peter Rodino to Committee on the Judiciary, December 11, 1973, IM,1, JCA2, Railsback Collection; "Rodino Outlines Progress of Impeachment Inquiry," news release, December 10, 1973, IM, 1, JCA2, Railsback Collection.

30 Representative Robert McClory speaking on impeachment, on December 18, 1973, Ninety-Third Congress, First Session, *Congressional Record* 119, Pt. 32: 42275–80; Robert McClory to Thomas Railsback, December 17, 1973, IM, 1, JCA2, Railsback Collection.

31 John Doar interview by Timothy Naftali, January 24, 2014, 22–25, 58–59, Richard Nixon Oral History Project, Richard Nixon Presidential Library and Museum, Yorba Linda, California; Columbia Oral Transcript, 118–23; Oral Transcript, 2, 6–11, RA.

32 Peter Rodino, "Statement of Appointment of John Doar As Special Counsel," December 20, 1973, IM, 1, JAC2, Railsback Collection; Peter Rodino to Committee on the Judiciary, "Materials for Press Conference on December 20," December 19, 1973, IM, 1, JAC2, Railsback Collection.

33 Mary Russell, "Republican to Direct Hill Impeachment Study," *Washington Post*, December 21, 1973.

34 John Doar to Members of the Judiciary Committee, January 29, 1974, IM, 1, JAC1, Railsback Collection; Hillary Clinton interview by Timothy Naftali, July 9, 2018, 13, Richard Nixon Oral History Project, Richard Nixon Presidential Library and Museum, Yorba Linda, California.

35 Thomas Railsback, June 11, 1975, FCI, 6–7, 54, Butler Papers; "Memorandum, Status Report of Minority Staff," Committee on the Judiciary, December 19, 1973, IM, 1, JAC2, Railsback Collection; Columbia Oral Transcript, 124–25.

36 Doar interview, 18–19, 26–27, Nixon Oral History.

37 Clinton Interview, 6–10, Nixon Oral History; William Weld interview by Timothy Naftali, September 28, 2011, 3, 9, Richard Nixon Oral History Project, Richard

Nixon Presidential Library and Museum, Yorba Linda, California; Michael Conway interview by Timothy Naftali, September 30, 2011, 5–6, Richard Nixon Oral History Project, Richard Nixon Presidential Library and Museum, Yorba Linda, California.

38 John Doar, "Memorandum to Members of the Judiciary Committee," January 29, 1974, IM, 1, JAC1, Railsback Collection; Thomas Railsback, notes, January 7 and 29, 1974, February 5, 1974, IM, 1, JAC6, Railsback Collection; House Committee Print, Committee on the Judiciary, House of Representatives, Ninety-Third Congress, Second Session, "Work on the Impeachment Inquiry Staff as of February 5, 1974," February 1974, 1–4; Bernard Nussbaum interview by Timothy Naftali, October 1, 2011, 11, Richard Nixon Oral History Project, Richard Nixon Presidential Library and Museum, Yorba Linda, California.

39 Walter Flowers, FCI/GT, 54, Tape 5, 23, 22; Endres interview, August 13, 2020.

40 Doar interview, 16, Nixon Oral History; Thomas Railsback, notes, January 29, 1974, IM, 1, JAC6, Railsback Collection; O'Brien interview, 15–16, Nixon Oral History; Raymond Thornton, June 13, 1975, FCI, 54, 19, Butler Papers; Hamilton Fish, June 26, 1975, FCI, 54, 9, Butler Papers; Brendan McNulty and Tim McNulty, *The Meanest Man in Congress: Jack Brooks and the Making of an American Century* (Montgomery, AL: New South Books, 2019), 308–12, 317–18.

41 "Congressman Peter W. Rodino Announces the Results of the January 24 Meeting of the Judiciary Committee's Advisory Committee on Its Impeachment Inquiry," press release, January 24, 1974, IM, 1, JAC2, Railsback Collection; Thomas Railsback, notes, January 24 and 31, 1974, IM, 1, JAC6, Railsback Collection.

42 John Gardner to Peter Rodino, January 22, 1974, and Peter Rodino to John Gardner, February 1, 1974, IM, 1, JCA1, Railsback Collection; Columbia Oral Transcript, 142–44; Oral Transcript, 2, 8–10, RA.

43 Columbia Oral Transcript, 107–110; Joe McCaffrey, notes on Rodino meeting, 262, 9, O'Neill Papers; "Memorandum Regarding Authority of the Committee on the Judiciary to Conduct Impeachment Investigation and Subpoenas," LEG, 184, 1, Albert Collection.

44 Committee on the Judiciary, House of Representatives, Ninety-Third Congress, Second Session, "Impeachment Inquiry: Hearings Before the Committee on the Judiciary," January–May 1974, Book I, 2–6, 26–27; Representative Rodino

speaking on impeachment, on February 6, 1974, Ninety-Third Congress, Second Session, *Congressional Record* 120, Pt. 2: 2349–50, 2051–63.

45 Oral Transcript, 4/9/03A, 4, RA; Peter Rodino, personal diary, 1974, PER119, 2, RA; "Rodino Office Calendar," 1974, PER113, 3, RA.

46 Oral Transcript, 5/14/99, 4–6, RA; interview with Ronna Freiberg, August 11, 2021.

47 Committee on the Judiciary, House of Representatives, Ninety-Third Congress, Second Session, "Work of the Impeachment Inquiry Staff as of March 1, 1974," House Committee Print, March 1974.

48 James M. Naughton, "Impeachment Panel Seeks House Mandate for Inquiry," *New York Times*, January 25, 1974; Leon Jaworski, *The Right and the Power: The Prosecution of Watergate* (New York: Reader's Digest Press, 1976), 25–30, 95–96.

49 James M. Naughton, "Rodino Fears Lag of Year in Inquiry," *New York Times*, January 23, 1974; Jaworski, *Right and Power*, 96–99.

50 "Impeachment Inquiry: Hearings," February 22, 1974, Book I, 102–28; Committee on the Judiciary, House of Representatives, Ninety-Third Congress, Second Session, "Procedures for Handling Impeachment Inquiry Material," House Committee Print, February 1974; Columbia Oral Transcript, 142–44.

51 Jaworski, *Right and Power*, 99–104; Sirica, *Set the Record Straight*, 215–17.

52 "Impeachment Inquiry: Hearings," March 5, 1974, Book I, 133–48; "Impeachment Inquiry: Hearings," March 7, 1974, Book I, 161–69.

53 Peter Rodino to John Sirica, March 8, 1974, and John Sirica to Peter Rodino, March 8, 1974, IM, 1, JCA6, Railsback Collection; "Text of Sirica Order and Opinion in Decision that Watergate Data Go to House," *New York Times*, March 19, 1974; Peter Rodino, statement, March 20, 1974, IM, 1, JCA6, Railsback Collection. An appeal of this decision was denied.

54 John Doar, memorandum, March 26, 1974, IM, 1, JCA5, Railsback Collection; John Doar to Committee on the Judiciary, March 27, 1974, IM, 1, JCA5, Railsback Collection; "The Briefcase and Its Role in Impeachment," New *York Times,* March 29, 1974.

55 Spencer Rich and Mary Russell, "Watergate Remarks Irk Democrats," *Washington Post*, January 31, 1974.

56 Thomas Railsback, notes, February 22, 1974, IM, 1, JCA6, Railsback Collection; John Doar to James St. Clair, February 25, 1974, IM, 1, JCA5, Railsback Collection.

57 R.W. Apple, "Nixon Is Unwilling to Yield More Tapes to House Unit," *New York Times*, March 13, 1974; John Herbers, "New Tack for Nixon," *New York Times*, March 15, 1974.

58 Peter Rodino, statement, March 13, 1974, IM, 1, JCA6, Railsback Collection; "Statement on Wrongdoing in High Places," Office of Majority Leader, March 14, 1974, 262, 9, O'Neill Papers.

59 Thomas Railsback, March 19, 1974, IM 3, personal notes, Railsback Collection; James St. Clair, memorandum, March 1974, IM, 1, JCA5, Railsback Collection; James St. Clair to John Doar, April 9, 1974, LEG, 184, 4, Albert Collection; William Cohen and Thomas Railsback, FCI/GT, Tape 4, 4–6, Butler Papers.

60 "Impeachment Inquiry: Hearings," March 21, 1974, Book I, 225–37; "Minority Members of the House Judiciary Committee," memorandum, April 3, 1974, IM, 1, JCA3, Railsback Collection; Peter Rodino, statement, April 11, 1974, LEG, 184, 4, Albert Collection.

61 Oral Transcript, 4, 10–11, RA; Columbia Oral Transcript, 64–65, 188–89; Committee on the Judiciary, House of Representatives, Ninety-Third Congress, Second Session, "Transcripts of Eight Recorded Presidential Conversations: Hearings Before the Committee on the Judiciary," May–June 1974, III-IV.

62 Columbia Oral Transcript, 70–72.

63 "Impeachment Inquiry: Hearings," April 4, 1974, Book I, 249–55; John Doar to James St. Clair, April 4 and April 11, 1974, IM, 1, JCA5, Railsback Collection; James St. Clair to John Doar, April 9, 1974, IM, 1, JCA5, Railsback Collection.

64 Peter Rodino to Richard Nixon, April 11, 1974, IM, 1, JCA5, Railsback Collection; "Impeachment Inquiry: Hearings," April 25, 1974, Book I, 334–56; Yale Oral Transcript, 23–24, 34–35, RA.

65 "Transcript of Nixon's Address to the Nation Regarding Controversy Over Tapes," *New York Times*, April 30, 1974; Carl Bernstein and Bob Woodward, "Nixon's Strategy: Blurring the Focus," *Washington Post*, April 30, 1974.

66 R.W. Apple, "Nixon Strategy Viewed as Seeking Divisions," *New York Times*, May 3, 1974; M. Caldwell Butler, May 1, 1974, Butler audio diary, Carton 47, Butler

Papers; Columbia Oral Transcript, 171–72, RA.

67 Oral Transcript, 4, 7–8, RA; Yale Transcript, 22–27, RA; James M. Naughton, "Rodino Aides Find Their Transcripts Vary from Nixon," *New York Times*, May 2, 1974.

68 "Impeachment Inquiry: Hearings," May 1, 1974, Book I, 442, 406–33.

69 Ibid., 438–59.

70 "President Should Be Impeached," *Los Angeles Times*, May 10, 1974; George Gallup, "Poll Supports Panel Refusal of Transcripts," *Star-Ledger*, May 5, 1974; Spencer Rich, "GOP Pressure for Resignation Grows," *Washington Post*, May 11, 1974.

71 Peter Rodino, statement on subpoenas, May 15, 1974, LEG, 184, 5, Albert Collection.

72 Peter Rodino to Richard Nixon, May 30, 1974, IM, 1, JCA5, Railsback Collection; John Doar to Committee on the Judiciary, May 29, 1974, IM, JCA3, Railsback Collection; Columbia Oral Transcript, 171–78.

73 Jaworski, *Right and Power*, 124–28.

74 Waldman, *Press Passes*, 96–100. For examples of Rodino's statements, see Peter Rodino, press statements, May 9, 15, 16, 22 and June 4, 5, 12, 1974, Carton 45, Rodino Releases Folder, Butler Papers.

75 Committee on the Judiciary, House of Representatives, Ninety-Third Congress, Second Session, "Impeachment Inquiry Procedures," May 2, 1974; Doar interview, 34–39, Nixon Oral History; Committee on the Judiciary, House of Representatives, Ninety-Third Congress, Second Session, "Statement of Information: Hearings Before The Committee on the Judiciary," May 9, 1974, Book I, III–V.

76 Mezvinsky, *Term to Remember*, 137–39; Holtzman, *Who Said It Would Be Easy*, 8; Nussbaum interview, 22–23, Nixon Oral History.

77 "Post Is Going To Have Its Problems-Nixon," *Washington Post*, May 16, 1974; "Impeachment Inquiry: Hearings," May 16, 1974, Book II, 703–708; William Cohen, June 17, 1975, FCI, 54, 19, Butler Papers.

78 "Impeachment Inquiry: Hearings," May 22, 1974, Book II, 803–808, May 31, 1974, Book II, 974–992; Columbia Oral Transcript, 138–42; Flowers, FCI, 54, 20–21, Butler Papers; Nussbaum interview, 4, 32, Nixon Oral History.

79 Fish, FCI, 54, 9, Butler Papers; Holtzman, *Who Said It Would Be Easy*, 44–46; Thornton, FCI, 54, 19, 22, Butler Papers; William Cohen, June 17, 1975, FCI, 54, 28, Butler Papers; Doar interview, 38–39, Nixon Oral History.

80 Waldman, *Press Passes*, 101–103; Breslin, *Good Guys*, 145–47; Mezvinsky, *Term to Remember*, 142–46.

81 Paul Houston, "Memo Says Nixon Told Mitchell to Plead Fifth," *Washington Post*, June 12, 1974; "Impeachment Inquiry: Hearings," June 13, 1974, Book II, 1303.

82 Marquis Childs, "Increasing the Odds Against Impeachment," *Washington Post*, June 18, 1974; David S. Broder, "Judiciary Panel Hit on Leaks," *Washington Post*, June 20, 1974.

83 Jack Nelson, "Rodino Denies Story on Vote to Impeach," *Los Angeles Times*, June 29, 1974; Representative Rodino speaking on press story, on June 28, 1974, Ninety-Third Congress, Second Session, *Congressional Record* 120, Pt. 16: 21735–36; Columbia Oral Transcript, 148–54; Flowers, FCI, 54, 24–25, Butler Papers.

84 "Impeachment Inquiry: Hearings," June 26, 1974, Book III, 1621–1711; Columbia Oral Transcript, 193–94, 220–22; Committee on the Judiciary, House of Representatives, Ninety-Third Congress, Second Session, "Testimony of Witnesses: Hearings Before the Committee on the Judiciary," July 1974.

85 David E. Rosenbaum, "Differences Cited in Panel Version of 8 Nixon Tapes," *New York Times*, July 10, 1974; "House Committee Issues the Voluminous Evidence from Watergate Inquiry," *New York Times*, July 12, 1974.

86 Cohen, FCI, 54, 14–15, Butler Papers; Fish, FCI, 54, 11, Butler Papers; Mezvinsky, *Term to Remember*, 163–70; Thomas Railsback, July 12, 1974, IM, 3, personal notes, Railsback Collection.

87 Committee on the Judiciary, House of Representatives, Ninety-Third Congress, Second Session, "Summary of Information: Hearings Before the Committee on the Judiciary," July 19, 1974; "Impeachment Inquiry: Hearings," July 19, 1974, Book III, 1923–1952, July 20, 1974, Book III, 1957–2034; James Reston Jr., *The Impeachment Diary: Eyewitness to the Removal of a President* (New York: Arcade Publishing, 2019), 44–46.

88 Carroll Kilpatrick, "Zeigler Reacts Angrily, Calls Doar Biased," *Washington Post*, July 20, 1974; "Impeachment Inquiry: Hearings," July 22, 1974, Book III, 2037–2096;

Committee on the Judiciary, House of Representatives, Ninety-Third Congress, Second Session, "Minority Memorandum on Facts and Law: Hearings Before the Committee on the Judiciary," July 22, 1974. Although the Republicans replaced Jenner right before this presentation, Rodino kept him on the committee payroll.

89 James Mann, FCI/GT, 54, 5, 8–9, Butler Papers; M. Caldwell Butler, personal notes, July 2–17, 1974, 48, Butler Papers; Flowers, FCI/GT, 54, 1,14–15, Butler Papers; Thomas Railsback, August 6, 1974, personal notes, 3, Railsback Collection; Columbia Oral Transcript, 246–57.

90 Thomas Mooney, "Day, Time, Place and Attendance of the Meeting of the Coalition," 54, Fragile Coalition Plans Folder, Butler Papers; "Drafts of Article I," 54, Fragile Coalition Plans Folder, Butler Papers; Columbia Oral Transcript, 194–215; Railsback, FCI, 17–19, 54, Butler Papers; Flower, FCI, 54, 26–28, Butler Papers.

91 Columbia Oral Transcript, 313–14; O'Brien interview, 31–38, Nixon Oral History.

92 Oral Transcript, 12/8/99, 3, RA; John P. McKenzie, "Justices Reject Privilege Claim in 8 to 0 Ruling," *Washington Post*, July 25, 1974. Hogan announced the previous day he was voting for impeachment. Lawrence Hogan to Republican colleagues, July 30, 1974, LEG, 184, 5, Albert Collection.

93 Committee on the Judiciary, House of Representatives, Ninety-Third Congress, Second Session, "Debate on Article of Impeachment: Hearings of the Committee on the Judiciary," July 24, 1974, 2–4.

94 R.W. Apple, "Panel's Pro and Con, Amid 2 Bomb Threats," *New York Times*, July 25, 1974.

95 "Impeachment Debate," July 25, 1974, 134–36, 110–13.

96 "Impeachment Debate," July 26, 1974, 150–53; Columbia Oral Transcript, 226–228.

97 "Impeachment Debate," July 26, 1974, 163–220; Columbia Oral Transcript, 190–93; Butler, personal notes, July 26, 1974, 48, Butler Papers; Waldman, *Press Passes*, 105–107.

98 Cohen, FCI, 54, 28–30, Butler Papers; Flowers, FCI, 54, 28–30, Butler Papers; Mann, FCI, 54, 5–6, Butler Papers.

99 "Impeachment Debate," July 26, 1974, 220, July 27, 1974, 252–328; Columbia Oral Transcript, 260–65.

100 "Impeachment Debate," July 27, 1974, 329–31; "How a Fragile Centrist Bloc

Emerged As House Panel Weighed Impeachment," *New York Times*, August 5, 1974.

101 Oral Transcript, 4/9/03A, 12–13, RA; Yale Oral Transcript, 40–41, RA.

102 R.W. Apple, "A Historic Charge," *New York Times*, July 28, 1974.

103 Mezvinsky, *Term to Remember*, 214–17.

104 Mann, FCI, 54, 6, Butler Papers; Columbia Oral Transcript, 267–69.

105 "Impeachment Debate," July 29, 1974, 333–447.

106 Columbia Oral Transcript, 292–95.

107 "Impeachment Debate," July 30, 1974, 449–560; Columbia Oral Transcript, 240–46; Reston, "Impeachment Journal," 66–67.

108 Representative Rodino on impeachment, on August 2, 1974, Ninety-Third Congress, Second Session, *Congressional Record* 120, Pt. 20: 26512; Peter Rodino to House colleagues, August 2, 1974, 282, 12, 9, O'Neill Papers; Thomas Railsback, August 6, 1974, IM, 3, personal notes, Railsback Collection; ad hoc committee to Speaker, August 5, 1974, LEG, 184, 5, Albert Collection.

109 Columbia Oral Transcript, 300–304; Woodward and Bernstein, *Final Days*, 374–79.

110 James M. Naughton, "An Impeachment Ordeal's Climax." *New York Times*, August 9, 1974.

111 Representative Rodino speaking on impeachment, Ninety-Third Congress, Second Session, *Congressional Record* 120, Pt. 22: 29219–29362; Committee on the Judiciary, House of Representatives, Ninety-Third Congress, Second Session, "Impeachment of Richard M. Nixon President of the United States: Report of the Committee on the Judiciary," August 20, 1974; Columbia Oral Transcript, 307–308. The unanimous committee vote on Article I was reflected in the majority and concurrent opinions.

CHAPTER NINE

1 Miles Benson, "Rodino Is Hot Property on the Lecture Circuit," *Washington Post*, September 1, 1974; David Nyhan, "Rodino Has Moved Center Stage with Clout that Reaches to '76,'" *Boston Globe*, May 11, 1975; O'Brien interview, 43, Nixon Oral History.

2 Leslie Oelsner, "Aide Doubtful that Ford Would Give Nixon Pardon," *New York Times*, August 10, 1974; John Herbers, "Decision Put Off," *New York Times*, August 29, 1974; Jaworski, *The Right and The Power*, 222–43.

3 Gerald Ford to Peter Rodino, August 21, 1974, WHCNF, Box 2692, Rodino Folder, Gerald R. Ford Presidential Papers, Gerald R. Ford Presidential Library, Ann Arbor, Michigan; Oral Transcript, 7/6/99, 6, RA; Columbia Oral Transcript, 163–64.

4 "Statement by the President in Connection with His Proclamation Pardoning Nixon," *New York Times*, September 9, 1974; Leon Jaworski to Philip Buchen, September 4, 1974, "Pardon of Richard M. Nixon and Related Matters: Hearings Before the Subcommittee on Criminal Justice of the Committee on the Judiciary," House of Representatives, Ninety-Third Congress, Second Session, 1974, 189–903.

5 Columbia Oral Transcript, 160–66; Yale Oral Transcript, 37–39, RA; "Survey Before Pardon Finds 58% Oppose It," *New York Times*, September 9, 1974; "terHorst Quits Post to Protest Pardon," *New York Times*, September 9, 1974.

6 Peter Rodino to Carl Albert, September 30, 1974, LEG, 168, 14, Albert Collection; Carl Albert to John Moss, October 7, 1974, LEG, 168, 14, Albert Collection; David E. Rosenbaum, "Rodino Rejects Revival of Impeachment," *New York Times*, September 10, 1974; James M. Naughton, "Congress Returns to Find Watergate Still a Burden," *New York Times*, September 12, 1974.

7 William Hungate to Gerald Ford, September 17, 1974, and September 25, 1974, "Pardon of Richard M. Nixon: Hearings," 193–98, 201–202. When Ford sent a perfunctory reply simply referencing his previous statements, Hungate followed up with a request that the White House send a representative to testify in person. Subcommittee member Elizabeth Holtzman began pressing for a full-scale investigation that would issue subpoenas to potential witnesses.

8 Oral Transcript, 3/23/99, 3–5, RA; Oral Transcript, 7/6/99, 5–6, RA; "Pardon of Richard M. Nixon: Hearings," 188.

9 James M. Naughton, "History Played Out on Familiar Stage," *New York Times*, October 18, 1974.

10 "Pardon of Richard Nixon: Hearings," 88–109; Oral Transcript, 3/23/99, 3–5, RA; Bob Kuttner, "House Democrats Urge Further Pardon Probe," *Washington Post*,

October 18, 1974. See also Benton L. Becker, "Memorandum of the History and Background of Nixon Pardon," September 9, 1974, Box 2, Nixon Pardon-Becker's Memorandum Folder, Benton L. Becker Papers, Gerald R. Ford Presidential Library, Ann Arbor, Michigan.

11 "Remarks of the President Upon His Announcing Nelson Rockefeller As Vice-President Delegate," August 20, 1974, Robert T. Hartman Files, Box 19, "Vice President-Announcement of Rockefeller Nomination," Ford Papers; Gerald Ford to Peter Rodino, WHCNF, September 10, 1974, 2692, Rodino Folder, Ford Papers; Linda Charlton, "Hearings Charted on Rockefeller," *New York Times*, September 17, 1974.

12 "Rodino Sees New Woe for Rocky," *Star-Ledger*, October 31, 1974.

13 Gerald Ford to Peter Rodino, November 11, 1974, WHCNF, 2692, Rodino Folder, Ford Papers; Peter Rodino to Gerald Ford, November 12, 1974, John Marsh Files, Box 29, Rockefeller, Nelson—Confirmation Hearings: General (1) Folder, Ford Papers; John Marsh to Gerald Ford, November 19, 1974, Marsh Files, 29, "Rockefeller, Nelson" Folder, Ford Papers.

14 "Nomination of Nelson A. Rockefeller to Be Vice President of the United States: Hearings Before the Committee on the Judiciary, House of Representatives," Ninety-Third Congress, Second Session, 1974, 1–3; Waldman, *Forgive Us Our Press Passes*, 116–18.

15 John Marsh to Gerald Ford, November 22, 1974, and December 10, 1974, Marsh Files, 29, Nelson Rockefeller Folder, Ford Papers.

16 "Debate on the Nomination of Nelson A. Rockefeller to Be Vice President of the United States: Meeting Held By the Committee on the Judiciary," House of Representatives, Ninety-Third Congress, Second Session, December 12, 1974; Representative Rodino, speaking on Rockefeller nomination, on December 19, 1974, Ninety-Third Congress, Second Session, *Congressional Record* 120, Pt. 23: 41426–27, 41516–17; Linda Charlton, "Senate Ceremony," *New York Times*, December 20, 1974.

17 Peter Rodino, "Remarks Before New Mexico Democratic Party Platform Convention," September 13, 1974, Press and Public Relations (PPR), Box 4, Folders 1 and 5, RA; Peter Rodino, itinerary, September 28–29, 1974, PER122, 11, RA.

18 William Greider, "Rodino Stumps for Party, the System," *Washington Post*, September 16, 1974; Frank E. Denholm to Peter Rodino, September 12, 1974, PER122, 10, RA.

19 William Greider, "Rodino Stumps for Party, the System," *Washington Post*, September 16, 1974.

20 Ibid.

21 Paul Boyd, "Rodino Flies to Add Charisma to Bonker Drive," *Seattle Post-Intelligencer*, October 27, 1974; Peter Rodino, itinerary, October 25–27, 1974, PER122, 18, RA; "Candidates Who Requested PWR's Assistance," memorandum, undated, PER122, 6, RA.

22 Larry Eckholt, "Warm Welcome for Rodino At U of I Law College Talk," *Des Moines Register*, October 26, 1974; Todd Engdahl, "Congressional Demos Aid State Candidates," *Oregonian*, October 27, 1974; Joseph F. Sullivan, "Confident Rodino Campaigns for Others," *New York Times*, November 2, 1974. Rodino also served as the grand marshal of Chicago's Columbus Day parade. Peter Rodino, itinerary, October 14, 1974, PER122, 13, RA.

23 James M. Naughton, "Democrats View Their Victory As Spur to Legislative Moves," *New York Times*, November 7, 1974; "Election-1974 results," memorandum to Peter Rodino, undated, PER122, 6, RA; Christopher Lydon, "Democrats Score Gains in Contests for Governor," *New York Times*, November 6, 1974.

24 Richard D. Lyons, "House Reformers Seek More Power," *New York Times*, November 14, 1974; Rowland Evans and Robert Novak, "Power Shift in the House," *Washington Post*, December 7, 1974; O'Neill, *Man of the House*, 282–285.

25 Miles Benson, "Common Cause Gives Rodino Top Rating Among House Chairman," *Star-Ledger*, January 14, 1975; Mary Russell, "Hill Chairmen Return to Meet with Freshmen," *Washington Post*, January 9, 1975; Richard D. Lyons, "House Democrats Oust 3 Chairmen," *New York Times*, January 23, 1975.

26 Mary McGrory, "Dream Goes on for Rodino," *Chicago Tribune*, July 28, 1975; Richard L. Madden, "A Year After Members of Impeachment Panel Reflect," *New York Times*, July 27, 1975.

27 "Extension of the Voting Rights Act: Hearings Before the Subcommittee on Civil and Constitutional Rights," Committee on the Judiciary, House of Representatives,

Ninety-Fourth Congress, First Session, 10, 2–13; Peter Rodino, handwritten notes, January 1975, LEG223, 2, RA.

28 Representative Rodino, speaking on voting rights extension, on July 28, 1975, Ninety-Fourth Congress, First Session, *Congressional Record* 121, Pt. 20: 25216–19; *The Voting Rights Act: Ten Years After* (Washington, DC: United States Commission on Civil Rights, January 1975), 39–57; Clarence Mitchell to Peter Rodino, May 15, 1975, LEG223, 3, RA; Richard L. Madden, "Congress Passes 7 Year Extension of Voting Rights," *New York Times,* July 29, 1975.

29 Fox Butterfield, "Many Americans Leaving Vietnam," *New York Times,* April 2, 1975; George Esper, "The Communist Takeover," *New York Times*, May 1, 1975; Flora Lewis, "Long Road to the Paris Pacts Had Misleading Signs, Pitfalls and Dead Ends," *New York Times*, May 1, 1975.

30 Kathryn M. Bockley, "A Historical Overview of Refugee Legislation: The Deception of Foreign Policy in the Land of Promise," *North Carolina Journal of International Law* 21, no. 1 (Fall 1995): 269–78.

31 Robert S. Ingersoll to Edward H. Levi, April 5, 1975, Theodore C. Marrs Files, Box 10, Indochina Refugees-Parole Authority (2) Folder, Gerald R. Ford Presidential Papers, Gerald R. Ford Presidential Library, Ann Arbor, Michigan; Philip Buchen to Gerald Ford, April 17, 1975, Marrs Files, 10, "Indochina Refugees-Parole Authority (2)," Ford Papers; "Emergency Program for Parole of Refugees From Vietnam," undated, Marrs Files, 10, "Indochina Refugees-Parole Authority (2)," Ford Papers; Representative Rodino, speaking on refugees, on April 22, 1975, Ninety-Fourth Congress, First Session, *Congressional Record* 121, Pt. 9: 11313.

32 David Binder, "Ford Asks Nation to Open Its Doors to the Refugees," *New York Times*, May 7, 1975; Linda Charlton, "Mail to Congress Against Refugees," *New York Times*, May 9, 1975.

33 Peter Rodino, "Statement Before Subcommittee on Immigration, Citizenship and International Law," May 7, 1975, LEG228, 13, RA; Max Friedersdorf to Gerald Ford, May 12, 1974, WHCNF, 2692, Rodino Folder, Ford Papers; David Binder, "Fund Bill Gains in House," *New York Times* May 8, 1975.

34 Oral Transcript, 4/16/99, 11, RA; "Statement by the President," December 24, 1975, White House press releases, Box 19, Ford Papers; Gerald Ford to Peter Rodino,

September 25, 1975, WHCNF, 2692, Rodino Folder, Ford Papers; L.C. Chapman to Peter Rodino, January 29, 1976, LEG228, 7, RA.

35 Miles Benson, "Rodino Emerges As Vocal Anti-Trust Leader," *Star-Ledger*, January 26, 1975; Miles Benson, "Price Warrior: Rodino Going After Farm Aid and Fuel Cost Structure," *Star-Ledger*, January 31, 1975.

36 Philip Shabecoff, "A Call for Action," *New York Times*, October 9, 1974; Representative Rodino speaking on antitrust, November 19, 1974, Ninety-Third Congress, Second Session, *Congressional Record* 120, Pt. 27: 36337–40; Carole Shifrin, "Anti-Trust Law Overhaul Approved by Congress," *Washington Post*, December 12, 1974; Gerald Ford to Peter Rodino, January 22, 1975, WHCNF, 2692, Rodino Folder, Ford Papers.

37 "Antitrust Parens Patriae Amendments: Hearings Before the Subcommittee on Monopolies and Commercial Law," Committee on the Judiciary, Ninety-Fourth Congress, First Session, 1975; Carole Shifrin, "Antitrust Measure Advances," *Washington Post*, May 8, 1975.

38 Morton Mintz, "House Bill to Strengthen Antitrust Laws Shelved," *Washington Post*, November 9, 1975.

39 Edward Walsh, "Ford Veto of Antitrust Bill Seen," *Washington Post*, March 18, 1976; Peter Rodino, "Dear colleague" letter, March 11, 1976, Marsh Files, 4, Antitrust Folder, Ford Papers; Paul O'Neal to John Marsh, March 12, 1976, Marsh Files, 4, Antitrust Folder, Ford Papers; Edward Levi to John Marsh, March 15, 1976, Marsh Files, 4, Antitrust Folder, Ford Papers.

40 Representative Rodino, speaking on merger notification, on August 2, 1975, Ninety-Fourth Congress, First Session, *Congressional Record* 122, Pt. 20: 25051–52; "Merger Oversight and H.R. 13131, Providing Premerger Notification and Statutory Requirements: Hearings Before the Subcommittee on Monopolies and Commercial Law," Committee on the Judiciary, House of Representatives, Ninety-Fourth Congress, Second Session, 1976, 1–2, 131–33. Emanuel Celler testified.

41 Alan Ransom to Peter Rodino, July 30, 1976, LEG230, 7, RA; Peter Rodino, "Dear colleague" letter, August 2, 1976, LEG230, 7, RA. The House also approved Rodino's bill to expand the scope of evidence that could be gathered during a preliminary investigation in civil cases involving antitrust violations, which was part of

the final omnibus bill.

42 Carole Shifrin, "Scott, Hart to Ask Antitrust Overhaul," *Washington Post*, March 2, 1975; Carole Shifrin, "Softened Antitrust Bill Clears Senate," *Washington Post*, June 11, 1976.

43 Alan Ransom to Peter Rodino, August 23, 1976, LEG230, 7, RA; Representative Rodino, speaking on antitrust, on September 16, 1976, Ninety-Fourth Congress, Second Session, *Congressional Record* 122, Pt. 24: 30868–30874, 30888; "Antitrust Legislation Is Signed by the President," *Washington Post*, October 1, 1976.

44 Marian R. Bruno, deputy director of the Federal Trade Commission, "Hart-Scott-Rodino at 25," remarks before the American Bar Association, June 13, 2002, www.ftc.gov; author's recollection. The Supreme Court's *Illinois Brick Co. v. Illinois* decision eliminated the awarding of treble damages to most consumers, and Rodino was not successful in his efforts to restore it.

45 Peter Rodino, speeches, 1975, PPR6, 5–11, RA; "Greater New Orleans Italian Cultural Society Ninth Annual St. Joseph Day's Banquet," program, March 19, 1975, PPR6, 3, RA; Peter Rodino, address to NAACP, June 21, 1975, POL73, 7, RA; Robert W. Maitlin, "Rodino Earns Coveted Award for Impeachment Role," *Star-Ledger*, July 24, 1975.

46 Martin F. Nolan, "How the Good Guys Finally Won," *New York Times*, May 11, 1975; George E. Reedy, "The Faking of the President," *Washington Post*, May 18, 1975.

47 Richard L. Madden, "A Year After, Members of Impeachment Panel Reflect," *New York Times*, July 27, 1975; Mary McGrory, "Dream Goes on for Rodino," *Chicago Tribune*, July 28, 1975; Michael Feinsilber, "Rodino Tells of Stormy Path to Impeachment Vote," *Star-Ledger*, July 27, 1975; Miles Benson, "Rodino Looks Back at the Impeachment Ordeal," *Star-Ledger*, July 31, 1975; Bob Weidrich, "Rodino Recalls the Nixon Ordeal," *Chicago Tribune*, August 4, 1975.

48 David Nyhan, "Rodino Has Moved Center Stage With Clout that Reaches to '76," *Boston Globe*, May 11, 1975; Oral Transcript, 4/16/99, 3–4, RA.

49 Interview with James Blanchard, June 11, 2021.

50 Itinerary, Democratic telethon, July 25–27, 1975, PER123, 17, RA; Robert Strauss to Peter Rodino, July 29, 1975, PER123, 17, RA; Jack Valenti to Robert Strauss,

September 15, 1975, PER96, 1, RA.

51 Ed Lang, "Rodino Visits Shores; Says He Won't Run," *North Dade Journal*, January 11, 1975; Al Nevler, "What About Rodino," *Seattle Post-Intelligencer*, December 3, 1974; Fortney Stark to Peter Rodino, March 25, 1975, PER95, 9, RA; Mary Hanna to Peter Rodino, April 1, 1975, PER95, 9, RA; James Lenon to Peter Rodino, October 23, 1975, PER95, 9, RA.

52 David B. Wilson, "As a Running Mate Rodino Offers a Number of Pluses," *Boston Globe*, July 4, 1976; Dick Zander, "On Paper at Least the Perfect Veep," *Newsday*, July 9, 1976.

53 Charles Rangel and Mario Biaggi to Democratic Colleagues, June 8, 1976, PER95, 11, RA; "Biaggi, Rangel Announce Support for Rodino as Possible Democratic Vice Presidential Nominee," press release, June 22, 1976, PER95, 11, RA; Mary McGrory, "O'Neill Has Made His Choice Known," *Washington Star*, June 25, 1976; Robert W. Maitlin, "O'Neill Pitching Hard for Rodino as the VP," *Star-Ledger* July 2, 1976.

54 Richard Benfield, "A 10-to-1 Shot for Second Spot," *The Record*, June 27, 1976; Peter Rodino, statement, June 22, 1976, PER95, 11, RA.

55 Stuart E. Eizenstat, *President Carter: The White House Years* (New York: Thomas Dunne Books, 2018), 90; Charles Kirbo interview, January 5, 1983, "The Jimmy Carter Presidential Oral History," Miller Center, University of Virginia, Charlottesville, Virginia; Jimmy Carter, *Keeping Faith: Memoirs of a President* (New York: Bantam Books, 1982), 35–39.

56 "Rodino Talks for an Hour with Top Carter Advisor," *Star-Ledger*, July 8, 1976; interview with John Russonello, June 26, 2021; Freiberg interview.

57 "Carter Screens Rodino and Calls Him Qualified," *Star-Ledger*, July 12, 1976; Oral Transcript, 4/9/03, 1–2, RA.

58 "Rodino Withdraws From the VP Race," *Star-Ledger*, July 13, 1976; Myron S. Waldman, "Rodino Bows Out, Cites Eye Ailment," *Newsday*, July 13, 1976; Peter Rodino, schedule for Democratic National Convention, July 13–15, 1976, PER96, 7, RA.

59 Peter Rodino, "Nominating Speech for Jimmy Carter," July 14, 1976, PPR15, 10, RA; James M. Naughton, "Democrats Turn to Nixon and Watergate as Issues," *New*

York Times, July 15, 1976; Jimmy Carter to Peter Rodino July 19, 1976, PER56, 12, RA. Also see Jonathan Alter, *His Very Best: Jimmy Carter, a Life* (New York: Simon & Schuster, 2020), 253–59.

60 Helen Dewar, "Carter Campaign Creates Ethnic Desk," *Washington Post*, August 22, 1976; Lou Cannon, "Ford, Carter Hustle Votes at Italian American Fete," *Washington Post*, September 17, 1976; Peter Rodino, campaign remarks, September 20, 1976, PER119, 3, RA; Joseph F. Sullivan, "Confident of Winning Re-Election, Rodino Will Campaign for Carter," *New York Times*, October 12, 1976; Linda Charlton, "Mondale Marches in Two Parades," *New York Times*, October 11, 1976.

61 David E. Rosenbaum, "Democrats Solidify Congress," *New York Times*, November 4, 1976; Oral Transcript, 4/9/03, 3, RA; Walter Mondale to Peter Rodino, November 22, 1976, PER57, 12, 12, RA.

62 Lou Cannon, "Carter Vows to Consult with Hill," *Washington Post*, November 24, 1976; Spencer Rich, "Shakedown Cruise," *Washington Post*, February 25, 1977; Frank Moore interview, July 30, 31, 2002, Oral History Project, Jimmy Carter Presidential Library and Museum, Atlanta, Georgia; William Cable interview, February 2, 1981, exit interviews, Carter Library.

63 O'Neill, *Man of the House*, 308–313; Spencer Rich, "Senate, White House Wrangle over Powers," *Washington Post*, March 12, 1977; Kai Bird, *The Outlier: The Unfinished Presidency of Jimmy Carter* (New York: Crown, 2021), 195–98.

64 Oral Transcript, 4/9/03, 3–4, RA; Hedrick Smith, "A Controversial Appointment," *New York Times*, December 21, 1976; Griffin Bell interview, March 23, 1988, Jimmy Carter Oral History Project, Miller Center.

65 John M. Goshko, "Bell Hill Hearings Shed Little Light on His Approach," *Washington Post*, January 17, 1977; Russonello interview; Oral Transcript, 3/17/99, 5–6, RA; Griffin Bell to Peter Rodino, September 12, 1977, June 9, 1978, August 7, 1978, PER56, 9, RA; Griffin B. Bell, *Taking Care of the Law* (New York: William Morrow and Company, 1982), 86–88.

66 Robert W. Maitlin, "Congress Woes," *Star-Ledger*, July 3, 1977; Robert W. Maitlin, "Rodino-Carter: Political Alliance," *Star-Ledger*, August 7, 1977; Saul Kohler, "Carter Calls Rodino for Tough Decisions," *Star-Ledger*, August 21, 1977; Oral Transcript, 3/17/99, 2–5, RA; Oral Transcript, 4/9/03, 3–4, RA.

67 Jimmy Carter to Peter Rodino, September 10, 1977, April 5, 1978, September 20, 1978, WHCNF, Box 2830, Rodino Folder, Presidential Papers of Jimmy Carter, Jimmy Carter Presidential Library and Museum, Atlanta, Georgia; Tim Kraft to Frank Moore, March 17, 1977, WHCNF, 2830, "Rodino" Folder, Carter Papers; Frank Moore to Jimmy Carter, September 12, 1977, WHCNF, 2830, "Rodino" Folder, Carter Papers; White House, "Exchange of Remarks Between the President and His Excellency Giulio Andreotti," July 26, 1977, SCR44, 139, RA.

68 White House staff, Congressional scheduling proposal, October 19, 1979, April 9, 1979, March 11, 1980, WHCNF, 2830, Rodino Folder, Carter Papers; Jimmy Carter to Peter Rodino, October 29, 1979, October 9, 1980, WHCNF, 2830, Rodino Folder, Carter Papers; daily diary of President Jimmy Carter, 1979–80, Carter Papers.

69 "A Ceremony for the Unveiling of the Portrait of the Honorable Peter W. Rodino Jr.: Proceedings Before the Committee on the Judiciary," Committee on the Judiciary, House of Representatives, Ninety-Fifth Congress, First Session, May 1977, 4–6; White House staff, Congressional scheduling proposal, March 21, 1977, WHCNF, 2830, Rodino Folder, Carter Papers; Gretchen Poston to Rosalynn Carter, May 16, 1977, WHCNF, 2830, Rodino Folder, Carter Papers.

70 General Services Administration, "Prospectus for Proposed Construction Under the Public Building Act of 1959," March 15, 1962, O'Brien Files, 20, Rodino Folder, LBJ Papers.

71 James Howard, H.R. 11739, February 5, 1976, copy in LEG156, 4, RA; "Transcript of the Proceedings of the Dedication of the Peter W, Rodino Jr., Federal Building," Newark, New Jersey, November 3, 1978, PER77, 1, RA; Jimmy Carter to Peter Rodino, November 17, 1978, WHCNF, 2830, Rodino Folder, Carter Papers.

72 Oral Transcript, 5/14/99, 8–11, RA; Oral Transcript, 4/21/99, 1–2, RA; Oral Transcript, 3/23/99, 7–11, RA.

73 Jimmy Carter to Marianna Rodino, June 28, 1978, PER74, 2, RA; Peter Rodino to Jimmy Carter, July 10, 1978, WNCNF, 2830, Rodino Folder, Carter Papers; daily diary of President Jimmy Carter, September 27, 1979, Carter Papers. For the other get well letters and cards, see PER74, 2, RA.

74 Russonello interview; "Rodino Curtails Washington Work Because of Wife's

Illness," *Asbury Park Press*, August 6, 1978; author's recollection.

75 David Wald, "Payne Will Challenge Rodino in Congressional Primary Race," *Star-Ledger*, February 16, 1980; David Wald, "Former Newark Judge Tosses Her Hat in Congressional Ring," *Star-Ledger*, February 22, 1980. Rodino's attempt to secure a more favorable district after the Democrats regained control of the New Jersey legislature was not successful. Peter Rodino to Brendan Byrne, May 21, 1975, POL82, 7, RA; Daniel Hayes, "Congressional Remap Bill Stalled," *Star-Ledger*, December 8, 1975.

76 Peter D. Hart Research Associates, "A Survey of Primary Voters' Attitudes in the Tenth Congressional District of New Jersey," March 1980, PER99, 7, RA; Peter Hart to Peter Rodino, March 13, 1980, PER99, 7, RA.

77 "Citizens for Rodino," campaign ads, schedules, brochures, May 1980, PER98, 14, RA; Jason Jett, "Rodino Rivals Speak Out at Newark Forum," *Star-Ledger*, May 20, 1980; Herb Jaffe, "Rodino, Ambrosio, Fenwick, Dwyer Win," *Star-Ledger*, June 4, 1980.

78 "Results in Races for U.S. Senate and the Make Up of the Newly Elected Congress," *New York Times*, November 6, 1980; Alter, *His Very Best*, 488–501, 577–95.

79 "Mrs. Rodino Dies at 70," *Star-Ledger*, December 4, 1980.

80 Jimmy Carter to Peter Rodino, December 3, 1980, PER56, 4, RA; Vincent B. Zarate, "DC Notables Attend Rites for Mrs. Rodino," *Star-Ledger*, December 7, 1980.

CHAPTER TEN

1 Robert Shogan, "Rep. Rodino Standing Firm Against Tide of Conservative Legislation," *Los Angeles Times* September 23, 1982; Mary Thornton, "House Judiciary Panel Bottles up Conservative Social Agenda," *Washington Post*, May 17, 1982.

2 Oral Transcript, 5/19/99, 12, RA.

3 Robert Cohen, "Rodino Pledges an Open Mind on Thurmond," *Star-Ledger*, November 16, 1980; Miles Benson, "Rodino Won't Bow to Conservative Tide," *Star-Ledger*, February 13, 1981; Nadine Cohodas, "House Judiciary Liberals Work to Retain Influence Amid Conservative Gains," *Congressional Quarterly*, February 21, 1981. See also Sean Wilentz, *The Age of Reagan: A History 1974–2008* (New York: HarperCollins, 2008), 127–50.

4 Steven V. Roberts, "House by 265 to 122 Votes to End Justice Dept. Role in Busing Cases," *New York Times*, June 10, 1981; Steven V. Roberts, "Antibusing Moves Passed by Senate After Long Fight," *New York Times*, March 3, 1982.

5 William French Smith to Peter Rodino, May 6, 1982, JGR Busing Folder (1), Box 6, John G. Roberts Files, Ronald Reagan Library, Simi Valley, California; William French Smith, *Law and Justice in the Reagan Administration: Memoirs of an Attorney General* (Palo Alto, CA: Hoover Institution Press, 1991), 20–29, 89–90; Steven V. Roberts, "Down in the Liberal Trenches with the Judiciary Committee," *New York Times*, August 22, 1982.

6 Oral Transcript, 5/19/99, 7–9, RA; "Constitutional Amendments Seeking to Balance the Budget and Limit Federal Spending: Hearings Before the Subcommittee on Monopolies and Commercial Law," Committee on the Judiciary, House of Representatives, Ninety-Seventh Congress, First and Second Session, 1981–1982; Dale Mezzacappa, "Rodino Fights to Keep Budget Amendment from Floor," *Philadelphia Inquirer*, July 21, 1982.

7 "New Right Took Its Best Shot and Missed," *Trenton Times*, August 22, 1982; "Committee Shorn of Amendment on Balanced Budget," *Washington Post*, September 30, 1982; Helen Dewar, "He Urges Voters to Take Names: Democratic Controlled House Rejects Balanced Budget Amendment," *Washington Post*, October 2, 1982.

8 Robert Cohen, "Rodino Sees Little Hope for New Rights Measure," *Star-Ledger*, April 30, 1981.

9 "House Coalition Wins on Extender to Keep Teeth in Voting Rights Act," *Star-Ledger*, October 6, 1981; Edward Walsh, "Defensive Tone Marks Speeches to Rights Group," *Washington Post*, April 30, 1981.

10 Smith, *Law and Justice*, 98–100; "House Gives Resounding 'Yes' to Renewal of Voting Rights Act," *Star-Ledger*, June 24, 1982; Peter Rodino, address before NAACP seventy-fifth anniversary convention, Kansas City, July 2, 1984, PER73, 7, RA.

11 "Rodino Offers a Bill to Curb Pistols," *New York Times*, April 10, 1981; Mary Thornton, "Gun Control Act Is Target of Senate Attack," *Washington Post*, December 10, 1981; "House Votes to Weaken Gun Control," *Washington Post*, April 11, 1986. Rodino did secure an exemption for handguns.

12 "Notes of John Daniel Consisting of A-P Parts," JGR/Environmental Protection Agency (Notes) Folder, 23, JGR, Reagan Library.

13 Peter Rodino to William French Smith, February 24, 1983, JGR/Environmental Protection Agency (General) Folder, 22, JGR, Reagan Library.

14 "Investigation of the Role of the Department of Justice in the Withholding of Environmental Protection Documents from Congress in 1982–83: Report of the Committee on the Judiciary," House of Representatives, Ninety-Ninth Congress, First Session, December 11, 1985, Volumes 1–4; Leslie Maitland Werner, "E.P.A. Inquiry Drags On," *New York Times*, May 4, 1985.

15 Oral Transcript, 4/16/99, 11, RA; Representative Rodino, speaking on immigration reform, on September 12, 1972, Ninety-Second Congress, Second Session, *Congressional Record* 118, Pt. 23: 30154–86; Rick Hutcheson to Stuart Eizenstat, July 21, 1977, Rodino Folder, 2839, WHCNF, Carter Papers; Stuart Eizenstat to Jimmy Carter, October 3, 1977, Rodino Folder, 2830, WHCNF, Carter Paper. One of Rodino's first decisions as the new chairman of the immigration subcommittee was to hire Arthur P. "Skip" Endres to work on the issue. Endres remained a senior adviser on immigration policy until Rodino 's retirement.

16 Peter Rodino to Thomas P. O'Neill, February 17, 1979, Thomas P. O'Neill to Peter Rodino, March 19, 1979, Peter Rodino to Thomas P. O'Neill, January 8, 1981, 360/13, O'Neill Papers; "U.S. Immigration Policy and the National Interest: The Final Report and Recommendations of the Select Commission on Immigration and Refugee Policy to the Congress and the President of the United States," March 1, 1981, 35–86, 405–406.

17 Craig Fuller, "Memorandum for the President," July 1, 1981, Illegal Aliens (1) Folder, Edwin J. Gray, "Memorandum for Martin Anderson," July 16, 1981, Illegal Aliens (2) Folder, Department of Justice, "US Immigration and Refugee Policy," July 30, 1981 all in Box 19, Martin Anderson Files (MAF), Reagan Library.

18 Robert Pear, "Senate Votes Sweeping Revisions of the Nation's Immigration Laws," *New York Times*, August 18, 1982.

19 Robert Pear, "House Unit Backs Immigration Bill," *New York Times*, September 23, 1982.

20 Robert Cohen, "Rodino Doubts New Aliens Bill," *Star-Ledger*, December 23, 1982;

David Hiller to Michael Uhlman, December 14, 1982, Immigration Reform and Control Act of 1983 (1) Folder, Box 7, William Barr Files (WBF), Reagan Library.

21 Endres interview, March 30, 2022; Charles Kamasaki, *Immigration Reform: The Corpse that Will Not Die* (Simsbury, CT: Mandel Vilar Press, 2019), 151–246.

22 "Peter Rodino Rides to the Rescue," editorial, *New York Times*, July 21, 1985.

23 Stephen Engleberg, "Rodino Plan Seen Aiding Chances of Bill on Aliens," *New York Times*, July 25, 1985; Oral Transcript, 4/21/99, 10–11, RA.

24 Robert Pear, "Senate Alien Bill Draws Criticism," *New York Times*, September 19, 1985; Robert Pear, "Senate Votes Bill Designed to Curb Illegal Migrants," *New York Times*, September 20, 1985.

25 Robert Pear, "Rodino Delays Immigration Bill to Seek Compromise on Farm Issue," *New York Times*, May 2, 1986; Robert Pear, "House Panel Approves a Comprehensive Measure on Immigration," *New York Times*, June 26, 1986.

26 Robert Cohen, "Rodino Suffers Sharp Setback as House Rejects Immigration Legislation," *Star-Ledger*, September 27, 1986.

27 Robert Pear, "Immigration Bill: How 'Corpse' Came Back to Life," *New York Times*, October 13, 1986; Andy Pazstor, "Languishing Immigration Bill Revived by Persistence, Luck and Compromise," *Wall Street Journal*, October 21, 1986.

28 Mary Thornton, "Immigration Changes Are Signed Into Law," *Washington Post*, November 7, 1986; Ronald Reagan to Peter Rodino, December 12, 1986, PER56, 30, RA; Tim Golden, "Mexicans Head North Despite Rules on Jobs," *New York Times*, December 13, 1991.

29 Alan Fram, "Peter Rodino: Capitol Hill's Invisible Man," *Home News*, November 6, 1983; Chuck Conconi, "Personalities," *Washington Post*, May 31, 1984; Robert Cohen, "Rodino Remembers Impeachment Hearing," *Star-Ledger*, July 22, 1984.

30 David E. Kyvig, *The Age of Impeachment: American Constitutional Culture Since 1960* (Lawrence, KS: University Press of Kansas, 2008), 267–77.

31 "Conduct of Harry E. Claiborne, U.S. District Judge, District of Nevada: Hearing Before the Subcommittee on Courts, Civil Liberties and the Administration of Justice," Committee on the Judiciary, House of Representatives, Ninety-Ninth Congress, Second Session, June 1986; "Impeachment of U.S. Judge Passes House," *New York Times*, July 23, 1986.

32 Representative Rodino, speaking on impeachment, October 7, 1986, Ninety-Ninth Congress, Second Session, *Congressional Record* 132, Pt. 20: 29136–149; House Judiciary Committee, "Scenario Exhibiting Articles of Impeachment in the Senate," undated, LEG171, 6, RA. The House presented four articles to the Senate.

33 Kyvig, *Impeachment*, 277–87; Daniel M. Freeman, *The House Was My Home: My Life on Capitol Hill and Other Tales* (Port Angeles, WA: Cadmus Publishing, 2020), 281–85.

34 "In the Matter of Certain Complaints Against United States District Judge Alcee L. Hastings: Report of the Investigative Committee to the Judicial Council of the Eleventh Circuit," three volumes, undated, LEG172, 4, 5, 6, RA; Terrence J. Anderson, "A Provisional and Preliminary Report on the Proceedings Against United States District Judge Alcee L. Hastings 1981–1986," January 16, 1987, LEG172, 3, RA; William Rehnquist to Speaker of the House, "Certification of the Judicial Conference of the United States," March 17, 1986, LEG172, 2, RA.

35 Peter Rodino to Frank Annunzio, March 27, 1987, LEG172, 2, RA.

36 Ruth Marcus, "Hastings Case Referred to Skeptical Lawmaker," *Washington Post*, March 19, 1987; Alan I. Baron to Subcommittee on Criminal Justice, June 14, 1988, LEG172, 2, RA; Freeman, *The House Was My Home*, 275–80.

37 "Senate Presented with Case for Judge's Ouster," *Star-Ledger*, August 10, 1988; Kyvig, *Impeachment*, 288–303.

38 Kenneth Guido to Peter Rodino, June 22, 1983, POL84, 13, RA; Kenneth Guido to New Jersey Democratic Congressional Delegation, April 2, 1984, POL85, 3, RA.

39 Peter D. Hart to Peter Rodino, March 26, 1984, PER103, 3, RA; Peter Rodino, "Statement on Candidacy For Re-Election," April 26, 1984, PER103, 1, RA; Joe White to Charles Scalera, May 1, 1984, PER103, 2, RA; Anthony F. Shannon, "Rodino Breezes in 10th District as the House Incumbents Triumph," *Star-Ledger*, June 6, 1984.

40 Peter Rodino, "Endorsement of Kenneth Gibson for Governor," May 18, 1981, PER99, 11, RA; "Rodino Backing Big Gibson Boost," *New Jersey Afro-American*, May 30, 1981.

41 Harvey Fisher, "Jackson Wants Black to Oust Rodino in '86," *The Record*, October 17, 1984.

42 Joseph F. Sullivan, "After 36 Years, Rodino's Base Remains Solid," *New York Times*, October 16, 1984.

43 New Jersey Coalition of Black Democrats, "Announcement of Conference," February 7, 1986, PER107, 11, RA; "Black Dems Name Slate for Exec, Congress," *Star-Ledger*, March 9, 1986.

44 Bayard Rustin to friends, February 21, 1986, PER107, 7, RA; Peter Rodino, "Announcement For Re-Election," March 7, 1986, PER107, 11, RA.

45 "Payne for Congress," campaign brochure, May 1986, PER109, 17, RA; Tuttle, *How Newark Became Newark*, 212–222; Joseph F. Sullivan, "Newark Result Casts Shadow on Primary," *New York Times*, May 18, 1986.

46 Jack Valenti to Peter Rodino, May 23, 1986, PER108, 21, RA; Charles Rangel to Verrick O. French, May 22, 1986, PER109, 7, RA; "Citizens for Rodino," radio advertisements, April 1986, PER107, 11, RA.

47 "Jesse Jackson Endorses Payne," *Star-Ledger*, May 30, 1986.

48 Richard Cohen, "Jesse Jackson: Blinded by Color," *Washington Post*, June 5, 1986; Joseph F. Sullivan, "Challenge to Rodino Closely Watched," *New York Times*, June 2, 1986.

49 Peter Rodino, "Statement on Jesse Jackson Visit," May 29, 1986, PER109, 4, RA; Oral Transcript, 7/13/99, 8–10, RA.

50 Joseph F. Sullivan, "Rodino Scores Easy Victory Over Councilman in Primary," *New York Times*, June 4, 1986.

51 Al Frank, "Republicans and Independent Rivals to Rodino Drop Out of House Race," *Star-Ledger*, September 25, 1986; Steve Chambers, "Black Issue Irks Rodino," *Asbury Park Press*, June 4, 1986; Alan C. Miller, "Watergate Role Secured Rodino's Place in History," *The Record*, June 4, 1986.

52 John G. Roberts to Fred Fielding, January 21, 1986, JGR Contra Aid (1) Folder, 11, Roberts Files, Reagan Library; Malcolm Byrne, *Iran-Contra: Reagan's Scandal and the Unchecked Abuse of Presidential Power* (Lawrence, KS: University Press of Kansas, 2014), 253–78.

53 Peter Rodino to Edwin Meese, December 11 and December 23, 1986, SF56, 2, RA; John Bolton to Peter Rodino, December 22, 1986, SF56, 1, RA.

54 Steven V. Roberts, "House Appoints 15 to Panel on Iran," *New York Times*,

December 18, 1986; Byrne, *Iran-Contra*, 279–314. See also William S. Cohen and George J. Mitchell, *Men of Zeal: A Candid Inside Story of the Iran Contra Hearings* (New York: Viking Penguin, 1988), 25–61.

55 Peter Rodino, "Opening Statement Before the Joint Hearings," May 5, 1987, LEG70, 9, RA; Robert Cohen, "Reagan Role Questioned by Rodino and Courter," *Star-Ledger*, May 17, 1987.

56 Maureen Dowd, "A Different White House" *New York Times*, July 29, 1987; Myron S. Waldman, "Probe Veteran Rodino Takes on Attorney General," *Newsday*, July 29, 1987; "Iran-Contra Investigation: Joint Hearings Before the Senate Select Committee on Secret Military Assistance to Iran and the Nicaragua Opposition and the House Select Committee to Investigate Covert Arms Transactions With Iran," House of Representatives, 100th Congress, First Session, Pt. 9, 276–90.

57 "Report of the Congressional Committees Investigating the Iran-Contra Affair," House report 100–433, 100th Congress, First Session, 1987, 644, 639–65, 3–22; Stephen Engelberg with David E. Rosenbaum, "What The Iran-Contra Committee Wish They Had Done Differently," *New York Times*, November 20, 1987.

58 Peter Rodino, "Statement Endorsing Joseph Biden for President," June 9, 1987, POL70, 1, RA; Robert Cohen, "Rodino Joins the Biden for President Team," *Star-Ledger*, May 1, 1987; David Wald, "Candidate's Withdrawal Leaves Jersey Supporters Angry and Disappointed," *Star-Ledger*, September 27, 1987.

59 Oral Transcript, 9/14/99, 10–12, RA.

60 Robert Cohen, "Rodino About-Faces Prepares to Run Again," *Star-Ledger*, July 19, 1987.

61 S.A. Paolantonio, "Political Future a Primary Question for N.J.'s Legendary Congressman," *Philadelphia Inquirer*, January 13, 1988; David Wald, "Rodino's On-Again, Off Again Retirement Keeps 10th District Dems Waiting," *Star-Ledger*, January 31, 1988.

62 Joseph F. Sullivan, "Black Politicians Pressure Rodino to Retire," *New York Times*, March 9, 1988; David Blomquist, "It's Time to Step Down, Rodino's Old Allies Say," *The Record*, March 14, 1988.

63 Lawrence Spinelli, notebook, January–March 1988, SF55, 17, RA; author's recollection.

64 Peter Rodino, statement, March 14, 1988, SF55, 17, RA.

65 "Chairman Rodino Retires, With Grace," editorial, *New York Times*, March 15, 1988; "Peter Rodino Chooses to Exit Gracefully," *Philadelphia Inquirer*, March 16, 1988; "Mr. Rodino Steps Aside," editorial, *Washington Post*, March 16, 1988.

66 William Brennan to Peter Rodino, March 17, 1988, PER65, 2, RA; "Retirement Clips," SCR82, RA.

67 SCR79, SCR80, SCR81, RA; S.A. Paolantonio, "N.J. Delegation Includes Rodino, Probable Successor," *Philadelphia Inquirer*, July 22, 1988; "Women's Caucus Hails Rodino as a 'Good Guy,'" *Star-Ledger*, September 14, 1988.

68 Robert Cohen, "Last Roll Call," *Star-Ledger*, October 21, 1988; author's recollection; "Rodino: An Ordinary Guy," January 1989, PPR042, 34, RA.

69 Oral History, 4/14/99, 1–2, and 3/17/99A, 1–2, 6–7, RA; Lawrence Spinelli to Peter Rodino, May 27, 1988, SF55, 15, RA; Jonathan Karp to Bill Berlin, October 24, 2002, PER172, 9, RA.

70 "Deposit and Dedication Agreement Between Seton Hall University and Peter Rodino," August 31, 1988, PER175, 1, RA; Peter Rodino, class notes, PER175, 2–4, 11 and PER176, 1–3, RA; Clifford D. May, "After 40 Years Making the Law, Rodino Now Teaches It," *New York Times*, January 25, 1989.

71 Joy Rodino interview, June 16, 2022; Joy Rodino, *Fifty-Two Words My Husband Taught Me: Love, Inspiration and the Constitution* (West Orange, NJ: DRJ Publishing, 2007); Sarah Hume to Merilee Jennings, August 9, 1993, PER188, 1, RA.

72 Kathy Kiely, "Ex-Chairman Advises from the Sidelines," *USA Today*, November 27, 1998; Oral Transcript, 7/13/99, 2, RA; Seton Hall University Press Office, "Requests for Rodino Interviews," September–December 1998, PER188, 2, RA.

73 Lizette Alvarez, "Sharp Divisions on Judiciary Panel," *New York Times*, September 14, 1998; Juliet Eilperin and John F. Harris, "House GOP Pushes Wide Clinton Probe," *New York Times*, September 30, 1998.

74 Peter W. Rodino Jr., "The Vote that Changed America," *New York Times*, July 27, 1999; David M. Halbfinger, "Warning on Impeachment, Based on the Past," *New York Times*, December 15, 1998; Tony Mauro, "Lost Lesson in Leadership," *USA Today*, June 7, 2001.

75 Donna De La Cruz, "A Nemesis of Nixon Takes a Look Back," *Philadelphia*

Inquirer, June 28, 2004; Stephen Steele, "Rodino Hospitalized for Artery Surgery," *Star-Ledger*, December 26, 1992.

76 Joy Rodino interview; Michael Kaufman, "Former Representative Peter W. Rodino Jr. Dies at 95, Led House Watergate Inquiry," *New York Times*, May 8, 2005; "Judiciary Chairman Steered Nixon Impeachment Hearing," *Palm Beach Post*, May 8, 2005.

77 Ron Marsico, "Watergate Icon Rodino Dies," *Star-Ledger*, May 8, 2005; Kate Wans, "Rodino Remembered for His Integrity," *Star-Ledger*, May 15, 2005; House Committee on the Judiciary, "Transcript of Proceedings," May 12, 2005, PER190, 3, RA.

78 "Funeral Mass of Peter Rodino," program, May 16, 2005, PER190, 2, RA; Paula A. Franzese, "Until the End He Kept a Good Heart," *Star-Ledger*, May 17, 2005; Ron Marsico, "A Final Thanks to Rodino," *Star-Ledger*, May 17, 2005.

79 Edward Kennedy to Joy Rodino, May 16, 2005, PER190, 3, RA.

INDEX

A

B

E

F

J

O

P

R

S

T